Understanding Consciousness

Understanding Consciousness, second edition provides a unique survey and evaluation of consciousness studies, along with an original analysis of consciousness that combines scientific findings, philosophy and common sense. Building on the widely praised first edition of the book, this new edition adds fresh research, and deepens the original analysis in a way that reflects some of the fundamental changes in the understanding of consciousness that have taken place over the last ten years.

The book is divided into three parts; Part I surveys current theories of consciousness, evaluating their strengths and weaknesses. Part II reconstructs an understanding of consciousness from first principles, starting with its phenomenology, and leading to a closer examination of how conscious experience relates to the world described by physics and information processing in the brain. Finally, Part III deals with fundamental issues such as what consciousness is and does, and how it fits into the evolving universe. As the structure of the book moves from a basic overview of the field to a successively deeper analysis, it can be used both for those new to the subject and for more established researchers.

Understanding Consciousness tells a story with a beginning, middle and end in a way that integrates the philosophy of consciousness with the science. Overall, the book provides a unique perspective on how to address the problems of consciousness and as such will be of great interest to psychologists, philosophers, neuroscientists and other professionals concerned with mind/body relationships, and all who are interested in this subject.

Max Velmans is currently Emeritus Professor of Psychology at Goldsmiths, University of London and Visiting Professor of Consciousness Studies at the University of Plymouth. He has been researching, writing and teaching consciousness studies for over thirty years and has over ninety publications in this area.

'This is an important book. It offers an excellent review of the whole range of philosophical and scientific attempts to understand consciousness, interwoven with a compelling account of the author's own preferred option (i.e "reflexive monism"), for which he is already well known. This further account of his views will be welcomed by all concerned' – **Christopher M H Nunn, Associate Editor, Journal of Consciousness Studies.**

'What an intellectually rich and readable journey through the tangled fabric of consciousness studies! The consciousness debate is enriched immeasurably by this fine and disciplined journey, with just a pinch of "mind-dust" to flavor the universe. Students of mind will find this to be among the finest and most disciplined journeys into the still dark corners of consciousness studies.' – **Jaak Panksepp, Bailey Endowed Chair of Animal Well-Being Science, College of Veterinary Medicine, Washington State University.**

Reviews of the First Edition:
'... this is among the best books written about consciousness over the last decade ... It sets a high standard in the natural philosophy of mind.' – **Professor Adam Zeman, Department of Clinical Neurosciences, Western General Hospital, Edinburgh, UK, in** *The Lancet*

'Understanding Consciousness presents a lucid, indeed masterly, account of the philosophical issues involved.' – **Professor Jeffrey Gray, Institute of Psychiatry, London, UK, in** *Times Higher Educational Supplement*

'... those who are engaged in the cognitive sciences should read this book so as to stimulate their own thinking ... the implications for the field are quire profound.' – **Professor Igor Aleksander, Imperial College, London, UK, in** *Trends in Cognitive Science*

'This is a fine book. In what has become a crowded field, it stands out as direct, deep, and daring. It should place Max Velmans amongst the stars in the field . . .' – **Professor Greg Nixon, Prescott College, Arizona, USA, in** *Journal of Consciousness Studies*

'This book is excellent. There are lots of books on consciousness, but few which mix the philosophical, psychological and neuroscientific, and even fewer which are written without an axe to grind . . . a lovely book . . . I'll be recommending it to everyone I see.' – **Professor John Kihlstrom, University of California at Berkley, USA**

'... a splendid assessment of and contribution to the debate about consciousness as it is currently being waged between psychologists, philosophers, some neuroscientists and AI people.' – **Professor Steven Rose, The Open University, UK**

'This is a splendid book . . . In my view it should have a profound and lasting effect upon the debate as to the nature and function of consciousness, and should stimulate much new thinking and investigation.' – **Professor David Fontana, University of Cardiff, UK and University of Algarve, Portugal**

'Following the best traditions, the book has an explanatory beginning, an unmissable middle and a happy end. . . . It is refreshing to find amongst the consciousness literature a book that is so accessible and focused. Velmans maintains a clarity rarely found in the deep abysses of philosophy, psychology and neurophysiology without departing from the point. Consequently, I would recommend this book equally both to the connoisseur of consciousness studies and to the mere aficionado.' – **Dora Brown, University of Surrey, in "The Psychologist", November 2000**

'Velmans launches a sustained and well-reasoned attack on the prevailing "orthodoxies" of functionalism and other reductionist so-called explanations of consciousness. . . . [In] arguing for his own position – his reflexive model – he deeply challenges the reader's assumptions. . . . The reflexive model touches on deeply provocative ideas which could yet catalyse the next step forward in understanding consciousness.' – **Les Lancaster, Liverpool John Moore's University, "Consciousness & Experiential Psychology", September, 2000**

'Max Velmans has written a fundamentally important book. At a time when many are expressing an increasing interest in our experience of "consciousness", he presents a coherent and comprehensive survey of the state of knowledge in this field. . . . But he does more than this . . . there is a level of original thinking in his writing that makes a useful contribution to the debate about one of the most complex issues of our time.' – **Joan Walton in "Caduceus", October, 2000**

'Being inspired with lucidity and a true interdisciplinary spirit, Understanding Consciousness is lasting in value.' – **Alexander Batthyany, University of Vienna, in "Theory & Psychology"**

Understanding Consciousness
Second edition

Max Velmans

Routledge
Taylor & Francis Group

LONDON AND NEW YORK

First published 2009 by Routledge
27 Church Road, Hove, East Sussex, BN3 2FA

Simultaneously published in the USA and Canada
by Routledge
270 Madison Avenue, New York, NY 10016

*Psychology Press is an imprint of the Taylor & Francis Group,
an informa business*

Copyright © 2009 Psychology Press

Typeset in Times by RefineCatch Limited, Bungay, Suffolk
Printed and bound in Great Britain by
TJ International Ltd, Padstow, Cornwall
Cover design by Design Deluxe

This publication has been produced with paper manufactured to strict
environmental standards and with pulp derived from sustainable
forests.

British Library Cataloguing in Publication Data
A catalogue record for this book is available from the British Library

Library of Congress Cataloging-in-Publication Data
Velmans, Max, 1942–
   Understanding consciousness / Max Velmans. – 2nd ed.
      p. cm.
   1. Consciousness. I. Title.
   BF311.V44 2009
   126–dc22

                                                    2008035695

ISBN: 978–0–415–42515–5 (hbk)
ISBN: 978–0–415–42516–2 (pbk)

Contents

Illustrations

Figures

Table

Preface to second edition

Consciousness is personal. Indeed it is so close to the core of our being that it has puzzled thinkers from the beginnings of recorded history. What is it? What does it do? How does it relate to the physical world and to the workings of our bodies and brains? At the dawn of the new millennium answers to these questions are beginning to emerge. However there is not one mind/body problem, but many. Some of the problems are empirical, some are conceptual, and some are both. This book deals with some of the deepest puzzles and paradoxes.[1]

In the nine years or so following the completion of the first edition of this book I have had the opportunity to debate and discuss the ideas presented here with many gifted scientists and philosophers, some sympathetic and some with competing views. Although I believe that my original analysis remains secure, these engagements have allowed me to clarify, deepen and update the argument at many points. To accommodate areas in which there has recently been considerable progress I have also added some new chapters and chapter sections, for example on the neural causes and correlates of consciousness, the potential (but disputed) relevance of quantum mechanics, the vexed problem of free will, and the rather mysterious fact that the phenomenal world seems to be out-there in space, when according to reductionist science it ought to be inside the brain. As before, this book charts a path through the mind/body labyrinth that incorporates these and many other seemingly disparate topics in what (I hope) is a simple, connected way.

A good story has a beginning, a middle, and an end, so this book is arranged in three parts. The first part, 'Mind–body theories and their problems', summarises currently dominant thinking about the nature and function of consciousness. We start, as we must in Chapter 1, with some initial definitions, and then go on in Chapter 2 to look at mind/body dualism, an ancient way of viewing the relation of mind to body that persists in some modern interpretations of quantum mechanics. In the Western tradition, this dualist splitting of the universe has largely given way to efforts to understand the universe in a unified materialist way, either in terms of its physical structure or in terms of the ways that it functions. Chapter 3 deals mainly with attempts to demonstrate that mind and consciousness are nothing more than *states of the brain*, a position variously known as 'central state identity theory', 'physicalism' or 'biological naturalism'. Chapter 4 turns to dominant traditions in psychological science that view mind or consciousness as *activities* (rather than states) – a tradition that has its roots in a form of behaviourism that was subsequently transformed by the emergence of cognitive science into a view known as 'functionalism' or, more precisely, as 'psychofunctionalism'. Chapter 5 broadens and completes this contemporary story, exploring the possibilities of mental functioning not just in brains but also in machines, with a careful look at 'computational functionalism', the view that mind and consciousness are nothing more than certain forms of functioning that might, in principle, be implemented in systems of many different kinds. While none of these positions is entirely satisfactory, all have rational grounds for their support. Rather than dismissing these commonly held views, the aim of Part I is to pinpoint both their strengths and weaknesses.

In spite of their depth of commitment to one or another theoretical position, many philosophers and scientists recognise that this classical dualist versus materialist debate leaves an uneasy tension. While dualism seems to be inconsistent with the findings of materialist science, materialist reductionism seems to be inconsistent with the evidence of ordinary experience. Our challenge is to understand consciousness in a way that does justice to both. With this in mind, Part II of this book, 'A new analysis: how to marry science with experience', goes back to first principles. Rather than seeking to defend any standard position, we start in Chapter 6 with a closer examination of experience itself. This has a surprising consequence. If one does this with care the old boundaries that separate the 'contents of consciousness' from what we usually think of as the 'physical world' can be seen to be drawn in the wrong place! What we normally think of as the 'physical world' is actually a *phenomenal world* or world of *appearances*. This turns the mind/body problem round on its axis as it forces one to re-examine how the 'contents of consciousness' relate to what we normally think of as the 'physical world'. There are, however, a number of ways in which these altered relationships can be understood. Chapter 7 compares three major, current alternatives, 'direct-realist physicalism', 'biological naturalism' and 'reflexive monism' – and Chapter 8 provides a deeper analysis of how the contents of consciousness, in the form of a phenomenal world, relate to the world described by theoretical physics. This broadened understanding of consciousness also forces one to completely re-examine the interrelation of subjective, intersubjective and 'objective' knowledge, along with the nature of empirical science, the topic of Chapter 9. To complete this reanalysis we finally turn to how the contents of human consciousness relate to what is happening in the human brain. Chapter 10 presents a close examination of how phenomenal experiences relate to the details of human information processing, and Chapter 11 summarises what is known about the neural causal antecedents and correlates of such experiences – with some further surprising conclusions. At first glance, these intricate relationships of consciousness, mind, matter and knowledge seem to form an impenetrable 'world knot'. But, as far as I can tell, it is possible to unravel it, step by simple step, in a way that is consistent with the findings of science and with common sense.

Part III of this book on 'reflexive monism' provides a new synthesis. Chapters 12 and 13 suggest what consciousness is and what it does. Chapter 14 then places consciousness within nature, developing a form of reflexive monism that treats human consciousness as just one manifestation of a wider self-conscious universe. Although the route to this position is new, the position itself is ancient. I find this reassuring. Understanding consciousness requires us to move from understanding the things we are conscious *of*, to understanding our role as conscious observers, and then to consciousness itself – an act of self-reflection which requires an outward journey and a return. If the place of return does not seem familiar, it is probably the wrong place.

I have many people to thank for their influence on my writings. First, my thanks to my students whose enthusiasm for learning about consciousness encouraged me to clarify my thoughts over the thirty-three years or so that I developed a course on 'The Psychology of Consciousness' at the University of London – and my special thanks to Anthony Freeman, John Kihlstrom, Chris Nunn, Guy Saunders and Steve Torrance for their kind suggestions about how to improve the first edition. I am also particularly grateful to the many, brilliant colleagues around the world with whom I have been privileged to discuss and debate. Many of you appear in these pages, but a far greater number have a place in the pages of my mind. My deepest gratitude goes to those few people who have been very close to me over many years. Thank you for keeping me watered and fed, and for your love and support. You know who you are. Much of what appears here is just our long conversation.

I hope that you enjoy reading this book as much as I have enjoyed writing it. For best results, try to resist starting at the end. As in all good stories, this ruins the plot.

Max Velmans
May, 2008

Note

1 I have dealt with other aspects of consciousness studies elsewhere. For example, Velmans and Schneider (2007) *The Blackwell Companion to Consciousness* provides fifty-five state-of-the-art tutorial reviews of current science and philosophy in consciousness studies written by many of the protagonists, which form ideal background reading for this book; the readings in Velmans (2000) *Investigating Phenomenal Consciousness: New Methodologies and Maps* also introduce a range of new methodologies appropriate to the study of subjective experience, along with a number of alternative 'maps' of the consciousness studies terrain.

Text acknowledgements

The author would like to thank the following for permissions granted.

An extract from 'Consciousness, Dreams and Virtual Realities' by A. Revonsuo (1995) in *Philosophical Psychology*, 8(1): 35–38. Carfax Publishing, Taylor & Francis Ltd (www.informaworld.com) Reprinted by permission of the publisher.

An extract from *Memories, Dreams, Reflections* by C.G. Jung (1983). Reprinted by permission of HarperCollins Publishers Ltd copyright © C.G. Jung (1983).

For the same extract from *Memories, Dreams, Reflections* by C.G. Jung, edited by Aniela Jaffe, translated by Richard and Clara Winston, translation copyright © 1961, 1962, 1963 and renewed 1989, 1990, 1991 by Random House, Inc. Used by permission of Pantheon Books, a division of Random House, Inc.

Every effort has been made to trace copyright holders and obtain permissions. Any omissions brought to our attention will be remedied in future editions.

Part I

Mind–body theories and their problems

1   What is consciousness?

Our conscious lives are the sea in which we swim. So it is not surprising that consciousness is difficult to understand. We consciously experience many different things, and we can think about the things that we experience. But it is not so easy to experience or think about *consciousness itself*. Given this, it is common within philosophy and science to identify consciousness with something smaller than itself, for example with some *thing* that we can observe, such as a state of the brain, or with some *aspect* of what we experience, such as 'thought' or 'language'. One of the themes of this book is that one can understand consciousness without reducing it in this way.

Our understanding of consciousness is also determined by our intellectual history. We are the inheritors of ancient debates. Is the universe composed of one thing (monism) or are there two (dualism)? Does the world have an observer-independent existence (realism) or does its existence depend in some way on the operations of our own minds (idealism)? Is knowledge of the world 'public' and 'objective', and knowledge of our own experience 'private' and 'subjective'? If so, how is it possible to establish the study of consciousness as a science? A second theme of this book is that we have to take stock of these ancient debates, but we do not have to be bound by the polarised choices that they offer.

Current Western philosophical and scientific thought is predominantly materialistic, inspired by the progress of natural science in understanding the material world. Yet, as Tarnas (1993) makes clear, the ultimate passion of the Western mind over 2,500 years has been to understand the ground of its own being. Being conscious is central to being human – and an understanding of consciousness has to be reflexive. From studying the things that we experience we progress to studying the experiencer and the experience. A third theme of this book is that it is possible to do so in a way that is consistent both with science *and* with 'common sense'.

What's the problem?

Traditionally, the puzzles surrounding consciousness have been known as the 'mind–body' problem. However, it is now clear that 'mind' is not quite the same thing as 'consciousness', and that the aspect of body most closely involved with consciousness is the brain. It is also clear that there is not one consciousness–brain problem, but many, which we will examine in the course of this book. As a first approximation, these can be divided into five groups, each focused on a few, central questions:

> **Problem 1.** What and where is consciousness?
>
> **Problem 2.** How are we to understand the *causal relationships* between consciousness and matter and, in particular, the causal relationships between consciousness and the brain?
>
> **Problem 3.** What is the *function* of consciousness? How, for example, does it relate to human information processing?
>
> **Problem 4.** What *forms of matter* are associated with consciousness – in particular, what are the neural substrates of consciousness in the human brain?
>
> **Problem 5.** What are the appropriate ways to *examine* consciousness, to discover its nature? Which features can we examine with first-person methods, which features require third-person methods, and how do first- and third-person findings relate to each other?

Are some problems hard and others easy?

In a now well known essay on the problems of consciousness, the philosopher David Chalmers suggested that they may be divided into the 'easy problems' and the 'hard problem'. 'Easy problems' are ones that can be researched by conventional third-person methods of the kind used in cognitive science, for example investigations of the information processing that accompanies subjective experience. The 'hard problem' is posed by subjective experience itself. As Chalmers notes:

> It is undeniable that some organisms are subjects of experience. But the question of how it is that these systems are subjects of experience is perplexing. Why is it that when our cognitive systems engage in visual and auditory information-processing, we have visual or auditory experience: the quality of deep blue, the sensation of middle C? How can we explain why there is something it is like to entertain a mental image, or to experience an emotion? It is widely agreed that experience arises from a physical basis, but we have no good explanation of why and how it so arises. Why should physical processing give rise to a rich inner life at all? It seems objectively unreasonable that it should, and yet it does. If any problem qualifies as *the* problem of consciousness, it is this one.
>
> (Chalmers, 1995, p. 201)

Given the strenuous efforts in the late twentieth century to demonstrate subjective experience to be nothing more than a state or function of the brain (see Chapters 3, 4 and 5), Chalmers's 'easy' versus 'hard' problem distinction provided a useful reminder that a purely third-person functional analysis of human information processing cannot reveal what it is like to have a subjective experience or explain why it arises.[1] However, this division of the problems of consciousness into 'easy' and 'hard' ones was, in turn, an over-simplification. As Chalmers himself accepted, even so-called 'easy' (empirically researchable) problems can in practice be very difficult to solve. It may also be that the 'hard' problem only seems unusually hard because we have been thinking about it in the wrong way. If so, changing some of our unexamined assumptions might be all we need to make the problem 'easy' – and this will be one of the themes of this book. Note, for example, that in contrast to consciousness, we usually take the existence of matter for granted, and we assume that physics does not present similarly 'hard' problems. But there are many, as we shall see in Chapter 14.

Given this, it seems more useful to sort the problems of consciousness into those that require empirical advance, those that require theoretical advance, those that require a re-examination of some of our pre-theoretical assumptions, and those that require some combination of all three. If, for example, the problem is 'What are the neural substrates of consciousness?', or, 'What forms of information processing are most closely associated with consciousness?', then conventional cognitive and neuropsychological techniques look as if they are likely to yield useful results. There are many questions of this empirical kind and, consequently, the new 'science of consciousness' is already very large (see, for example, the extensive reviews and readings in Velmans and Schneider, 2007).

Examples of empirical questions and investigations within neuro-psychology include:

- The search for the neural causes and correlates of major changes in normal, global conscious states such as deep sleep, rapid eye movement dreaming, and the awake state.
- The search for added neural conditions that support variations in conscious experience within normal, global states, such as visual, auditory and other sensory experiences, experiences of cognitive functioning (the phonemic and other imagery accompanying thinking, meta-cognition, etc.) and affective experience.
- The search for neural conditions that support altered states of consciousness in psychopathology and in non-pathological altered states, such as the hypnotic state, some drug-induced states, meditation, and mystical states.

Examples of empirical questions and investigations within cognitive psychology include:

- Examination of the timing of conscious experience: when in the course of human information processing (for example in input analysis) does a conscious experience arise?

- The determination of functional conditions that suffice to make a stimulus conscious: for example, does material that enters consciousness first have to be selected, attended to and entered into working memory or a 'global workspace'?
- The investigation of functional differences between preconscious, unconscious, and conscious processing, for example in studies of non-attended versus attended material.

Questions about how best to study consciousness are also approachable but subtle, in that they require one to develop epistemology *and* methodology.[2]

But questions about the fundamental nature, causal efficacy, and function of consciousness have proved to be notoriously difficult. There are paradoxes that need to be resolved. For example, at first glance, it seems obvious that consciousness has causal efficacy. There is extensive evidence that brain states have causal influences on conscious experiences, and there is extensive evidence that experiences can have causal influences on the body and brain (earlier experiences and thoughts, for example, influence later actions). However, neural material and the 'stuff' of conscious experience seem to be very different, so it is not easy to envisage *how* these might have causal influences on each other. Causal interactions between seemingly very different energies do occur in physics (for example, the interactions between electricity and magnetism), but the differences between consciousness and the brain seem to be of a different order. One might ask, 'How could something *subjective* have causal interactions with something *objective*?'

Similarly, it seems obvious that consciousness has a function. Indeed, according to evolutionary theory consciousness *must* have a function, otherwise it would not have evolved to be so central in our lives. There have been many proposals in the scientific literature about what that function might be. Common suggestions are that consciousness is necessary to deal with novelty or complexity, to provide feedback, to enable memory and learning, to enable language and problem solving, to enable imaginal short- and long-term planning in advance of carrying out acts in the real world, to enable creativity and so on.

However, these proposals face a central dilemma: once one can specify *how* such functions work in information processing terms, one no longer seems to need consciousness to explain the working of the system which embodies that processing. One can envisage the same processes operating in mechanical or electrical systems unaccompanied by any subjective conscious experiences. So, what, if anything, does subjective experience *add* to effective functioning? Answers to such questions lie in the borderlands of philosophy and science.

Problems 1 to 5 also interconnect. If one is not clear about what consciousness is, how can one develop methods to study it, or hope to find its neural substrates in the brain? Nor can questions about causal efficacy be dissociated from questions about function. If consciousness has no causal influence on neuronal activity, it is not easy to see what its function in the brain's activity could be. Showing how these questions interconnect, and finding a path through the paradoxes, is one of the main purposes of this book.

But we need to start somewhere – and it is natural to approach the first question first. 'What *is* consciousness?' Let us begin with some simple definitions and distinctions.

Defining consciousness

According to Thomas Nagel (1974), consciousness is 'what it is like to be something'. Without it, after all, it would not be like anything to exist. It is generally accepted in philosophy of mind that this does capture something of the essence of the term. At the same time, as George Miller (1962) pointed out, 'Consciousness is a word worn smooth by a million tongues.' The term means many different things to many different people, and no universally agreed 'core meaning' exists. This is odd, as we each have 'psychological data' about what it is like to *be conscious* or to *have consciousness* to serve as the basis for an agreed definition.

This uncertainty about how to define consciousness is partly created by the way global theories about consciousness (or even the nature of the universe) have intruded into definitions. For example, 'substance dualists' such as Plato, Descartes and Eccles believe the universe to consist of two fundamental kinds of stuff, material stuff and the stuff of consciousness (a substance associated with soul or spirit). 'Property dualists' such as Sperry and Libet take consciousness to be a special kind of property that is itself nonphysical, but which emerges from physical systems such as the brain once they attain a certain level of complexity. By contrast, 'reductionists', such as Crick (1994) and Dennett (1991), believe consciousness to be nothing more than a state or function of the brain. Within cognitive psychology, there have been many proposals which identify consciousness with some aspect of human information processing, for example with working memory, focal attention, a central executive, and so on.

We will examine the arguments for and against consciousness being a substance, property, state, or function of the brain in Chapters 2 to 5. The only point we need to note for now is that these definitions of consciousness start more from some *theory* about its nature than from the *phenomenology of consciousness itself*. This is to put the cart before the horse. We will proceed in the opposite direction, starting with the phenomenology and moving only gradually (in Parts II and III of this book) to a global theory. For this we need to go back to first principles.

To what does the term 'consciousness' refer?

As with any term that refers to something that one can observe or experience, it is useful, if possible, to begin with an *ostensive definition*. That is, to 'point to' or 'pick out' the *phenomena* to which the term refers and, by implication, what is *excluded*. In everyday life there are two contrasting situations which inform our understanding of the term 'consciousness'. We have knowledge of what it is like to be conscious (when we are awake) as opposed to having no memory of being conscious (when in dreamless sleep). We also understand what it is like to be conscious *of* something (when awake or dreaming) as opposed to not being conscious of that thing.

This everyday understanding provides a simple place to start. A person, or other entity, is conscious if they experience *something*; conversely, if a person or entity experiences nothing they are not conscious. Elaborating slightly, we can say that when consciousness is present, *phenomenal content* is present. Conversely, when phenomenal content is absent, consciousness is absent.[3]

This stays very close to everyday usage and, to begin with, it is all that we need. To minimise confusion, I will also stay as close as possible to everyday, natural language usage for related terms. In common usage, the term 'consciousness' is often synonymous with 'awareness' or 'conscious awareness'. Consequently, I will use these terms interchangeably. For example, it makes no difference in most contexts to claim that I am 'conscious of' what I think, 'aware of' what I think, or 'consciously aware' of what I think.[4] The 'contents of consciousness' encompass all that we are conscious of, aware of, or experience. These include not only experiences that we commonly associate with ourselves, such as thoughts, feelings, images, dreams, body sensations and so on, but also the experienced three-dimensional world (the phenomenal world) beyond the body surface.

Some important distinctions

In some writings 'consciousness' is synonymous with 'mind'. However, given the extensive evidence for nonconscious mental processing, this definition of consciousness is too broad.[5] In this book, 'mind' refers to psychological states and processes that may or may not be 'conscious'.

In other writings 'consciousness' is synonymous with 'self-consciousness'. As one can be conscious of many things other than oneself (other people, the external world, etc.), this definition is too narrow. Here, self-consciousness is taken to be a special form of *reflexive* consciousness in which the object of consciousness is the self or some aspect of the self.

The term 'consciousness' is also commonly used to refer to a state of wakefulness. Being awake or asleep or in some other state such as coma clearly influences what one can be conscious of, but it is not the same as being conscious in the sense of having 'phenomenal contents'. When sleeping, for example, one can still have visual and auditory experiences in the form of dreams. Conversely, when awake there are many things at any given moment that one does *not* experience. So in a variety of contexts it is necessary to distinguish 'consciousness' in the sense of 'phenomenal consciousness' from wakefulness and other states of arousal, such as dream sleep, deep sleep, and coma.[6]

Finally, 'consciousness' is sometimes used to mean 'knowledge', in the sense that if one is conscious of something one also has knowledge of it. The relation of consciousness to knowledge turns out to be very important. However, at any moment, much knowledge is nonconscious, or implicit (for example, the knowledge gained over a lifetime, stored in long-term memory). So consciousness and knowledge cannot be co-extensive. We return to this in Part III of this book.

The above, broad definitions and distinctions have been quite widely accepted in the contemporary scientific literature (see, for example, Farthing, 1992; and readings in Velmans, 1996a and Velmans and Schneider, 2007), although it is unfortunate that various writers continue to use the term 'consciousness' in ways that have little to do with its everyday meaning. Agreeing on definitions is important. Once a given reference for the term 'consciousness' is fixed in its *phenomenology*, the investigation of its nature can begin, and this may in time transmute the meaning (or sense) of the term. As Dewey (1910) notes, to grasp the meaning of a thing, an event or situation is to see it in its relations to other things – to note how it operates or functions, what consequences follow from it, what causes it, and what uses it can be put to. Thus, to understand what consciousness is, we need to understand what causes it, what its function(s) may be, how it relates to nonconscious processing in the brain, and so on. As our scientific understanding of these matters deepens, our understanding of what consciousness *is* will also deepen. A similar transmutation of meaning (with growth of knowledge) occurs with basic terms in physics such as 'energy', and 'time'.

Notes

1 An earlier analysis of the difficulties of incorporating the phenomenology of consciousness into a purely third-person information processing model of the mind was also made from within cognitive science itself by Velmans (1991a, 1991b). This is a somewhat different way to express why consciousness is a 'hard' problem – and we will return to various aspects of this problem and how to resolve it in Chapters 4, 5, 10 and 13.

2 See Chapter 9, and additional readings in Varela and Shear, 1999; Velmans, 2000; Jack and Roepstorff, 2003, 2004.

3 This may seem obvious to the point of being trivial. However, in the philosophical and scientific literature this restricted use of the term consciousness, sometimes known as 'phenomenal consciousness', has been challenged. For example, a number of theorists have argued that there are other forms of consciousness such as 'access consciousness' (Block, 1995), 'executive consciousness', 'control consciousness' and so on. In Chapters 4 and 9, I argue that such proposals are counterproductive for the reason that they import *nonconscious* information processing operations

(e.g. the nonconscious operations involved in accessing information throughout the brain) into the ordinary meaning of 'consciousness', making it more difficult to be clear about how the phenomenology of consciousness *relates* to such nonconscious information processing. It is also worth noting that Eastern philosophies refer to a state of 'pure consciousness', without any phenomenal contents (Fontana, 2007; Shear and Jevning, 1999; Shear, 2007). As this possibility does not have a direct bearing on the issues on which we focus, we can safely leave it to one side for now, without dismissing it.

4 Note that in some theories 'awareness' is thought of as a form of low-level consciousness that is distinct from full consciousness. This is not a serious problem for the present usage, provided that the situation described has some phenomenal content (for example where one is dimly aware of a stimulus). However, confusions arise in situations where the term 'awareness' is applied to situations where there is no relevant phenomenal content, for example when 'awareness' refers to preconscious information processing, or, worse, to the nonconscious information processing which *accompanies* consciousness (as proposed by Chalmers, 1995). In the present usage, being 'aware of' nonconscious information processing is a contradiction in terms.

5 See, for example, Dixon (1981), Kihlstrom (1987), Velmans (1991a), Reber (1993), de Gelder *et al.* (2001), Wilson (2002), Goodale and Milner (2004), Jeannerod (2007), Kihlstrom *et al.* (2007), Merikle (2007).

6 For various purposes it remains useful to distinguish the conditions for the existence of consciousness (for example the difference between being awake and in deep coma) from the added conditions which determine its varied phenomenal contents (for example having visual rather than auditory experiences). However, for the purposes of my analysis I will retain the convention that unless one is conscious *of* something one is not conscious. A useful introduction to some of these problems of definition is given by Güzeldere (1997).

2 Conscious souls, brains and quantum mechanics

The ancient history of dualism

The belief that humans are more than material bodies extends well beyond the twilight of recorded history. In palaeolithic graves one finds not only tokens of respect for the dead but also provisions for an afterlife. Quarters of venison, shellfish, flint instruments and funeral furniture imply a belief that the dead have needs and means for satisfying them similar to our own (Luquet, 1996). Egyptian mythology is specific. The land of the dead lies in the West, at the entrance to the desert. There, in the kingdom of Osiris the hearts of departed souls are weighed in judgement. Those found to be pure may dwell in happiness for ever in the kingdom. Hearts of the guilty are devoured by Amemait, part lion, part hippopotamus, part crocodile.

Early Orphic and Pythagorean mystery teachings also held the soul to be immortal. But, in the philosophy of the ancient Greeks, the 'soul' begins to have properties that we now associate with consciousness and mind. For Socrates, the ability to *reason* comes from the soul. It is not just *psyche* – some insubstantial shadow of the body that dwells in Hades when the body dies, but rather it is man's true self or *nous*, that faculty of intuitive insight that allows one to distinguish good from evil and aspires to choose the good. The aim of life, for Socrates, is the perfection of the soul, achieved by *knowledge*, particularly knowledge of oneself.

According to Plato, the material body *interacts* with the soul. In the acquisition of knowledge, the body influences the soul through the operation of its senses, but the reasoning soul provides man's only means of understanding the true nature of the world. The body and its sensations provide a world of ever-changing appearances, but these are mere reflections of the unchanging patterns or universal forms that underlie the structure of the world. Being itself a universal form, the soul has intuitive knowledge of the forms, which it can recover through its power of reason. The soul is also the 'form of life' which has the ability to make the body move and act. In short, in Platonic thought the soul is a *knowing agent*. It is the source of consciousness and reason, and through the exercise of will, it manipulates the body. The body in turn acts on the soul, forming impressions on its consciousness via the senses.

This is classical, *dualist-interactionism*. In the seventeenth century this was given a more concrete form in the writings of the French philosopher and mathematician René Descartes.

The dualist-interactionism of René Descartes

In an intellectual climate dominated by the conviction that the material universe consisted of nothing but 'insensate corpuscles' or 'atoms', Descartes found it difficult to believe that the bodies and brains of animals and man could be anything other than machines, whose operations are entirely determined by mechanical principles. Like other aspects of the physical world they are composed of a substance which is extended in space (*res extensa*) and their behaviour may be understood in terms of the way bits of *res extensa* move and interact.

Yet, there are some human capacities, Descartes argued, which simply *cannot* be explained in mechanistic terms. In his *Discourse on the Method* (Part V) he suggests that,

> if there were machines which have a resemblance to our body and imitated our actions as far as it was morally possible to do so, we should always have two very certain tests by which to recognise that, for all that, they were not real men. The first is, that they could never use speech or other signs as we do when placing our thoughts on record for the benefit of others. For we can easily understand a machine's being constituted so that it can utter words, and even emit some responses to action on it of a corporeal kind, which brings about a change in its organs; for instance, if it is touched in a particular part it may ask what we wish to say to it; if in another part it may exclaim that it is being hurt, and so on. But it never happens that it arranges its speech in various ways, in order to reply appropriately to everything that may be said in its presence, as even the lowest type of man can do. And the second difference is, that although machines can perform certain things as well as or perhaps better than any of us can do, they infallibly fall short in others, by which means we may discover that they did not act from knowledge, but only from the disposition of their organs. For while reason is a universal instrument which can serve for all contingencies, these organs have need of some special adaption for every particular action. From this it follows that it is morally impossible that there should be sufficient diversity in any machine to allow it to act in all events of life in the same way as our reason causes us to act.
>
> (in Haldane and Ross, 1931; also cited in Flew, 1978, p. 127)

Thus, for Descartes, the capacity for language and the faculty of reason provide a flexibility, an ability to respond appropriately to every novel situation, in man, which could never be accomplished by any mechanistic system.

Box 2.1 An old argument about whether a computer can think

Descartes' argument that no mechanism could use language appropriately or solve problems bears an uncanny resemblance to the test proposed by the mathematician Alan Turing for deciding whether a computer can 'think'. In this test a number of judges are required to distinguish between a computer and a human using only the replies that they provide to any questions put to them. To eliminate irrelevant cues all questions and answers are typewritten, and the judges are placed in a separate room. If the ability of the judges to identify the computer (on the basis of this linguistic exchange) does not differ significantly from chance, then, Turing asserts, the machine may be said to 'think'. The main difference between Descartes and Turing is that Descartes believes machines will always fail this test whereas, 300 years later, Turing thinks they will eventually succeed. We will discuss whether or not Turing is right in Chapter 5.

Although these arguments were presented over 300 years ago they have a contemporary relevance (Box 2.1).

Descartes also believed that the same principles can be used to distinguish humans from 'brutes' (his rather anthropocentric term for other animals):

> For it is a remarkable fact that there are none so depraved, or stupid without even excepting idiots, that they cannot arrange different words together, forming of them a statement by which they make known their thoughts; while on the other hand there is no other animal, however perfect and fortunately circumstanced it may be, which can do the same. It is also a very remarkable fact that although there are many animals which exhibit more dexterity than we do in some of their actions, we at the same time observe that they do not manifest dexterity at all in many others. Hence the fact that they do better than we do, does not prove that they are endowed with mind, for in this case they would have more reason than any of us, and would surpass us in all other things. It rather shows that they have no reason at all, and it is nature which acts in them according to the disposition of their organs, just as a clock, which is only composed of wheels and weights, is able to tell the hours and measure the time more correctly than we do with all our wisdom.
>
> (ibid.; also cited in Flew, 1978, p. 138)

Descartes' clear separation of man from the rest of nature was also driven by his epistemology. Like the Greek rationalists before him, Descartes was sceptical about the sensory world. Secure knowledge, he believed, could not be grounded in the world of appearances provided by the senses, as one cannot rule out the possibility that these are illusory or even a dream. Only the rational mind can provide secure knowledge. And to a mind prepared to doubt everything only one thing could be certain – the fact that it *was* something which experienced doubt. The existence of the thought guarantees the existence of the thinker. 'Cogito, ergo sum' – *I think, therefore I am*. Descartes therefore concludes that the ability to think is the indubitable essence of man. And it exists *only* in man, not in other animals.

As we will see in Chapter 8, contemporary research into nonhuman animal language and reasoning does not support Descartes' opinions of other animals. However, Descartes believed that this separation of man from the rest of nature is a consequence of the fact that man alone has a rational, immaterial soul. It is this which enables him to think, speak, feel, and have conscious sensations. Indeed, in Descartes' view, it is impossible that matter alone could have conscious thought no matter how it is arranged. Rather, these capacities must be manifestations of a second, fundamentally different substance in the universe – *res cogitans*, a substance which thinks. Man, then, is a duality – a union of *res extensa*, in the form of a material body and brain extended in space, and *res cogitans*, an immaterial soul or mind.[1]

In clearly separating man's extended substance from his thinking substance, Descartes is often thought to be responsible for the mind–body problem in its modern form. How, for example, could substances as different as these interact? Descartes proposed that causal interactions between body and mind operate in a hydraulic fashion. Stimulation of the sense organs produces motions in the 'animal spirits' contained in the nerves, which produce motions in the pineal gland, and these produce perceptions in the soul. Conversely, the exercise of free will by the soul produces movements in the animal spirits in the pineal gland, which are transmitted via the nerves to the muscles. The pineal was thought to be the principal interface between body and soul, partly because of its central position in the brain. It is well placed to influence and be influenced by the movements of animal spirits initiated either by the soul or by the sense organs. Descartes also noted that there is only one such gland (in contrast to other organs of the brain known to Descartes, which tend to come in pairs). So it might be the point at which sensory influences from separate sense organs (e.g. the two eyes) converge, to produce a unified experience of the world in the soul.

In the light of current understanding of the brain this model of animal spirits, nerves and pineal gland seems antiquated. However, dualist-interactionist *philosophy* (which has persisted over the millennia) must be distinguished from specific, *neurophysiological* theories about the way that conscious minds might interact with brains. A contemporary defence of dualist-interactionist philosophy has been given by Foster (1991), and variants of dualist-interactionism have been defended in the twentieth century by some of the most eminent neurophysiologists, including Charles Sherrington

(1942) and Wilder Penfield (1975), and, in some depth, by John Eccles (1980, 1989). As we will see below, it also persists, in various forms, in some current theories about the role of consciousness in quantum mechanics.

Dualism in modern science

In some respects, it is not surprising that defenders of dualism were to be found in twentieth-century science, even amongst researchers most closely involved with investigations of the brain. The existence of consciousness seems undeniable. Yet, the most detailed histological examination of the brain does not reveal it. Nor does science, now or then, fully explain it. As Eccles noted in 1980:

> nowhere in the laws of physics or in the laws of derivative sciences, chemistry and biology, is there any reference to consciousness or mind. . . . Regardless of the complexity of electrical, chemical or biological machinery there is no statement in the 'natural laws' that there is an emergence of this strange non-material entity, consciousness or mind. This is not to say that consciousness does not emerge in the evolutionary process but merely to state that its emergence is not reconcilable with the natural laws as presently understood.
>
> (Eccles, 1980, p. 20)

Eccles concluded from this that 'the self-conscious mind' (his terminology) must have some nonmaterial existence. At the same time, Eccles argued that the self-conscious mind must have causal effects on brain functioning, or it could not have evolved. Theories that explain mental functions entirely in terms of brain functions are, he claimed, in conflict with the principle of biological evolution:

> Since they all . . . assert the causal ineffectiveness of consciousness per se, they fail completely to account for the biological evolution of consciousness, which is an undeniable fact. There is firstly, its emergence and then its progressive development with the growing complexity of the brain. In accord with evolutionary theory only those structures and processes that significantly aid in survival are developed in natural selection. If consciousness is causally impotent, its development cannot be accounted for by evolutionary theory. According to biological evolution mental states and consciousness could have evolved and developed only if they were causally effective in bringing about changes in neural happenings in the brain with consequent changes in behaviour. That can occur only if the neural machinery of the brain is open to influences from the mental events of the world of conscious experiences, which is the basic postulate of dualist-interactionist theory.
>
> (Eccles, 1980, p. 20)

According to Eccles, the causal role of consciousness has two aspects. First, the 'self-conscious mind' integrates the information arriving at the neural modules of the neocortex from the sense organs to provide a unified stream of consciousness. Second, in willed movement, the self-conscious mind excites appropriate assemblages of neurons controlling motor responses. In essence, this is the same theory championed by Plato and Descartes. The mind influences the body through the exercise of free will, and the body influences the mind by providing sensory information, which the mind integrates into perceptual experience. Eccles, of course, updates Descartes' neurophysiology, replacing the pineal gland with modularly arranged neurons in the dominant hemisphere which are 'open' to the influences of the self-conscious mind, thereby 'liaising' between mind and brain. That is,

> The self-conscious mind is actively engaged in reading out from the multitude of liaison modules that are largely in the dominant cerebral hemisphere. The self-conscious mind selects from these modules according to attention and interest, and from moment to moment integrates its selection to give unity even to the most transient experiences. Furthermore, the self-conscious mind acts upon these modules modifying their dynamic spatio-temporal patterns. Thus it is proposed that the self-conscious mind exercises a superior interpretative and controlling role. A key component of this hypothesis is that the unity of conscious experience is provided by the self-conscious mind and not by the neural machinery of the liaison areas of the cerebral hemisphere. Hitherto it has been impossible to develop any neurophysiological theory that explains how a diversity of brain events come to be synthesised so that there is a unified conscious experience of a global or gestalt nature.
>
> (Eccles, 1980, p. 49)

In his extensive writings on this subject, Eccles developed other, detailed proposals. For example, while Eccles accepted that both hemispheres of the brain have a form of consciousness, he focused on the 'liaison brain' in the dominant hemisphere, as he believed that only this is *fully* conscious. That is, only the dominant hemisphere 'knows that it knows' and can communicate its awareness – essential requirements, he maintained, for a 'conscious self'.

These claims, based on findings with 'split-brain' patients, need not concern us for now. The above extracts demonstrate how an ancient philosophical position might, *in principle*, be reinterpreted to fit in with modern science. They provide an initial basis for assessing the viability of dualist-interactionism as a modern theory of mind.

Unfortunately, these 'scientific' arguments offered by Eccles in defence of his position are very weak ones. Eccles based his conclusion that consciousness was a nonmaterial entity on its exclusion from a 1980s understanding of natural laws and the scope of natural science. But our understanding of natural laws and the scope of science is in principle revisable, as the subsequent re-emergence of Consciousness Studies as a major scientific discipline makes clear. Eccles just takes it for granted that the emergence and biological evolution of consciousness following Darwinian principles is 'an undeniable fact', but, while this is a common assumption, it is not a 'fact' that has in any way been established by science, and other ways of viewing the relationship of consciousness to biological evolution exist (see Chapter 14). The force of this argument also depends on whether or not one accepts dualism. If consciousness is a nonmaterial entity of the kind Eccles proposes, then to deny it a causal role might be regarded as contrary to evolutionary theory (provided that one is willing to extend Darwinian evolutionary theory to nonmaterial entities). But if consciousness turns out to be nothing more than a state or function of the brain, as various reductionist theories suggest (see Chapters 3 to 5), then there is no problem about it having a causal role and, therefore, no inconsistency with evolutionary theory.

Nor is there any evidence in support of modules in the dominant hemisphere in the brain being 'open' to the manipulations of a nonmaterial mind. In any case, as we will see in Chapter 11, there are now various neurophysiological theories that deal with 'how a diversity of brain events come to be synthesised so that there is a unified conscious experience' (commonly known as 'neural binding') without any nonmaterial intervention.

Quantum dualist interactionism

In an attempt to provide a fuller understanding of how a nonmaterial consciousness might intervene in neural activity, Beck and Eccles (1992, 2003) subsequently developed a detailed model of how conscious will exercises motor control (and other brain functions), by influencing quantum mechanical events in a way that momentarily increases the probability of exocytosis, the release of neurotransmitter substance at synaptic clefts that causes post-synaptic neurons to fire. When such influences operate over a large number of synapses, they argue that this can have major psychological effects. As quantum mechanical effects are in any case probabilistic they argue that this offers a natural explanation for voluntary movements caused by mental intentions without violating physical conservation laws. A similar argument for the effects of quantum mechanics on the brain is offered by Stapp, when he notes that,

> Quantum mechanics deals with the observed behaviors of macroscopic systems whenever those behaviors depend sensitively upon the activities of atomic-level entities. Brains are such systems. Their behaviors depend strongly upon the effects of, for example, the ions that flow into nerve terminals. Computations show that the quantum uncertainties in the ion-induced release of neurotransmitter molecules at the nerve terminals are large (Stapp, 1993, p. 133, 152). These uncertainties propagate in

principle up to the macroscopic level. Thus quantum theory must be used in principle in the treatment of the physical behavior of the brain, in spite of its size.

(Stapp, 2007a, p. 300)

However, Stapp rejects Beck and Eccles's way of applying quantum mechanics to consciousness–brain interactions, on the grounds that biasing the probabilities of quantum statistical rules is actually in conflict with the rules, and therefore in conflict with the standard model of quantum mechanics.[2] According to Stapp, there is no need for the operations of consciousness to be in conflict with the rules, as, following Bohr's famous 'Copenhagen Convention' (later extended by Von Neumann and then by Stapp himself), consciousness already plays a central causal role in the operations of quantum mechanics.

Why? In the quantum world observed phenomena depend critically on the choices experimenters make about the observational arrangements that they use. Photons can for example appear to behave either as waves or as particles depending on the experimental setup, and the measurement of, say, the position of an electron affects it in such a way that one can no longer measure its momentum (so the decision to measure position excludes the possibility of knowing about its momentum). In classical physics, one can interpret such observer-dependencies epistemically, as a limitation on what we can know about the world via physical experiments, rather than ontologically, as a fact about the autonomously existing physical world itself. However, in various interpretations of quantum mechanics, this epistemic versus ontological distinction becomes blurred.

For example, the Copenhagen Convention argues that quantum mechanics does not describe an autonomously existing external world. Rather, it describes the observations made by conscious observers that are consequent on certain measurement operations. As Stapp notes, this incorporation of the *observer's knowledge* into the mathematics of quantum mechanics involves a major shift in what physics is about:

> The quantum conception of the relationship between the psychologically and physically described components of scientific practice was achieved by abandoning the classical picture of the physical world that had ruled science since the time of Newton, Galileo, and Descartes. The building blocks of science were shifted from descriptions of the behaviors of tiny bits of mindless matter to accounts of *the actions that we take to acquire knowledge* and of the *knowledge that we thereby acquire*.

(Stapp, 2007b, p. 883)

This is clearly an *epistemic* claim about how physics is done, and what physics is about. However, in the same paragraph, he goes on to suggest that,

Science was thereby transformed from its seventeenth century form, which effectively excluded our conscious thoughts from any causal role in the mechanical workings of Nature, to its twentieth century form, which focuses on our active engagement with Nature, and on what we can learn by taking appropriate actions.

(ibid.)

In stressing that classical physics 'effectively excluded our conscious thoughts from any causal role in the mechanical workings of Nature', Stapp clearly implies that in quantum mechanics consciousness *does* play a causal role in the mechanical workings of Nature – which is a claim about the *ontology* of both consciousness and Nature. But then he adds, by way of explanation, that in quantum mechanics our choices enter into 'what we can learn [about Nature] by taking appropriate action', which reverts back to an epistemic claim about the role of observer choices in the acquisition of physical knowledge. It is important to note these subtle shifts when assessing the status of what Stapp (2007a) refers to as 'Quantum dualist interactionism'.

As noted above, classical 'dualist interactionism' refers to the view that autonomously existing conscious experiences can have two-way causal interactions with the brain. In order for consciousness to influence brain states, there must be some 'gap' in neural causal chains for consciousness to operate. In the realm of classical physics no such gaps are apparent. So it is commonly assumed that the physical world is 'causally closed'.

However, according to Stapp the same 'causal closure' does not apply in quantum mechanics. The Copenhagen Convention accepts that the decisions made by experimenters about what to measure are not themselves described by the quantum rules. If conscious agents can freely choose the probing questions they will physically pose, and such choices are not themselves determined by known physical laws, then physics no longer forms a closed system. Consequently, in the new physics there is a natural place for conscious choices to have a real effect on physics.[3]

Note, however, that, once again, this argument for the causal efficacy of consciousness involves a blurred distinction between two meanings, in this case two meanings of 'the causal closure of the physical world'. One might for example accept that physics is 'open' in the sense that physicists are free to choose the physical measurements that they want to make, and that these choices are not described by the quantum rules, while rejecting the suggestion that neurobiological processes in the brain have causal 'gaps' that provide space for the intervention of such 'conscious choices'.[4]

In various interpretations of quantum mechanics there is in any case ambiguity, and associated controversy, about where in the observation process a choice about what to observe and a subsequent observation is made. For example, according to the 'Copenhagen Convention', the original formulation of quantum theory developed by Niels Bohr, there is a clear separation between the process taking place in the observer (Process 1) and the process taking place in the system that is being observed (Process 2), but the observer is defined very broadly:

> The observer consists of the stream of consciousness of a human agent, together with the brain and body of that person, and also the measuring devices that he or she uses to probe the observed system. Each observer describes himself and his knowledge in a language that allows him to communicate to colleagues two kinds of information: *How he has acted* in order to prepare himself – his mind, his body, and his devices – to receive recognizable and reportable data; and *What he learns* from the data he thereby acquires. This description is in terms of the conscious experiences of the agent himself. It is a description of his intentional probing actions, and of the experiential feedbacks that he subsequently receives.
>
> (Stapp, 2007b, p. 886)

This 'Process 1' taking place in the 'observing' part of the system is necessarily described in ordinary language and the language of classical physics. By contrast, 'Process 2', which is taking place in the system being probed, is described in the symbolic language of quantum mechanics. Prior to an observation being made all possible states of the observed system exist in 'superposition', with probabilities of becoming actual described by the Schrödinger wave equation. The transition from possible to actual states does not occur until an observation is made. Once made, the act of observation 'collapses' the possible states into one, actual, measured state (to which the Schrödinger wave equation no longer applies).

But this leaves an unresolved issue: if the 'observer' includes the measuring instrument (e.g. a Geiger counter) as well as the body, brain and conscious experience of the observer, then what aspect of the measurement process causes the collapse is open to debate. It could, for example, be the case that quantum events are actualised at the time that they are recorded by a Geiger counter, rather than when they are consciously experienced – which would have little consequence for the causal impact of conscious experience on the physical world.[5]

However, in a later extension of quantum theory, Von Neumann demonstrated that there is nothing in the formalism to exclude *any* of the physical systems involved from the quantum mechanical description of the observed system, including the measuring instruments, body, and even brain of the conscious observer. Whether one places the cut between the observer and the physical observed world, or places it at the interface between the observer's brain, body and external world on the one hand, and the observer's conscious experience on the other, does not alter the mathematics of quantum mechanics or its predictions. Nor does this alter the essential idea that the mathematics describes what the subject experiences when he probes the world in a certain way. Consequently, to remove this ambiguity, Von Neumann redrew the boundary between the observer and the observed at the interface of conscious experiences and the brain. In this reformulation, conscious experiences themselves become the choosing agents, and the quantum potentials that they probe and directly affect are *in their own brains*!

As Stapp observes,

> This placement of the cut does not eliminate the need for Process 1. It merely places the physical aspect of the Process 1 psychophysical event in the brain of the conscious agent, while placing the conscious choice of which probing question to pose in his stream of consciousness. That is, the conscious act of choosing the probing question is represented as a psychologically described event in the agent's mind, which is called by Von Neumann (1955, p. 421) the 'abstract ego'. This choice is physically and functionally implemented by a Process 1 action in his brain. The psychologically described and physically described actions are the two aspects of a single psychophysical event, whose physically described aspect intervenes in the orderly Process 2 evolution in a mathematically well defined way.
>
> (Stapp, 2007a, p. 304)

To differentiate the conscious part of Process 1 (the 'conscious ego') from the physically embodied part, Stapp (2007c) refers to it as 'Process 0'. Stapp believes that such quantum dualist interactionism neatly sidesteps the classical problems of mind–body (or consciousness–brain) interaction (see Stapp, 2007a, p. 305). According to the Von Neumann/Stapp theory, consciousness (Process 0) chooses what question to ask; through the mediation of Process 1 this interacts with Process 2 (the developing possibilities specified by the quantum mechanics of the physical system under interrogation, including the brain) – and Nature supplies an answer, which is in turn reflected in conscious experience (making the entire process a form of dualist-interactionism).

It is not surprising, however, that a theory designed to make sense of observer–observed interactions in quantum mechanics 'neatly sidesteps' the classical problems of consciousness–brain interaction, as quantum mechanical theories were never intended to address such problems! A central claim of the Von Neumann/Stapp theory, for example, is that it is the observer's conscious free will (Von Neumann's 'abstract ego' or Stapp's 'Process 0') that chooses how to probe nature. But *how* such choices are made by the 'abstract ego' and *how* the phenomenology of consciousness could affect the brain in ways not already affected by its neural correlates (by the operation of Process 1) remain obscure, as we will see below.

The plausibility of dualist-interactionism

It is remarkable that dualist-interactionism has persisted in a form very similar to that proposed by the ancient Greeks for over 2,500 years. Although it is framed in terms of current neuropsychology, the mind–body theory of John Eccles is little changed from that of Plato and Descartes. As before, the self-conscious mind is a nonmaterial entity with an independent existence (dualism). It receives information from the senses, and exercises control over the body through the exercise of will (classical interactionism). Von Neumann and Stapp similarly view consciousness as an agent that exercises choice, whose operations are not determined by the physical system with which it interacts, although, in perception, it is affected by that physical system. One likely reason for the persistence of this view is that now, as then, it gives a simple, straightforward account of the following facts:

1   Bodies and brains *seem* to be very different from minds and consciousness. Arms and legs for example seem to be made of completely different 'stuff' from thoughts and feelings. No one can find consciousness by examining bits of the brain. It is intuitively plausible therefore to suggest that body and mind (or brain and consciousness) are different *types* of thing.
2   There is extensive evidence that the body and brain affect mind and consciousness via the senses (for example that the visual system affects visual experience). There is also extensive evidence that mind and consciousness affect the body and brain (for example in the way that visual experiences, thoughts, and conscious choices influence subsequent actions). It is plausible therefore to suggest that mind and consciousness *interact* with body and brain.

As far as it goes, nothing could be simpler – and for this reason, dualist-interactionism forms a natural place of departure for alternative theories of consciousness or mind. Any alternative theory would have to account for the same facts in an equally plausible way. Yet in contemporary science and philosophy of mind there are very few defenders of dualist-interactionism. Why?

The problems of dualist-interactionism

1 Dualism tells us little about the nature of consciousness

Within dualism the ontological nature of consciousness, mind, or soul remains essentially mysterious. According to Descartes, it is *res cogitans*. But what kind of 'substance' is a 'substance that thinks'? In his clean separation of *res cogitans* from *res extensa* (the stuff of the material world), Descartes is often thought to have ushered in the modern era. The stuff of the world is purely mechanical, following mathematically describable laws. These can be discovered by empirical research and are, therefore, in the province of natural science. Consciousness, mind or soul, being nonmaterial, cannot be investigated empirically. Consequently, it is in the province of theology and metaphysics. In the seventeenth century, this separation of responsibilities was liberating for science, enabling the investigation of matter to proceed without interference from the church.

However the cost of splitting the universe into two fundamentally different substances was to block any empirical investigation of consciousness and mind. Three hundred years later, this separation appears to have outlived its cultural value. Eccles made much of the fact that current science does not explain consciousness (see above). Given its historical exclusion from scientific investigation by both scientists *and* theologians, this is hardly surprising. But the same constraints may not apply to future science. Given the success of science in explaining mysteries once thought to be beyond any natural explanation (the origins of life, the evolution of man), many scientists and philosophers now believe a natural explanation is possible for consciousness and mind.

2 Consciousness is not the same as mind or soul

The classical dualist-interactionist position is not easily translated into a contemporary understanding of consciousness, mind and brain. As noted above, Plato, Descartes and Eccles make no clear distinctions between the terms 'consciousness', 'mind', and 'soul'. But, in the modern context, these terms have different meanings. 'Consciousness' is not easy to define. However, as pointed out in Chapter 1, one can begin to define it ostensively by contrasting situations where it is present and absent, for example, situations where one is conscious *of* something as opposed to not being conscious of that thing. That is, consciousness can partly be defined in terms of the presence or absence of phenomenal content. 'Mind', by contrast, refers to psychological processes that may or may not have associated conscious contents. There is considerable evidence for example for a 'cognitive unconscious'. And 'soul' traditionally refers to some essential aspect of human identity that survives bodily death.

Put this way, the distinctions between consciousness, mind and soul should be clear. It should be obvious, for example, that one can investigate the conditions under which consciousness (of a stimulus) is present or absent, or the operations of mind (reasoning, the use of language, etc.), by means of psychological research, irrespective of one's convictions about the survival of the soul.

3 Thought does not exemplify the whole of conscious experience

Historically, dualism has associated consciousness, mind or soul with the ability to reason. For Descartes, the best exemplar of conscious experience is *thought*. Thoughts do have conscious manifestations, for example verbal thoughts may be experienced in the form of phonemic imagery or 'inner speech'. However, the phenomenal properties of such thoughts do not exemplify the *whole* of conscious experience. As you read this sentence for example you have a visual experience of print on a page, attached to a book, extended in three-dimensional phenomenal space. This visual, phenomenal world seems to have properties (or 'qualia') very different from verbal thoughts. To understand consciousness one needs to discover how its phenomenology relates to processes in the brain, the external world and so on. Conversely, if we *start* with an inaccurate (or partial) description of its phenomenology we are unlikely to arrive at an accurate understanding. A brief mention of this point will do for now. In Part II of this book, I show how a more accurate phenomenology leads to a different understanding of consciousness.

4 The problem of causation

Dualist-interactionism takes the causal interaction of consciousness and brain to be well substantiated by the evidence of ordinary experience. Eccles also asks, 'If consciousness doesn't do anything, how could it have evolved?' However, the *mechanism* by which interaction takes place is far from clear. As Hume (1739), Moore (1910), and Russell (1948) have pointed out, differences in *appearance* between entities and events do not in themselves eliminate the possibility of their causal interaction – witness the mutual influence of magnetic fields and electric currents. Yet, if consciousness or mind is truly immaterial and 'soul-like' then the differences between it and the material world seem to be more fundamental than any differences that obtain amongst physical energies and events. How could something 'extended' interact with something that 'thinks'? How could experienced *wishes* or *desires* affect the behaviour of *neurons*? And how could *electrochemistry* give rise to *subjective experiences*? Little wonder that Spinoza (1677) and Leibniz (1686) judged the causal interaction of *res cogitans* and *res extensa* to be literally inconceivable (Box 2.2).

Extensive investigations of the brain have deepened this puzzle. According to dualist-interactionism the activities of the brain cannot be fully understood without the causal intervention of a nonmaterial consciousness or mind. But, on the basis of present evidence, the brain appears to operate on entirely physical principles. Viewed from the perspective of classical physics, there appear to be no 'gaps' in neural causal chains for nonmaterial causes to fill. In this sense, the physical world appears to be *causally closed*. Nonmaterial causation also seems to contravene the Conservation of Energy Principle. In order to do work in the physical universe one requires energy. If mental events are to influence physical ones, physical energy must be created from some nonmaterial source, and the total physical energy of the universe thereby increased. Equally, for physical events to influence mental ones, energy must be drawn from the physical universe. However, according to the Conservation of Energy Principle energy can neither be created nor destroyed.

Box 2.2 How could the conscious mind and the body have causal interactions?

Spinoza and Leibniz recognised the causal interaction of the conscious mind (or soul) with the body to be one of the hardest problems of consciousness. To resolve it Spinoza developed a form of 'dual-aspect theory', to which we return in Chapters 11 and 13. Leibniz, on the other hand, proposed a form of 'non-interactionist dualism' or 'parallelism' in which the causal interaction of the body and the soul is an illusion. In actual fact, he argues, God has formed the body and the soul into a pre-established harmony – like two perfectly aligned clocks, each keeping time exactly with the other. This perfect correlation produces the appearance of a causal relation although neither actually influences the other. Needless to say, this attempt to solve a mystery by recourse to a deeper one has few adherents in modern scientific thought.

Given our state of incomplete knowledge about consciousness, mind and physical matter, one cannot rule out the possibility that such interactions take place. It might be, for example, that in consciousness–brain interactions energy is 'borrowed from' and 'paid back' to the physical universe leaving the total in balance.[6] According to Hart (1995), consciousness might itself be a 'form of energy' currently unknown to physics, in which case conservation of energy would have to include the energy of consciousness, and transforms from physical to consciousness energies could, in principle, be found. Alternatively, it might be the case that consciousness interacts with the brain's microstructure. As noted above, another suggestion, made by Eccles (1989) and Beck and Eccles (1992, 2003), is that mental events might intervene in very small degrees in the unstable equilibrium of the brain at the microscopic probabilistic level – a form of influence that might not be inconsistent with physical determinism at the macroscopic level. Through a multiplier effect, such small influences might have macroscopic effects.

Whether the neurobiology of synaptic transmission would actually allow such quantum mechanical effects is highly controversial (see in particular Smith, 2008). In any case, as Stapp (2007a) points out, such biasing would be inconsistent with the rules of quantum mechanics. The Schrödinger wave equation describes the probability of quantum mechanical events being actualised with *great precision*. Either this remains true for quantum mechanical events in the brain, or it does not. If it remains true, then any momentary biasing of probabilities (by conscious free will) would have to be compensated for by subsequent biasing against those probabilities, otherwise the shape of the probability function would be changed. Alternatively, the Schrödinger wave equation does not apply at the loci of conscious intervention in the brain.

As Stapp points out, there is *another* sense in which the world described by physics is not causally closed – the sense in which experimenters are free to choose the measurements they make which in turn have a powerful influence on what they observe. Following Von Neumann, he suggests that the same process operates at the interface of conscious experience and the brain. However, in their present forms, such quantum mechanical accounts of the causal interaction of consciousness and brain suffer from problems that are just as serious as those of macroscopic accounts. Quantum mechanical effects occur within the brain at the microcosmic level just as they do in the rest of the material world, but there is little evidence as yet that these have measurable, macrocosmic effects.[7] Nor is it clear how perturbations at the microcosmic level could be translated into *psychologically relevant* macro-effects. Solving a problem or speaking a language, for example, are highly complex forms of human information processing that require the manipulation of symbols, grounded in meanings, which can be related to global knowledge of the world. This applies even more to the 'conscious choices' made by physicists about how to make measurements that might have theoretical significance in physical experiments. It is by no means clear how such *operations on representations of the world* could be determined by some nonmaterial consciousness, momentarily affecting quantum mechanical events. Events at the quantum mechanical level do not determine the way conventional computers operate on representations. So, unless the brain turns out to be a 'quantum computer', interventions at the quantum mechanical level would seem to be at the wrong level of grain.

And there are other reasons to be cautious about the applications of quantum mechanics to neuropsychology. It seems reasonable to suppose that a 'collapse' of a superposition of quantum states of, say, a photon by the conscious experience of an observer involves the observer having some form of visual experience. While this might not be inconsistent with the mathematics of quantum mechanics, it is paradoxical in terms of the processes involved in visual perception as it would seem to require *backward causation in time* (Box 2.3).

However, the *central* problem for dualist accounts of causality remains the *phenomenology* of consciousness. According to Eccles the self-conscious mind controls activities in the motor cortex through the exercise of free will. But how could a consciously experienced wish to do something activate neurons or move muscles? The processes required to activate neurons are not even *represented in consciousness*! For example, the phenomenology of a 'wish' includes no details of where our motor neurons are located, let alone how to activate them. *The same argument applies at the quantum mechanical level.* 'Experiencing a wish' reveals nothing of the momentary probabilities of quantum mechanical states, let alone how to alter them. Nor, following Von Neumann and Stapp, does the phenomenology of a conscious choice reveal anything about how to intervene in the developing quantum process within one's own brain. Consciousness without phenomenology is not consciousness

---

Box 2.3 A paradox for quantum dualist interactionism: how could a visual conscious experience actualise its own prior cause?

Although it only takes one photon arriving at the retina to trigger a visual experience, the vitreous humour of the eye scatters light, so that even under optimal conditions, it requires from five to eight photons to trigger that experience (see Chapter 8). Studies of the visual system and other sensory systems also make it clear that conscious experiences do not arise at the instant that input stimuli arrive at the cortex. Instead, a period of preconscious processing occurs that involves neural activation, analysis, synthesis and so on. This takes time. Experiments reviewed by Libet (1996), for example, suggest it takes at least 200 milliseconds for neural states to form in a way that is adequate to support a tactile conscious experience (see Chapter 10). In short, within neuropsychology, consciousness *of* external events is thought to take place later in time than the occurrence of the events themselves and, perhaps, hundreds of milliseconds later in time than the arrival time of the neural activation they produce at the sensory cortex. The relevance of quantum mechanics to an understanding of how such systems operate is not obvious. According to the Stapp/Von Neumann interpretation a photon is only actualised once it results in a visual experience. But how could a *resulting* conscious experience 'actualise' its own *prior cause*? This would seem to require backward causation in time! And are we also to say, following Von Neumann and Stapp, that preconscious processes responsible for creating neural conditions that are adequate to support a conscious experience also only become 'actualised' once the visual experience arises? Note that such paradoxes would remain if there is *any* delay between the input stimulus and the consequent experience. That is, the problems remain even if Libet's figure of a minimal 200-millisecond delay turns out to be an overestimate.

---

at all (see Chapter 1). Consequently, if some aspect of the mind does control the momentary activities of neurons at the microcosmic level, that aspect of the mind must be *nonconscious*. This paradoxical relation of conscious phenomenology to nonconscious processing is discussed, in depth, in Chapters 4 and 10.

5 The problem of function

Both Descartes and Eccles support their case for a nonmaterial, self-conscious mind by listing capacities that could not be carried out by a purely material brain. Descartes, for example, focuses on language and reasoning, and Eccles on information integration. These claims have to be re-evaluated in the light of advances in artificial intelligence, and increased understanding of the brain.

It remains true, to the present day, that no existing machine can use language and reasoning with an appropriateness and flexibility approaching that of humans. But in restricted domains, where the rules and procedures are relatively well understood, machine performance is impressive – for example, mathematical calculation, or the ability to play chess, triumphantly demonstrated by the 1996 defeat of Grandmaster Gary Kasparov by IBM's 'Deep Blue' (cf. Newborn, 1997). Given such restricted successes, it is no longer self-evident that there is anything about the nature of physical systems as such that prevents more sophisticated functioning.[8] It would appear to be our limited understanding of our own mental processing that limits our ability to simulate or emulate such abilities in machines. Indeed, within cognitive psychology, one criterion for a 'good theory' is that it be sufficiently well specified to be instantiated in a machine.

Whether, in humans, there is some *general* ability to respond appropriately in all circumstances over and above such specialised skills remains to be seen. The human brain remains far more complex than any existing machine, and there is extensive cognitive neuropsychological evidence that its operation is largely 'modular'. That is, the brain's sophisticated functioning results from the interaction of large numbers of relatively specialised processors. It may be that, in addition, there is a *general* human capacity or intelligence that can be applied to many situations, along the lines suggested by Descartes. Indeed the relative contribution of specialised versus general skills has been a central topic for researchers of 'intelligence' for around 100 years. However, there is no reason, as yet, to doubt that such generalised functioning, once instantiated in the brain, follows physical principles.

6 The problem of explanatory adequacy

A more fundamental problem with dualist-interactionist explanations of human functioning is that they do not offer a genuine *alternative* to physical or functional explanations. For example, Descartes claims that *res cogitans* provides a general-purpose intelligence without suggesting *how* it does so. Eccles asserts that the self-conscious mind 'reads' information displayed on dominant hemisphere, 'selects' according to 'attention' and 'interest', and 'integrates' its selection to give unity to experiences. But he says nothing about *how* the self-conscious mind achieves such things. Stapp finds a gap in quantum mechanics where consciousness can exercise choices about how to interrogate the physical world, but again says nothing about *how* those choices are made – and quantum mechanics offers no answers. The processes involved in reading, selectively attending to, integrating, and responding to information have been extensively investigated in cognitive psychology for around fifty-five years (see Chapters 4 and 10), and it is abundantly clear that such functions require complex systems. If the self-conscious mind performs such functions it would itself have to be *a complex system* (like the brain). To encode information it would also have to possess discriminable states that need to be embodied somehow in a structure that can be accessed. But if the self-conscious mind is nonmaterial, without spatial location and extension, what kind of structure could this be? In short, all the problems of explaining how such functions operate in the brain simply regress, with added complications, to the self-conscious mind.

In sum, classical dualism offers 'explanations' which themselves require explanation. It also 'splits' the world in ways that make it difficult to put it back together again. Given this, it is not surprising that monists have searched for a more unified theory of consciousness and mind.

Notes

1 In Descartes' dualism no clear distinction is made between the terms 'soul', 'mind', and 'consciousness', so for exposition of his position I use the terms interchangeably. Later, I will argue that this loose conflation of terms is a source of major confusion in contemporary debates, which needs clarification before genuine progress can be made.

2 Stapp also rejects the suggestion that conscious influences are carried out by a disembodied soul. Rather, they reflect the operations of one aspect of a dual-aspect, psychophysical mind. As the latter proposal is also an important feature of the reflexive monism developed in this book, we return to it in depth in Chapters 11 and 13.

3 Hans Primas (2002) made the similar point that physical experiments require one to fix boundary conditions and initial conditions that are not given by the fundamental laws of nature, both in classical physics, and even more obviously in quantum mechanics. So, in this sense, conscious agents influence the findings of physics, and again, in this special sense, the physical world is not causally closed.

4 Indeed, there are good reasons to believe that 'free choice' or, more generally, 'free will', in the form that we experience it, is compatible with causal closure at the level of classical physics, a position known as 'compatibilism'. We examine this in depth in Chapter 14.

5 As it happens, most physicists have moved on to the view that interactions of a quantum particle with its environment (for example with the billions of particles that make up a macroscopic Geiger counter) produce a decoherence of the superposition of quantum states of that particle which fixes it into a given state – in which case the consciousness of an observer is not required. As this is an alternative to quantum dualist interactionism (rather than a version of it) I will not go into decoherence theory here. But see Thomas (2007) and Greene (2004, ch. 7), for lucid explanations.

6 The notion that energy may be briefly 'borrowed' and 'paid back' to the universe is used in subatomic physics to account for phenomena such as the tunnelling of electrons through electrical fields, the escape of alpha particles from radioactive nuclei and the existence of 'virtual' particles.

7 Critics of the QM approach to consciousness have pointed out that the heat and noise of the brain are too great to support QM effects. Hameroff and Penrose (1996) have suggested quantum mechanical effects might nevertheless operate within microtubules, protein structures found in the skeleton of neurons. These microtubules normally exist in quantum coherent states, whose (gravitation-induced)

collapse corresponds to elementary acts of consciousness. They also suggest ways in which such effects might combine to allow the brain to operate as a 'quantum computer'. This highly original, but controversial proposal has been extensively criticised by Grush and Churchland (1995), defended by Penrose and Hameroff (1995), and further criticised by Atmanspacher (2006), Stapp (2007a), and Smith (2008). The Hameroff–Penrose model is closer to a dual-aspect theory of consciousness–brain than interactionist-dualism, but I mention it here on the grounds that it is one of the most detailed models of consciousness–brain activity at the QM level.

8 Modern versions of the 'argument from capacity' are equally controversial. According to Penrose (1994) certain mathematical problems are noncomputable using classical computing systems although they are computable by minds. He suggests that such problems might be soluble by a 'quantum computer' – in which case, the brain itself might be a quantum computer. However, a quantum computer is still a *physical system*, so this is not an argument in support of the intervention of a nonmaterial consciousness or mind.

3 Are mind and matter the same thing?

How to collapse dualism into monism

There are three ways to collapse mind–matter dualism into monism:

1 Mind and physical matter might be aspects or arrangements of something more fundamental that is in itself neither mental nor physical (dual-aspect theory; neutral monism; pan-psychism).
2 Physical matter might be nothing more than a particular aspect or arrangement of mind (idealism).
3 Mind might be nothing more than a particular aspect or arrangement of physical matter (physicalism; functionalism).

Current Western philosophy and science largely favours option 3, so this will be the main focus of our analysis. However, each of these positions has been defended in the philosophy of mind, and being out of current fashion does not mean they are entirely wrong. Let us examine them briefly, in turn.

Dual-aspect theory

Spinoza (1677), like Descartes, viewed mind ('thinking being') and body ('extended being') as very different in kind, yet intimately conjoined in their activity. For Spinoza, however, the differences between mind and body are so great that their causal interaction is inconceivable. Rather, mind and body are different aspects of one underlying reality (which he variously refers to as 'Nature' or 'God'), and it is for this reason that they appear intimately conjoined. That is,

> Mind and body are one and the same thing, conceived first under the attribute of thought, secondly, under the attribute of extension. Thus it follows that the order of concatenation of things is identical, whether nature be conceived under the one attribute or the other; consequently the order of states of activity or passivity in our body is

> simultaneous in nature with the order of states of activity and passivity
> in the mind . . .
>
> (Spinoza, 1677)

In its original form, this theory threatens to solve a mystery by introducing a greater one (the unfathomable nature of 'Nature', or 'God'). However, the related notion that *consciousness* and aspects of *brain activity* may be thought of as one process with two sides was later taken up by Lewes (1877), Romanes (1885), Gunderson (1970), and Nagel (1986). Later, Velmans (1991a, 1991b) and Chalmers (1996) developed this into different dual-aspect theories of information. We return to these in Chapters 13 and 14.

Neutral monism

According to Ernst Mach (1885), William James (1904) and Bertrand Russell (1948), mental events and physical ones are not aspects of some more *fundamental* reality but simply different ways of *construing* the world as perceived. On this view, there is only one, neutral stuff of which the perceived world is composed, which Mach refers to as 'sensations', James as 'pure experience', and Russell as 'events'. Although the terms they use to describe the perceived world differ, the central argument used to support neutral monism is the same: what we observe in the world is neither intrinsically mental nor physical. Rather, we *judge* what we experience to be 'mental' or 'physical' depending on the network of relationships under consideration.

Mach (1885), for example, writes that,

> The traditional gulf between physical and psychological research . . . exists only for the habitual stereotyped method of observation. A colour is a physical object so long as we consider its dependence upon its luminous source, upon other colours, upon heat, upon space, and so forth. Regarding, however, its dependence upon the retina . . . it becomes a psychological object, a sensation. Not the subject, but the direction of our investigations is different in the two domains.

Or, as William James (1904) puts it, a room in which one sits enters simultaneously into two histories – 'one of them is the reader's personal biography, the other is the history of the house of which the room is a part'. In so far as the room is one's present field of consciousness it is 'the last term of a train of sensations, emotions, decisions, movements, classifications, expectations, etc, ending in the present, and the first term of a series of similar "inner" operations extending into the future'. On the other hand, it is also the end product of a very different series of physical operations, 'carpentering, papering, furnishing, warming' and so on, and it is the potential recipient of future physical operations – 'As your field of consciousness it may never have existed until now' – As a physical room it may have 'occupied that spot and had that environment for thirty years' (Box 3.1).

Box 3.1 How an entity in the world can be both mental and physical

There is a clear sense in which some experienced entities in the world are both mental and physical. From one point of view this *WORD* is an experience – one might for example investigate how it comes to be seen as *WORD* rather than WORD by tracing the activities of different sets of feature analysers which code for line orientation in the brain. At the same time, this *WORD* has physical properties determined by the nature and texture of the paper on which it is written, the ink used in the print, and so on. These different ways of analysing *WORD* do not alter its *phenomenology*. Only the network of relationships of interest changes.

Given the supposed, unbridgeable 'gap' separating the physical world from conscious experience, it is important not to lose sight of this simple (often neglected) point – and we will return to it in Chapter 6. However, one needs a lot more than this to solve the mind–body problem. For example, one still has to relate the phenomenal world to the very different world described by physics.[1] And it is not so easy to be 'neutral' about the status of events more traditionally regarded as the contents of consciousness, such as images, dreams, emotions and thoughts. These are clearly 'mental', but how, in the sense that the neutral monists intend, could they be 'physical'? Such experiences appear to differ from tables, chairs, floors, etc., not only in terms of the network of relationships into which they enter, but also in terms of their intrinsic qualities (or 'qualia'). That is, in contrast to physical objects they have no solidity, permanence, location, or extension in space.

And what of the causal interactions between consciousness and the brain which have so troubled dualist theories? How, in neutral monism, can the brain 'produce' experiences or experienced wishes affect neurons? According to Russell (1948) such questions pose no special problems, provided that 'causation is regarded – as it usually is by empiricists – as nothing but invariable sequence or concomitance' (p. 276). Given this, he concludes that,

> The whole question of the dependence of mind on body or body on mind had been involved in quite needless obscurity owing to the emotions involved. The facts are quite plain. Certain observable occurrences are commonly called 'physical', certain others 'mental'; sometimes 'physical' occurrences appear as causes of 'mental' ones, sometimes vice versa. A blow causes me to feel pain, a volition causes me to move my arm. There is no reason to question either of these causal connections,

or at any rate no reason which does not apply to all causal connections equally.

(Russell, 1948, p. 276)

In a sense, Russell is right. If we knew the necessary and sufficient neural conditions for a given conscious experience, these would count as the 'neural causes' of that experience. That is, if we could reproduce the neural conditions, we could reproduce the experience! The reverse is equally true. When we have a conscious wish to move an arm, we can usually do so. But this alone would not give us an *understanding* of how neuronal events could give rise to subjective experiences which seem so unlike neuronal events, or vice versa. Nor does it deal with the problem that, viewed macroscopically, the physical world appears to be causally closed. If one assumes that every experience has a neurophysiological correlate, then whenever an experience (such as a volition) appears, its neural correlates would also appear, thereby filling any 'gaps' in the neural causal chain, in which case there is no 'room' for any mental intervention. And if one already has a complete causal account of what is going on in neural terms, why introduce added, conscious causes? To these problems, neutral monism provides no solutions.

The reduction of body to mind

If one cannot bridge the mind–body gap by being 'neutral' about whether events are mental or physical, perhaps they have to be one thing or the other. But then one has to choose which one has ontological primacy. Historically, this choice has been determined by decisions about what counts as reliable knowledge, and particularly by decisions about whether to trust what one experiences. According to the Greek Rationalists, experience is illusory. Only innate knowledge of reality accessed through our ability to reason can provide knowledge of the true structure of the world (the universal forms). By contrast, British Empiricists such as John Locke (1690) believed that, at birth, the mind is a blank slate (a *tabula rasa*) on which the world makes impressions via the senses. Concepts and theories of the world are constructed by the mind on the basis of sensations, and their reliability depends entirely on the extent to which they can be seen to reduce to or derive from such sensations. That is, sensations provide the 'bedrock' of knowledge. They are as close to the world as one can get. Ironically, this sceptical, empiricist position provided the foundation for Berkeley's Idealism – the view that things exist only in so far as they exist *in the mind*.

John Locke himself had no doubts that the physical world is real. Like Descartes, he thought it to be composed of 'insensate corpuscles' (atoms) whose movements stimulate our sense organs by direct contact. This mechanical stimulation is transmitted via the 'nerves' to the brain which then produces effects in the mind, in the form of 'ideas' or 'ideas of sensations' such as ideas of solidity, motion, colour, smell and taste. According to Locke, sensations differ in how accurately they represent the physical causes that produce them. 'Primary sensations' such as sensations of 'extension', 'figure' (shape), 'solidity' and 'motion' mirror qualities that actually inhere in matter (they are attributes of the corpuscular world of seventeenth-century physics). 'Secondary sensations', although produced in the mind by the motions of material particles, do not represent what the particles themselves are like. For example, sound is a sensation produced in us by the motion of particles in the air, heat is a sensation produced in us by the motion of particles of which objects are composed, sensations of light are produced by the motions of particles impinging on the eye, and so on.

Locke's model is valuable in that it makes an initial attempt to ground a theory of knowledge in a theory of how the brain and the physical world interact (it does not divorce epistemology from ontology) – and, in rough outline, it is not far from contemporary views about the way sensations relate to the world described by physics (light is produced by photons, sound by the vibrations of air molecules, heat by molecular Brownian motion, etc.). But the model poses as many problems as it addresses. How could 'motions in the nerves' become 'sensations in the mind'? If mental events are quite different from physical or mechanical ones then what is their nature? And, on what basis can Locke judge the *resemblance* of sensations to the physical entities that they represent. To make a judgement about resemblance, one would need to make a comparison. But within Locke's empiricist epistemology there seems to be no way to make this comparison. According to Locke, abstractions about the fundamental nature of the world are only reliable in so far as they reduce to or can clearly be seen to derive from sensations. Sensations are as close to the real world as one can get. So there are no means (within empiricist philosophy) for knowing through sensations, concepts or theories the nature of a physical world that is, in many respects, quite *different* from our sensations.[2]

Berkeley's Idealism

Bishop George Berkeley (1710) agreed with Locke that 'secondary qualities' commonly attributed to material objects can, strictly speaking, only be said to exist in the mind of the perceiver. When we speak of colours, sounds, tastes and so on we are referring to aspects of what we experience. However, for Berkeley, this applies equally to 'primary qualities', which Locke believed to have an independent existence in the material world. When we speak of bodies being 'extended' or being 'solid' or having a certain 'shape' we are referring to how we *experience* those bodies, just as much as when we speak of colours or tastes. And, if all the 'qualities' normally attributed to material objects are in fact forms of experience in the mind of the perceiver, then what, asks Berkeley, is the sense of speaking of an unperceivable 'material' world which somehow 'lies behind' what we perceive? There is no such world! The abstractions of physics are simply convenient and useful ways to describe and interrelate what we do experience. In fact, the only sense in which objects or qualities of objects may be said to exist is in so far as they *are* experiences. '*Esse est percipi*' – to be is to be perceived![3]

With this argument, Berkeley solves a number of problems. If the 'real' world is just the world we *experience*, then there is no need to worry about how the events we perceive might 'represent' the 'material causes' which bring them into being. The 'material causes' have no real existence – they are simply abstractions, and themselves products of the mind. Their usefulness (following empiricist philosophy) depends entirely on how they reduce to or can be seen to derive from what we do experience. Nor is there any need to puzzle over how material causes could possibly produce mental effects, or any need to ask whether there are two fundamentally different 'substances' in the universe (mental and physical). According to Berkeley's analysis, the only existing 'substance' is a mental one!

Problems with idealism

Like neutral monism, idealism tends to skate over the qualitative differences between events normally thought to be 'in the mind' such as thoughts and dreams, and entities like chairs and tables normally thought to be in the external physical world; the fact that all such events are *experienced* does not alter the fact that they are *experienced to be different*. Nor does it tell us anything about how volitions, percepts and the like relate to brain activity.

But the main, unfortunate consequence of Berkeley's thesis is that if things are *not* experienced they *do not exist*. Rather like our dreams – if we do not dream them, they are not there. This consequence seems absurd. If you bring an egg to the boil, then leave the kitchen for 3.5 minutes, you get a soft-boiled egg whether you are watching it or not. So how can experiencing the egg be the sole grounds for its existence? Berkeley, too, found such consequences unacceptable. But, there was *One*, he pointed out, who perceived all – so the 'choir of Heaven and furniture of Earth' do exist continuously, for they exist as ideas 'in the mind of God'.

Being an Irish bishop, this 'solution' served a number of purposes. Not only did it resolve certain problems in epistemology and certain paradoxes surrounding the mind–body problem, but it also provides a good reason for the existence of God. God is the stabilising principle which gives an otherwise erratic universe continuous existence. However, those of a secular bent were not impressed. As the philosopher Geoffrey Warnock points out, when Berkeley first published this thesis in 1710, 'Some thought he was insane, and some that he could not be wholly serious; some thought he was corrupted by an Irish propensity to paradox and novelty; almost no one took him seriously' (Warnock, 1972, p. 34) (Box 3.2).

In Bertrand Russell's classic *A History of Western Philosophy* (first published in 1946), Berkeley's Idealism is given a detailed treatment as one important position in philosophy of mind. In the materialist 1990s, it hardly

---

Box 3.2 A little poem from Ronald Knox to George Berkeley

There was a young man who said, 'God
Must think it exceedingly odd
   If He finds that this tree
   Continues to be
When there's no one about in the Quad'.

     REPLY

Dear Sir:
   Your astonishment's odd:
I am always about in the Quad
   And that's why the tree
   Will continue to be,
Since observed by
   Yours faithfully
       God.

---

received a mention (e.g. it received just ten words in the 642 pages of Guttenplan (1994) *A Companion to the Philosophy of Mind*), and it has little influence on current Western psychology and philosophy. However, as with dual-aspect theory and neutral monism, I have re-introduced idealism on the grounds that, even viewed from the perspective of Western science, it is not *entirely* wrong. A version of idealism is to be found, for example, in the 'Copenhagen' interpretation of quantum mechanics (see Chapter 2), and, while it may be absurd to suggest that the existence of the macroscopic material world depends on its being perceived, it is not absurd to suggest that this is true of the *phenomenal world* (the world *as perceived*). A different form of idealism – that the *manifest* world depends for its existence on consciousness and mind – also plays a central role in Eastern philosophies that derive their sources of evidence largely from introspective investigations of consciousness and mind. We examine how the material world relates to the phenomenal world, and how to make sense of idealism versus realism in Chapter 8.

The reduction of mind to body

Given the problems with Berkeley's Idealism, it may be that reducing the physical to the mental is to collapse the mind–body problem in the wrong direction. Far more common in the twentieth and early twenty-first century has been the reduction of the mental to the physical.

Like dualism, materialism was given an explicit form by the ancient Greeks. According to Leukippos and his pupil Democritus there is nothing in the universe other than 'atoms and the void'. Even the soul is composed of atoms that permeate the atoms of the body. According to Thomas Hobbes (1651), man is just a machine – 'For what is the heart, but a spring; and the nerves, but so many strings, and the joints but so many wheels, giving motion to the whole body . . .?' Sensory experience, he thought, is only a 'motion in the brain' produced by the motions of matter in the external world. There can be no other intrinsic quality in experiences, argues Hobbes, 'for motion produceth nothing but motion'.

Such views are clear antecedents to the modern and widely shared intuition amongst natural scientists that descriptions of the world given by physics, for example the equations of quantum mechanics, are more fundamental and ultimately more 'real' than our everyday talk of minds and experiences. In the words of the Cambridge physicist Stephen Hawking (1988), if we could develop a theory that unified all the known physical forces of the universe 'we would know the mind of God' (see Chapter 8).

Hawking, no doubt, only meant to refer to one aspect of 'God's thinking'. But, to many students of consciousness and mind, such claims for the all-embracing explanatory power of a grand unified theory (GUT) are in any case wildly optimistic. The explanatory power of scientific theories can only be assessed in terms of the phenomena they are designed to explain. Given that those working on GUT have not, by and large, *addressed* the many problems surrounding consciousness and mind, it would be surprising indeed if GUT explained them. As noted in Chapter 2, we cannot even be certain, at the present time, that quantum mechanical phenomena are psychologically relevant. Nor, if we return to classical physics, do Newton's laws of *motion* tell us anything about human *motivation* (what 'moves' people), let alone how humans solve problems, have emotions and, ultimately, become aware of their own existence. There is, however, a more plausible form of 'Physicalism' which claims mind and consciousness to be nothing more than *states of the brain*. This claimed identity between mind, consciousness and states of the central nervous system is sometimes known as 'central state identity theory'.

Reducing consciousness to a state of the brain

It has long been suspected that there is a *causal relation* between mind, consciousness and brain (Box 3.3). However, the claim that mind and consciousness are *nothing more than* states of the brain is far more radical. If this claim can be justified, then the fundamental puzzles surrounding the mind–body relationship, and (in its modern form) the consciousness–brain relationship, would be solved. Clearly, if consciousness is nothing more than a state of the brain (a C-state, say), it should be possible to understand it within the existing framework of natural science. Causal relations between

---

Box 3.3 How states of consciousness depend on states of the brain

According to Hippocrates of Cos (460–357 BC),

> Man ought to know that from the brain and from the brain only,
> arise our pleasures, joys, laughter and jests, as well as our sorrows,
> pains, griefs and fears. Through it, in particular, we think, see, hear,
> and distinguish the ugly from the beautiful, the bad from the good,
> the pleasant from the unpleasant, in some cases using custom as a
> test, in others perceiving them from their utility. It is the same thing
> which makes us mad or delirious, inspires us with dread and fear,
> whether by night or by day, brings sleeplessness, inopportune mis-
> takes, aimless anxieties, absent-mindedness, and acts that are con-
> trary to habit.
>
> (from Jones, 1923; cited in Flew, 1978, p. 32)

---

consciousness and brain would translate into the causal relations between
C-states and other brain states, and the functions of consciousness would
simply be the functions of C-states within the global economy of the brain.
The methods for investigating consciousness would then be third-person
methods of the kind already well developed in neurophysiology and cognitive
science.[4]

With such a potential prize in view, philosophical and scientific theories
of consciousness over the last fifty years have in the main assumed, or tried
to show, that some form of materialist reductionism is true. Given the
dominance of this approach we need to examine it in some depth.

How could conscious experiences be brain states?

Given the apparent differences between the 'qualia' of conscious experiences
and brain states it is by no means *obvious* that they are one and the same.
Physicalists such as Ullin Place (1956) and J.J.C. Smart (1962) accepted that
these apparent differences exist. They also accepted that descriptions of
mental states and descriptions of their corresponding brain states are not
identical in meaning. However, they claimed that with the advance of neurophysiology these descriptions will *be discovered* to be statements about one
and the same thing. That is, a contingent rather than a logical identity will be
established between consciousness, mind and brain.

Smart (1962) summarises this position in the following way:

> Let us first try to state more accurately the thesis that sensations are

brain-processes. It is not the thesis that, for example, 'after-image' or 'ache' means the same as 'brain-process of sort X' (where 'X' is replaced by a description of a certain brain process). It is that, in so far as 'after-image' or 'ache' is a report of a process, it is a report of a process that happens to be a brain process. It follows that the thesis does not claim that sensation statements can be translated into statements about brain processes. Nor does it claim that the logic of a sensation statement is the same as that of a brain process statement. All it claims is that in so far as a sensation statement is a report of something, that something is a brain process. *Sensations are nothing over and above brain processes.*

(p. 163; my italics)

In short, there is a distinction to be drawn between how things seem, how we describe them, and how they really are.

It is important to remember that no discovery that reduces consciousness to brain has yet been made. Central state identity theory, therefore, is partly an expression of faith, based on precedents in other areas of science. Consequently, arguments in defence of this position have focused on the *kinds of discovery which would need to be made* for reductionism to be true. We need to examine these with care.

C.D. Broad noted in 1925 that materialism comes in three basic versions: *radical, reductive* and *emergent*. Radical materialism claims that the term 'consciousness' does not refer to anything real (in contemporary philosophy this position is usually called 'eliminativism'). Reductive materialism accepts that consciousness does refer to something real, but claims that science will discover that real thing to be nothing more than a state (or function) of the brain. Emergentism also accepts the reality of consciousness but claims it to be a higher-order property of brains; it supervenes on neural activity, but cannot be reduced to it.

Eliminative materialism

The atomism of Democritus and the 'man as machine' metaphor of Hobbes are early examples of eliminativism. More recent attempts to 'do away with consciousness' divide into (a) those which deny its existence outright, (b) those which argue that the term 'consciousness' and its associated concept do not refer to anything sufficiently clear to make the term (and concept) usable, and (c) those which argue that our theories about consciousness (our 'folk psychologies') are so crude and fallacious that they are bound to be replaced, without remainder, by some future neuroscience.

In a commentary on my 1991 article 'Is human information processing conscious?', the philosopher Georges Rey (1991), for example, denies that consciousness exists, comparing my faith in the existence of consciousness to a theologian's faith in the existence of God:

Why in the world should one believe in such a God? Why should one believe in such a consciousness? In both cases, of course, people have been tempted to say, 'Because I have direct access to it.' But such first-person breast beating begs the question … the challenge … is to come up with some *non-question-begging* reason to believe consciousness exists. I doubt there is any to be had.

As noted in Chapter 2, Descartes, using the same 'method of doubt', came to the opposite conclusion. One might, he argued, doubt the existence of the material world. But, when in doubt, one cannot deny the existence of doubt itself, and, therefore, the existence of thought and consciousness. If Descartes is right, Rey's doubt about the existence of consciousness is self-defeating. Unless one has consciousness one cannot have doubts! In my reply to Rey (Velmans, 1991b, section 7.3) I also pointed out that to deny the existence of consciousness is to deny *everything* that one experiences. If consciousness does not exist, neither do its contents. That is, Rey questions not just the existence of love and hate, pleasure and pain, and other inner events such as thoughts, images and dreams – but also the experienced body and the *entire phenomenal world*, including visual experiences of meter readings, brain events in others, and so on. This is to saw away the branch on which the eliminativist position sits. That is, if consciousness does not exist, observations do not exist.[5] And if observations do not exist, science does not exist – in which case neurophysiology does not exist and one can forget about trying to reduce consciousness to a state of the brain.

Sloman (1991) (in the same set of commentaries) attacks the *concept* of consciousness, claiming that 'people who discuss consciousness delude themselves in thinking that they know what they are talking about. … it's not just one thing but many things muddled together' – rather like our 'multifarious uses of "energy" (intellectual energy, music with energy, high energy explosion, etc.)'. Stanovich (1991) likewise points out that 'the term "consciousness" fractionates into half a dozen or more different usages'. This, he claims, makes it a 'botched concept; a psychiatric institution is too good for it; it deserves the death penalty'. Given this, they argue, one can make no generalisations about it.[6]

Sloman and Stanovich are right to stress the importance of definitions. As noted in Chapter 1, no universally agreed definition of the term 'consciousness' exists. Consequently, a good deal of confusion has arisen in consciousness studies from different implicit and explicit usages of the term. Yet there is nothing to prevent organised discussion of a *specific* usage of 'consciousness', and provided that this usage is agreed, there is nothing to prevent its scientific investigation. In this monograph I restrict the term 'consciousness' to situations where phenomenal content is present (where one is conscious *of* something – see Chapter 1). The conditions that determine whether one is conscious of something can be investigated experimentally. In psychology there is a large experimental literature dealing with conscious versus preconscious or unconscious processing. In psychophysics, for example, it is traditional to investigate the conditions under which subjects become conscious of a given stimulus (stimulus thresholds), or become conscious of changes in the stimulus (difference limens). In ordinary life there seem to be clear situations where one is conscious (of things) when awake, versus not conscious (of anything) in deep sleep. In short, while it is important to be mindful of confusing usages, there are good reasons for retaining the term.

The philosopher Patricia Churchland's attempt to eliminate phenomenal 'consciousness' from science focuses on its role in our common-sense *theories* (folk psychologies) about what is going on in our minds. In folk psychology we typically explain our actions in terms of our conscious wishes, beliefs, reasons, and so on. Rather like 'phlogiston' in explaining the role of combustion or 'élan vital' in explaining what gives organic matter life, such folk psychological terms, she claims, will disappear from future, more advanced explanations of mind. Folk psychological theories will be replaced by the more exact theories of psychological science and, in time, these will be replaced by more exact neurophysiological theories. As psychological theories operate at a higher level of analysis than neurophysiological theories their terms of analysis do not always correspond. However psychological theories influence the development of neurophysiological ones and vice versa. As such theories continue to co-evolve, their convergence will increase until, in some distant future, the higher level, psychological theories will be reduced to the more fundamental, neurophysiological theories. When this happens, she claims, consciousness will have been shown to be nothing more than a state of the brain. As she puts it:

> In the sense of 'reduction' that is relevant here, reduction is first and foremost a relation between theories. Most simply, one theory, the *reduced* theory T_R, stands in a certain relation (specified below) to another more basic theory T_B. Statements that a phenomenon P_R reduces to another phenomenon P_B are derivative upon the more basic claim that the *theory* that characterises the first reduces to the *theory* that characterises the second.
>
> (Churchland, 1989, p. 278)

Whether or not folk psychological *theories* can always be usefully replaced by the more mechanistic theories of psychological science, and whether these, in turn, can always be reduced to neurophysiological accounts is open to debate (Box 3.4).

But even if a reduction of psychological to neurophysiological theory (in a given case) is possible, this would not reduce conscious *phenomena* to being nothing more than states of the brain. As the philosopher William Wimsatt (1976) pointed out, such eliminativist arguments confuse *interlevel* reduction (the reduction of psychological phenomena to neurophysiological phenomena) with *intralevel* reduction (Box 3.5).

Box 3.4 Psychological concepts that are difficult to reduce to neurophysiological concepts

Some psychological concepts are in part *defined* by one's interactions with *other human beings*, such as 'empathy' or a desire for 'intimacy' or 'fame'. While the cognitive and affective aspects of such mental states will have corresponding brain states, the meaning of these terms is partly *social and relational*. Consequently, such concepts (and associated theories) cannot be reduced without remainder to states of the brain. Recent 'enactive' and 'embodied' theories of perception and cognition also stress the importance of the *active engagement of organisms with the surrounding physical world* in their explanations of how the mind works. Some aspects of visual perception for example are difficult to explain without reference to sensory-motor interactions with the world (see discussions in Chapters 5 and 8, and reviews by Noë, 2002, 2007).

Note that this difference between interlevel and intralevel reduction has nothing to do with the special properties of consciousness as such. Overt human behaviour for example is a higher level phenomenon that can in principle be described from an entirely 'third-person' perspective. On occasion, a (lower level) neurophysiological explanation of behaviour might give a better understanding of that behaviour than a (higher level) cognitive psychological account. But it does not make sense to claim that the neurophysiological causes somehow eliminate or replace the resulting *behaviour*. Even if one can explain the detailed neuromuscular antecedents of some motor response, the overt response remains.

Box 3.5 The difference between interlevel and intralevel reduction

Intralevel reductions involve the replacement of a *given theory by a more powerful theory* that operates *at the same level of explanation* (the replacing theory explains the same phenomena in a more powerful way). A classical example is the reduction of Newtonian to Einsteinian physics. In such reductions one may obtain a genuine replacement of the reduced theory; for example Newtonian physics turns out to be nothing more than a special case of relativity theory. In interlevel reductions, on the other hand, lower level theories about causal relations amongst lower level phenomena are used to *explain* higher level phenomena, but the lower theories and phenomena do not *replace* the higher level phenomena.

In short, higher level to lower level theory reduction is not equivalent to higher level phenomenon reduction, and the inability of a reducing neurophysiological *theory* to eliminate consciousness as a *phenomenon* has nothing to do with the nonmaterial *nature* of consciousness. Given this, might a *non-eliminative* reduction be possible? Genes were shown to be nothing more than DNA molecules. Lightning was shown to be nothing more than the motion of electrical charges through the atmosphere. So, even if one cannot *eliminate* consciousness, perhaps science will discover it to be nothing more than a state of the brain!

What non-eliminative reductionism needs to show

There is nothing hypothetical about our own conscious experiences. To each and every one of us, our conscious experiences are observable *phenomena* (psychological *data*) which we can describe with varying degrees of accuracy in ordinary language. *Other* people's experiences might be 'hypothetical constructs', as we cannot observe their experiences in the direct way that we can observe our own, but that does not make our own experiences similarly hypothetical. Nor, as we have seen above, are our own conscious experiences 'theories' or 'folk psychologies'. With deeper insight we might be able to improve our theories *about* what we experience, but this would not replace, or necessarily improve, the experiences themselves.

In essence, then, the claim that conscious experiences are nothing more than brain states is a claim about one set of phenomena (first-person experiences of love, hate, the smell of mown grass, the colour of a sunset, etc.) being nothing more than another set of phenomena (brain states, viewed from the perspective of an external observer). Given the extensive, *apparent* differences between conscious experiences and brain states, this is a tall order. Formally, one must establish that, despite appearances, conscious experiences are *ontologically identical* to brain states.

Instances where phenomena viewed from one perspective turned out to be one and the same as seemingly different phenomena viewed from another perspective do occur in the history of science. A classical example is the way the 'morning star' and the 'evening star' turned out to be identical (they were both found to be the planet Venus).

But viewing consciousness from a first- versus a third-person perspective is very different from seeing the same planet in the morning or the evening. From a third-person (external observer's) perspective one has *no direct access* to a subject's conscious experience. Consequently, one has no third-person data (about the experience itself) which can be compared to or contrasted with the subject's first-person data. Neurophysiological investigations are limited, in principle, to isolating the neural correlates or antecedent causes of given experiences. This would be a major scientific advance. But what would it tell us about the nature of consciousness itself?

Common reductionist arguments and fallacies

Reductionists commonly argue that if one could find the neural *causes* or *correlates* of consciousness in the brain, then this would establish consciousness *itself* to be a brain state (see, for example, Place, 1956; Crick, 1994). Let us call these the 'causation argument' and the 'correlation argument'. I suggest that such arguments are based on a fairly obvious fallacy: for consciousness to be nothing more than a brain state, it must be *ontologically identical* to a brain state. However, *correlation* and *causation* do not establish *ontological identity*.

These relationships have been persistently confounded in the literature, so let me make the differences clear (see Table 3.1).

Table 3.1 Ontological identity, correlation and causation

	Symmetrical	*Obeys Leibniz's Law*
Ontological identity	Yes	Yes
Correlation	Yes	No
Causation	No	No

Ontological identity is *symmetrical*: if A is identical to B, then B is identical to A. Ontological identity also *obeys Leibniz's Law*: if A is identical to B, all the properties of A are also properties of B and vice versa (for example all the properties of the 'morning star' are also properties of the 'evening star').

Correlation is also *symmetrical*: if A correlates with B, then B correlates with A. But correlation *does not obey Leibniz's Law*: if A correlates with B, it does not follow that all the properties of A and B are the same. For example, height in humans correlates with weight, but height and weight do not have the same set of properties.

Causation, by contrast, is *asymmetrical*: if A causes B, it does not follow that B causes A. If a rock thrown in a pond causes ripples in the water, it does not follow that ripples in the water cause the rock to be thrown in the pond. And causation *does not obey Leibniz's Law* (flying rocks and pond ripples have very different properties).

Once the obvious differences between causation, correlation and ontological identity are laid bare, the weaknesses of the 'causation argument' and the 'correlation argument' are clear. Under appropriate conditions, brain states may be shown to cause or correlate with conscious experiences, but it does not follow that conscious experiences are nothing more than states (or, for that matter, functions) of the brain. To demonstrate that, one would have to establish an ontological identity in which all the properties of a conscious experience and a corresponding brain state were identical. Unfortunately for reductionism, few if any properties of experiences (accurately described) and brain states appear to be identical.

In short, the causes and correlates of conscious experience should not be confused with their *ontology*. As it happens, various *nonreductionist* positions such as dualist-interactionism and epiphenomenalism *agree* that consciousness (in humans) is causally influenced by and correlates with neural events, but they *deny* that consciousness is nothing more than a state of the brain. As no information about consciousness *other than its neural causes and correlates* is available to neurophysiological investigation of the brain, it is difficult to see how such research could ever settle the issue. The *only* evidence about what conscious experiences are like comes from first-person sources, which consistently suggest consciousness to be something other than or additional to neuronal activity. Given this, I conclude that reductionism via this route *cannot be made to work* (cf. Velmans, 1998a).[7]

False analogies

Faced with this difficulty, reductionists usually turn to analogies from other areas in science, where a reductive, causal account of a phenomenon led to an understanding of its ontology that is very different from its phenomenology. Francis Crick (1994), for example, makes the point that, in science, reductionism is both common and successful. Genes for example turned out to be nothing but DNA molecules. So, in science, this is the best way to proceed. While Crick recognises that experienced (first-person) 'qualia' pose a problem for reductionism, he suggests that in the fullness of time it may be possible to describe the *neural correlates* of such qualia. And, if we can understand the nature of the correlates, we may come to understand the corresponding forms of consciousness. By these means science will show that 'You're nothing but a pack of neurons!'

It should be apparent from the above that finding the neural correlates of consciousness won't be enough to reduce people to neurons! The reduction of consciousness to brain is also quite unlike the reduction of genes to DNA. In the development of genetics, 'genes' were initially hypothetical entities inferred to exist to account for observed regularities in the transmission of characteristics from parents to offspring. The discovery that genes are DNA molecules shows how a theoretical entity is sometimes discovered to be 'real'. A similar discovery was made for bacteria, which were inferred causes of disease until the development of the microscope, after which they could be seen. Viruses remained hypothetical until the development of the electron microscope, after which they too could be seen. These are genuine cases of materialist reduction (of hypothetical to physical entities).

But it would be absurd to regard conscious experiences as 'hypothetical entities', waiting for their neural substrates to be discovered to make them real. Conscious experiences are first-person *phenomena*. To those who have them, they provide the very fabric of subjective reality. One does not have to wait for the advance of neuroscience to know that one has been stung by a bee! If conscious experiences *were* merely hypothetical, the mind–body problems, and in particular the problems posed by the phenomenal properties of 'qualia', would not even exist.

Ullin Place (1956) focuses on causation rather than correlation. As he notes, we now understand lightning to be nothing more than the motion of electrical charges through the atmosphere. But mere correlations of lightning with electrical discharges do not suffice to justify this reduction. Rather, he argues, the reduction is justified once we know that the motion of electrical charges through the atmosphere *causes* what we experience as lightning. Similarly, a conscious experience may be said to be a given state of the brain once we know that brain state to have *caused* the conscious experience.

I have dealt with the fallacy of the 'causation argument' above. But the lightning analogy is seductive because it is half true. That is, *for the purposes of physics* it is true that lightning can be described as nothing more than the motion of electrical charges. But there are three things that need to be accounted for in this situation, not just one – an event in the world, a perceiver, and a resulting experience. Physics is interested in the nature of the event in the world. However, psychology is interested in how this physical event interacts with a visual system to produce *experienced lightning* in the form of a perceived flash of light situated in a phenomenal world. This experienced lightning may be said to *represent* the same event in the world which physics describes as a motion of electrical charges. But the *phenomenology of the experience itself* cannot be said to be nothing more than the motion of electrical charges! Prior to the emergence of life forms with visual systems on this planet, there presumably was no such phenomenology, although the electrical charges which now give rise to this experience did exist.

In sum, the fact that motions of electrical charges cause the experience of lightning does not warrant the conclusion that the *phenomenology* of the experience is nothing more than the motion of electrical charges. Nor would finding the neurophysiological causes of conscious experiences warrant the reduction of the phenomenology of those experiences to states of the brain.[8]

Faced with this problem, some reductionist philosophers claim that psychologists are just not interested in phenomenology (Box 3.6). Hardcastle (1991) for example makes this (false) suggestion – and goes on to offer similar reductionist arguments to those above, noting that,

> science regularly and nonproblematically redescribes the way the world seems to us from a first-person perspective in third-person objective terms. To wit, objects which appear red to us do so because they reflect a certain wavelength of electromagnetic radiation. Surfaces which seem warm to us do so because their mean molecular kinetic energy is above a certain level relative to the MMKE of our skin. There is no reason why consciousness should not be reducible in the same way.

As does Place (1956), Hardcastle erroneously assumes that if cause C is shown to produce effect E, then E reduces to C. A sensation of redness might

---

Box 3.6 Should psychologists be interested in phenomenology?

According to Hardcastle (1991) the inability to capture first-person experiences within third-person accounts is of little concern. If consciousness is not captured by (a third-person) psychology, so be it; 'consciousness could simply be outside the domain that psychologists are trying to capture. . . . Whether an information processing model is complete depends on what it is explaining.' The short answer to this is that conscious phenomenology has been of concern to experimental psychology from its very beginnings in the psychophysics of Gustav Fechner (1860) and this concern is retained in modern consciousness studies (see, for example, readings in Velmans and Schneider, 2007).

Dennett goes even further, arguing that psychologists *should not* be interested in phenomenology. In vision research, for example, 'Every investigable issue that comes up for . . . a psychologist seems to have a parallel version in the land of robot vision' (in discussions following Velmans, 1993a, p. 99). Given that one can understand robot functioning in entirely third-person terms, why should we worry about first-person phenomenology? But this, again, misrepresents what psychologists actually do. In some areas of psychology, conscious phenomenology *is* and always has been an investigable issue – for example, in the study of sensory systems (the study of colour vision, pitch perception, olfaction, etc.). And, without reports of subjective experience, large tracts of psychological research would simply disappear (free recall in memory, perceptual illusions, studies of emotions, dreams, and so on). For a detailed discussion of this issue see the online debate between Dennett and Velmans (2001), and subsequent papers by Dennett (2003) and Velmans (2007c). We return to this issue in Chapters 8 and 9.

---

be caused by certain electromagnetic wavelengths interacting with the colour coding mechanisms of the visual system, but this does not establish the resulting *sensation* to be nothing more than 'electromagnetic radiation'. For the purposes of physics it may be useful to redescribe visual stimuli in the world as electromagnetic radiation. But the ability of the visual system to translate electromagnetic frequencies into colour sensations is what is of interest to psychology – and to redescribe the *sensations* as electromagnetic radiation does not make sense!

Given that such examples of supposed reduction of first-person experience to third-person science (DNA, lightning, colour, heat, etc.) are not really examples of first-person reduction at all, perhaps a nonreductive materialism is more appropriate. For example, according to Sperry (1969, 1970, 1985) and

Searle (1987, 1992, 1994a, 1997, 2007), conscious states cannot be redescribed (now or ever) in neurophysiological language. Rather, they have to be described just as they seem to be. Searle, for example, believes *subjectivity* and *intentionality* to be essential features of consciousness. Conscious states have 'intrinsic intentionality', that is, it is intrinsic to them that they are *about* something. According to Searle, this distinguishes conscious states from physical representations such as sentences written on a page. Conscious readers might interpret these *as if* they are about something (such physical representations have 'as-if intentionality'), but they are just marks on a piece of paper and not about anything in themselves. Subjectivity, too, 'is unlike anything else in biology, and in a sense it is one of the most amazing features of nature' (Searle, 1994a, p. 97). Nevertheless, Searle maintains that conscious states are just higher order features of the brain. As he later observes, 'Sometimes philosophers talk about naturalizing consciousness and intentionality, but by "naturalizing" they usually mean the first-person or subjective ontology of consciousness. On my view, consciousness does not need naturalizing, for it is already a part of nature as the subjective, qualitative biological part' (Searle, 2007, p. 329).

Emergentism

In classical dualism, consciousness is thought to be a nonmaterial substance or entity different in kind from the material world, with an existence that is independent of the existence of the brain (although in normal life it interacts with the brain). 'Emergentism' in the form of 'property dualism' retains the view that there are fundamental differences between consciousness and physical matter, but views these as different kinds of property of the brain. That is, consciousness is *not reducible* to something 'physical' in the manner suggested by central state identity theory, but its existence is still *dependent* on or *supervenient* on the workings of the brain. For this reason its protagonists sometimes describe this position as 'non-reductive physicalism' – although whether this position is truly non-reductive is open to question as we shall see.

As Guttenplan (1994) notes, whether a conscious property that emerges from the brain is better thought of as 'mental' or 'physical' is arguable. So labelling this position can be a delicate matter. Given their insistence that mental properties do not reduce to the physical properties of neurons or to other physical properties that can be described in entirely 'third-person' terms, both Sperry and Searle could be described as property dualists. However, Sperry (1985) considers his position to be a form of monism (for the reason that all mental properties are properties of the brain), and Searle actually describes his position as 'physicalism' or, in his most recent writings, as 'biological naturalism'.[9]

Searle (1987), for example, argues (as I have) that *causality* should not be confused with *ontological identity* (see my critique of reductionism above), and his case for physicalism appears to be one of the few to have addressed this distinction head-on. The gap between what *causes* consciousness and what conscious *is* can be bridged, he suggests, by an understanding of how microproperties relate to macroproperties. The liquidity of water is caused by the way H_2O molecules slide over each other, but is nothing more than (an emergent property of) the combined effect of these molecular movements. Likewise, solidity is caused by the way molecules in crystal lattices bind to each other, but is nothing more than the higher order (emergent) effect of such bindings. In similar fashion, consciousness is caused by neuronal activity in the brain and is nothing more than the higher order, emergent effect of such activity. That is, consciousness is just a 'subjective' *physical macroproperty* of the brain.

Searle's argument is ingenious, but it needs to be examined with care. The brain undoubtedly has physical macroproperties of many kinds. Like other physical systems, its physical microstructure supports a physical macrostructure. However, the physical macroproperty of brains that is most closely analogous to 'solidity' and 'liquidity' is 'sponginess', not consciousness! There are, of course, more psychologically relevant 'objective' macroproperties, such as the blood flow patterns picked up by PET scans or the magnetic and electrical activities detected by fMRI and EEG. But why should increased blood flow constitute 'subjectivity', or why would it be 'like anything' to be an electrical potential or magnetic field? While some of these properties undoubtedly *correlate* with conscious experiences, there is little reason to suppose that they are *ontologically identical* to conscious experiences.[10]

One might also question how Searle's property dualism could really be a form of *physicalism*. Searle insists that consciousness is a *physical* phenomenon, produced by the brain in the sense that the gall bladder produces bile. But he also stresses that *subjectivity* and *intentionality* are defining characteristics of consciousness. Unlike physical phenomena, the phenomenology of consciousness cannot be observed from the outside; unlike physical phenomena, it is nearly always *of* or *about* something. But, according to him, this 'traditional notion of the mental, that distinguishes it from the physical, contains a serious mistake. The mistake is to suppose that the essential features of consciousness prevent it from being an ordinary part of the physical world' (Searle, 2007, p. 330). Note, however, that, put this way, the debate about how the 'physical' relates to the 'mental' becomes a debate about how these terms should be used, rather than a debate about how the ontology of consciousness relates to the ontology of entities and events more usually thought of as 'physical'. Even if one accepts that consciousness is, in some sense, caused by or emergent from the brain, given its subjectivity and intentionality why call it 'physical' rather than 'mental' or 'psychological'? Merely *relabelling* consciousness, or moving from micro- to macroproperties, doesn't really close the gap between 'objective' brains and 'subjective' experiences.[11]

It is interesting to note that Roger Sperry (1969, 1970) developed a similar *emergent interactionist* position. Like his contemporary John Eccles, Sperry found it difficult to believe that biochemical and physiological data will ever provide an account of mental phenomena. Nor did he believe consciousness to be a mere epiphenomenon, or passive by-product of cerebral activity. Rather, according to Sperry, consciousness is a holistic property of the brain that both emerges from brain activity and 'supervenes'[12] over or regulates the neural activity from which it emerges.[13]

Sperry (1969) argues that just as holistic properties of organisms have causal effects that determine the course and fate of constituent cells and molecules, the conscious properties of cerebral activity may have causal effects on brain functions that control the details of nerve impulse traffic. For example, if the corpus callosum is intact, consciousness co-ordinates and unifies the activity of the two halves of the brain. In this way, he claims, consciousness can be seen to be 'an integral part of the brain process itself and an essential constituent of the action. Consciousness in the present scheme is put to work. It is given a use and a reason for being, and for having evolved' (Sperry, 1969, p. 533).

How might a holistic property both *emerge from* and *regulate* the pattern of nerve impulse traffic? One analogy suggested by Dewar (1976) is the phenomenon of 'mutual entrainment'. The term 'entrainment' refers to the synchronisation of an oscillator to an input signal. This occurs, for example, when television receiver oscillators controlling the vertical and horizontal lines 'lock into' transmitting frequencies to produce a given picture on the screen. Examples of entrainment, Dewar notes, may also be found at many levels of biological organisation – a particularly apposite case being the way 'biological clocks' governing circadian rhythms can be locked into varying periods (of around twenty-four hours) to produce altered cycles of day–night activity in animals.

'Mutual entrainment' occurs when two or more oscillators interact in such a way as to pull one another into synchrony. This occurs, for example, when different alternating-current generators feeding the national grid are pulled into synchrony by what Norbert Wiener (the father of cybernetics) referred to as a 'virtual governor' in the system. Although the generators may be far distant from each other and may start up and stop at idiosyncratic times, once 'online' they are made to speed up or slow down to produce alternating current in phase with that of all the other machines feeding the grid. As Dewar points out, the 'virtual governor' is not located in any one place in the system, but rather pervades the system as a whole, so that it does not have a 'physical existence' in the usual sense. It is an emergent property of the entire system. In similar fashion, Dewar suggests, consciousness is 'a holistic emergent property of the interaction of neurons which has the power to be self-reflective and ascertain its own awareness'.

This analogy becomes particularly interesting in the light of recent discussions of the 'binding problem'. Although we experience objects as unified wholes, there is extensive evidence that different features of objects are encoded in spatially separated regions of the brain. Crick (1994), for example, cites evidence for the existence of twenty-seven distinct areas in the visual system that encode different visual features. Given their spatial separation in the brain, and the potential participation of any given feature in the representation of an indefinitely large number of objects, how on any given occasion does the brain 'bind' a particular set of feature representations together to support a unified experience? One 'binding' process suggested by Von der Malsburg (1986) involves the synchronous or correlated firing of diverse neuron groups representing currently attended to objects or events. Although this possibility remains tentative, evidence for the existence of such binding processes (involving rhythmic frequencies in the 30 to 80 Hz region) has been reviewed by Crick and Koch (1990, 1998), Engel and Singer (2001), Gray (1994), and Singer (2007).[14] Crick and Koch (1990) proposed that such synchronous bindings are the neural basis of consciousness.

Whether or not mutual entrainment controls neural binding, there seems to be little doubt that mechanisms that control the co-ordination of nerve impulse traffic exist. Given the well integrated nature of normal conscious experiences, it also seems reasonable to propose that such binding processes operate prior to the formation of, or co-occur with, such experiences. However, there is nothing to guarantee that such properties are sufficient to cause consciousness let alone are identical to consciousness. It is not clear, for example, how what is normally thought of as control circuitry involving feedback, feedforward, mutual entrainment and so on could in itself produce consciousness (it presumably does not do so in thermostats, guided missile systems, and the national grid).

Significantly, 40 Hz synchronised oscillations have been found in the visual systems of anaesthetised cats (Crick, 1994, p. 245), suggesting that such integrated operation can take place in the absence of normal experience. An apparent dissociation between consciousness and 40 Hz synchronous oscillations has also been found in humans by Schwender *et al.* (1994). Schwender and his co-workers were interested in the effects of nonspecific versus receptor-binding anaesthetics on auditory processing in primary auditory cortex of patients undergoing cardiac surgery. Nonspecific anaesthetics act on all excitable biological membranes, producing a general depression of neural activity. Receptor-specific anaesthetics block the receptors of specific neurotransmitters (e.g. opioids bind to mu, kappa and delta opioid receptors in the central nervous system). While nonspecific and receptor-binding anaesthetics both produce surgical anaesthesia, Schwender *et al.* found that they had very different effects on auditory processing. Nonspecific anaesthetics blocked auditory processing, but receptor-specific anaesthetics did not. In particular, evoked potentials at frequencies of around 40 Hz, associated with processing in primary auditory cortex, were suppressed under nonspecific anaesthetics but continued under receptor-binding ones. To assess the effects of such physiological differences, Schwender *et al.* played taped stories of Robinson Crusoe and his companion Friday to anaesthetised subjects (during the operation). After the operation none of the patients had any explicit, conscious memory of the tape. However, seven of the thirty subjects given the receptor-binding anaesthetic produced Robinson Crusoe as an associate to 'Friday' in an implicit memory test, whereas none of the nonspecific group did so. This suggested that the 40 Hz activity that took place during receptor-binding anaesthesia was associated with useful auditory processing. It is possible for example that it provided 'binding' for the output of auditory analysers operating on the taped input (along the lines suggested by Crick and Koch, 1990). However, the 40 Hz activity did not prevent surgical anaesthesia, nor did it enable conscious recall. That is, 'binding' may not be sufficient for consciousness.[15]

Conversely, the discovery of such control mechanisms in the brain permits alternative, entirely physiological accounts of its directed, integrated activity. With such mechanisms in place, no added intervention by conscious awareness is required. In this regard, it is important to note that we are *not aware* of any active directing of nerve impulse traffic in our brains. Paradoxically, therefore, any conscious intervention would have to be unconscious! It also remains entirely unclear how what we normally think of as consciousness or awareness *could* operate in this 'supervisory' way.

The strengths and weaknesses of emergentism

Emergentism tries to 'naturalise' dualism. Neural microproperties cause conscious macroproperties. In treating consciousness as an emergent property, emergentism accepts that there are significant differences between conscious experiences and the micro-activities of the brain, without positing the existence of some nonmaterial entity (consciousness, mind or soul) that lies outside the province of natural science. In Sperry's interactionism consciousness is also given an important role in the activities of the brain, thereby providing a reason for its emergence consistent with evolutionary theory.

But the problems that remain are serious. Demonstrating the brain to have physical macroproperties that are supervenient on its physical microproperties is one thing; *identifying* those physical macroproperties with the properties of *consciousness* is another. Searle, as shown above, tries to settle the issue by *fiat*. Subjective, intentional conscious experiences are simply *declared* to be physical states. But this doesn't really help much. The ontology of these 'new' physical states is not really clarified by renaming them. Nor does the transition from microproperties to macroproperties *explain* how brains, viewed from a third-person perspective, could themselves have a first-person perspective. And the problem of *how* ordinary physical states could *interact* with such extraordinary 'subjective', 'intentional' states remains.

Almost forty years ago, Bindra (1970) made a similar criticism of Sperry, pointing out that his case for subjective experience having a causal influence on neural activity rests on nothing more than a 'semantic equating of conscious awareness with higher order cerebral organisation'. The same accusation can be levelled at Dewar (1976), and at the more recent identification of consciousness with 40 Hz synchronous neuronal oscillations by Crick and Koch (1990). Given the integrated nature of consciousness, 'mutual entrainment' might be one form of higher order cerebral organisation to which consciousness is linked. But the unargued transition from the 'synchronisation of oscillations' to the 'power to be self-reflective and ascertain its own awareness' is just too quick.

At this point, the difficulties of asserting consciousness to be integral to the physical workings of the brain, yet at the same time something other than physical activity, should be apparent. Ironically, Eccles (1980) accused Sperry of being a reductionist, while Bindra (1970) accused him of unnecessary mystification. Similar caveats apply to the case developed by Searle (1992, 1997, 2007). In asserting consciousness to be neither a mysterious 'substance' or 'entity', nor merely the higher order *neural* activity of the brain, emergent property dualism seeks to occupy some middle ground. Arguably, however, it hovers, without firm support, between nonmaterialist dualism and materialist reductionism.

Notes

1 Neutral monists differ in how they address this. Mach (1885), for example, adopts phenomenalism – the view that statements about sense data are the only firm foundation for scientific knowledge. Causal or other laws in science simply summarise the relations between perceived events in an economic way. Hypothetical constructs relating to physical realities that one cannot directly observe are no more than convenient fictions and hence there is no underlying reality to explain. By contrast, Russell (1948) considers the world described by physics to be real. To cope with how it differs from the world as perceived he proposes the existence of two spaces, 'physical space' and 'psychological space'. Physical space is the space–time structure described by relativity theory. Psychological space contains the everyday objects of the three-dimensional phenomenal world. The relation of the experienced world to the world described by physics can then be determined in terms of how these two spaces relate to each other.

2 Modern empirical science is not hampered by this problem because it accepts the Greek rationalist intuition that through the power of reason, expressed in the ability to theorise, develop mathematical formalisms and so on, it is possible to generate descriptions of the world that go beyond the evidence of the senses. It is central to the scientific method that such theories be open to empirical testing (verification, falsification, etc.), but a commitment to empirical testing requires no commitment to an empiricist epistemology. Cognitive psychology, for example, does not accept the simple hierarchical empiricist model of the way concepts derive from sensations, theories from concepts, and so on (knowledge of the world is thought to be concept-driven as well as data-driven).

3 Ernst Mach's *phenomenalism* is similar, in its insistence that what we think of as material objects are actually arrangements of 'sensations' while hypotheses or theories are just convenient ways of thinking about our sensations.

4 Functionalism, the view that mind and consciousness are nothing more than *functions* of the brain, has similar potential benefits for natural science. Given the differences between a physical brain *state* (specifiable in terms of neurochemistry, neurophysiology, etc.) and a brain *function* (specifiable in terms of more abstract, causal relationships into which that state enters), I will consider functionalism separately, in Chapters 4 and 5.

5 I give a fuller justification of this claim once we examine the relation between observations and experiences in more detail in Chapters 6 and 9.

6 Sloman's attempt to fragment consciousness is followed by an attempt to eliminate it from the analysis of mind altogether, to be replaced by a study of *capabilities*. 'If we give up the idea of a unique referent, we can instead survey relevant phenomena, analyze their relationships to other capabilities . . . and try devising mechanisms capable of generating all these capabilities, including self-monitoring capabilities.' He goes on to discuss architectures that might support monitoring, information integration and higher level control. As I noted in Velmans (1991b, section 7.3), the study of such capabilities and the architectures that instantiate them is extremely important. But, ultimately, psychology has to make sense of the phenomenology of consciousness too – and a psychology that speaks *only* of capabilities and their embodying architectures *has nothing to say about phenomenal consciousness at all* whether fragmentary or unified (see Chapter 5).

7 Some philosophers have tried to finesse such arguments by adopting a different point of departure. Armstrong (1968) and Lewis (1972) for example define sensations not in terms of their first-person qualia, but in terms of the causal relationships into which sensations enter. If sensations are nothing more than causal relationships then they might turn out to be identical to brain states or processes which fulfil the same causal relationships. However, if conscious qualia cannot be reduced to causal relationships (see also Chapters 4 and 5) such reductive definitions of conscious phenomenology beg the question.

8 Note that the reduction of perceived lightning to electrical charges works for the purposes of physics for the reason that these are alternative representations of the same event out in the world (event L, say). The perceived lightning is a phenomenal representation of L (phenomenal L) produced by the visual system, and the description 'a motion of electrical charges' is a more abstract representation of L developed by physics (physical L). Given that these are alternative representations of the same event (they have the identical referent L) it makes sense to choose the one that is most useful for physics on the basis of its explanatory power. It is reasonable to suppose that the phenomenology of perceived lightning also has *neural correlates* in the visual system, which in turn code information about L in some neural form (neural L). *Reductive materialism* claims that phenomenal L is nothing more than neural L (that the phenomenal experience of lightning is nothing more than its neural correlates). This claimed *ontological identity* runs into the standard problems outlined above (that correlates are not identities, that the properties of neural codes are not the same as phenomenal properties, etc.). However, there is something identical in neural L and phenomenal L – that is, they encode *identical information* about L, albeit in different neural and phenomenal formats. In Chapter 13, I give an account of this relationship between phenomenal L and neural L in terms of a nonreductive, dual-aspect theory of information.

9 To confuse matters further, Davidson (1970), who develops a similar position, prefers to call it 'anomalous monism'.

10 In fact Searle admits that there is an essential difference between consciousness and other physical properties such as liquidity and solidity. Liquidity and

solidity (viewed from the perspective of physics) are reducible to molecular behaviour, but consciousness cannot be reduced to neuronal behaviour (Searle, 2007, p. 211). Or later, 'consciousness only exists if it is experienced as such. For other features, such as growth, digestion, or photosynthesis, you can make a distinction between our experience of the feature and the feature itself. This possibility makes reduction of these other features possible. But you cannot make that reduction for consciousness without losing the point of having the concept in the first place. Consciousness and the experience of consciousness are the same thing' (ibid., p. 213).

11 Searle (1997) tries to resist the charge that he is a property dualist for the reason that property dualism makes it difficult for him to be a true physicalist. Instead he argues that his position should really be called property *n*-ism, where the value of *n* is left open. As he notes, 'There are lots of real properties in the world: electromagnetic, economic, gastronomical, aesthetic, athletic, political, geological, historical, and mathematical to name but a few. . . . The really important distinction is not between the mental and the physical, mind and body, but between those real features of the world that exist independent of observers – features such as force, mass, and gravitational attraction – and those features of the world that depend on observers – such as money, property, marriage and government' (p. 211). According to Searle, 'though all observer-relative properties depend on consciousness for their existence, consciousness is not itself observer-relative' (p. 211). This needs a little clarification, as there is an obvious sense in which consciousness *is* observer-relative – that is, without an experiencing observer one cannot have an experience. What Searle is getting at is that the consciousness of a given observer is intrinsic *to that observer* (unlike, say, money, which is not an intrinsic property of anything). Searle's distinction between intrinsic features of the world and observer-relative ones is important and we will return to it in our analysis of functionalism in Chapter 4. However, the gap between subjective, intentional properties and non-subjective, non-intentional properties is not closed by expanding the number of cases of the former or the latter to an arbitrarily large *n*. Nor is it closed by introducing a further observer-relative versus intrinsic property distinction – as it is the *intrinsically* 'first-person' nature of conscious experience that seems to make it *intrinsically different* from physical properties (as they are usually conceived).

12 Davidson (1970) is credited for entering the term 'supervenience' into philosophical discussions of the mind–body problem. In his usage, however, the term merely denotes a *dependency* of the mental on the physical, without *reducibility* of the mental to the physical. Sperry's (1969) usage gives consciousness a function, suggesting that it *governs* that from which it *emerges*. See Kim (1993, 2005, 2007) for extensive discussions of different usages of the term 'supervenience' within philosophy of mind.

13 Another version of emergent interactionism has recently been proposed by the neurophysiologist Benjamin Libet (1996). For Libet, consciousness is an emergent field that has the power to veto behaviours that are preconsciously planned and readied for action by the brain. We consider this possibility in Chapter 10.

14 Shastri and Ajjanagadde (1993) also gave a detailed, innovative account of how such variable bindings might propagate over time, as attended-to representations change, within neural networks, and Metzinger (1995) considered the philosophical implications, for example how such momentary bindings might solve the homunculus problem, and provide the basis for the experience of an integrated self.

15 Significantly, in their latest writings on the subject, Crick and Koch (2007) have moved away from the suggestion that such bindings are a sufficient neural basis for consciousness, and in similar fashion, Singer (2007) now regards such bindings as a *prerequisite* for conscious experience.

4 Are mind and consciousness just activities?

Classical dualist and monist theories of consciousness argue about whether it is a substance, entity, or property that is distinct in some way from the material world. In psychological science, however, mind and consciousness have more commonly been thought of as *activities*.

Faced with the task of converting their discipline from a 'discourse' (logos) about the 'soul' (psyche) to an experimental science, psychologists' views of mind and consciousness have been determined, in part, by the available experimental methods. This influence of the *method* of enquiry on the *topic* of enquiry was taken to extremes in behaviourism, which dominated psychology throughout the first half of the twentieth century.

The first psychological laboratory

Behaviourism is best understood as a reaction to introspectionism, the early form of 'experimental' psychology that it replaced. Following on the creation of psychophysics by Gustaf Fechner (1860), Wilhelm Wundt founded the first psychological laboratory at the University of Leipzig in 1879. For Wundt, however, the task of psychology was the scientific study of the 'mind' and, for him, the study of 'mind' required the study of consciousness. With his experimental method, controlled, measurable stimuli were used to bring about given conscious states. Rather like chemical compounds these states were thought to have a complex structure and the aim of experimentation was to analyse the entire structure into its fundamental, component elements. This was to be achieved by trained subjects carefully introspecting and reporting on their detailed, moment to moment experiences.

This categorising of conscious states presented a formidable task and extensive inventories were developed, for example in the laboratories of Külpe (1901) and Titchener (1915). However, in the early years of the twentieth century, this programme fell into disrepute. How can one give a definitive list of the contents of consciousness? In his analysis of this period, Boring (1942) noted that Külpe's laboratory discovered less than 12,000 distinct sensations, whereas Titchener's laboratory discovered more than 44,435. These differences appeared to be largely due to differences in how subjects had been trained to attend to and describe what they experienced, and without agreement in the field about the fine details of the introspective method, disagreements between different laboratories were difficult to settle. Worse, given the privacy of individual experience and the *sole* reliance on subjective reports, introspective findings were difficult to falsify. Güzeldere (1997), for example, recounts the famous debate between followers of Titchener and Külpe about the existence of 'imageless thought':

> Titchener was convinced that all conscious thought involved some form of imagery, at least some sensory elements. However, subjects from Külpe's laboratory came up with reports of having experienced thoughts with no associated imagery whatsoever. The debate came to a stalemate of, 'You cannot experience X,' of Tichenerians versus 'Yes, we can!' of Külperians . . .
>
> (p. 15)

Other reasons for the demise of introspectionism had more to do with the prevailing, positivist, intellectual climate. Psychologists were keen to reformulate their discipline along the lines of natural science. John Watson (1913), for example, argued that the subject matter of psychology should not just be restricted to humans, but should include other animals. The introspective method does not allow this for the reason that other animals cannot make verbal reports about what they experience. Nor, he argued, does it make much sense to speculate about what they experience. Psychology, therefore, should confine itself to a study of overt behaviours, the stimuli which produce them, and observable physiological functions such as the behaviour of nerves, glands, muscles and so on. Thus refocused, psychology would become a behavioural form of biological science.

In short,

> Psychology as a behaviorist views it is a purely objective experimental branch of natural science. Its theoretical goal is the prediction and control of behavior. Introspection forms no essential part of its method nor is the scientific value of its data dependent upon the readiness with which they lend themselves to interpretation in terms of consciousness.
>
> (Watson, 1913, p. 158)

Indeed, 'The time has come when psychology must discard all reference to consciousness; when it need no longer delude itself into thinking that it is making mental states the object of observation . . .' (ibid., p. 163).

Methodologically, there are clear advantages to be gained from this refocusing of psychological enquiry. The organism's responses may be measured with precision and, being publicly observable, allow intersubjective agreement or the settling of disagreement. Watson's commitment to behaviourism, however, was more than methodological. In his view mental events are *irrelevant* to psychological enquiry – and some mental events are in any case nothing more than the behaviour of internal organs. For example, thinking (Descartes' prime exemplar of nonmaterial mind) was, for Watson, nothing more than minute muscular activity of the vocal tract.

Methodological and analytic behaviourism

Clearly, if inner variables such as consciousness or mind reduce to behaviour, and behaviour is entirely under stimulus control, then nothing is lost by restricting psychology to the study of responses and the stimuli that produce them. In this way *methodological behaviourism*, which is basically a thesis about how psychological research should be carried out, and *analytic behaviourism*, a reductive thesis regarding the ontological nature of consciousness or mind, are mutually supportive. Consequently, behaviourist psychologists often adopted aspects of both positions.

B.F. Skinner (1953), for example, shared Watson's belief that the aim of psychology is the prediction and control of behaviour. This, he argued, involves a causal chain composed of three links:

1   An operation performed on the organism from without (e.g. water deprivation)
2   An inner condition (e.g. physiological or psychological thirst)
3   A kind of behaviour (e.g. drinking)

Skinner argued that the second link in this chain is useless in the control of behaviour unless we can manipulate it directly, and this, he believed, cannot be done. Our knowledge of neurological states is insufficient to allow prediction and control of behaviour, and, he suggests, it may always be so. In any event, the first link in the chain (the external stimulus configuration) determines the behaviour of the second link, which in turn determines overt behaviour. Consequently, we may safely focus on the first link to achieve prediction and control. He therefore concludes, 'The objection to inner states is not that they do not exist but that they are not relevant to functional analysis' – a clear commitment to methodological behaviourism.

At the same time, Skinner tries to strengthen his thesis by demonstrating that talk of intervening mental events is mostly vague and metaphysical. For example, if someone forgets something (an observable behaviour) we speak, metaphorically, of his 'mind' being 'absent'. Other mental accounts, he claims, simply restate the facts of observed behaviour and are, therefore, redundant. For example, 'He eats because he is hungry' is, arguably, no more informative than to say 'he eats'. Such attempts to translate statements about mental events into statements about observable responses exemplify Skinner's *analytic* behaviourism.

Around the 1950s the attempt to translate statements about consciousness or mind into statements about behaviour was given considerable impetus by philosophers such as Gilbert Ryle (1949) and Ludwig Wittgenstein (1953).[1] Nevertheless, behaviourism has been all but abandoned in contemporary psychology and philosophy of mind.

Difficulties with behaviourist analyses of consciousness

Watson's theory that thought is nothing more than the minute movements of articulatory muscles was heroically put to the test by S.M. Smith who temporarily paralysed all his muscular activity with curare. He reported afterwards that his ability to think and remember while paralysed was unimpaired – thereby falsifying the 'minute muscle movement' theory of thought (cf. Smith *et al.*, 1947). Recent studies of locked-in syndrome lead to the same conclusion (see Chapter 11).

Analytic behaviourism is, in any case, counterintuitive. There is an old joke about two behaviourists conversing after sex. 'That was great for you', says one to the other, 'But how was it for me?' The joke is amusing because it is absurd. We do not learn about our own joys and griefs second-hand, from observations of our behaviour by others, or, entirely, from observations of our own behaviour. We simply feel them.

As Chappell (1962) noted, 'If behaviorism were true, I could find out that I myself had a pain by observing my behavior, but since I do not find out that I have a pain, when I do, by observing my behavior . . . behaviorism is not true' (p. 10).

Conversely, we are often *not* able to determine the mental states of others even if they make no attempt to conceal these states and their overt behaviour is clearly visible. Again, as Chappell comments,

> If behaviorism were true I could always in principle find out when you had a pain by observing your behavior, but since I cannot always find out, even in principle, that you have a pain when you do, whereas I can always observe your behavior it follows that behaviorism is not true.
>
> (ibid., p. 10)

There are also many instances where overt behaviour is *inconsistent* with what one thinks, feels or otherwise experiences. For example, one may experience hunger without eating (if one is on a diet), or eat in spite of the fact that one is not hungry (e.g. if one's mother insists!) – and one may conceal or lie about one's intentions and so on.

Even if one tries to express some experience faithfully in overt behaviour it is not always possible to do so. For example, the phenomenology of experience cannot always be unambiguously and exhaustively described in words ('translated into verbal behaviour'). This was, in fact, one of the stumbling blocks of introspectionism.

Given the many dissociations between conscious states and overt behaviour, the attempt to *reduce* conscious states to overt behaviour seems ill-conceived.

Are mental states just 'dispositions' to behave?

However, there are subtler versions of behaviourism which are not so easily dismissed, for example Gilbert Ryle's (1949) suggestion that mental states reduce not to overt behaviour but rather to 'dispositions to behave'. While there may be no immediate, overt response to which a given mental state refers, people are always *disposed* to behave in one way or another and it is to such dispositions, argues Ryle, that mental terms refer. Just as there is no army over and above the soldiers, brigades and divisions within it, and there is no university over and above the buildings and academic activities that take place within them, there are no mental states, he claims, over and above the dispositions to behave that we observe. For example, the difference between the presence and absence of intelligence can only be judged by intelligent behaviour, and not by the presence or absence of some Cartesian 'ghost in the machine'. Those who propose mind or consciousness to be some entity or state quite separate from such dispositions to behave are guilty, according to Ryle, of a simple 'category error'.

Ryle's dispositional analysis seems at least partly true of some mental concepts. Intelligence does seem to refer, in part, to people's disposition to behave in some ways rather than others, for example in ways that improve their social standing or success. If one removes the disposition to behave in an intelligent way from 'intelligence', what is left? However, such a reduction to dispositions to behave seems counterintuitive for terms which refer to the phenomenology of experience. How can one translate the phenomenal qualia of visual images or after-images, or the smell of Columbian coffee, or the sound of an Indian sitar into behavioural dispositions?

In his book, *A Materialist Theory of Mind* (1968), the Australian philosopher D.M. Armstrong attempted to do just that. Armstrong's case involved the application of two central propositions:

(a) Mental states (of whatever kind) are nothing but states of a person apt for bringing about certain sorts of behaviour.
(b) States of a person apt for bringing about certain sorts of behaviour are nothing but states of the brain.

In this way, Armstrong tried to eliminate phenomenal qualia by a two-stage reduction, combining dispositional behaviourism with central state identity theory. Consider, for example, the nature of perception. According to Armstrong, perception is just, 'a matter of acquiring capacities to make physical discriminations within our environment' (p. 83), and 'nothing but the acquiring of true or false beliefs concerning the current state of the organism, body and environment' (p. 209). 'Our perceptions, then, are not the basis for our perceptual judgements, nor are they mere phenomenological accompaniments of our perceptual judgements. They are simply the acquirings of these judgements themselves' (p. 226).[2]

In short, according to Armstrong, there is nothing about perceptions which is additional to the capacity to make discriminations based on the acquiring of true or false beliefs about the organism and environment. Such a reanalysis, he argues, has two advantages. It both captures the 'inner character of perception' and creates 'a logical tie between the inner event and the outer behaviour' (ibid., p. 248).

There are obvious difficulties with this thesis. If perception is nothing more than a *belief* about ourselves or our environment (encoded in some brain state) then how can one account for cases where we do not believe what we perceive? In the illusion shown in Figure 4.1, the inner lines appear to be bent. However, use of a straight edge shows the lines to be straight. Yet, believing

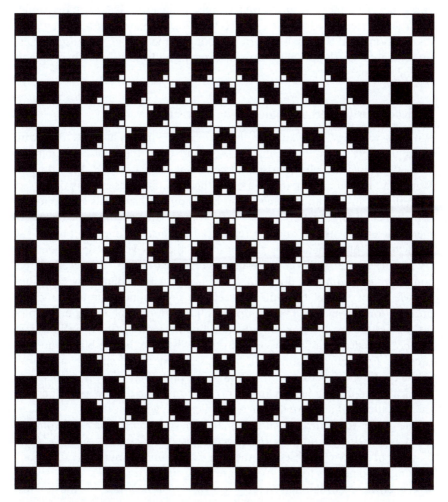

Figure 4.1 A visual illusion: 'Flying Squirrel'. Reproduced with kind permission of Professor Akiyoshi Kitaoka, Ritsumeikan University, Kyoto, Japan.

the lines to be straight does not alter their bent appearance. If so, phenomenal appearance cannot merely be the acquiring of true or false beliefs.

The reduction of conscious perception to the capacity to make physical discriminations is also inconsistent with the extensive evidence for human ability to make discriminations below the threshold of conscious awareness (cf. Dixon, 1981; Kihlstrom, 1996; Cheesman and Merikle, 1984, 1986; Merikle, 2007). The existence of this ability has been known for over 100 years. Pierce and Jastrow (1885), in what may have been the first psychology experiment published in America, studied the ability of subjects to make weight and brightness discriminations by reducing the difference between standard and comparison stimuli until subjects had zero confidence about which stimulus was the brighter or heavier one. However, when forced to guess they were more accurate than chance, indicating that some discrimination ability remained below the level of subjective awareness. Given such dissociations, and the persisting irreducibility of the 'qualia' of consciousness to behaviour, analytic behaviourism, even in a dispositional form, seems unlikely to succeed.[3]

Difficulties with methodological behaviourism

Within psychology, the waning influence of behaviourism had less to do with its implausible account of consciousness and mind than with the inability of methodological behaviourism to carry out its manifesto. According to Watson and Skinner it matters little whether mental states exist as they exert little, if any, autonomous influence on behaviour. Behaviour is controlled by stimulus configurations combined with appropriate schedules of reinforcement. Given the stimuli and the reinforcement history, one can predict the behaviour. Unfortunately for this position, there is very little evidence in its favour. Brewer (1974), for example, reviews evidence that even simple conditioning in humans does not occur unless it is mediated by conscious knowledge of the relationship between the conditioned stimulus and the unconditioned response. For example, a puff of air (an unconditioned stimulus) causes the eye to blink (an unconditioned response). If the puff of air is reliably preceded by a flash of light this too will cause the eye-blink (the light becomes a conditioned stimulus), but this only occurs if subjects are aware of the contingency between the light and the puff of air. That is, even simple classical conditioning in humans seems to require the intervention of cognitive mediators, which have no place in radical behaviourist theory.

The ability to predict *complex* human behaviour on the basis of stimulus input is extremely poor. As the psychologist Charles Tart puts it, 'After 50 years of behaviorist research, the best way of finding out what somebody is going to do next, is to ask, "What are you going to do next?" '[4]

The critique of Skinner's (1957) book *Verbal Behavior* by the linguist Noam Chomsky (1959) suggested that the problems of explaining language in behaviourist terms were insurmountable. In real-life situations, given a stimulus, it is very difficult to predict a human verbal response, as what people say does not appear to be entirely under stimulus control. For example,

A typical example of 'stimulus control' for Skinner would be the response to a piece of music with the utterance Mozart or to a painting with the response Dutch. These responses are asserted to be 'under the control of extremely subtle properties' of the physical object or event. Suppose instead of saying Dutch we had said Clashes with the wallpaper, I thought you liked abstract work, Never saw it before, Tilted, Hanging too low, Beautiful, Hideous, Remember our camping trip last summer?, or whatever else might come into our mind when looking at a picture (in Skinnerian translations, whatever other responses exist in sufficient strength). Skinner could only say that each of these responses is under the control of some other stimulus property of the physical object. If we look at a red chair and say red, the response is under the control of the stimulus 'redness'; if we say chair, it is under the control of the collection of properties (for Skinner, the object) 'chairness', and similarly for any other response. This device is as simple as it is empty. Since properties are free for the asking (we have as many of them as we have nonsynonymous descriptive expressions in our language, whatever this means exactly), we can account for a wide class of responses in terms of Skinnerian functional analysis by identifying the 'controlling stimuli'. But the word 'stimulus' has lost all objectivity in this usage. Stimuli are no longer part of the physical world; they are driven back into organism. We identify the stimulus when we hear the response. It is clear from such examples, which abound, that the talk of 'stimulus control' simply disguises a complete retreat to mentalistic psychology. We cannot predict verbal behaviour in terms of the stimuli in the speaker's environment, since we do not know what the current stimuli are until he responds. Furthermore, since we cannot control the property of a physical object to which an individual will respond, except in highly artificial cases, Skinner's claim that his system, as opposed to the traditional one, permits the practical control of verbal behaviour is quite false.

(Chomsky, 1959, p. 51)

Rather than behaviour being determined in a rigid mechanistic fashion by impinging stimuli, human beings are able to select and interpret the information to which they attend and they may respond in ways that are flexible, adaptive and potentially novel. Faced with such a 'loose coupling' between external stimuli and overt response, psychologists in the second half of the twentieth century turned once more to a study of inner mental events – to a *cognitive psychology* which investigates the states and processes which *enable* human beings to produce the behaviour that they do. This resurgent interest in cognitive processes within psychology was extensively cross-fertilised by theoretical developments in other disciplines – by information theory, signal

---

Box 4.1 The beginnings of cognitive psychology

The arrival of cognitive psychology as a discipline distinct from behaviourism was heralded by Ulric Neisser's famous 1967 book *Cognitive Psychology*, but the beginnings were much earlier. Donald Broadbent in Cambridge, for example, produced the first flow diagram of selective attention in 1958. This is turn built on the prior develop-ment of flow diagrams in systems analysis and employed the use of 'filters' and 'channels' with 'limited information capacity', imported from electrical engineering. Useful accounts of the influences which led to the emergence of cognitive psychology, along with an analysis of its debts to and divergences from behaviourism, are given by Lachman *et al.* (1979) and Gardner (1987).

---

detection theory, control theory, and systems analysis in engineering, by developments in linguistics, and, above all, by the impact of computers (Box 4.1). Cognitive psychology remains the dominant paradigm in Western psychological science, and it has a distinct *functionalist* approach to the analysis of consciousness and mind.

The emergence of functionalism in psychological science

Functionalism in modern psychology treats mind and consciousness as func-tions of the brain, typically specified in information processing (or more recently in neural network) terms. However, the earliest attempt to under-stand consciousness and mind in a functionalist way probably appears in Aristotle's discussions of the soul – for souls, he argues, are simply the *forms in which life is expressed*. In organisms, these forms are defined largely by their capacities and modes of functioning. Thus, plants have a 'vegetative' soul defined by their capacity to grow, decay, feed and reproduce; animals have a 'sensitive' soul defined by their capacity to perceive and desire; only humans have a 'rational' soul, defined by the capacity to think.[5]

Within psychology, the view that mind and consciousness may be viewed as functions or processes dates back to William James (1890). However this only became properly established around the late 1950s with the introduction of information processing theories of cognitive functions, the development of artificial intelligence, and the computer simulation of human behaviour. Once established, cognitive psychology replaced behaviourism almost as quickly as behaviourism had replaced introspectionism. By the late 1960s, models of the mind no longer consisted of stimuli, responses and a 'black box' representing the brain (containing, at most, a few internal mediating stimuli and responses), but a wealth of mental processes arranged into relatively

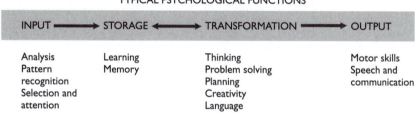

Figure 4.2 A rough outline of where some of the mental functions studied by psychology fit into the flow of human information processing.

autonomous information processing systems which encode input information, store it, transform it, and produce appropriate output. A schematic diagram of where some of the processes studied by psychology fit into the flow of information (from input to output) is shown in Figure 4.2.

Initial ideas about where consciousness fits into human information processing

How does consciousness relate to such processing? According to James (1890) the current contents of consciousness define the 'psychological present' and are contained in 'primary memory' (a form of short-term working store). The contents of 'secondary memory' (a long-term memory store) define the 'psychological past', and while they remain in secondary memory they are unconscious. James also suggested that stimuli that enter consciousness are at the focus of attention, having been selected from competing stimuli to enable effective interaction with the world. Stimuli at the focus of attention are also given significance and value by their contextual surround – a conscious 'fringe' or flowing consciousness 'stream'. These ideas, developed around 100 years ago, eventually became the focus of much psychological research.

However, in the early years of cognitive psychology, references to consciousness were made only in passing, in discussions that were really focused on the details of information processing. For example, Broadbent (1958) mentions consciousness in his 'filter' model of selective attention. This model was intended to account for the finding that subjects have a limited capacity to process information arriving simultaneously at the sense organs. A cocktail party is typical, in that one can fully attend to only one of the many conversations occurring at any given moment (Cherry, 1953). The conversation to which one attends enters consciousness, but the other non-attended conversations form a kind of background 'buzz'. As Broadbent put it, this is evidence for an 'information processing bottleneck' in the system. So the brain needs to select the information to which to attend. How is this done? In Broadbent's initial model (based on the evidence available in the 1950s) selection is achieved by a preconscious 'sensory filter' which performs a rough *physical* analysis of input stimuli. It then selects the information which will be passed through the bottleneck of the brain's 'limited capacity decision channel' (LCDC) for further processing. Only information that enters the LCDC is analysed for meaning, becomes conscious, and may be used to organise a response. James's linking of consciousness to primary memory was also reintroduced into experimental psychology by Waugh and Norman (1965), but, again, their work had more to do with the relation of primary to secondary memory than consciousness. Nevertheless, by 1962, George Miller, in his classic *Psychology: The Science of Mental Life*, felt able to assert that while most psychologists confess they do not know what consciousness is, 'They are sure it is not a substance – a material thing – but a process or group of processes, which occurs in some objects and not in others' (Miller, 1962, p. 40).

In the late 1960s theories of selective attention and memory converged. That is, a number of models appeared each summarising a large body of research in which selection, attention, and transfer of information between primary and secondary memory were combined into one integrated system (e.g. Atkinson and Shiffrin, 1968; Norman, 1969). In the model proposed by Donald Norman (1969), for example, stimuli arriving in parallel at the sense organs are initially subject to analysis of a preconscious, automatic kind so that they may be identified (by matching them to traces in secondary memory formed by previous experience with those stimuli). Once matched, they are assessed for significance. Only the most 'pertinent' of the input stimuli are selected for further processing by a limited capacity attention system, thereby entering consciousness.[6] Conscious processing contrasts with preconscious processing in that it is voluntary and flexible. Attended-to stimuli may be processed in a variety of ways – for example, they may be rehearsed and stored in secondary memory, they may enter into problem solving, or they may form the basis of some overt response. Information that is not selected for more detailed attention remains unconscious and is eventually lost from the system (see Figure 4.3).

While such theories *associated* consciousness with particular forms and stages of processing (typically with focal attention or primary memory), they remained uncommitted about the *nature* of this association. However, from around 1970 a number of papers appeared in which the *ontological identification* of consciousness with a form of processing becomes explicit. Following Broadbent (1958), for example, Posner and Warren (1972) asserted that the use of a limited capacity central processing system 'becomes the central definition of a conscious process and its non-use is what is meant by a process being automatic'. Posner and Boies (1971) also pointed out that tasks involving the limited capacity central processor can be interfered with by other tasks which compete for the use of the limited capacity central processor. They argued, therefore, that susceptibility to interference provides one way of defining which processes are conscious by experimental means. Rehearsal of a stimulus and choosing an appropriate output response, for example, can both be disrupted by competing tasks and are (on this definition) 'conscious processes'. Simultaneous recognition of

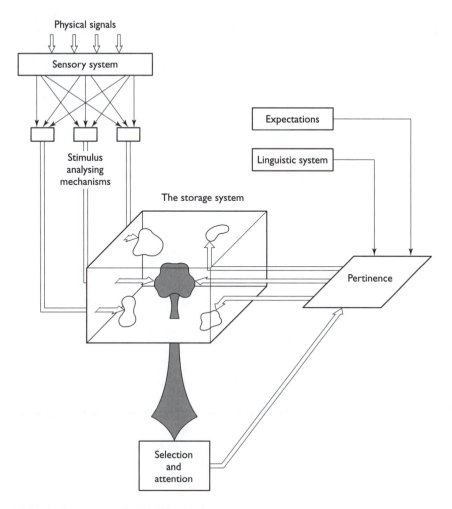

Physical signals

Sensory system

Stimulus
analysing
mechanisms

The storage system

Expectations

Linguistic system

Pertinence

Selection
and
attention

The selection process. Both the physical inputs and the pertinence of information determine what will be selected for further processing. Physical inputs pass through the sensory system and stimulus analysing mechanisms before exciting their representation in the storage system. Simultaneously, the analysis of previously encountered material, coupled with the history of expectations and the rules of perception, determine the class of events assumed to be most pertinent at the moment. That material which receives the greatest combined excitation is selected for further attention.

Figure 4.3 A 'late-selection' model of selective attention (from D. Norman, *Memory and Attention: An Introduction to Human Information Processing.* Copyright © 1969, John Wiley and Sons, Inc. Reprinted with permission).

different input stimuli, on the other hand, appears, at least to a degree, to proceed in a parallel, automatic fashion, without mutual interference, and is 'preconscious' (see Figure 4.3 above).

Comparisons were also made between the operations of the limited capacity central processor and an 'executive monitor programme' sometimes used in large computing installations to allocate processing resources efficiently to the many simultaneous tasks in which the system is engaged (Shallice, 1972; Bower, 1972; Bjork, 1975). Bjork (1975), for example, outlined a model of human information processing in which 'an explicit central processor is proposed as a kind of executive consciousness that controls and governs the system; without the involvement of the central processor, nothing happens in the system beyond the formation of input traces'.

If consciousness just *is* a 'central processor' or a 'central executive system' then it clearly does something useful in the activities of brain. As Darwin's friend, the naturalist George Romanes, noted in 1885, this is exactly what one would expect from evolutionary theory – for,

> Is it not itself a strikingly suggestive fact that consciousness only, yet always, appears upon the scene when the adjustive actions of any animal body rise above a certain level of intricacy. . . . Surely, this large and general fact points with irresistible force to the conclusion, that in the performance of these more complex adjustments, consciousness or the power of feeling or the power of willing are of some use. Assuredly on the principles of evolution, which materialists at all events cannot afford to disregard, it would be a wholly anomalous fact that so wide and important a class of faculties of mind should have become developed in constantly ascending degrees throughout the animal kingdom, if they were entirely without use to animals. . . . we never meet, on any large or general scale with organs or functions which are wholly adventitious. Is it to be supposed that this general principle fails just when its presence is most required, and that the highest functions of the highest organs of the highest animals stand out of analogy with all other functions in being in themselves functionless? To this question I, for one, can only answer unequivocally, No.
>
> (cited in Vesey, 1970, p. 182)

The notion that consciousness is necessary, or at any rate useful, in the performance of *complex* tasks, particularly when these are novel, or require flexibility, is a recurring theme in subsequent psychological theory. Following James (1890), many psychologists have also identified consciousness with 'focal attention' or with the contents of 'primary memory'. Up to the early 1990s, for example, 'preconscious' processing was commonly identified with 'pre-attentive' processing, whereas 'conscious' processing was identified with 'focal-attentive' processing (e.g. Baars, 1991; Mandler, 1975, 1985, 1991;[7] Miller, 1962). Following James (1890) and Waugh and Norman (1965), there were also many identifications of consciousness with primary memory or some similar short-term working store.[8] More recently, James's views about the role of 'fringe consciousness' have also been reintroduced into cognitive psychology by Mangan (1993, 2003, 2007). James stressed that the significance and value of conscious material at the focus of attention are indicated by the relatively vague feelings that surround it. Mangan argues that such feelings provide *contextual* information about conscious material at the focus of attention, in a highly condensed form. For example, the goodness-of-fit of currently focused-on material with prior material stored in long-term memory may be manifest in consciousness as a simple feeling of its 'rightness' or 'wrongness'.[9]

Within cognitive psychology, various attempts have also been made to spell out the evolutionary functions of consciousness in finer detail.[10] Mandler (1975), for example, argued that,

> relational processes operate primarily if not exclusively on conscious content. In addition to choice, these include evaluation, comparison, grouping, categorization and serial ordering. In short, practically all novel relational orderings require that the events to be ordered must be simultaneously present in the conscious field. . . . Once relations have been established and stored subsequent evaluations are frequently unconscious.

According to Mandler (1975), such conscious operations confer a number of evolutionary advantages. For example:

1   Consciousness enables the covert testing of possible ways of interacting with the immediate environment, that is 'the consideration of complex input–output contingencies – including ones the organism has never previously performed', eliminating the need for overt testing of those actions which might have harmful consequences.
2   Consciousness makes it possible to reformulate long-range plans – involving retrieval of information from secondary memory, modification of that information, storage of the new plans and so on.
3   Consciousness provides a 'troubleshooting function' for systems which normally operate unconsciously but only become conscious when they fail. For example, if one is driving a car and the brakes suddenly fail, awareness is immediately redirected to the task in hand, enabling 'repair work' to get under way.

In sum, Mandler concluded that,

> Many of these functions permit the organism to react reflectively instead of automatically, a distinction that has frequently been made between humans and lower animals. All of them permit more adaptive transactions between the organism and the environment. Also, in general, the functions of consciousness permit a focusing on the most important and species relevant aspects of the environment.[11]
>
> (Mandler, 1975, p. 57)

In similar fashion, Dixon (1981) identified consciousness with 'an action system in which the final product of interactions between sensory-inflow, stored information and need states is delivered up for the elaboration of plans and responses' (p. 3). This conscious action system, according to Dixon, evolved to

> hallmark those features of the external scene which were at any one time of maximum importance to survival and upon which plans of action could be based. A second and related function of a consciousness system would be the provision of a means whereby organisms could contemplate their own need states, to mediate between inner and outer demands, and given the limited capacity of the effector system, to establish priorities for action.
>
> (ibid.)

Baars (1988) attempted to integrate some of these ideas by positioning consciousness within a 'Global Workspace' architecture of the brain. In their review of cognitive models of consciousness, Baars and McGovern (1996) point out that the brain has hundreds of different types of *unconscious specialised processors*, such as feature detectors for colours, line orientation and faces, which can act independently or in coalition with one another, thereby bypassing the limited capacity of consciousness. These processors are extremely efficient, but restricted to their dedicated tasks. The processors can also receive global messages and transmit them by 'posting' messages to a limited capacity, *global workspace* whose architecture enables system-wide integration and dissemination of such information. Such communications allow new links to be formed between the processors, and the formation of novel expert 'coalitions' able to work on new or difficult problems. Baars *et al.* (1997) liken this global workspace to a 'theatre of consciousness in the society of the mind'.

A further element of this model of the mind is provided by the *unconscious contexts* within which activities on 'central stage' take place.

> Contexts are coalitions of expert processors that provide the director, playwright and stagehands behind the scenes of the theatre of the mind. They can be defined functionally as *knowledge structures that constrain conscious contents without being conscious themselves*, just as the playwright determines the words of the actors on stage without being visible.
>
> (Baars and McGovern, 1996, p. 89)

Contexts are provided by past experiences (stored in memory), expectations, beliefs and so on.

As do prior theories which *identify* consciousness with information 'at the focus of attention', 'in a working store', 'in a limited capacity decision channel' and so on, Baars and McGovern (1996) assert that '*information in the global workspace corresponds to conscious contents*' (p. 89). Accordingly, they give consciousness a central role in the economy of mind that corresponds to the *functions of the global workspace*. Within their model, the global workspace is essential for organising novel, complex activities. So Baars and McGovern give consciousness many things to do:

1   By relating input to its context, consciousness defines input, removing its ambiguities in perception and understanding.
2   Consciousness is required for successful problem solving and learning, particularly where novelty is involved.
3   Making an event conscious raises its 'access priority', increasing the chances of successful adaptation to that event.
4   Conscious goals can recruit subgoals and motor systems to carry out voluntary acts. Making choices conscious helps to recruit knowledge resources essential to arriving at an appropriate decision.
5   Conscious inner speech and imagery allow us to reflect on and, to an extent, control our conscious and unconscious functioning.
6   In facing unpredictable conditions, consciousness is indispensable in allowing flexible responses.

'In sum, consciousness appears to be the major way in which the central nervous system adapts to novel, challenging and informative events in the world' (ibid., p. 92). Romanes (1885) came to a similar conclusion, as we have seen.

Recurring themes in cognitive models of consciousness

There are many differences in the detail of cognitive models of consciousness, for example, in the way selection, attention, primary memory and the operations of a limited capacity central processor relate to each other. Nevertheless in their attempts to relate consciousness to such functioning, there are a number of recurring themes. It is generally agreed that the initial processing of information arriving at the sense organs proceeds, at least to some extent, in a parallel, automatic, preconscious fashion. When a stimulus is sufficiently well identified to be judged more important or 'pertinent' than competing stimuli it may be selected for more detailed attention. It is only if this happens that the stimulus enters primary memory (or some equivalent short-term 'working memory'), in which case it enters consciousness and may be subject to further processing of a novel, flexible kind. In this there is a trade-off between the greater range of processing resources that can be allocated to a given, attended-to task, and the smaller number of tasks that can be at the focus of attention at any given moment. Attentional processing may involve categorisation, choice, planning, reorganisation, retrieval from and transfer to secondary memory and so on. As a result of such processing, information at the focus of attention is integrated in a coherent way, and becomes generally available (widely disseminated) throughout the system, providing the basis for a co-ordinated, adaptive, overt response. While novel, complex tasks require such conscious processing for their successful execution, once they are well learnt they may be dealt with in an automatic, unconscious way.[12]

The strengths of functionalism in cognitive psychology

In many respects, psychofunctionalism seems intuitively plausible. Psychologists study mental processes. So it is hardly surprising that psychological theories might, indeed, be theories of mental processes. The identification of mind with certain modes of functioning also reconciles the intuition that the mind is somehow embodied in the brain with the contrary intuition that the mind does not seem to have a specific spatial location in the brain.

Psychofunctionalism also seems consistent with our natural language usage of many mental terms. For example our ability to think, solve problems and so on seems to relate to our capacity to function in certain ways. Likewise, when comparing ourselves with other humans or other animals, it is common to assess our mental abilities in functional terms. Historically, this has been accepted even by dualists such as Descartes. Indeed, for Descartes, man's ability to use language and to respond appropriately to changing situations gives him capacities which are beyond any machine or any nonhuman animal (see Chapter 2). One might or might not agree with Descartes that this is evidence for a thinking, nonmaterial soul (*res cogitans*). But it seems difficult to deny that theories that specify the detailed processes involved in language, thinking, problem solving and so on illuminate at least some aspects of the nature of mind.

For our present purposes we do not need to consider the extensive experimental work which led to the development of the many models of conscious and nonconscious processing outlined above (we consider this evidence in more depth in Chapter 10). Suffice it to say that the evidence in support of broad functional links between consciousness, attention and primary memory along the lines described above is considerable (for reviews see, for example, Velmans, 1991a; Baars and McGovern, 1996; Mandler, 1997; Styles, 1997; Pashler, 1999). The above, broad outline of how mental processes are organised is also supported by everyday experience. It is easy to demonstrate for example that one attends to only a small amount of the information that arrives at the sense organs. Just notice, as you read, the pressure of your feet against the floor, the range of environmental sounds, the sensation of your own breathing, and so on. These other inputs only enter consciousness once one allocates attention to them. So it is reasonable to suppose that there must be a process which governs selection of input, allocation of attentional resources and entry into consciousness. The observation that complex, novel tasks require conscious attention is also evident to anyone learning to drive a car or play a musical instrument. Once in consciousness, an event also becomes part of one's 'psychological present' – which makes it possible for it to become part of one's psychological past, involving storage in long-term memory, the possibility of later recall and so on.

In short, the cognitive psychological approach, which treats mind as a complex system that can be analysed into its constituent functions and processes, seems to be both productive and plausible (unlike behaviourism, which ignored or denied the existence of mind). Information processing accounts have also significantly advanced our understanding of the processes most closely associated with consciousness in the economy of mind. In principle, functional accounts of mental operations can also be combined with neurophysiological accounts of how the wetware of the brain operates (as in cognitive neuropsychology) with potentially unifying results. One might have doubts about whether it makes sense to *reduce* functional descriptions of the mind to neurophysiology, but few would deny that it makes sense to investigate the manner in which mental functions are *embodied* in neurophysiology.

According to Mandler (1975, 1997), this division of labour, in which cognitive theories describe the mind and neurophysiological theories describe the brain, has clear implications for the mind–body problem. That is, 'Once it is agreed that the scientific mind–body problem concerns the relationship between two sets of theories, the enterprise becomes theoretical and empirical, not metaphysical' (Mandler, 1997, p. 494).

The weaknesses of functionalism in cognitive psychology

Unfortunately, matters are not quite that simple. To the extent that mind can be thought of in process terms, it is true that the relation of mind to brain concerns the relation of mental processes to the neural wetware that embodies them. But, as noted in Chapter 1, 'mind' needs to be distinguished from 'consciousness' for the reason that mental processes may or may not be conscious. *Theories* of mind (or brain) also need to be distinguished from mind (or brain) itself (as noted in Chapter 3, theory reduction is not equivalent to phenomenon reduction). Crucially, such theories, expressed in functional, information processing terms, are 'third-person' accounts of what is going on. That is, they are inferences about intervening processes based on observations of input–output contingencies. Neurophysiological accounts are similarly based on 'third-person' observations of the brain. By contrast, consciousness is, in essence, a 'first-person' phenomenon (we cannot observe someone else's consciousness from the outside, so if we did not have it ourselves, we would not suspect it was there). Consequently, one cannot take it for granted that third-person functional accounts of mind or brain are also accounts of consciousness.

The truth of this is evident from the fact that, for many years, cognitive accounts of mental processes now thought to be closely associated with consciousness made little if any reference to consciousness. Theories of selective attention, for example, focused on how processing capacity was allocated, on determining the stage of input analysis at which stimulus selection takes place, and on how pre-attentive processing differs from focal-attentive processing. Theories of short-term memory tried to specify its capacity, the principles governing information entry to and loss from the memory system, the modes of encoding used, and so on. While there are good reasons to believe that phenomenal consciousness in humans is closely associated with attentional processing and short-term memory, the *nature* of this association is not what is at issue in such cognitive investigations. Consequently, it is not clearly specified in such information processing accounts. In the models above, for example, there are no 'bridging laws' or 'transform equations' which cross the gap from third-person information processing accounts to first-person accounts of phenomenal experience. Cognitive theories which place consciousness in an information processing 'box' simply *assume* or *define* it to be ontologically identical to a given form of processing in the brain (largely *ignoring* its phenomenology). Such theories typically move, without blinking, from relatively well justified claims about the forms of information processing with which consciousness is *associated*, to entirely unjustified claims about what consciousness *is* or what it *does*. Baars and McGovern (1996), for example, move without any discussion, from the somewhat ambiguous claim that 'information in the global workspace *corresponds* to conscious contents',[13] to the claim that consciousness actually *carries out the functions of the global workspace.* However, such manoeuvres beg the question; that is, they assume or posit *what they need to establish.*

Information at the 'focus of attention', in 'primary memory' or in a 'global workspace' might, for example, cause or correlate with what we experience. But it is important to distinguish *causation* and *correlation* from *ontological identity*. Conflation of these basic relationships is a common flaw in reductionist accounts. As we have already examined this in depth in Chapter 3, I will not repeat the analysis here. We all know what it is like to have conscious experiences. Taken together, they comprise our *entire phenomenal worlds.* How the phenomenal 'shape' and 'qualia' of these experienced worlds *relate* to neurally encoded information at the focus of attention is not self-evident. Rather than ignoring this issue, it needs investigation. One cannot explain what consciousness is or what it does, without explaining what this *phenomenology* is, or what it does. Discussions of information processing which ignore its phenomenology are not discussions of consciousness.

It is instructive to note that psychological theories that take the identity of consciousness with information processing for granted tend to be vague about the phenomenology–information processing relationship at just the points where they need to be clear. As we have seen, early cognitive theories often used the term 'conscious' loosely, to describe a *property* of a process, for example a property of the LCDC, focal-attentive processing, or primary memory. This associated certain forms of processing with consciousness but entailed no commitment about whether consciousness as such actually *does anything* – consciousness might for example be an epiphenomenal property that *accompanies, emerges from* or *is produced by* certain forms of processing.

By contrast, George Miller (1962) took the bolder position that consciousness *is* 'a process or group of processes'. Indeed he went on to claim that 'the selective function of consciousness and the limited span of attention are complementary ways of talking about one and the same thing' (ibid., p. 65). If consciousness *is* a brain process that selects items for attention then it clearly does something important in the workings of the brain.

Miller derived this suggestion from the work of William James. However, James's own characterisation of the consciousness–attention relation was ambiguous. As he pointed out in his *Principles of Psychology*, not only do the sense organs themselves select, in that they respond to just a portion of the energies described by physics, but also selective attention,

> out of all the sensations yielded, picks out certain areas as worthy of its notice and suppresses all the rest. . . . [Thus,] the mind is at every stage a theater of simultaneous possibilities. Consciousness consists in the comparison of these with each other, the selection of some, and the suppression of the rest by the *reinforcing and inhibiting agency of attention.*
>
> (James, 1890, Vol. 1, p. 288; my italics)

Miller (along with many other commentators) takes this to mean that consciousness *does* the selecting. However James actually states that *the agency of attention* compares, selects and so on. Consciousness 'consists in' the ongoing comparison, selection and suppression which are undertaken by attentional processing. What 'consists in' means in this passage is not entirely clear. It could mean, 'is nothing more than', in which case Miller's interpretation is justified; or it could mean, 'is constituted by', or 'is constructed by', in which case consciousness *results* from focal-attentive processing. These fine distinctions matter for the reason that the first interpretation makes no sense – how could consciousness select what enters consciousness? To determine what enters consciousness a *preconscious* selection must take place (this is taken for granted in most modern theories of selective attention).

Indeed, in a later chapter of his 1962 book, Miller begins to examine the role of consciousness with greater care – and what he finds threatens to undermine *all* the identities and functions claimed for consciousness outlined above, including those that he himself suggests.

Are the detailed activities of mind conscious?

Miller asks us to examine what we are actually aware of when we 'think'. If we attend to this carefully, Miller argues, it becomes apparent that 'thinking' is a *preconscious* process (Box 4.2). Significantly, Karl Lashley (1958), one of the most prominent psychologists of his era, came to the same conclusion.

Box 4.2 No activity of mind is ever conscious

George Miller arrives at the view that no activity of mind is conscious by attending to what we actually experience when we try to think or remember something, or experience an emotion or a motivation to do something:

> The fact that the process of thinking has no possible access into consciousness may seem surprising at first, but it can be verified quite simply. At this moment, as you are now reading, try to think of your mother's maiden name.
>
> What happened? What was your conscious awareness of the process that produced the name? Most persons report they had feelings of tension, of strain unrelated to the task, and then suddenly the answer was there in full consciousness. There may have been a fleeting image or two, but they were irrelevant. Consciousness gives no clue as to where the answer comes from; the processes that produce it are unconscious. It is the result of thinking, not the process of thinking, that appears spontaneously in consciousness.
>
> (Miller, 1962, p. 71)

And,

> What is true of thinking and of perceiving is true in general. We can state it as a general rule. No activity of mind is ever conscious. In particular, the mental processes involved in our desires and emotions are never conscious. Only the end product of these motivational processes can ever become known to us directly.
>
> (ibid., p. 72)

This contention is in any case supported by the very existence of cognitive psychology as a scientific discipline. If the complex processes which enable us to select information, attend to it, plan, organise, determine priorities, respond appropriately and so on, were available to consciousness, there would be no need for careful experiment and theoretical inference to determine their operations. One could simply observe these activities introspectively, much as one can observe the way cogs, springs and levers drive the hands of a mechanical clock.[14] However, working out *how* we are able to do these things has proved to be very difficult, even at the functional level. And we have no introspective access whatsoever to the neurophysiological activities in our own brains.

So which is it to be? Either consciousness is a 'process or group of processes' which does something in the activities of mind, or 'no activity of mind is ever conscious', in which case consciousness is an epiphenomenon – 'the result of thinking' and not the 'process of thinking'. Miller can't have it both ways! While the former option is consistent with functionalism, the latter clearly is not – for if consciousness is not an activity of mind then all the problems supposedly solved by functionalism are raised again. After all, what is an 'epiphenomenon', where is it located, how is it produced, how could it have evolved, and so on? The logical possibility that consciousness might be both the 'result of thinking' and a 'process' would not resolve matters – for what kind of mental process could it be that plays no part in the activities of mind?

Other functionalist theories of consciousness face similar problems. If consciousness just *is* a kind of functioning which can be specified in third-person information processing terms, then it must *have* a function that is specifiable in those terms.[15] But if we are *not aware* of carrying out the claimed functions how can they be conscious? We return to this issue in depth in Chapter 10.

For those who are not yet convinced that there is a problem, I leave the conundrum in Box 4.3.

Box 4.3 A conundrum: is it possible for consciousness to do something to or about something that it is not conscious of?

If the answer is NO
We are not aware of the activity of our own brains.
So we conclude that consciousness as such does not influence brain activity.

If the answer is YES
We are not aware of the activity of our own brains.
So consciousness must influence brain activity *unconsciously*.
So we conclude that consciousness as such does not influence brain activity.
Yet consciousness is central to human *being*.
Without it our existence would be like *nothing*.
So the notion that consciousness does nothing makes no sense.

Notes

1 See readings in Chappell (1962), and a discussion of some of the subtleties by Byrne (1994).
2 This hybrid position is not easy to categorise. Armstrong is clearly committed to a form of dispositional behaviourism. However, given his ultimate reduction of phenomenal states to states of the brain, he is also a central state identity theorist (see Chapter 3). Given his attempt to recast the ordinary meanings of terms which

refer to conscious states into the causal relations which mediate between stimulus and response, Armstrong is also sometimes thought of as a 'conceptual functionalist' or an 'analytic functionalist' (Byrne, 1994). A similar view was later developed by the philosopher Daniel Dennett, as we will see in Chapter 5.

3 The attempt to remove the phenomenal aspects of perception from perception produces many further difficulties. Armstrong finds it necessary to argue, for example, that the colours of surfaces are not aspects of perception. Rather, he claims, they 'are nothing but physical properties of physical objects or processes' (ibid., p. 272). This, he maintains, follows from the distinction between a surface being red, which is a physical property of a surface, and a surface looking red, which is an aspect of perception. As he points out, unless he manages to exclude qualities of objects such as 'redness' from perception he would have to abandon his whole analysis (ibid., p. 272), for how could the colour of a surface out in the world be nothing more than the capacity to make certain discriminations? But in what sense is there some observer-independent 'redness' in the world? There is nothing intrinsically red about electromagnetic wavelengths in the region 700 nanometers. Animals without colour vision or humans with red–green colour blindness may be able to detect light in this region without it looking red. Although it is a logical possibility that redness is somehow 'really there' (and that such humans and animals simply do not see it) it is more parsimonious to regard the existence of redness and other perceptual qualia as being contingent on the interactions of physical energies with the visual (and other perceptual) systems of conscious beings. We return to this issue in depth in Chapters 6, 7 and 8. Other versions of Armstrong's theory have been developed – for example, by Lewis (1972, 1994), and Shallice (1972) – but these face related difficulties to which I will return in the analysis of *functionalism* below.

4 Personal communication, September, 1996. According to Tart this wry comment on behaviourism originated somewhere on the US West Coast in the late 1960s.

5 See, in particular, Aristotle's *De Anima*, Book 2, chs 1 and 2, or Flew (1978), pp. 72–81, for relevant extracts. In contrast to Plato's dualism in which idealised forms have an autonomous transcendent existence, Aristotle's forms are immanent in their embodying substance. Consequently, in Aristotle's cosmology there is no room for personal immortality as the body's 'soul' is not viewed as a separate incorporeal substance (any more than the function of cutting can be seen as separate from the axe). Aristotle is unclear on this point, however, as he also appears to believe that *intellect*, which enables humanity to comprehend the forms, cannot entirely be reduced to an aspect of bodily functioning, but participates in the one, divine intellect (*nous*) which is immortal and transcendent (see, for example, Tarnas, 1993, pp. 55–62).

6 In Broadbent's (1958) model, information is selected for attentional processing on the basis of a preliminary physical analysis. Consequently, this is known as an 'early selection' model. Norman's (1969) model suggests that a rudimentary, preconscious analysis for *meaning* also takes place (enabling the 'pertinence' of a stimulus to be assessed), before a selection is made. So this is known as a 'late selection' model. The evidence for preconscious meaning analysis is extensive (for reviews see Velmans, 1991a; Styles, 1997).

7 This identity was challenged by Velmans (1991a), and Baars (1997a) subsequently changed his position from identifying focal-attentive processing with consciousness to viewing it as a *gateway* to consciousness; the identity implicit in Mandler's writings was also somewhat equivocal. We return to a fuller evaluation of this literature below.

8 Examples include Norman (1969), Atkinson and Shiffrin (1968), Mandler (1975), and, in more detail, Ericsson and Simon (1984), and Baddeley (1993).

9 According to Mangan, the unconscious process that produces such feelings may

resemble the computation discovered by Hopfield (1982), in which the goodness-of-fit of an immense number of interacting, neuron-like nodes is condensed into a single metric or index.

10 See, for example, Mandler (1975, 1985, 1997), Crook (1980), Dixon (1981), Johnson-Laird, (1988), Baars (1988, 2007), Shallice (1978, 1988), and Schacter (1990). A useful summary of the way the theories of Mandler, Shallice, Johnson-Laird, and Schacter relate to that developed by Baars (1988) is given in Baars and McGovern (1996).

11 In a later review of his own twenty years of theorising on this issue, Mandler (1997) concluded that, 'Given our recent insights into the parallel and distributed nature of (unconscious) mental processing, the human mind (broadly interpreted) needed to handle the problem of finding a buffer between a bottleneck of possible thoughts and actions of comparable "strengths" competing for expression and the need for considering effective action in the environment. Consciousness handles that problem by imposing limited capacity and seriality' (p. 490). This returns to the basic insights developed by James (1890) and Broadbent (1958). Following James, Mandler (1997) also identifies the capacity of conscious contents with the capacity of primary memory.

12 Elements of such cognitive psychological theorising have also been incorporated into many philosophical and neurophysiological theories of consciousness. Prominent examples include Dennett's (1978) identification of consciousness with the information stored in a hypothetical 'buffer memory M', Block's (1995) reification of information accessibility into a distinct form of 'access consciousness' (which he separates from phenomenal consciousness), and the necessity of short-term memory to consciousness in the thalamocortical reverberatory loop model of Crick and Koch (1990). Crick and Koch's (1998) assertion that, 'the biological usefulness of visual consciousness in humans is to produce the best current interpretation of the visual scene in the light of past experience . . . and to make this interpretation directly available, for a sufficient time, to the parts of the brain that contemplate and plan voluntary motor output, of one sort or another, including speech', combines a number of these recurring cognitive psychological themes.

13 Interpreted weakly, 'corresponds' could mean 'is associated with' or 'correlates with'; however, Baars and McGovern go on to interpret this in the strong sense of 'is identical to'. While the weak interpretation poses no theoretical problems, the identity claim does pose problems, as we shall see.

14 Various mental activities do of course *result* in conscious experiences in the forms of percepts, thoughts, feelings and so on, and they are in this sense 'conscious'. Given this, the claim that 'no activity of mind is ever conscious' needs to be unravelled with care, along with its implications for the causal role (if any) of consciousness. We return to this issue in depth in Chapter 10.

15 If it does not *have* a function it makes no sense to claim that it *is* a function (one can't have functionless functions). The converse does not of course apply, i.e. consciousness might have a function without *being* a function (as claimed for example in dualist-interactionist theory).

5   Could robots be conscious?

Descartes believed that mere physical mechanisms could never think flexibly
and use language in the ways that humans do. Nor, lacking *res cogitans*
(substance that thinks), could they be conscious. However, the ability to think,
use language and be conscious even in *humans* cannot really be *explained* by
adding an immaterial substance 'that thinks', for the simple reason that all
questions about *how* it is possible for humans to think, use language, etc.
simply regress to *res cogitans* (see Chapter 2). Language and thought require
the use of rules and procedures that need to be instantiated in some medium
that can carry out such rules and procedures. Cognitive psychology takes it
for granted that the embodying medium is the brain. Functionalism in cognitive psychology (psychofunctionalism) makes the added assumption that
mind and consciousness *are nothing more than* forms of processing in the
brain. Formally, mental or conscious states are identified with the *causal
relationships* that state enters into with perceptual input, overt responses and
other mental or conscious states. From this point of view, the study of mind
and consciousness simply *is* the study of the rules and procedures people use
when they think, solve problems, use language and so on, typically specified
in information processing or neural network terms.

As we have seen in Chapter 4, there is good reason to believe that the
functioning of mind in humans can be usefully described in such third-person
terms, although first-person phenomenal consciousness does not fit naturally
into such descriptions. Furthermore, whatever one's doubts might be about
the *reducibility* of first-person consciousness to third-person accounts of
functional relationships, there seems little doubt that mind and consciousness
in humans are closely *associated* with the activity of the brain, and that the
brain is a physical system. Given this, what is there to prevent physical systems
other than brains *also* having associated mind and consciousness?

According to *computational functionalists*, there is nothing to prevent mind
and consciousness in nonhuman systems for the reason that mental operations are nothing more than computations. The mathematician Alan Turing
(1950), for example, suggested that if independent judges cannot distinguish
the answers given by a computer to questions put to it from those of a human
being, then the machine may be said to 'think'. And the philosopher Hillary

Putnam (1960) claimed the relation between mind and brain to be 'analogous to the relation between the logical operations carried out by a computer and the physical structure of the machine'.

Such logical operations may be likened to psychological operations in that they describe functioning in a computer that is similar to logical operations in brains, and, Putnam later notes, in that they have the interesting property of being neither 'mental' (in a Cartesian sense) nor 'physical'. Rather, 'As Aristotle saw, psychological predicates describe our form, not our matter' (Putnam, 1975, p. 279).

Note that functions are easily dissociable from structures. A system with a given physical structure may fulfil many different functions. A given computer may, for example, be programmed to solve equations, control factory processes, simulate human cognitive functioning and behaviour, and so on. Conversely, the same function can be embodied in many different physical structures. The earliest computers for example were built out of vacuum tubes which were replaced by transistors and subsequently by integrated circuits.[1]

Following the development of artificial intelligence (AI) and the computer simulation of mental functions, it became common in cognitive science to think of the brain/mind relationship as analogous to the distinction between the 'hardware' of a computer (the physical structure) and the 'software' (the programming) of the machine.[2] That is, many psychofunctionalists are also computational functionalists. However, it is important to note that psychofunctionalism does not *entail* computational functionalism. Psycho-functionalism claims mind and consciousness to be nothing more than functions of the *brain*. According to *computational functionalism* the biochemical composition of the brain is *irrelevant* to mind and consciousness. In short, mind and consciousness are *exportable*; whatever the physical properties of a system might be, if it embodies the same functions defined entirely in terms of the causal relations between input, internal elements in the system and output, it has the same mind.

How to make mechanical systems into minds

Descartes' seventeenth-century doubts about whether any machine can think are hardly surprising. In ancient Greece, Ethiopia and China men had already built machines that mimicked the behaviour of the human body. But simulating the functions of the human mind proved to be more difficult. The first digital calculating machine was constructed by Blaise Pascal in 1642 and later refined by Leibniz to the point where it could add, multiply, divide and extract square roots (cf. McCorduck, 1979). Impressive though this machine was, its functions were fixed.

The first attempt to build a general purpose, programmable calculator was made by the English mathematician Charles Babbage. This 'Analytic Engine', which occupied Babbage from 1833 to the end of his life in 1871, had a processing unit controlled by punched cards which, he hoped, would allow it to analyse and tabulate any mathematical function. In the words of his close associate, Lady Lovelace, the Analytic Engine 'would weave algebraic patterns the way the Jacquard loom weaved patterns in textiles' (cited in Morrison and Morrison, 1961).

But Babbage never completed his project – and the first general purpose digital computers were constructed in World War II. Building on the theoretical work of Alonzo Church, Alan Turing and others, the first was devised by Thomas Flowers, a British Post Office engineer, to decode German ciphers, in the Ultra project set up at Bletchley Park in 1943. ENIAC, another machine used to generate bombing tables, was built in the Moore School of Engineering at the University of Pennsylvania. In spite of their superior speed and general purpose computing abilities neither these machines nor their immediate successors were thought of as exercising reason or emulating other functions of the human mind. In this they resembled Charles Babbage's Analytical Engine – and, as Lady Lovelace noted in a memoir, 'The Analytical Engine has no pretensions whatever to originate anything. It can do whatever we know how to order it to perform' (ibid.).

Some of the intellectual steps necessary for the creation of more 'thoughtful' machine behaviour had, however, already been taken. In 1854, the Irish logician George Boole, building on the work of Leibniz, William Hamilton and Augustus de Morgan, had developed a means of expressing the propositions of logic and the relations between such propositions in terms of simple symbols and rules for operating on those symbols. This 'algebra' was, in turn, expressible in terms of a binary code (consisting solely of zeros and ones). In 1937, Claude Shannon, an engineering student at MIT (Massachusetts Institute of Technology), obtained his master's thesis for demonstrating that Boolean algebra can be used to describe the behaviour (the sequencing of 'on' and 'off' states) of relays and switching circuits. Consequently, the possibility emerged that logical operations could be embodied in the operations of a machine.

In spite of this, the gap separating logical operations carried out by switching circuits from 'thought' remained wide. In the 1950s, however, there was a dawning realisation that it might be possible to bridge the gap separating humans from machines from the *human* side. That is, human functions could themselves be thought of in terms of the operation of systems that encode, store, retrieve and transform information. Conversely, once simple machine language operations were appropriately combined into complex, interconnected systems they could generate higher level functions that, to some extent, resembled those performed by humans. In 1955, for example, Newell, Simon and Shaw working at the RAND Corporation in America, developed these insights into a new programming language, IPL1 (and later, IPL2), capable of expressing procedures and strategies of the kind which appear to be used by humans, in the form of instructions suitable for driving the operations of a machine. Armed with this they produced the 'Logic Theorist', a programme embodying strategies for solving problems of logic (Newell and Simon, 1956; Newell *et al.*, 1960).

At the time, the results appeared to be a stunning success. The Logic Theorist proved thirty-eight of the first fifty-two theorems of Russell and Whitehead's *Principia Mathematica*, including a shorter and more elegant proof of Theorem 2.85 than that given in the original work. This was followed afterwards by the 'General Problem Solver' (GPS), a programme incorporating a variety of general purpose strategies for solving problems, derived in this case from the self-reports of human problem solvers. Even more impressive than the Logic Theorist, this early simulation programme was eventually developed to the point where it could solve problems in eleven different domains. These included chess, theorem proving, missionaries and cannibals, integration, and parsing sentences, thereby capturing something not only of the manner but also of the flexibility of human problem solving (cf. Newell and Simon, 1972). Given that proficiency in these domains is one method of assessing intelligence in humans, it is understandable that for many workers in Artificial Intelligence this provided convincing evidence of intelligence in a machine.

By the early 1980s, for example, chess programmes were beginning to beat international masters. In 1980 the US's North Western University's Chess 4.7 programme beat international master, David Levey, in a tournament game. And in 1982 the Chess Champion Mark V system, marketed in Hong Kong by Scisys, beat the UK grandmaster John Nunn five times out of six. In addition, the Mark V found three correct solutions to a celebrated chess problem thought to have only one solution. The problem was originated by Russian expert, L. Zagorujko, in 1972. The problem had been widely publicised in newspapers and journals throughout the world, but no human being had found a solution other than the one proposed by Zagorujko. Nunn was unable to find the solution, but the Mark V confounded the experts by finding Zagorujko's solution and two alternatives of its own (cf. Simons, 1983, p. 76). Later, IBM's 'Deep Blue' defeated the then reigning international champion Gary Kasparov (Newborn, 1997). In March 2007, Rybka, the 2007 World Computer-Chess Champion created by international master Vasik Rajlich, defeated international grandmaster Jaan Ehlvest in a six-game match with three wins and three draws, in spite of a one-pawn handicap (randomly selected) and half the thinking time offered to the grandmaster.

Since that time there have been many further advances in the computer simulation of human mental abilities, although not all human abilities have proved easy to simulate in this way. Symbol manipulation according to rules and procedures is natural to implement in serial, digital computers. Consequently, these have been useful devices for simulating cognitive operations that follow serial, logical rules. However, some abilities that are simple for humans have proved to be extremely difficult to implement in such machines. For example, the complex patterns presented by faces and speech exhibit statistical regularities which are difficult to characterise in terms of invariant features and fixed rules for their identification, making them difficult to recognise via such symbol manipulation techniques. What is difficult for one machine architecture, however, may not be difficult for another. Over recent decades, for example, there have been extensive developments in the pattern recognition of faces, speech and so on. Recent systems use multilayered, artificial neural nets whose internal connections are either strengthened or weakened over a learning period (according to pre-set 'learning rules'), depending on whether or not they contribute to successful recognition of the to-be-recognised pattern.[3] In such systems it is not necessary to specify the defining features of complex patterns *a priori* – when appropriate forms of feedforward and feedback are applied, the system simply 'relaxes' into states which optimise recognition performance. Such neural nets have the added advantage over serial computers of appearing closer in their architecture and operation to neurons in living brains.

The ability of neural nets to accomplish aspects of such tasks in a relatively simple way and their potential for linking cognitive science to neuroscience are, like the digital computer before them, having a major influence on psychological models of the 'brain's mind' (an example of theory 'co-evolution' of the kind described by Churchland, 1989). For our purposes, it does not matter which, if either, approach becomes dominant – and it may even be that symbolic, rule-based approaches and neural network approaches are complementary, for example in situations where the psychological phenomena can be well described by rules, while the mechanisms for learning the rules can be well described in terms of neural networks. This might apply, for example, to the grammatical rules underlying use of language (cf. Abrahamsen and Bechtel, 2006). Whether or not this turns out to be true, the ability of artificial systems to simulate or emulate some areas of cognition once thought to be exclusive to the human mind is now quite impressive.

But what can't machines do?

According to Descartes, no machine could reason or use language in the appropriate ways that humans do for the reason that such flexibility is beyond the capacity of material 'stuff' no matter how it is arranged. Within AI circles it is now commonly thought that the limits of machine performance have more to do with our limited ability to *specify* what is required to carry out a given task than anything about mechanisms as such. However, there are reasons to suspect that it may not be possible to give a formal specification of the procedures required to carry out all tasks. This may be true not just for the pattern recognition of faces and speech discussed above but also for the global meanings and knowledge of the world which form the very ground of human thought and the use of human language. For Turing the inability of human judges to distinguish typewritten answers given by a machine from those of a human is a sufficient test of whether a machine can think. But, as the psychologist Robert Green (1981) has pointed out, there are more demanding tasks which can be carried out by humans (with appropriate training) that might not be specifiable in terms of the symbol manipulations according to rules which form the programmes of Turing machines. For example:

> Of the more intriguing tasks that have been explored using computers, that of translating from one language to another is of especial relevance. In the heady days of the 1950s it was believed that, given sufficient time, money and singleminded expert effort, all the problems relating to machine translation were in principle capable of solution. Over the years it became painfully clear that some of the problems associated with semantic content might prove to be ultimately intractable. As Lock (1975) points out, human translators and computers go about their business in very different ways. So far as human translators are concerned, 'The commonly accepted model, that he takes the words and grammar of Language A and replaces them with the words and grammar of Language B, is simply wrong. No translator works that way. What he really does is to read or listen to the text in Language A to get the idea . . . then he expresses the same meaning in Language B. Meaning is the substance of communication. Words and grammar are arbitrary conventions which have evolved over the years and differ from one language to another.'
>
> (Green, 1981, p. 177)

Differences in machine and human routes to language translation might not matter if each effectively accomplished the same task. Unfortunately, natural languages are notoriously context-sensitive and ambiguous, which makes exact translation from one language to another extremely difficult. As Green notes, this led to various attempts to construct 'pivot languages' based on logical principles common to all languages, in which each statement in any given actual language would have a single, unambiguous meaning, which could then be translated into any other language. A pivot language might, for example, have fifty-one separate terms for the word 'head' corresponding to its fifty-one natural language meanings. The varied ways in which natural languages use surface syntax to combine individual meanings into compound meanings might also be formalised by translating the surface forms into some common 'deep' structure or logical syntax of the kind used in transformational grammars, with the result that, in the deep structure, every statement is exact and unique. If ambiguous surface structures can be translated into unambiguous deep structures it might be possible to translate compound meanings accurately from one natural language to another. Such a task would be immense, but let us suppose that, in principle, it could be achieved. If so, the abilities of human translators would *still* be superior to those of machines. As Green points out,

> Whereas natural language is very fuzzy round the edges, which is

what makes poetry possible, the pivot language would not tolerate such vagueness. The elliptical, allusive, evocative properties of natural language would have to be sacrificed in order to arrive at a semantically unambiguous formulation. The pivot language would be sterile, lacking the richness and flavour of a natural language. Retranslating out from the pivot language into the target language would reintroduce all the fuzziness associated with that target language, but this fuzziness would not coincide with the fuzziness associated with the source language. Human translators can do better than this by catering for the fuzziness, catching the nuances, and trying to match the allusive, evocative aspects of the material in both the source and target languages. This is partly what makes the art of translation so challenging and rewarding for a human translator and also why machine translation is regarded as more suitable for technical material than poetry.[4]

(ibid., p. 179)

What is needed, Green concludes, is the ability to trade not just in words but in *ideas*. The same may be said of other tasks which humans perform with relative ease. Consider, for example, the sixteen statements in Box 5.1. Green suggests that any reasonably intelligent adult will sort these into eight, similar-meaning pairs with little difficulty.

Why might this task be difficult for a machine? In these pairs, similar ideas are conveyed by sentences composed of entirely different words embedded in different surface forms (compare, for example, (f) and (n)) and their meaning cannot be understood without a global understanding of the physical and social world. This is difficult for machine translation as it involves far more than the manipulation of individual word semantics according to syntactic rules. Yet, as Green notes,

Our human subject faces no such problems. He goes straight for the meaning, being utterly indifferent to logical syntax or any other niceties. The whole point of the comparison between the performance of man and machine is that there seems to be no way of getting from the form of language to its real content without a sapient, sentient being transducing mere quantifiable information into immanent wholistic meaning.

(ibid., p. 181)

At first glance, this seems to recapitulate the arguments of Descartes: only a sapient, sentient being could use language in the appropriate ways that humans take for granted. Unlike Descartes, however, Green's intent is not to place an unbridgeable divide between humans and machines. Rather, his aim is to define the gap more accurately in order to cross it. So, in what way could a machine truly learn the art of human language?

As we know, an ordinary person is constantly being bombarded with

Box 5.1 Can you do something that no existing computer can do?

Try sorting the following sixteen sentences into eight similar-meaning pairs.

(a) A nod is as good as a wink.
(b) An unfortunate experience produces a cautious attitude.
(c) Every cloud has a silver lining.
(d) Fine feathers make fine birds.
(e) Hints are there to be taken.
(f) Idealists can be a menace.
(g) It is an ill wind that blows no good.
(h) Least said, soonest mended.
(i) Never count your chickens before they are hatched.
(j) Never judge a sausage by its skin.
(k) Once bitten, twice shy.
(l) Reality imposes its own limitations.
(m) Some disagreements are best forgotten.
(n) The road to hell is paved with good intentions.
(o) There's many a slip twixt cup and lip.
(p) You can't make a silk purse out of a sow's ear.

You should be able to do it if you focus on the *idea* that each sentence conveys rather than on its grammar or constituent words. According to Green (1981) the odds against getting this correct by random combinations are over 13 million to one – and no machine, currently on the stocks, using a general language translating programme that combines individual word meanings following syntactic rules would do better than chance.

information of all sorts through a variety of channels. Setting aside all the technical difficulties, let us suppose that we can produce a machine capable of handling . . . different forms of input – auditory, visual, tactual, gustatory and so on, together with appropriate means for manipulating the environment so that it can perform the same kind of experiments that a baby does when it grabs a wooden brick and tries to chew it. Essentially, what we are after is a self-programming computer that can be brought up in the family and learn empirically. If the conceptual leap seems too big it may be bridged by Washoe and Helen Keller, taken either separately or in tandem.

Linguistic skills then develop naturally instead of being imposed. Rather than placing a ready made dictionary and a set of rules into the computer, it acquires a vocabulary and the appropriate rules by a gradual process of self-instruction. The autodidact, employing an inductive-deductive strategy, learns by comparing the various kinds of input in situational contexts, forming categories, attaching labels and generally sorting the chaos into a form and order that enables predictions to be made and effective goal seeking action to be taken. As McNamara (1973) so succinctly puts it, '. . . the main thrust in language learning comes from the child's need to understand and express himself.' Or, even more pointedly, '. . . the infant uses meaning as a clue to language, rather than language as a cue to meaning.'

(ibid., p. 184)

Green argues that a machine of this kind would pass Turing's test without difficulty – and, given that only a sentient being could appreciate meaning in this full sense, such a machine would also be conscious.

These arguments, presented over twenty-five years ago, have a contemporary relevance. For example, the philosopher Aaron Sloman (1997a, 1997b) has developed a research programme to specify how the more complex functional architectures associated with human mind and consciousness might develop as a consequence of machine interaction with the world (see review in Sloman and Chrisley, 2003), and in recent years this and similar programmes have received added impetus from theories that view human perception and cognition itself as fundamentally 'embodied' and dependent on interaction with the world.[5] Yet, even today, natural language in artificial systems remains a problem. Efforts to teach sensory-motor and cognitive skills to a robot infant, 'Cog', have, for example, been under way for over a dozen years under the direction of Rodney Brooks and Lynn Andrea Stein at MIT. Although the conditions that enable learning had to be pre-programmed into the robot, its 'nervous system' is a massively parallel architecture designed to learn from interaction with the world. Initial learning included the recognition, manipulation, and avoidance of objects and so on, but the ultimate aims were more ambitious. The philosopher Daniel Dennett (a member of this team) reported that:

> One talent that we have hopes of teaching to Cog is a rudimentary capacity for human language. And here we run into the fabled innate language organ or Language Acquisition Device made famous by Noam Chomsky. Is there going to be an attempt to build an innate LAD for our Cog? No. We are going to try to get Cog to build language the hard way, the way our ancestors must have done over thousands of generations. Cog has ears (four, because it is easier to get good localization with four microphones than with carefully shaped ears like ours!) and some special-purpose signal-analyzing software is being developed to give Cog a fairly good chance of discriminating human speech sounds, and probably the capacity to distinguish different human voices. Cog will also have to have speech synthesis software . . . to have Cog as

well-equipped as possible for rich and natural interactions with human beings.

(Dennett, 1995, p. 480)

It was anticipated that, given such basic equipment, language acquisition would involve a long learning process as it takes a long time for a child to grow into an adult. The team also intended to equip Cog with a 'motivation structure', with internally programmed goals and preferences which roughly map onto human desires. Ultimately, it was hoped that Cog would learn how to report on its own internal states. And, if all this can be made to work, Dennett claimed, we will have as much reason to believe in Cog consciousness as in consciousness in other humans.

Twelve years later (October, 2007), the list of achievements reported on the Cog programme website is instructive.[6] Cog appears to be able to make human-like eye movements and head and neck orientation behaviours; it can reach to a visual target, imitate head nods, make oscillatory arm movements and play the drums; it is also capable of some face and eye detection. However language learning is not even mentioned in its list of current research programmes.

Would Cog really be conscious?

It has to be said that twelve years is not a long time in the broad sweep of science – and how well Cog (or some other system) might learn to use natural language remains to be seen. But, suppose that Cog did learn to 'trade in ideas'. Would that be enough to conclude that it is conscious? If other minds are judged to be conscious *solely* in terms of what they can *do* this conclusion might be hard to resist. One can argue of course that we do *not* attribute consciousness to others primarily in terms of what they do. Rather, we infer consciousness in others by extrapolation from consciousness in ourselves (we return to this below). But suppose, for the sake of argument, that such attributions of sentience on the basis of observed functioning are legitimate. What would that tell us about consciousness in a machine?

It should be apparent that the conditions under which we would *attribute* mind and consciousness to other beings can be distinguished from claims about the *ontological nature* of what we attribute. Green, Dennett, and Sloman, for example, are philosophical descendants of Ryle (1949) in attributing mind and consciousness to a functioning system solely on the basis of its behaviour, or dispositions to behave. They nevertheless have different opinions about the nature of consciousness.

Dennett (1991), for example, develops an *eliminative* position (similar to that of Ryle). For him, terms like 'mind' and 'consciousness' are *nothing more than attributions* that we make on the basis of observed behaviour. They are essentially fictional attributions which may be quite useful to make in ordinary life, but they do not correspond to anything real either in brains or in machines. Rather, they correspond in a rough way to aspects of 'virtual machine' functioning which enable systems with appropriate architectures to display functioning of psychologically interesting kinds.[7] Sloman and Logan (1998) develop a slightly different *reductionist* position. For them, mental terms also denote aspects of virtual machine functioning. But, while everyday concepts of consciousness and mind are irretrievably confused, these terms nevertheless denote functions which can be precisely expressed in 'information level' design descriptions[8] (of the kind commonly suggested in cognitive psychology). In contrast, Chalmers (1996) develops an *emergentist* position. For him, mind is nothing more than functioning, but consciousness is *supervenient* on functioning and *not reducible to* it.[9] Green, on the other hand, remains neutral about which of these three options to adopt (personal communication).

It should be clear that these different versions of functionalism have very different implications for so-called 'conscious machines'. Dennett argues that we have as much reason to believe in Cog consciousness as in human consciousness for the reason that he *does not believe that human consciousness really exists* (at least in the sense that we normally understand it).[10] Sloman agrees with Dennett that mental terms refer to 'virtual machine' functions of certain kinds but insists that such functions are nevertheless real. That is, the qualia of consciousness exist *but only as modes of functioning in virtual machines*. For Chalmers, consciousness supervenes on functioning without reducing to it. Consequently, machines that function in ways that are indistinguishable from humans have conscious experiences that are indistinguishable from those of humans. Such experiences are real, nonphysical, emergent phenomena both for humans and for machines. For the moment I will focus on the more traditional eliminativist and reductionist positions. We will return to Chalmers's position when considering the distribution of consciousness in the universe in Chapter 14.

Can we get rid of qualia?

Within the sciences, it is generally agreed that colours, sounds and so on are not inherent properties *of the physical world*. Rather, such conscious 'qualia' are produced in our experience by the action of physical energies on our perceptual systems. Such experiences do not exist without experiencers. But few would go so far as to deny the existence of conscious 'qualia' altogether. Dennett, however, tries to do just that when he writes,

> Philosophers have adopted various names for the things in the beholder (or properties of the beholder) that have been supposed to provide a safe home for the colors and the rest of the properties that have been banished from the external world by the triumphs of physics: *raw feels, phenomenal qualities, intrinsic properties of conscious experiences, the qualitative content of mental states*, and, of course, *qualia*, the term I use. There are

subtle differences in how these terms have been defined, but I am going to ride roughshod over them. I deny that there are any such properties. But I agree wholeheartedly that there seem to be.

(Dennett, 1994, p. 129)

What science has actually shown us is just that light-reflecting properties of objects . . . cause creatures to go into various discriminative states. . . . These discriminative states of observers' brains have various primary properties (their mechanistic properties due to their connections, the excitation states of their elements, and so forth), and in virtue of these primary properties, they . . . have secondary, merely dispositional properties. In human creatures with language, for instance, these discriminative states often eventually dispose the creatures to express verbal judgements alluding to the color of various things. The semantics of these statements makes it clear what colors supposedly are: reflective properties of the surfaces of objects or of transparent volumes. . . . And that is just what colors are in fact. . . . Do not our internal discriminative states also have some special intrinsic properties, the subjective, private, ineffable properties that constitute the way things look to us (sound to us, smell to us, and so forth)? No. The dispositional properties of those discriminative states already suffice to explain all the effects: the effects on both peripheral behavior (saying 'Red!', stepping on the brake, and so forth) and internal behavior (judging 'Red!', seeing something as red, reacting with uneasiness or displeasure if red things upset one). Any additional qualitative properties or qualia would thus have no positive role to play in any explanations, nor are they somehow vouchsafed to us directly in intuition. Qualitative properties that are intrinsically conscious are a myth, an artifact of misguided theorizing, not anything given pretheoretically.

(ibid., p. 130)

Dennett tries to explode this 'myth' we all engage in, by examining situations in which humans clearly seem to use qualia to carry out tasks, and then showing that the same task can be carried out without qualia by a robot. Suppose, for example, that one is asked to compare billiard-table-felt-green and Granny-Smith-apple-green in the 'mind's eye' in order to decide which has the paler hue. We seem, in such instances, to retrieve information from memory that enables us to compare one subjective experience directly with another, on the basis of which we make our response. But a robot fitted with a TV camera and suitable colour coding equipment (of the kind available off the shelf) could perform the same discrimination without using representations that are *themselves* coloured, and in actual fact, Dennett suggests, we do the same:

Nothing red, white, or blue happens in your brain when you conjure up an American flag, but no doubt something happens that has three physical variable clusters associated with it – one for red, one for white, and one for blue, and it is by some mechanical comparison of the values of those variables with stored values of the same variables in memory that you come to be furnished with an opinion about the relative shades of the seen and remembered colors.

(ibid., p. 136)

While the brain no doubt performs such comparisons via different physical processes from those of the robot, according to Dennett, there is no reason to claim any less phenomenal content for the discriminative states of the robot than for discriminative states of the brain. The 'qualia' of consciousness have no real existence, either in humans or in machines.

Problems with Dennett's eliminativism

To the watchful reader, the sleight-of-hand in this argument should be clear. Note that Dennett tries to eliminate colour qualia in four steps:

1   He translates first-person accounts of *what it is like to experience* colour 'qualia' (the experience of Granny-Smith-apple-green etc.) into third-person accounts of how systems might *perform tasks* (how they might achieve colour discrimination, colour naming, stop on red, and so on).
2   He shows how the task might be performed by brains or machines without the use of representations that are themselves coloured.
3   He concludes that 'qualia' are not needed for functional explanations.
4   He concludes that 'qualia' do not exist.

Step 1 is fundamental to computational functionalism (in its normal eliminative and reductionist forms). If one cannot reduce first-person accounts of what it is like to experience something into third-person accounts of how systems function *without leaving something important out*, these versions of functionalism cannot get off the ground. Yet it seems obvious that something important is left out. Once one strips conscious qualia away from accounts of how a system processes information or of how they are disposed to behave, one has removed all reference to how things appear from a first-person perspective. Consequently, these accounts no longer tell one *anything* about *what it is like to experience something*. For example, it might be possible to specify the precise functional correlates of sharp pains, shooting pains and burning pains in information processing terms. But unless one had actually experienced such pains one would not know how these *feel*.[11] Overt behaviour or dispositions to behave are even less informative, as there are no rigid links that connect experience with behaviour. If I am in pain, I might be disposed to be stoical or to make a big fuss without altering the pain I feel. Conversely, I might respond in exactly the same way to pains that are qualitatively distinct (see the discussion of behaviourism and the reasons for its demise in psychology in Chapter 4).

The absence of any rigid link between 'qualia' and behaviour is even clearer in machines. As Dennett notes, qualia are actually *irrelevant* to accounts of how machines might discriminate between colours. His robot-with-TV-camera, for example, might *actually* experience Granny-Smith-apple-green as billiard-table-felt-green (and vice versa), or as pale blue versus dark blue, or it might have no experiences whatsoever. Provided that it translates electromagnetic energies into internal physical variables that suffice for machine discrimination, its behaviour might remain indistinguishable from that of a human being *whichever is the case*. But the converse of this is that machine discrimination alone tells us *nothing* about machine experience – and certainly nothing about human experience.

Given that Dennett's stated intention is to explain conscious experience, and not just how brains and machines perform tasks (his 1991 book is called *Consciousness Explained*), this is a rather large omission – to which we return below.

But first let us consider steps 2, 3 and 4. Step 2 is easily justified. There is little doubt that accounts can be given of brain or machine functioning in physical or information processing terms that make no appeal to the 'qualia' of conscious experiences. Indeed, viewed from a third-person perspective, it is difficult to see how conscious qualia *could* affect the behaviour of neurons or silicon chips (as the physical world appears causally closed). And, if one examines the experimental literature regarding the relation of conscious qualia to human information processing with care, one comes to the same conclusion (see Chapters 4 and 10, and Velmans 1991a).

Step 3 (that qualia are not needed for functional explanations) then follows from step 2. However, step 4 does not follow from step 3. The primary evidence for conscious experience in humans is *first-person* evidence. Computational functionalism (in its eliminative and reductionist forms) tries to show that mental terms denote nothing more than causal relations (intervening between input and output) in functioning systems, which can be specified in entirely third-person, information processing terms. If such causal relationships can be fully specified without *reference* to the qualia of consciousness, one can conclude that conscious qualia are irrelevant or superfluous to such third-person accounts. But it does not follow that conscious qualia have no useful place in 'first-person' accounts, or that they do not exist.[12]

Can qualia be reduced to the functioning of virtual machines?

The reductive, functionalist response is to *question* the value of 'first-person' accounts, and to argue that qualia can be fully *explained* in third-person, functional terms. If one can specify the architecture of a system that behaves *as if* it experiences qualia, understands meaning, operates from a 'first-person' perspective and so on, there is, they claim, *nothing left to explain*. Sloman and Logan (1998), for example, develop a theory of architectures capable of functioning as if they experienced qualia of many different kinds. *Intro-spective reports*, for example, require systems capable of self-monitoring and self-control. They note that the 'reports' generated by such systems are really about virtual machine states or internal physical and physiological states, but for Sloman and Logan, the same is true for 'qualia' in humans. Thus:

> Phenomena described by philosophers as 'qualia' may be explained in terms of high level control mechanisms with the ability to switch atten-tion from things in the environment to *internal* states and processes. . . . These introspective mechanisms may explain a child's ability to describe the location and quality of its pain to its mother, or an artist's ability to depict how things look (as opposed to how they are). Software agents able to inform us (or artificial agents) about their own internal states and processes may need similar architectural underpinnings for qualia.
>
> (Sloman and Logan, 1998, p. 4)

According to Sloman (1997b), provided that it has an appropriate archi-tecture there is every reason to believe that such a machine could fall in love. How do we go about specifying the appropriate architecture? 'Read what poets and novelists and playwrights say about love, and ask yourself: what kinds of information processing mechanisms are presupposed.' Sloman notes for example that X is in love with Y *implies* X's thoughts are constantly drawn to Y. This requires a capacity for reflection, self-monitoring, and self-control (and, one might add, a systematic bias in focal attention, accompanied by a *loss* in self-control and the ability to focus attention on anything else).

Discovering architectures which enable machines to simulate the mental functioning of humans is undoubtedly useful in the construction of more interesting machines, and it seems likely that an analysis of such architectures will make a useful contribution to our understanding of the operation of the human mind. Functional analyses may also tell us something important about which forms of processing relate most closely to conscious experience in the human brain (see for example the discussion of *information dissemin-ation* in Chapter 4). However, Sloman (1997a, 1997b) and Sloman and Logan (1998) also wish to say something fundamental about the *ontological nature* of conscious experience. They hope to show that if the behaviour of con-scious humans can be explained in functional terms, then conscious qualia can be *reduced* to 'information states' within a 'virtual machine'.

As Sloman and Chrisley (2003) subsequently put it,

> we start with the tentative hypothesis that although the word 'conscious-ness' has no well-defined meaning, it is used to refer to a cluster of aspects of information processing in humans and other animals. On that basis we can enhance our understanding of what these aspects might be by designing, building, analysing, and experimenting with virtual-machine

architectures which attempt to elaborate the hypothesis. This activity may in turn nurture the development of our concepts of consciousness, along with a host of related concepts, such as 'experiencing', 'feeling', 'perceiving', believing', 'wanting', 'enjoying', 'remembering', 'noticing', and 'learning', helping us to see them as dependent on an implicit theory of minds as information processing virtual machines.

(p. 134)

Following this strategy, Sloman and Chrisley translate the problem of 'qualia' and the problem of 'other minds' into questions about how *we can get access to our own mental states or those of others*, where such states are entirely defined in information processing terms. Thus redefined, the problems become easy. For example, according to Sloman and Chrisley, the problem of 'qualia' 'arose out of philosophical discussions of our ability to attend to aspects of internal information processing' (p. 165), and that possibility is inherent in any system that has an appropriate self-referential architecture. Once one specifies the architecture, one has solved the problem. They also suggest that,

> evolution apparently solved the 'other minds problem' before anyone formulated it, both by providing built-in apparatus for conceptualising mental states in others at least within intelligent prey species, predator species and social species, and also by 'justifying' the choice through the process of natural selection, which tends to produce good designs.

(p. 160)

It should be apparent that, broadly speaking, this reductive strategy is similar to Dennett's eliminative strategy discussed above. However, as before, it is one thing to explain how information is accessed or how conscious humans might perform other tasks in third-person information processing terms, but another thing to explain the nature and function of phenomenal 'qualia'. If qualia are really nothing more than accessible information states within a virtual machine then why do they *seem* to be subjective, private, coloured, painful and so on? Information states in a machine are, after all, 'objective',[13] publicly accessible, and not themselves coloured or painful, as Dennett makes clear. And, given that having subjective, first-person experiences would make no difference to a machine's information processing (defined in purely third-person terms), what is the *function* of such first-person *seemings*? If they really are nothing more than information states of the kinds found in virtual machines, why should evolution have provided us with such a (supposedly) faulty insight into our own minds?

Transposed qualia

Given the entrenched nature of philosophical commitments on these issues, it may be that arguments in favour of one position or the other will never be decisive. But what if there were unambiguous third-person experimental evidence that *clearly dissociates input–output functioning from their accompanying qualia*? In the 1970s and early 1980s I carried out such experiments while developing a frequency transposing hearing aid for the sensory-neural deaf.[14] Sensory-neural deafness is produced by damage to the hair cells of the cochlea and/or the auditory nerve that carries signals from the cochlea to auditory projection areas in the brain. The neurons responsible for higher frequencies are more sensitive to damage than those in the lower frequencies. Consequently, the sensory-neural deaf commonly have residual hearing only in the lower frequencies, and are not able to hear speech components with energies in the higher frequencies, such as the sibilant and stop consonants that form the beginnings and ends of the words sip, ship, chip, tip, and pip. For example, when residual hearing extends only up to around 1 kHz, only the middle vowel of these words can be heard and all the words sound much the same. Amplification does not help as this simply sends high frequency signals of greater intensity into neural circuitry that can no longer transmit them to the brain. To ameliorate this, I developed a frequency transposing hearing aid that selects a band of frequencies from 4 kHz to 8 kHz that contains major energy components of sibilant and stop consonants, lowers their frequency to the 0 Hz to 4 KHz range, and combines these transposed consonant components with amplified, but otherwise unaltered, speech signals that are already in the low frequency residual hearing range (e.g. the lower formants of vowel sounds).

To a normal hearing person most of the transposed consonants sound like lower frequency versions of the originals. But the technique also produces some distinct changes in qualia. In particular 'sip' sounds more like 'ship' – and the original 'sh' in 'ship' sounds even more 'shooshy' (even more sibilant), so that it becomes unlike any normally produced speech sound, although it remains readily identifiable and distinct from both the original and transposed versions of 's'. As the transposed versions of 's' and 'sh' and similar consonants were audible to many sensory-neural children we then used these sounds to assist them in learning to articulate such consonants, using a combination of imitation and auditory feedback. Speech training using transposed speech was carried out in the conventional way; for example, to learn how to articulate the sound 's', children had to try to imitate the speech therapist until the sound they produced matched the sound made by the therapist.

Why is this of philosophical interest? Using a combination of low frequency filtering and amplitude compression it is possible to simulate various forms of low frequency residual hearing – and, using such simulations, one can be confident that the transposed sounds heard by a deaf child are systematically different from the originals heard by a normal hearing person. One can be confident for example that once the sound 's' is processed by the equipment and further restricted by the bandwidth of the damaged ear/brain system, it sounds more like a filtered version of 'sh'. *However this change in qualia makes no difference to the speech training situation.* To teach a child to say 's', the therapist has to produce an 's' in the normal way, even though, to the child, the sound that the therapist produces sounds more like a 'sh'. For the child to imitate 's' successfully, he or she also has to say 's' in the normal way (with the tip of the tongue placed just behind the teeth to form a small aperture with the roof of the mouth) so that, once again, the therapist hears the child produce an 's' while the child hears something more like a 'sh'. The same applies to other normal and transposed speech sounds. To produce a normal 'sh', the aperture produced by the hump of the tongue and the roof of the mouth has to be positioned further back (towards the throat), whether one hears the sound that results as a normal 'sh' or as a transposed version of the original.

What applies to speech production also applies to speech perception. All the functional discriminations enabled by normal contrasts between 's' and 'sh' (such as the difference between sip and ship) are enabled by transposed versions of 's' and 'sh' (provided that the residual hearing range is sufficient to allow their discrimination). For example, if a deaf child presented with a transposed version of 'sip' is asked to report whether they hear 'sip' or 'ship', they would say the word 'sip' in a normal way (even though the sound that they hear is more like 'ship'). In short, *in this situation, the qualia of ordinary and transposed speech sounds are functionally indistinguishable.* Indeed, without added information about how transposition works, a deaf child might never know that transposed versions of 's' and 'sh' were any different from the versions heard by those with normal hearing; similarly, unless a normal hearing person knew that the deaf child was equipped with a transposing aid, they might never know that the child was functioning with transposed speech as opposed to amplified versions of normal speech. And here is the point: if functionally equivalent speech perception and production can be associated with different speech qualia, there must be something about the differences between such qualia that cannot be reduced to how speech perception and production function – a clear dissociation of qualia from input–output functioning.[15]

Can qualia be reduced to the exercise of sensory-motor skills?

It might of course be that virtual machine functionalism is only a partial story. Human brains are embodied, and bodies are, in turn, embedded in and interact with the surrounding world. Consequently, there has been a recent resurgence of interest in 'enactive' theories that view perception and cognition in terms of embodied interactions with the environment rather than being solely dependent on 'inner representations of the world' stored in the brain.

This fosters a rather different understanding of mental processing. For example, theories of visual perception commonly assume that we have a detailed and complete inner representation of the external world built up over successive eye saccades out of the degraded information arriving at the retinas. If such a complete representation were updated moment-by-moment, then we should always notice changes in the visual field (by comparing current input with complete records of the world developed from prior input). But experimental findings on inattentional and change blindness suggest that we don't. Studies of inattentional blindness such as that by Simons and Chabris (1999) indicate that we do not see what we do not attend to *even when we are directing our gaze at it*. Equally surprising, studies of change blindness such as that by Simons and Levin (1998) demonstrate that we do not notice *major changes* in what we are gazing at unless fast transitions capture our attention, or we happen to be focusing our attention on the precise features that change. Taken together, such findings provide persuasive demonstrations that what we notice about the perceived world is less complete and detailed than we usually think.

To account for such findings, the *enactive* view suggests that we perceive perhaps five to six features of the world at any given moment (wherever we gaze) but we are free to pick up any other features, as we need them, by *exploring the world* (e.g. with eye movements). The reason we think that the visual world is rich in detail and colour is because the world itself does have this detail and colour, and we see this wherever we look. We do not need to build up a complete, detailed, inner representation of the world because the world itself stores all the relevant information. If true, this would be a genuine advance in our understanding of how perception works (that we pick up just five or six visual features at each fixation) and about the nature of consequent inner representations of the world (that they are limited to the features that are picked up and are, therefore, not complete). The dynamic interaction between internal information and external information (picked up on a need-to-know basis) also suggests that internal information may sometimes be formatted in a way that is suited to such ongoing activities, for example as a set of procedures for action, rather than being iconic or propositional (see, for example, readings in Noë, 2002).

If true, this would be a genuine advance in our understanding of how visual perception works. But what about our understanding of consciousness? While questions about perceptual functioning and about the nature of conscious phenomenology are, in principle, separable, a number of enactive theorists claim them to be connected: according to them, if one understands perceptual functioning in an enactive way as mastery of a set of sensory-motor skills, one can also understand the nature of conscious experience including its 'qualia' in this way, thereby (hopefully) resolving this 'hard' problem of consciousness. For example, O'Regan *et al.* (2004) ask, 'What is it exactly about phenomenal consciousness which makes it seem inaccessible to normal scientific inquiry? What is so special about "feel"?' Their reply is that, 'Feel is . . . not "generated" by a neural mechanism at all, rather, it is exercising what the neural mechanism *allows the organism to do*.' The feel of driving a Porsche for example does not reside in any given moment, but rather in the fact that you are currently engaged in exercising the Porsche driving skill. And, 'If the feel of Porsche driving is constituted by exercising a skill, perhaps the feel of red, the sound of a bell, the smell of a rose also correspond to skills being exercised.'

Applying a similar strategy to an understanding of machine consciousness, Kiverstein (2007) writes,

> I will argue that a dynamic sensorimotor (DSM) account of conscious experience can help us to see how it might be possible for a machine to have a subjective point of view. *According to the DSM account, conscious experience is an activity of perceptually exploring the world in which one exercises one's sensorimotor knowledge.* Sensorimotor knowledge is a form of practical knowledge where what the subject has mastery of are the dynamics which govern sensorimotor behaviour.
>
> (p. 128; my italics)

It should be apparent from earlier discussions above that this reductive identification of conscious 'feel' with the exercising of a sensory-motor skill is a variant of reductive functionalism, even though it locates the relevant functioning in the skilful interaction of organisms with the surrounding world rather than in causal relationships that are exclusively located within the brain. Given this, it is not surprising that the view has similar problems.

As with other versions of reductionism, the entire force of the argument derives from a *redefinition* of consciousness (see for example the italics in the quote from Kiverstein above). Once one accepts the redefinition one is, so to speak, home and dry, as there is no obvious reason why sensory-motor skills might not be incorporated into a machine. As Kiverstein goes on to argue, 'The DSM account claims that it is exercise of sensorimotor knowledge which is constitutive of conscious experience. . . . If this is right, a creature could enjoy conscious experience just by exercising its mastery of sensorimotor dynamics in actively sensing the world' (p. 128). He then goes on to argue that such machines have their own first-person perspective – but again *redefines* this in terms of having a vantage point on the world from the particular physical location that the machine occupies, as opposed to the normal meaning which is to have direct access to *what it is like to have a given experience.*

But why, one can ask, should driving a Porsche or any other skill *feel like anything at all?* One can hardly deny that human functioning of different kinds often does feel like something for humans. However human functioning can often be dissociated from its normal feel. For example, once they are well learnt, consciously performed skills can often be performed unconsciously, so it does not follow that skilful functioning itself fully *explains* the accompanying feel.

If it is a *contingent*, not a *necessary*, fact that certain kinds of functioning in humans have certain kinds of feel, then switching one's emphasis away from neural mechanisms as such, to 'what neural systems allow an organism to do', gets one no closer to understanding why that enabling of skill should have a feel at all. Piloting a 747 no doubt feels like something, to *a human pilot*, and the way that it feels is likely to have something to do with human biology. But why should it feel the same way to an electronic autopilot that replaces the skills exercised by a human being? Or why should it feel like anything to be the control system of a guided missile system? Anyone versed in the construction of electronic control systems knows that if one builds a system in the right way, it will function just as it is intended to do, *whether it feels like anything to be that system or not.* If so, functioning in an electronic (or any other) system is logically tangential to whether it is like anything to be that system, leaving the hard problem of why it happens to feel a certain way in humans untouched.

In sum, eliminative and reductive versions of computational functionalism come at a cost. They largely dismiss the phenomenology of the phenomena (the conscious experiences) that they seek to explain.[16] And they attempt to collapse our first-person perspective to what can be seen from a third-person perspective without really explaining why we should have a first-person perspective, with associated 'qualia', at all.

Is it possible to develop a nonreductive computational functionalism?

But might it be possible to develop a *nonreductive* computational functionalism that does not reduce consciousness to behaviour but explains the phenomenology of conscious experience itself? According to John Searle (1994a), conscious experiences have various properties that seem to differentiate them from other aspects of the world. For example, subjectivity and qualia are essential features of conscious experience, and many conscious states are intentional[17] (they are about something or meaningful to the agent which has them). Searle argues that such features are emergent properties of the physical brain (see Chapter 3). But why restrict consciousness to the brain? If consciousness is emergent, might not such features emerge from *any* computational system with an appropriate architecture and sufficient complexity?

In his famous Chinese Room thought experiment, Searle has argued that this cannot be true of GOFAI (Good Old-Fashioned AI) systems that simply run programmes, i.e. which operate on symbols according to rules. This thought experiment asks you to

> Imagine that you carry out the steps in a program for answering questions in a language you do not understand. I do not understand Chinese, so I imagine that I am locked up in a room with a lot of boxes of Chinese symbols (the database); I get small bunches of Chinese symbols passed to me (questions in Chinese), and I look up in a rule book (the program)

what I am supposed to do. I perform certain operations on the symbols in accordance with the rules (that is, I carry out the steps in the program) and give back small bunches of symbols (answers to the questions) to those outside the room. I am the computer implementing a program for answering questions in Chinese, but all the same I do not understand a word of Chinese. And this is the point: *if I do not understand Chinese solely on the basis of implementing a computer program for understanding Chinese, then neither does any other digital computer solely on that basis, because no digital computer has anything I do not have*.

(Searle, 1997, p. 11)

According to Searle, if such programmes do not understand meaning they do not have minds (and certainly not conscious minds). That is:

1 Programmes are entirely syntactical (they consist of symbols manipulated according to rules).
2 Minds have semantics (they understand meaning).
3 Syntax is not the same as, nor by itself sufficient for, semantics.

Therefore, programmes are not minds.

Searle originally put this argument in *Behavioral and Brain Sciences*, in 1980. Later, in 1997, he suggested that, if anything, his original argument conceded too much to the strong AI position. Strong AI claims that computation is *intrinsic* to mind. But the constituents of programmes, that is, symbols and syntactic rules, are not even intrinsic properties of computers. The natural sciences typically deal with features of the world that are intrinsic in this sense. Such features are observer-independent, in that their existence does not depend on what anybody thinks (examples include mass, photosynthesis, and electrical charge). Intrinsic features can be contrasted with observer-dependent features that exist only 'in the eye of the beholder'. Social sciences are often concerned with properties that are observer-dependent or observer-relative in this sense, in that their existence depends on how humans treat them, use them, or otherwise think of them. Some bits of green paper, for example, are 'money', *but only because we think of them as money*, and the same is true of symbols and syntax. English written sentences for example consist of symbols arranged according to syntactic rules. Intrinsically, however, they are ink marks on paper. Ink marks have intrinsic chemical properties, but they become symbols for some human beings only because, through training, they have learnt to *treat* and *use* such ink marks as words in English. Electrical states in computers can *become* symbolic for the same reasons. They are intrinsically physical, but they can become symbols to appropriately trained humans who treat and use them as symbols. Indeed, the same can be said of computation itself:

computation is an abstract mathematical process that exists only relative to conscious observers and interpreters. Observers such as ourselves have found ways to implement computation on silicon-based electrical machines, but that does not make computation into something electrical or chemical.

(ibid., p. 17)

If Searle is right, a computer isn't even a computer to a computer! Symbols, syntax and computation are in the eye of the beholder, and a computer just isn't a beholder any more than a book beholds the symbols on its printed pages. By contrast, 'My present state of consciousness is intrinsic in this sense: I am conscious regardless of what anybody else thinks' (Searle, 1997, p. 15).[18]

Searle stresses that these are not arguments against the usefulness of computers in *simulating* mental processes, or a denial that computers can act *as if* they can think, love and so on (he calls this 'weak AI'). Nor is this intended to prove that machines cannot think. For him, the brain is a machine (a biological one) and the brain can think – and it is possible that consciousness somehow *emerges* from silicon much as he believes it to emerge from the biological matter of the brain. These are, however, arguments against those versions of computational functionalism which claim that implementing the right programme in any hardware at all *is all there is to having a mind* (Searle calls this 'strong AI'). In short, they are arguments about the limitations of programmes rather than about the limitations of silicon or other nonbiological substances.

Now, one might agree that these are powerful arguments against GOFAI systems (typically housed in a PC), whose every operation whether self-generated or not must be interpreted and used by some independent human user. But what about a robot? As Green (1981) pointed out, machine language translators operating on symbols according to rules do not 'trade in ideas' (in this, his argument has interesting parallels to those of Searle). But what of a robot with sense organs and effector systems whose internal representations of the world were developed by direct sensory-motor interaction with it – a robot that learns, in effect, much as a baby does? Wouldn't the representations of the world in its own internal states resulting from the success or failure of its history of interactions be genuinely 'about something' to the robot, particularly if they guided its future interactions with the world? After all, meaningful representations in humans do not arrive *magically*. They have a developmental history, charted for example in extensive studies of how children learn the meanings of words. Word *forms* are essentially arbitrary (different languages use different verbal forms for similar meanings), so, initially, they are no more meaningful to humans than they are to machines. Through the early language game played by children with parents, verbal symbols need to somehow become *grounded* in the world.

This need for 'symbol grounding' has been well documented by the psychologist Stevan Harnad (1990, 1991). Harnad agrees with Searle that a system that does nothing more than operate on symbols according to rules could never learn to understand a language. Its efforts would resemble those of a human learning a first language equipped with nothing more than a dictionary. Unless symbols in the dictionary are somehow *already meaningful*, each symbol would simply be explicated in terms of more meaningless symbols, and there would be no way to get off 'the symbol/symbol merry go round' to meaning and understanding.

However, Harnad suggests that meaning can be achieved by 'symbol grounding', that is by linking the symbols to real events in the world, via internal iconic representations of sensory input. Such iconic representations first have to be categorised into recurring, elementary features (which correspond to perceived features of the world). The association of symbols with such recurring feature categories would allow symbols to pick out the class of features or objects that they 'name', thereby 'grounding' the symbols. Once symbols are grounded in elementary features, the composition of symbols into strings would allow the generation of complex feature combinations that would inherit their grounding from their elementary constituents. For example, once the symbols 'horse' and 'stripes' are grounded in appropriate feature categories, one can derive 'zebra' ('zebra' = 'horse' and 'stripes'). Connectionist systems, he suggests, might achieve the pattern recognition of elementary invariances in input required for feature or object categorisation in a natural, endogenous way. Cognitive systems that manipulate symbols according to rules might then become grounded simply by incorporating a connectionist 'front end'.

Could robots have unconscious minds?

Whether or not such proposals about how symbols become grounded are correct in their details, it seems reasonable to suggest that words acquire meanings via their associations with internal representational states, and that representations in the brain become grounded, at least in part, through causal relationships between internal representations, actions and external events. Now, if that is the way symbols become meaningful for humans, why can't the same associations of symbols to grounded representations be developed in robots? If this is possible, wouldn't the symbols be 'about something' (semantic) to the robot? And, if one concedes *that* much, given the Chinese Room criteria, would not the machine then have a mind?

There might not, of course, be 'anybody at home' in the robot (as Harnad points out). That is, 'symbol grounding' might be sufficient for robot semantics and therefore for robot mind, and yet not be sufficient for robot *consciousness*. Indeed, Searle (1997) insists that his Chinese Room argument is about semantics rather than consciousness. As he stresses, symbols and syntax are not sufficient 'for the understanding of the semantics of language *whether conscious or unconscious*' (p. 128; my italics). Given this, it might be that information processing that is grounded in representations developed through sensory-motor interactions with the world is in some sense constitutive of *unconscious* mind in machines.

This possibility needs to be taken seriously for the reason that much of the *human* mind is unconscious. Human information processing, for example, is largely preconscious or unconscious. Information stored in long-term memory is largely unconscious (only a tiny proportion of a lifetime's experiences is conscious at any given moment) and such information is arguably 'about something' *whether or not it is conscious*. While it remains unconscious, for example, it may influence actions, enter into the creation of expectations, affect judgements, create emotional reactions to ongoing events and so on. Preconscious semantic processing is also required for many skills that we think of as 'conscious'. Reading, for example, requires the preconscious identification of the many possible meanings of individual words, the analysis of syntax, and an appropriate combination of individual word meanings into the global meaning of sentences and overall text. It is clear from this that intentionality (in the sense of being about something) has to be teased away from 'consciousness'. Following Brentano it has been traditional to think of intentionality as definitive of conscious experiences. While it may be true that consciousness is nearly always consciousness of something, it also appears to be true that unconscious states, for example, in human memory, are genuinely about something to the person who has them; that is, unconscious semantics also exist in the human mind (for example, in representations of the world stored in long-term semantic memory).

Note, however, that talk of preconscious and unconscious processing in humans is contextualised by the existence of *consciousness* in humans. That is, preconscious processing *precedes* (related) conscious experience and unconscious processing *contrasts* with processing that has manifestations in conscious experience (see Chapter 10). The existence of human consciousness also contextualises the well accepted contrast between conscious and unconscious mind. If consciousness were entirely absent in a silicon robot it might be more accurate to describe its functioning as *nonconscious* rather than as 'unconscious'. In humans, unconscious or preconscious 'semantic processing' is also very different from 'conscious meaning and understanding' in that the latter is associated with *phenomenal contents* which are (by definition) not present in unconscious representational states. Examples of such contents include 'feelings of understanding' or 'puzzlement' that might accompany reading and speech perception, along with the experience of visual or auditory verbal forms (Mangan, 1993). If a robot were entirely nonconscious, such feelings and visual or auditory experiences would be absent, in which case its semantically encoded states would never become 'consciously meaningful' and its 'understanding' would never be 'conscious understanding'. Whether it nevertheless makes sense to speak of a *nonconscious mind* in such a machine then depends on the *criteria* one applies for the attribution of mind of any kind (we return to this below).

Can one incorporate what it is like to be something into robot consciousness?

To see how far we can take this line of argument let us suppose that it is reasonable to attribute at least a 'nonconscious mind' to robots provided that they pass appropriate third-person functional tests, for example, if their symbols are 'grounded' and they can 'trade in ideas'. In humans, mental processes sometimes operate with associated consciousness and sometimes not, so it seems reasonable to allow for both possibilities in other animals and machines. It also follows that the necessary and sufficient conditions for the existence of unconscious (or nonconscious) *mind* are not co-extensive with the conditions for *consciousness*. Given this, what else would be needed for robot consciousness?

As we have seen, third-person causal relations between input, intervening states and output would not be enough, as a robot's symbols might be grounded in causal relationships with the world and still not have 'anybody at home'. But, suppose that 'what it is like to be a conscious being' was *itself* translated into a functional description and *that* functioning was built into a robot. Wouldn't that finally be enough to guarantee robot consciousness?

This approach has been developed in an initial way by Aaron Sloman and his colleagues, as we have seen above. The German philosopher Thomas Metzinger (1997, 2003) has also developed added functional descriptions of many aspects of phenomenal content, including, for example, fundamental properties such as 'having a first-person perspective', feeling that experiences are '*my* experiences', and so on. According to him, perspectivalness (having a first-person perspective) is a higher order property of phenomenal space as a whole, in which 'I' am an immovable centre. This 'I' or 'self' is experienced as being identical through time. The contents of phenomenal self-consciousness form a coherent whole, and I am acquainted with those contents before initiating any intellectual operations. They also have the quality of 'mineness'; for example, I always experience my thoughts and my emotions as belonging to me and voluntary acts as initiated by me.

Such phenomenal properties, Metzinger suggests, can be explained by a 'phenomenal self-model' located within a more general model of reality. This model can be described abstractly, as a set of causal relations (although Metzinger assumes that it will also possess a true biological description, for example, as complex patterns of neural activation developing over time). Thus, 'perspectivalness' requires the existence of a single, coherent and temporally stable model of reality, which is representationally extended around a single, coherent and temporally extended phenomenal subject (a model of the part of the system that is having the experience). To have the attribute of phenomenal 'mineness' a representational state must be embedded within the currently active self-model – a condition which is not met in some pathological conditions, for example, in florid schizophrenia, where consciously experienced thoughts are not experienced as *my* thoughts. If the coherence of the global self-model is in some way impaired, other syndromes arise, for example, in multiple personality disorders and the anosagnosias (such as Anton's syndrome where sufferers deny their own blindness).

These ideas constitute 'work in progress', but it should be clear that they introduce something of what it is like to have a first-person perspective, which is missing from models of the mind based on purely third-person input–output relationships. That is, Metzinger takes it for granted that first-person data regarding *what it is like to be a self* with a perspective on the world are relevant to functional modelling. However, his project is still 'functionalist' in that his aim is to *translate* first-person phenomenology into third-person functional descriptions (in the hope that this can be done without leaving anything important out). Such a project has clear benefits to the development of machines that behave more like human beings. The location of a self model within a world model is central for example to a number of current developments in robotics (Benjamin *et al.*, 2006; Bongard *et al.*, 2006; Chella and Macaluso, 2006; Vaughan and Zuluaga, 2006; Holland, 2007; Aleksander, 1996, 2007).

Could semantic transparency produce phenomenal consciousness?

But couldn't an entirely *nonconscious* machine incorporate a model of its own nature and ongoing states developing over time, embedded in a model of some wider reality? Metzinger entirely agrees – a representational model of the self, located in a wider reality, could be instantiated in a system without instantiating *phenomenal* 'perspectivalness', 'selfhood' and 'mineness'. So he suggests one further, vital step that would enable the transition from the *representational* property of 'self-modelling' to the *phenomenal* property of 'selfhood'. The transition can be made, he suggests, if the representational states are 'semantically transparent', that is, if they do not contain the information (within their own content) that *they are models*. Under such circumstances the system 'looks through' its own representational structures, as if it were in direct and immediate contact with their content. Consequently, 'we experience ourselves as being in direct and immediate contact with ourselves' (rather than with *models* of ourselves).

While this suggestion is worth considering, it raises some obvious questions. Who or what is it in the system that 'looks through' its own representational structures? Within computational functionalism, the only thing that could 'look' would be other parts of the system. But how could one part of a system 'look through' another part of the system? Alternatively, if 'transparency' is just a metaphor for a system not knowing that its representations are just models, would supply of that knowledge make phenomenal consciousness disappear? If so, it should be possible to test this for oneself. The notion that phenomenal representations are just models of what the world is really like is a central theme of Chapters 6, 7 and 8 of this book, and this is widely accepted in psychological research. Yet (in my own experience) even a *firm conviction* that one's own phenomenal representations are just models does not remove their qualia.

Conversely, consider a thought experiment involving two near-equivalent machines. Machine 1 has all the functions that Metzinger requires to build a conscious robot. However, in addition, it has meta-representations that supply the knowledge that its representations are just models. If Metzinger is right, this added knowledge should *block* the development of phenomenal qualia. In machine 2, we simply remove a few lines of machine code from machine 1, either removing the meta-representations or making them inaccessible to the rest of the system. But it seems counterintuitive that such a simple trick would be enough to make the mysterious richness of phenomenal consciousness suddenly appear.

Metzinger's theorising is interesting for the reason that it gets progressively closer to the *structure* of human consciousness. It takes phenomenology seriously, and begins to reveal some of the functional organisation implicit in what we normally experience. This, in turn, is likely to be useful in the search for the processes that support human consciousness within the brain. But it remains the case that an entirely third-person, functional description *even of phenomenal consciousness itself* leaves something important out. It is true, for example, that phenomenal contents model a self in the world, and that these models do not normally contain the information that they are merely representations. It is also true that the same property of 'transparency' could be instantiated in any system whose 'global' representation of 'self' within some embedding social and physical reality does not contain the information that it *is* a representation. But there is little reason to believe that the simple act of removing meta-information about the ontological status of (or information processing precursors of) a representation would transform it into phenomenal consciousness. A robot might have an executive system which operated on the basis of higher order global representations of itself and the world (rather than on the basis of sub-processes which create such representations) and *still not have anybody at home*.

Agnosticism about robot consciousness

Given that we do not know the necessary and sufficient conditions for consciousness in the human brain, we cannot, of course, rule out the possibility that the robot *is* conscious. According to dualists such as Descartes, something nonmaterial would need to be added to the machine in the form of *res cogitans*, a substance that thinks. A nonmaterial soul, for example, might just decide to inhabit a suitably well appointed robot! Or, it might just be a fact of the universe that functioning of any kind is invariably associated with experience (as argued by Chalmers, 1996). Or silicon might just have the same causal powers to 'produce' experience as the human brain (a possibility that Searle (1997) does not dismiss). Alternatively, silicon functioning might be accompanied by a distinctively 'silicon experience'! We will discuss these options further, along with a possible way of deciding between them, in Chapter 14. For now, however, the simple message is that on the basis of third-person criteria or evidence alone, *we cannot tell*. Indeed, we could know *everything there is to know* about robot system functioning, and *still* not know whether it was conscious. And, if third-person functional accounts alone cannot tell us whether or not a robot is conscious, or what it is like to have robot consciousness, they cannot be complete accounts of consciousness. Nor can third-person functioning be all there is to having a conscious mind.

Given such caveats, recent builders of 'conscious machines' are often more cautious about their claims (cf. Aleksander, 2007). Franklin (2003), for example, constructed software to handle the assignment of new billets to seamen, via email, in just the way that a conscious human being might, by incorporating a 'global workspace' architecture of the kind suggested by Baars (1988) to underlie consciousness in humans. However, Franklin was careful to claim only that the system was *functionally conscious* (behaved *as if* it were conscious), while remaining agnostic about its phenomenal consciousness.

In recognition of this more cautious approach, Torrance (2007) introduces a useful distinction between weak and strong MC (machine consciousness) that is analogous to the older distinction between weak and strong AI. As he notes, 'Weak MC seeks to model functional analogues to (or aspects of) consciousness. Strong MC aims to develop "machines" that are (supposedly) *genuinely* conscious' (p. 154). And he goes on to explain that,

> Those who see themselves as engaged in weak MC will describe their activity in terms of modelling various aspects of natural consciousness with the purpose of better understanding the latter. Those who set themselves strong MC goals will be aiming to produce machines which have psychologically real (and perhaps ethically significant ...) states of consciousness.[19]

(p. 155)

First-person and third-person criteria for the existence of mind

Deciding whether a robot has a conscious mind, an unconscious or nonconscious mind, or no mind at all is complicated by the fact that the term 'mind' shares some of the ambiguities of the term 'consciousness'. We do not have a precise, agreed understanding of what 'mind' is in humans any more than we agree about consciousness. But there is nevertheless a core of intuitive understanding of what 'mind' and 'consciousness' refer to in our own case. In the first instance, our understanding derives from experience of our own mind – from what it is like to *have a mind* or to *be conscious*.

Indeed, according to Searle (1990), unless a mental state is potentially conscious it is *not* a mental state, and in his later work this connection to consciousness (which he calls the 'Connection Principle') becomes the *sole* criterion for 'having a mind'. On this first-person criterion, an entirely nonconscious robot would not have an 'unconscious mind', or even a 'nonconscious mind', and an account of system functioning would not be an account of what makes a mind at all.[20]

But there are ancient, competing intuitions. To have a 'mind' is also to have certain modes of functioning and capacities. This intuition dates back to Aristotle, and recurs in Descartes' attempts to demonstrate that man cannot be just a machine, on the grounds that no machine could ever use language or respond appropriately to continually changing circumstances in the ways that humans do. Such criteria can also be used to judge the presence of mind in *others*. It is hardly surprising, therefore, that modern cognitive science has focused on these, rather than on first-person criteria – with consequent, considerable advances in the understanding of the mental processes which enable human adaptive functioning (whether these be conscious or not). From this perspective, 'mind' is what *enables* us to 'think', to 'understand', to communicate, to experience ourselves as beings embedded in a world, and so on. In so far as such functioning manifests in observable behaviour, such criteria can also be applied to making judgements about the presence of 'mind' in nonhuman animals and in robots.

If one applies *only* such third-person, functional criteria, a robot might be judged to have a mind (of a kind) even if we remain agnostic about whether it is conscious. For example, if it possesses internal representations that are made 'semantic' by virtue of causal relations which link them to real world events, combined, say, with a representation of itself (a self-model) which locates the robot within a wider representation of the world.

Irresolvable philosophical debates arise when either first- or third-person criteria are applied *exclusively*, that is, if one insists on viewing mind only in terms of what it is like to experience (from a first-person perspective), or only in terms of capacities or functions which can be observed from a third-person perspective. In arguing that states become mental only by virtue of their connection to conscious experience, Searle adopts first-person criteria to the exclusion of third-person criteria. In arguing that states become mental only through their causal relationships with input, output and other intervening states, computational functionalists such as Dennett and Sloman adopt third-person criteria to the exclusion of first-person criteria.

This use of first- versus third-person criteria would not create a problem if they were perfectly correlated (if whenever one experienced mind or consciousness in a given way one behaved or functioned in a given way and vice versa). But we know from the human case that this is not so. Experience of given kinds may or may not be accompanied by behaviour of given kinds (see the discussion of behaviourism in Chapter 4). Consequently, overt behaviour or functioning may be indicative of accompanying experience but it cannot be definitive of it. Conversely, first-person experience is indicative of the nature of mind but not definitive of it, for the reason that the workings of mind are largely unconscious. We have little first-person insight into the processes that enable us to speak, read or understand, or even of the myriad fine-motor adjustments that enable us to walk. Consequently, these and nearly all other cognitive abilities have to be inferred from third-person behavioural or neurophysiological evidence. Functional models of how such processes operate in the human brain developed by cognitive psychology and related sciences are, therefore, models of the activities of mind.

Human minds enable adaptive functioning *and* have manifestations in conscious experience. Given this, I argue (in Part II of this book) that it is inappropriate to *choose between* first-person and third-person accounts of the mind. A complete psychology requires *both*.

The strengths and weaknesses of functionalism

The view that mind can, at least in part, be understood in terms of capacities and functions seems consistent with our natural language usage of many mental terms. For example, our ability to think, solve problems and so on seems to relate to our capacity to function in certain ways. Treating 'mind' as a system property is also one way to reconcile the conflicting intuitions that mind has no precise location but is nevertheless, somehow, 'in' the brain. As Aristotle noted, capacities have to do with the way matter is *formed*.

As we have seen in Chapter 4, functionalism in cognitive psychology treats mind and consciousness as forms of information processing in the brain, and this approach has proved to be very productive in the development of psychological theory. Computational functionalism has also fostered the development of more interesting machines, progressing from simple calculators to machines able to handle logic, solve problems and emulate many other aspects of human information processing. In recent years there has also been considerable interest in developing embodied robotic systems that can learn from interactions with the world, including some that are able, in some sense, to model themselves in relation to the world. Such developments have provided a deeper understanding of what any system would need to do in order to operate in a 'mind-like' fashion, and even to behave as if it were conscious.

However, it is important to remember that, within philosophy of mind, computational functionalism is not treated as a partial explanation of mind or merely one useful approach to understanding its nature. Rather, it is a *reductive* thesis that takes the nature of mind and consciousness to be *nothing more than* a set of functions which can be exported to any system able to house them. Given this, it is also important to remember that a system might behave *as if* it were conscious without *being* conscious. Nor is 'mind' co-extensive with 'consciousness', for the simple reason that some mental processes are unconscious. Consequently, once we have specified what unconscious mind is, we still have to specify what conscious mind is, and what the nature and function of phenomenal consciousness itself might be.

It should be apparent that any problems for psychofunctionalism as a reductive thesis must also be problems for computational functionalism, and we have examined some of these problems in Chapter 4 and in the analysis above. As noted, one can give a purely 'third-person' account of 'mental' functioning in the brain (or other systems) in terms of information transformation from input to output, without mentioning 'first-person' consciousness; consequently, much of twentieth-century psychology ignored it. In recent years, functionalist theories have addressed this issue by proposing internal forms of representation that also incorporate various aspects of what it is like to be conscious, such as a 'phenomenal self-model' located within a more general model of reality, getting progressively closer to how humans appear to function in the world. But how a 'phenomenal self-model' (in a brain or in a machine) becomes a *consciously experienced self* remains a mystery.

Is the consciously experienced self *reducible to* a phenomenal self-model, or some other aspect of functioning that can be entirely described in third-person terms? There are good reasons to believe that phenomenal consciousness in humans is *closely associated* with certain forms of brain processing; focal-attentive processing, for example, appears to be one of the *causal antecedents* of conscious experience, and information in primary memory, a 'global workspace', or a 'phenomenal self-model' might *correlate* with conscious contents. However, *causation* and *correlation* do not establish *ontological identity* (see the discussion of the differences between correlation, causation, and ontological identity, and the limits these differences place on reductionism in Chapter 3).

For consciousness to *be* a function that can be specified in information processing terms, it must also *have* a function that can be specified in those terms. However, careful examination of typical 'conscious processes' (such as speaking, reading and so on) reveals that the information processing which enables them is *preconscious* (see Chapters 4 and 10). Other functions which have recently been claimed for consciousness, such as 'information dissemination' or 'information integration' in the brain, are actually *unconscious* (we have no awareness whatsoever of integrating or disseminating information in our own brains). In Chapter 10, I show how these problems generalise to all information processing accounts. If so, it might make sense to think of *preconscious* or *unconscious* mental processing in functional terms, but how one might reconcile this with *phenomenal consciousness* being nothing more than an information processing function is not clear.

Broadly speaking, functionalism treats the problems of mind and consciousness as equivalent to the problem of *other minds*, knowable only in terms of what they *do*. That is, it adopts the convention that only third-person data about the nature of mind and consciousness are legitimate. The fundamental problem with this is that phenomenal consciousness is, in essence, a first-person phenomenon. Our primary knowledge about consciousness derives from *being* conscious. In sum, functionalism is a useful, but partial, theory of mind. We are not just human *doings*, we are also human *beings*.

Notes

1 A given function must of course be embodied in *some* (token) physical structure. But it need not be a structure of a given type. Consequently functionalism is consistent with a physical 'token identity theory', but not with a physical 'type identity theory'. On this view, a given mental state is nevertheless a *function* of a given type, defined in terms of the causal relationships it enters into within the economy of mind.

2 This analogy is only approximate. Commonly employed computer functions can be 'hard-wired' into the system (as are the programmes which execute addition and subtraction in a calculator) and are, therefore, technically an aspect of the machine hardware. Equally, inherited as opposed to environmentally programmed brain functions may be, at least in part, 'hard-wired' in the brain. The changes in connectivity in neural networks consequent on learning in the brain or in artificial systems may similarly be thought of as changes in functioning embodied in changes in structure.

3 See the monumental collection of readings in Arbib (2002) or overviews by Smolensky (1994) and Bechtel and Abrahamsen (2002).

4 It is interesting to note that the search engine 'Google' has in recent years developed a statistically based automatic translation system for web pages that bypasses all such complications. Rather than using a rule-based approach that requires well defined vocabularies and grammars, it simply feeds the computer billions of words of text, both monolingual text in the target language, and aligned text consisting of examples of *human translations* between the languages in question. The system then applies statistical learning techniques to build a translation model. Although Google have achieved some good results with this blockbuster technique, they admit that it still does not approach the fluency of a native speaker or possess the skill of a professional translator.

5 See, for example, Varela *et al.* (1993), Noë (2004, 2007), Rockwell (2005), Wheeler (2005), and the discussion below.

6 See www.ai.mit.edu/projects/humanoid-robotics-group/cog/capabilities.html

7 With an appropriate architecture, sufficiently complex systems can operate in many different ways, that is, they can instantiate many different 'virtual machines' whose internal organisation may be very different from the architecture of the physical system which embodies them. Parallel distributed processing for example is commonly simulated in conventional, serial computers. The simulation of human mental functions in computers requires the creation of such virtual machines for the reason that these need to function in the ways humans are thought to function.

8 Information level design descriptions refer to various internal, semantically rich short- and long-term information structures and processes. These include short-term sensory stores, long-term associations, generalisations about the environment and the agent, stored information about the local environment, currently active motives, motive generators, planning mechanisms and so on.

9 There is a sense in which most functional properties of systems which have been regarded as psychologically interesting are 'emergent'. Short-term memory and focal-attention for example only emerge (as functions) in systems of appropriate complexity. But these are properties that are traditionally described in third-person terms. Computational functionalists differ in how they treat first-person properties such as subjectivity, and qualia. It is in his treatment of first-person properties that Dennett is an eliminativist and Sloman a reductionist. Metzinger (1997) takes a less reductionist position in that he tries to give a functional description of subjectivity as such without reducing it to something else – although whether first-person properties can be fully captured in third-person terms is

arguable (see below). Chalmers argues that functional relations alone determine mind and consciousness, so I have included his views within 'computational functionalism'. However, he also insists that consciousness does not *reduce* to functioning, making his a hybrid position which is difficult to categorise; sometimes he describes it as 'naturalistic dualism' and sometimes as 'double-aspect' theory.

10 While Dennett does not deny that 'consciousness exists' he explicitly denies that conscious 'qualia' exist (see below). In short, what he accepts as existing is not what people normally mean by 'consciousness' (see discussions in Velmans, 2001, 2007c).

11 This is sometimes referred to as 'the knowledge argument' and it has been extensively discussed in philosophy of mind, famously, for example, by Nagel (1974) and Jackson (1986). See Alter (2007) for a review.

12 In Velmans (1991a) I have reviewed extensive experimental evidence and argument in support of the view that human information processing operates without the intervention of conscious phenomenology (just as Dennett, 1994, claims). For example conscious phenomenology usually comes too late to enter into the processes to which it most closely relates (see Chapter 10). But this evidence *presupposes the existence of conscious phenomenology* whose nature and timing can be related to specific forms of information processing in the brain. My conclusion, given the evidence, was that conscious phenomenology exists, but cannot be thought of in third-person information processing terms. That is, one cannot reduce it to 'third-person' causal relations in the way that functionalism suggests. If so, we may need alternative, nonreductive ways of thinking about consciousness, how first-person causal accounts relate to third-person accounts, and so on (see Chapter 13).

13 I have placed the term 'objective' in scare quotes for the reason that the objective versus subjective distinction may be more accurately construed as an intersubjective versus subjective distinction, as we will see in Chapter 9.

14 See Velmans (1973a, 1973b, 1975), Velmans and Marcuson (1983), Velmans *et al.* (1982), and Velmans *et al.* (1988).

15 Readers familiar with the philosophical literature will recognise the similarity of this research, and the arguments associated with it, to much debated 'spectrum inversion' thought experiments (see, for example, Block, 1994; Van Gulick, 2007). As it happens, spectrum inversion can be achieved by a similar transposition technique: one cannot produce negative frequencies, so if one slides frequencies down the frequency axis through zero, they shift in phase by 180 degrees and start to move up the frequency axis again. Consequently if one subtracts 4 kHz from each frequency in a band of frequencies in the 0 to 4 kHz region, it inverts, so that 4 kHz becomes 0 Hz, and what was 0 Hz becomes 4 kHz. As suspected in the speculative literature, the effects of this are quite complex, so I have used a simpler example of frequency transposition to demonstrate an entirely practical way of dissociating functions from their normally associated qualia.

16 This is sometimes justified by drawing analogies with reductionism in biology, e.g. the elimination of *élan vital* in favour of mechanistic explanations of life, or the reduction of genes to DNA molecules. As shown in Chapter 3, such analogies are false. That is, reducing *first-person appearances* to *third-person descriptions* of the brain states or functions which cause or correlate with them is quite different from reducing a *preliminary, perhaps fallacious third-person account* of a given phenomenon to a *more basic or advanced third-person account*.

17 Searle believes that not all conscious states are intentional, for example pains are just pains; they are not about something else. In Chapter 8, I develop the view that *all* conscious states are 'about something' for the reason that they are fundamentally *representational* in nature. Pains, for example, represent actual damage, or potential sources of damage to the organism.

18 In Chapter 9, I offer a rather different analysis, in which I argue that all observed properties (phenomena) including those we usually think of as 'physical' are, in a sense, observer-relative. While the existence of some *entities* may be observer-independent, the way they appear to us as *phenomena* cannot be observer-free. This is true in an obvious sense for my own consciousness. Its existence may not depend on 'what anybody else thinks', but it certainly depends on what *I* think (and I am an observer too). I merely footnote this because these caveats do not bear on the main thrust of Searle's argument – namely, that simply running a programme, or even less, simply *being* a programme, would not suffice to make a computer or a programme into a mind.

19 As Torrance points out, his weak versus strong MC also corresponds to the distinction sometimes made in the field between functional and phenomenal consciousness (Franklin, 2003), which is in turn linked to Block's distinction between phenomenal and access consciousness. Torrance also notes that some defenders of strong MC would deny that any sensible distinction can be made between functional and phenomenal consciousness, which is not surprising as they usually (but misleadingly) *define* phenomenal consciousness in functional terms, as noted above.

20 This stress on the 'Connection Principle' marked a shift in Searle's position, as 'being potentially conscious' is not quite the same as 'having semantics' (the Chinese Room criterion), for the reason that unconscious states in humans can also have semantics (see above). Searle (1990) did try to connect the two criteria by arguing that only conscious states are truly 'intentional' (truly about something). If so, those rules and procedures without access to consciousness, inferred by cognitive science to characterise the operations of the unconscious mind, are, according to Searle, not mental at all. Rather, they have no ontological status. They are simply ways of describing some interesting facets of purely physiological phenomena. What is crucial, according to Searle, is whether a state has *aspectual shape*. That is, what characterises the 'mental' is that 'whenever we perceive or think about anything, it is always under some aspects and not others that we think about that thing'. A conscious desire for water, for example, is not the same as a conscious desire for H_2O, although the referent of the desire may be the same in both cases. But how can an unconscious state have aspectual shape? Only in so far as it has the potential to be conscious, claims Searle, for aspectual shape 'cannot be exhaustively or completely characterised solely in terms of third person, behavioral, or even neurophysiological predicates' (Searle, 1990, section II, step 3). Without reference to consciousness, for example, there would be no way of distinguishing a desire for water from a desire for H_2O. It is true, of course, that there are indefinitely many ways of characterising any object (for example we can characterise a given glass of water in terms of whether it comes from the Yangtze river or not, whether one prefers it to wine, and so on). In Velmans (1990b) however, I argue that it does not follow from this that unconscious representations do not have 'aspectual shape'. In fact, it is not possible to construct semantic memories in cognitive theory or semantic networks in artificial systems without specifying how each 'node' in the network (each representation of an object or event) relates to other nodes in the network. A given 'thought' or 'mental episode' is then specified by a given pattern of activation in the network – and it is this which gives each state an 'aspectual shape'. Unconscious representational states do not have phenomenal contents, so Searle is right to conclude that a desire for water rather than H_2O cannot be fully known without reference to subjective experience, but this is because conscious 'desire' and the phenomenal characteristics of water simply *are* aspects of experience. Given this, the presence (or absence) of subjective phenomenal contents becomes the *only* difference between conscious and unconscious representational states. 'Intentionality' may

then be thought of as a functional property to do with 'symbol grounding' (see above). This dissociation between intentionality and phenomenal consciousness opens up the possibility that some states, judged to be 'mental' on the Chinese Room criterion, are not mental on the 'Connection Principle'. This does not happen for conscious states (which are in any case 'about something') or for those unconscious representational states that *can* become conscious, as these fulfil *both* criteria. In normal vision, for example, the representational states that enable one to discriminate between simple visual stimuli such as X and O are 'mental' both because they are about something (the visual stimuli) and because they are conscious. But the ability of blindsighted subjects to make the same discrimination without any accompanying visual experience indicates that the ability to discriminate does not *require* a connection to consciousness (Weiskrantz, 1997). For these individuals the connection to visual consciousness in the blind portion of their retinal field has literally been severed (by striate cortex lesions), but, functionally, their ability to discriminate is (partially) spared. Given that the representational states that enable a given discrimination in the normal and blindsighted conditions are likely to be very similar, it seems rather arbitrary to declare one to be 'mental' and the other not. It seems more natural to apply 'third-person' functional criteria to *unconscious* states (they are 'mental' if they enter into the operations of mind), and to apply both third-person (functional) and 'first-person' criteria to conscious states (they are conscious mental states if they *both* enter into the activities of mind *and* have phenomenal contents – see Velmans, 1990b, and discussion below).

Part II

A new analysis: how to marry science with experience

- Consciousness creates form,
therefore matter is a product
of consciousness

- reality is a big thought
  - a dream

~ all life ~~experiences~~ the
is the
same consciousness, but
having different experiences

~ unified consciousness
oneness?

6 Conscious phenomenology and common sense

How can we describe phenomenal consciousness accurately? It is well accepted that descriptions of phenomena cannot be entirely theory-free. As the philosopher Karl Popper puts it, even basic terms in science are 'theory-laden'. Thus, 'observations, and even more observation statements and statements of experimental results, are always interpretations of the facts observed; they are interpretations in the light of theories' (Popper, 1972, p. 107, note 3).

In accounts of consciousness the influence of pre-existing theory on phenomenal descriptions has been extreme. Dualists describe consciousness as consisting of immaterial 'qualia'; physicalists attempt to redescribe those qualia in terms of brain states; functionalists insist that they can be described as a set of causal relationships; and so on. In developing such accounts, the protagonists do, of course, make reference to examples of conscious phenomenology. But, with some notable exceptions, they have been more intent on squeezing the phenomenology into some pre-existing theory than on broadening existing theory to encompass the fullness of the phenomenology itself.[1]

These classical accounts of consciousness have been shaped by a history of ideas that, in the Western tradition, come to us from the ancient Greeks – from the dualist-interactionism of Plato, the functionalism of Aristotle, and the materialism of Democritus (who believed all things to be nothing more than atoms and the void). Indeed, some ideas about the nature of consciousness and its relationship to the material world are so deeply ingrained in our culture that they *are taken for granted by dualists and materialists alike*, thereby providing the point of departure for their 2,500-year-old debate. To escape the impasse, I believe that we need to re-examine these presuppositions.

What *are* these presuppositions? Try reading the statements in Box 6.1 and decide which of them is true.

Dualist influences on contemporary thought

In spite of the problems of dualism, and the tendency to dismiss it in current philosophical writing, it continues to exert a major influence on

Box 6.1 What do you take for granted about the nature of consciousness?

Consider each one of the statements below and decide whether it is true or false.

1   The soul is different from the body; when the body dies the soul continues to exist.
2   Consciousness is a property of the soul; matter cannot have consciousness, no matter how it is arranged.
3   Human beings have consciousness; nonhuman animals do not have consciousness.
4   Physical objects as-perceived are quite distinct from our percepts *of* those objects.
5   The contents of consciousness are *observer-dependent* in that they exist only in the mind of the observer; the physical objects we see around us, by contrast, are observer-independent, in that they exist independently of the mind of the observer.
6   The contents of consciousness are *subjective*; perceived physical objects are *objective*.
7   The contents of consciousness are *private*; perceived physical objects are *public*.
8   The contents of consciousness do not seem to be *located* anywhere, or if they are, they may loosely be said to be located 'in the mind' or 'in the brain'; the physical objects we perceive, by contrast, have clear locations in the three-dimensional space surrounding our bodies.
9   The contents of consciousness do not seem to have *spatial extension*, i.e. they do not have dimensions such as length, breadth and width; the physical objects we perceive, by contrast, do have spatial extension.
10 The contents of consciousness seem to be *insubstantial* in that they do not have properties such as hardness, solidity and weight; perceived physical objects such as chairs and tables, by contrast, do have such properties.

If you decided that *any* of the statements above are true, then, implicitly or explicitly, you have been influenced by a dualist understanding of consciousness.

contemporary belief and thought *even on those who oppose it*. It is natural, for example, to think of one's *own* consciousness, at least in part, in a dualist way. According to classical dualist-interactionism each of claims 1 to 10 is true. Claims 1 and 2 relating to the soul are taken directly from Descartes. Claim 3 also comes from Descartes, although some non-dualists have argued for the same sharp separation of man from other animals (e.g. Carruthers, 1998; Humphrey, 1983). In general, however, materialist reductionists *deny* claims 1 to 3, and, for our present purposes, we are more interested in what dualists and reductionists *share*. For this, we need to examine claims 4 to 10, which deal with the way the contents of consciousness relate to the perceived, physical world.

There are few who would disagree with propositions 4, 5, 6 and 7, for the reason that these can be equally well accommodated within either dualism or its most commonly defended reductionist alternatives (that consciousness is nothing more than a state or function of the brain). These claims relate to the *separation of the observer from that which is observed*. Claim 4 makes the point that conscious experiences are *in* the observer (in his mind or brain) as opposed to being in the world (where the perceived objects are); consequently the existence of the experiences, but not of the perceived objects, is observer-dependent (claim 5). Claims 6 and 7 relate to how experiences can be *known*. Being 'in the mind or brain' they are private and subjective, in contrast to the public, objective, physical world. Dualists sometimes conclude from this that experiences must be studied by private, subjective methods; reductionists frequently conclude from this that the study of experiences cannot be a science.

Propositions 8, 9 and 10 which deal with what conscious experiences seem to be like ('qualia' in philosophy of mind) also derive from Descartes, and they, too, command widespread assent, in that many dualists and reductionists would agree that this is how experiences *seem* to be. Dualists and reductionist merely disagree about whether experiences are *really* how they *seem*. For dualists the absence of location, extension, and any other substantial, physical properties is consistent with consciousness being non-material. For reductionists such 'seemings' provide the departure point for their programme of research – the aim of which is to establish that conscious experiences are nothing more than states or functions of the brain.

If I am right about the pervasive influence of dualism (even on those who oppose it) you will have agreed with some or all of propositions 4 to 10. That, at any rate, applies to the many hundreds of students and colleagues to whom I have put these claims – and prior to 1976, I believed them myself. Together, they define the 'gap' which seems to separate the contents of our conscious experiences from the physical objects that we perceive. But I now believe propositions 4 to 10 to be false. Why? Because they systematically *misdescribe* the phenomenology of conscious experience. Let me explain.

What and where are experiences?

Suppose I ask you to *point* at your experiences. According to Descartes, experiences are formed out of *res cogitans*, a substance that thinks, which has no location or extension in space. The material world is composed of *res extensa*, a substance that has both location and extension in space. If this is right, then one cannot really point at experiences, as they have no location. At best, one might be able to point at the place where conscious experiences interface with the material world. According to Descartes this is at the pineal gland located in the centre of the brain.

Modern reductionist philosophers argue that experiences are nothing more than states or functions of the brain. It might be difficult to point with any precision at such states or functions, as they are likely to be distributed properties of large neuronal populations. Nevertheless, if one *had* to point at experiences one would point at the brain.

In short, classical dualists and reductionists disagree vehemently about *what* conscious experiences are, but they agree (roughly) about *where* they are. In so far as experiences can be located at all, that location is somewhere in the brain. This, in turn, places experiences in a given spatial relationship to the external, physical world.

How to position experiences in relation to the brain and physical world

Implicit in assertions 4 to 10 is a dualist model of perception of the kind shown in Figure 6.1. This assumes perception to involve a simple, linear, causal sequence (viewed from the perspective of an external observer E). Light rays travelling from the physical object (the cat as-perceived by E) stimulate the subject's eye, activating her optic nerve, occipital lobes, and associated regions of her brain. Neural conditions sufficient for consciousness are formed, and result in a conscious experience (of a cat) in the subject's mind. This model of visual perception is, of course, highly oversimplified, but for now we are not interested in the details. We are interested only in where external physical objects, brains and experiences are *placed*.[2]

It will be clear that there are two fundamental 'splits' in this model. First, the contents of consciousness are clearly separated from the material world (the conscious, perceptual 'stuff' in the upper part of the diagram is separated from the material brain and the physical cat in the lower part of the diagram). This conforms to Descartes' view that the stuff of consciousness (*res cogitans*, a substance that thinks) is very different from the stuff of which the material world is made (*res extensa*, a substance that has extension and location in space). Second, the perceiving *subject* is clearly separated from the perceived *object* (the subject and her experiences are on the right of the diagram and the perceived object is on the left of the diagram).

It is clear from this simple model why consciousness is often thought to

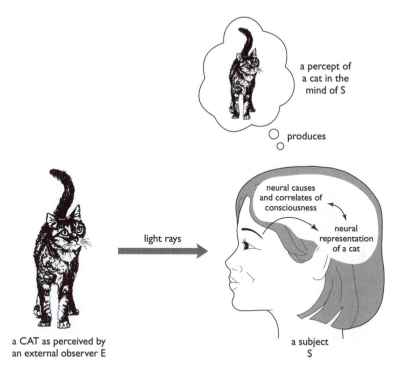

a percept of
a cat in the
mind of S

produces

neural causes
and correlates of
consciousness

neural
representation
of a cat

light rays

a CAT as perceived by
an external observer E

a subject
S

Figure 6.1 A dualist model of perception (adapted from M. Velmans (1998) 'Physical, psychological and virtual realities', in J. Wood (ed.) *The Virtual Embodied.* London: Routledge).

elude scientific study. From E's perspective, the physical cat and the subject's brain are (potentially) visible; they appear to be public, objective, and viewable from an external, third-person perspective. Consequently, a scientific study of cats and brains presents no philosophical problems. By contrast, S's experience of a cat seems to be private, subjective, and viewable only from S's first-person perspective. If so, how can it form a datum for science?

Dualists have, traditionally, been content to accept that there may be aspects of human experience that are beyond science. However, the problems of assimilating such dualism into a scientific worldview are serious (see Chapter 2). Consequently, it is not surprising that twentieth-century philosophy and science tried to naturalise dualism by arguing or attempting to show that conscious experiences are nothing more than states or functions of the brain. A reductionist model of visual perception is shown in Figure 6.2.

The causal sequence in Figure 6.2 is the same as in Figure 6.1, with one added step. While reductionists generally accept that the subject's experience of a cat *seems* to be insubstantial and 'in the mind', they argue that it is *really* a state or function of the brain. In short, the reductionist model in Figure 6.2 tries to resolve the conscious experience – physical world split by eliminating

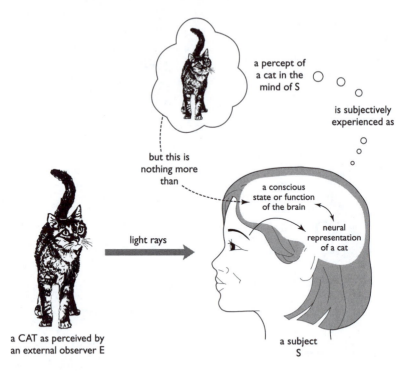

a percept of
a cat in the
mind of S

is subjectively
experienced as

but this is
nothing more
than

a conscious
state or function
of the brain

neural
representation
of a cat

light rays

a CAT as perceived by
an external observer E

a subject
S

Figure 6.2 A reductionist model of perception (adapted from M. Velmans (1998) 'Physical, psychological and virtual realities', in J. Wood (ed.) *The Virtual Embodied*. London: Routledge).

conscious experience or reducing it to something physical that E (the external observer) can in principle observe and measure. That is, it tries to collapse how things appear from the subject's first-person perspective (the conscious experience of the cat) to the brain states (or functions) that can be observed from E's third-person perspective. But reductionism *retains* the split (implicit in dualism) between the observer and the observed. The perceived object (on the left side of the diagram) remains quite separate from the conscious experience *of* the object (on the right side of the diagram).

A common-sense view of conscious phenomenology

In Velmans (1990a, 1993a, 1996b, 2008a) I have argued that this debate about whether experiences reduce to states or functions of the brain starts in the wrong place. Why? Because, in various ways, dualist and reductionist theoretical accounts of consciousness discount or deny the importance of the phenomenology of most ordinary experiences, thereby fostering a misleading impression about what it *is* that does, or does not, reduce to states of the brain. Most experiences appear to be neither a state of some non-extended substance that thinks, nor a state or function of the brain. For Descartes the prime exemplar of conscious experience is verbal *thought* ('I think therefore I am') which manifests in consciousness in the form of phonemic imagery or inner speech, and it is true that claims 4 to 10 describe the phenomenology of verbal thoughts fairly well. Thoughts *do* seem to be different from physical objects as-perceived as well as being observer-dependent, subjective, private, insubstantial, and without a clear location and extension in space (although many would claim them to be loosely 'in the head' or 'in the brain').

But it is a mistake to extrapolate from one example of conscious experience to the whole of conscious experience. Let me illustrate with a very simple example. Suppose you stick a pin in your finger and experience a sharp pain. Within philosophy of mind pain is often regarded as a paradigm case of a conscious, mental event (it is private, subjective and so on). But *where* is this pain? Given their theoretical presuppositions, dualists and reductionists do not find this an easy question. For dualists, all experiences are rather like 'thoughts' which are not really anywhere, while for reductionists, experiences are really neural states or functions distributed around the brain. However, if *forced* to point they would point (vaguely) at the brain. I take this to be a very simple question. The pain one experiences is in the finger. If one had to point at the pain one should point at where one *feels the pain* (where the pin went in). Any reader in doubt on this issue might like to try it.

Let me be clear that this sharp difference of opinion is about the location and extension of the pain *experience* and not about its *antecedent physical causes* (for example, the deformation and damage to the skin produced by the pin). One might, for example, have identical physical deformation and damage to the skin of the finger without the pain if the finger were anaesthetised. Nor is this a dispute about the neural causes and correlates of pain. I agree that the proximal neural causes and correlates of pain are located in the brain. But the neural causes and correlates of a given experience are not *themselves* that experience. In science, *causes* and *correlates* are not *ontological identities*.

I have pointed out the fundamental differences between causes, correlates and identities in Chapter 3, so I will not repeat this analysis here. By way of a reminder, a simple example from physics should suffice. If one moves a wire through a magnetic field this causes an electrical current to flow through the wire. Conversely, if one passes an electric current through a wire this causes a surrounding magnetic field. But that does not mean that the electrical current is ontologically identical to the magnetic field. The current is in the wire and the magnetic field is distributed in the space around the wire. Although they are intimately related, they cannot be the same thing for the reason that they are in different places.[3] Similarly, activation of appropriate pain circuitry in the brain may cause an experience of pain (phenomenal pain) in the finger, but these cannot be the same thing if they are in different places. The same argument applies to the neural *correlates* of phenomenal pain, as these correlates are also obviously in the brain, while the phenomenal pain remains in the finger.

No, I am not being facetious. In terms of its phenomenology, the pain really is in the finger and *nowhere else*. And this simple example demonstrates a general principle which leads one away from the dualist model in Figure 6.1 and the reductionist model in Figure 6.2 towards a 'reflexive' model of how conscious phenomenology relates to the brain and the physical world in Figure 6.3 (cf. Velmans, 1990a). The damage produced by a pin in the finger, once it is processed by the brain, winds up as a phenomenal pain in the finger, located more or less where the pin went in. That is why the entire process is called 'reflexive'. Figure 6.3 illustrates a similar process with a phenomenal cat. As before, an entity or event stimulates sense organs and initiates perceptual processing, although in this case the initiating entity is located beyond the body surface in the external world. As before, afferent neurons and cortical projection areas are activated, along with association areas, long-term memory traces and so on, and neural representations of the initiating event are eventually formed within the brain – in this case, neural representations of a cat. But the entire causal sequence does not end there. S also has a visual experience of a cat and, as before, we can ask what this experience is like. In this case, the proper question to ask is, 'What do you see?'[4] According to dualism, S has a visual experience *of* a cat 'in her mind'.

produces an
experience of

a CAT in the world as
perceived by the subject

neural causes
and correlates of
consciousness

neural
representation
of a cat

light rays

a CAT as perceived by
an external observer E

a subject
S

Figure 6.3 A reflexive model of perception (adapted from M. Velmans (1998) 'Physical, psychological and virtual realities', in J. Wood (ed.) *The Virtual Embodied*. London: Routledge).

According to reductionists there seems to be a phenomenal cat 'in S's mind' but this is really nothing more than a state of her brain. According to the reflexive model, and the broader 'reflexive monism' (RM) that I develop later in this book, while S is gazing at the cat, her only visual experience *of* the cat is the *cat she sees out in the world*. If she is asked to point to this phenomenal cat (her 'cat experience'), she should point not to her brain but to the cat as-perceived out in space beyond the body surface. In this, S is no different from E. The phenomenal cat experienced by S is as much out-there in the phenomenal world as the cat experienced by E. That is, an entity in the world is reflexively *experienced* to be an entity in the world.[5] Once again, if you have any doubts, why not find a cat and try it.

Of course, not all the entities and events we experience have such a clear location and extension in three-dimensional phenomenal space. Some experiences appear to be located on the surface of or internal to the body (touch sensations, visceral sensations, etc.) and are usually reflexively located where the stimuli that caused those sensations activated our sense organs. We also have 'inner' experiences such as verbal thoughts, images, feelings of knowing, experienced desires and so on. Such inner experiences really do seem to have a phenomenology of the kind described in propositions 4 to 10. One might argue that verbal thoughts have a rough location, in that they seem to be 'in the head' (in the form of inner speech) rather than in one's foot, or free-floating out in space, but they are not clearly located in the manner of pains and cats. However, the reflexive process is the same. The cognitive processes that give rise to thoughts, feelings of knowing and so on originate in the mind/brain, although these processes are unlikely to have a precise location in so far as they engage the mass action of large, distributed, neuronal populations (cf. Dennett and Kinsbourne, 1992). Consequently, in so far as these processes are experienced at all, they are reflexively experienced to be roughly *where they are* (in the head or brain).[6]

There is far more to be said about conscious phenomenology and its relation to the brain and physical world. But, if I am right so far, even a cursory examination of what we *actually* experience poses a fundamental challenge to dualist and reductionist ways of characterising what *it is* that they need to explain. As noted above, both dualism and reductionism assume experiences to be quite different from the perceived body and the perceived external world (perceived bodies and worlds are out-there in space, while experiences *of* bodies and worlds are either 'nowhere' or in the mind or brain). But the reflexive model suggests that in terms of *phenomenology* there is no actual separation between the perceived body and experiences *of* the body or between the perceived external world and experiences *of* that world. It goes without saying that when one has a conscious thought, there isn't some *additional* experience *of* a thought 'nowhere', or in the mind or brain. But neither is there a phenomenal pain nowhere, or in the mind or brain, *in addition* to the pain one experiences in the finger if one stabs it with a pin. And there isn't a phenomenal cat nowhere, in the mind, or in the brain, *in addition* to the cat one sees out in the world. According to the reflexive model, this additional experience is a theoretical fiction, and that is why the dualist versus reductionist argument about the nature of this experience cannot be resolved. Applying Occam's razor gets rid of both the fiction and the argument.

But the reflexive model does not get rid of conscious phenomenology. Thoughts, pains and phenomenal cats are experienced to have very different qualities or 'qualia', along with different locations and extensions, but they are nevertheless aspects of what we experience. Together, such inner experiences, bodily sensations, and externally experienced entities and events comprise the contents of our consciousness – which, together, form the constituents of our everyday phenomenal world.

Given that the reflexive model conforms closely to everyday experience, it should be easy to grasp the essence of the argument so far. Descartes' focus on *thought* as the prime exemplar of conscious experience led him to suggest that experiences are a state of 'thinking stuff' that has no location and extension in space – and reductionists commonly agree that experiences *seem* to have such ephemeral qualities (that is why they want to give them a more secure ontology in states or functions of the brain). While I agree that thoughts and other 'inner' experiences appear to have such qualities, most other experiences do not have those qualities. On the contrary, most experienced phenomena seem to have a clear location and extension in phenomenal space.

Who else says this?

To those immersed in dualist or reductionist modes of thought this proposed expansion of the contents of consciousness to include those aspects of the phenomenal world that we normally think of as the 'physical world' may seem radical, and the notion that many experiences have at least a *phenomenal* location and extension might appear strange. But, thus far, this proposal is hardly new. In one or another form it appears in the work of George Berkeley (1710), Immanuel Kant (1781), C.H. Lewes (1877), W.K. Clifford (1878), Ernst Mach (1885), Morton Prince (1885), William James (1890, 1904), Edmund Husserl (1931), A.N. Whitehead (1932), Charles Sherrington (1942), Bertrand Russell (1948), Wolfgang Köhler (1966), and Karl Pribram (1971, 1974, 1979, 2004). Similar analyses of what consciousness *seems* to be like have also recently been given by Antti Revonsuo (1995, 2006), Steven Lehar (2003, 2006), Michael Tye (1995, 2007), Shepard and Hut (1997), Hans Dooremalen (2003), Jeffrey Gray (2004), Rupert Sheldrake (2005), and Ted Honderich (2006).

William James (1904), for example, suggests that to convince oneself about where experiences are the observer only needs to

> begin with a perceptual experience, the 'presentation', so called, of a physical object, his actual field of vision, the room he sits in, with the book he is reading as its centre, and let him for the present treat this

complex object in the commonsense way as being 'really' what it seems to be, namely, a collection of physical things cut out from an environing world of other physical things with which these physical things have actual or potential relations. Now at the same time it is just those self-same things which his mind, as we say, perceives, and the whole philosophy of perception from Democritus's time downwards has been just one long wrangle over the paradox that what is evidently one reality should be in two places at once, both in outer space and in a person's mind. 'Representative' theories of perception[7] avoid the logical paradox, but on the other hand they violate the reader's sense of life which knows no intervening mental image but seems to see the room and the book immediately just as they physically exist.

And Whitehead (1932) anticipates the 'reflexive model' (in somewhat anthro-pocentric fashion) when he suggests that,

> The mind in apprehending also experiences sensations which, properly speaking, are projected by the mind alone. These sensations are projected by the mind so as to clothe appropriate bodies in external nature. Thus the bodies are perceived as with the qualities which in reality do not belong to them, qualities which in fact are purely offsprings of the mind. Thus nature gets credit which should in truth be reserved for ourselves; the rose for its scent; the nightingale for its song; and the sun for its radiance. The poets are entirely mistaken. They should address their lyrics to themselves, and should turn them into odes of self-congratulation on the excellency of the human mind. Nature is a dull affair, soundless, scentless, colorless, merely the hurrying of material, endless, meaningless.
>
> (p. 54)

More recently, Tye (1995) has tried to accommodate the same observation by suggesting that perceptual experiences are *transparent*:

> Why is it that perceptual experiences are transparent? When you turn your gaze inward and try to focus your attention on intrinsic features of these experiences, why do you always seem to end up attending to what the experiences are *of*? Suppose you have a visual experience of a shiny, blood-soaked dagger. Whether, like Macbeth, you are hallucinat-ing or whether you are seeing a real dagger, you experience redness and shininess as outside you, as covering the surface of a dagger. Now try to become aware of your experience itself, inside you, apart from its objects. Try to focus your attention on some intrinsic feature of the experience that distinguishes it from other experiences, something other than what it is an experience *of*. The task seems impossible: one's awareness seems always to slip through the experience to the redness and shininess, *as instantiated together externally*. In turning one's mind

inward to attend to the experience, one seems to end up scrutinizing *external* features or properties.

(p. 135)

One insight, of course, does not make a theory. James, for example, is a neutral monist, Whitehead is a process theorist, and Tye is a physicalist. The reflexive model that I elaborate below (and the broader reflexive monism it exemplifies) differs in essential ways from each of these positions (although it also incorporates many shared elements).

A reflexive model of how consciousness relates to the brain and the physical world

The reflexive model of perception suggests that all experiences result from a preconscious reflexive interaction of an observer with an observed. The resulting experiences can be subdivided into three categories:

1   The experienced external world (the phenomenal world) which seems to have location and extension.
2   The experienced body (the phenomenal body or body image) which seems to have location and extension.
3   'Inner' experiences (thoughts, images, feelings of knowing and so on) which have no clear location and extension in phenomenal space, although they can be loosely said to be 'in the head or brain'.

Figure 6.3 illustrates one example of a reflexive interaction resulting in an experience (a visual percept) of a phenomenal cat. In this case, the initiating stimulus (the observed) is an entity located in space beyond the body surface that interacts with the visual system of the observer to produce an experienced entity out in space beyond the body surface. As noted earlier, a similar reflexive interaction takes place when the initiating stimulus is on the surface of (or within) the body, or within the brain itself, to produce experienced entities and events on the surface of (or within) the body, or 'in the head or brain' itself.

What is going on? Following current conventions in the psychology of perception, I assume that the mind/brain constructs a 'representation' or 'mental model' of what is happening in the world, body or mind/brain itself, based on the input from the initiating stimulus, sensory-motor interactions with the world, expectations, traces of prior, related stimuli stored in long-term memory, and so on (cf. Rock, 1997). Such mental models encode information about the entities and events that they represent in formats determined by the sensory modality that they employ. Visual representations of a cat, for example, include encodings for shape, location and extension, movement, surface texture, colour, and so on.

How do these neural encodings relate to the subject's visual experiences? In

Velmans (1991b) I suggested that the way information in a given mental model appears to be formatted depends on the *observational arrangements*. The information encoded in the mental model appears in different forms to the subject (S) and the external observer (E) for the reason that the means available to S and E for accessing the information in that mental model differ.

An external observer, inspecting a subject's brain, has to rely on his own exteroceptive systems (typically vision) aided by physical equipment (PET scans, fMRI and so on). Viewed in this way (from this third-person perspective), a visual mental model in the subject's brain might appear in the form of neural activation in a series of relatively distinct feature maps distributed throughout the subject's visual system. We do not know precisely what is required to make such neural representations conscious. However, given the integrated nature of visual experiences, it is reasonable to assume that when such distributed neural activities do become conscious they must be bound together in some way, perhaps through synchronous 40 Hz oscillations (see Chapters 3 and 11). We may also expect there to be observable (physical) influences on the pattern of activity embodied in the mental model from existing memory traces (corresponding to the effects of expectation, stored knowledge and so on). Whatever the fine detail turns out to be like, viewed from E's perspective, the information (about the cat) in S's mental model is likely to take a neural or other physical form. In terms of what E can directly observe of S's mental model, this is the end of the scientific story.

However, the observational arrangement by which the subject accesses the information in her own mental model is entirely different. As with E, the information in S's mental model is translated into something that she can observe or experience, but all she experiences is a phenomenal cat out in the world. While she focuses her attention on the cat she does not become conscious of having a 'mental model of a cat' in the form of neural states. Nor does she have an experience of a cat 'in her brain'. Rather, she becomes conscious of what the neural states *represent* – an entity out in the external world. In short, the *information* encoded in S's mental model (about the entity in the world) is *identical* whether viewed by S or by E, but the way the information appears to be *formatted* depends on the perspective from which it is viewed. In this respect, the reflexive model of perception adopts a dual-aspect theory of information.[8]

Let me illustrate with a simple analogy. Let us suppose that the information encoded in the subject's brain is formed into a kind of neural 'projection hologram'. A projection hologram has the interesting property that the three-dimensional image it encodes is perceived to be out in space, in *front* of its two-dimensional surface, provided that it is viewed from an appropriate (frontal) perspective and it is illuminated by an appropriate (frontal) source of light. Viewed from any other perspective (from the side or from behind) the only information one can detect about the object is in the complex interference patterns encoded on the holographic plate. In analogous fashion, the information in the neural 'projection hologram' is displayed *as* a visual, three-dimensional object out in space only when it is viewed from the appropriate, first-person perspective of the perceiving subject. And this happens only when the necessary and sufficient conditions for consciousness are satisfied (when there is 'illumination by an appropriate source of light'). Viewed from any other third-person perspective the information in S's 'hologram' appears to be nothing more than neural representations in the brain (interference patterns on the plate).

The projection hologram is, of course, *only* an analogy,[9] but it is useful in that it shares some of the apparently puzzling features of conscious experiences. Viewed from an external observer's perspective, the *information* displayed in the three-dimensional holographic image is encoded in two-dimensional patterns on a plate, but there is *no* sense in which the subject's three-dimensional image is *itself* 'in the plate'. Likewise, according to the reflexive model there is no sense in which the phenomenal cat observed by S is 'in her head or brain'. In fact, the three-dimensional holographic image *does not even exist* (as an image) without an appropriately placed observer and an appropriate source of light. Likewise, the existence of the phenomenal cat requires the participation of S, the experiencing agent, and all the conditions required for conscious experience (in her mind/brain) have to be satisfied. Finally, a given holographic image only exists *for* a given observer, and can only be said to be located and extended where that observer *perceives* it to be.[10] S's phenomenal cat is similarly private and subjective. It can only be said to be out in phenomenal space beyond the body surface to the extent that she perceives it to be out in space beyond the body surface.[11]

What is perceptual projection?

Unconscious mind/brain processes construct experienced realities in which our phenomenal heads appear to be enclosed within three-dimensional, phenomenal worlds, not the other way around. But the neural mental models that encode information about these three-dimensional experienced realities *are* 'in the head or brain'. Given this, how do phenomenal cats and other phenomenal objects that are perceived to be located and extended in space get to be out there? It is clear that nothing *physical* is projected by the brain. There are for example no light rays projected through the eyes to illuminate the world, contrary to the beliefs of ancient Greek thinkers such as Empedocles (cf. Zajonc, 1993). Rather, 'perceptual projection' is a *psychological effect* produced by unconscious perceptual processing.

In short, perceptual projection is an effect that requires explanation; perceptual projection is not itself an explanation. The projection hologram has a number of features that might be usefully incorporated into a causal explanation of such effects, but it is not intended to be a literal theory of what is taking place in the mind/brain. Right now, we just don't know how it is done. Of course, not fully understanding *how* it happens does not alter the fact *that* it happens – and the evidence for perceptual projection is considerable. I have reviewed this elsewhere (in Velmans, 1990a), so below I merely list some examples, to remove any doubts that the phenomenon is real.

Projected pain

Doctors take it for granted that pains can be located in the body and that their precise location provides a useful indicator of the nature of bodily damage or disease – a view that patients accept as simple, common sense. However, philosophers of mind treat pain as a paradigm case of a conscious mental event, and take it for granted that, however it *seems*, pain is really 'in the mind or brain'. I prefer to defend common sense and will return to this debate in Chapter 7. For the moment we are merely interested in appearances, for the reason that perceptual projection (of pain beyond the brain) is a *subjective, psychological effect*. In so far as pains *seem* to be in the body (beyond the brain) they exemplify this effect.

Of course, pains are usually felt to be in the region of the affected sensory end organs (a pin in the finger produces pain in the finger), and sense organs attached to the peripheral nervous system are, in a sense, extensions of the brain. Given this, one might argue that pain is not projected beyond the 'extended brain'. But this argument won't work for phantom limbs. Livingston (1943) for example provides a case history of

> a physician, who had long been a close friend of mine, (who) lost his left arm as a result of gas bacillus infection. . . . The arm was removed by a guillotine type of amputation close to the shoulder and for some weeks the wound bubbled gas. It was slow in healing and the stump remained cold, clammy, and sensitive. . . . In spite of my close acquaintance with this man, I was not given a clear impression of his sufferings until a few years after the amputation, because he was reluctant to confide to anyone the sensory experiences he was undergoing. He had the impression, that is so commonly shared by layman and physician alike, that because the arm was gone, any sensations ascribed to it must be imaginary. Most of his complaints were ascribed to his absent hand. It seemed to be in a tight posture with the fingers pressed closely over the thumb and the wrist sharply flexed. By no effort of will could he move any part of the hand. . . . The sense of tenseness in the hand was unbearable at times, especially when the stump was exposed to cold or had been bumped. Not infrequently he had a sensation as if a sharp scalpel was being driven repeatedly, deep into . . . the site of his original puncture wound. Sometimes he had a boring sensation in the bones of the index finger. The sensation seemed to start at the tip of the finger and ascend the extremity to the shoulder, at which time the stump would begin a sudden series of clonic contractions. He was frequently nauseated when the pain was at its height. As the pain gradually faded, the sense of tenseness in the hand eased somewhat, but never in a sufficient degree to permit it to be moved.

In the intervals between the sharper attacks of pain, he experienced a persistent burning in the hand. The sensation was not unbearable and at times he could be diverted so as to forget it for short intervals. When it became annoying, a hot towel thrown over his shoulder or a drink of whisky gave him partial relief.

(cited in Melzack, 1973)

By way of treatment, Livingston administered a novocaine injection of the upper thoracic sympathetic ganglia of both sides. This removed the pain (for a number of months) but not the phantom limb. Rather, 'To our mutual surprise, he (now) felt that he could voluntarily move each of his phantom fingers' (ibid).

Projected tactile sensations

Further examples of the same projection effect are provided by tactile sensations, which are subjectively located on the surface of the skin, and by kinaesthetic sensations in our limbs (Box 6.2).

As with pains, such tactile projections also take place in phantom limbs. Melzack (1973), in his review of such experiences, reports that,

Most amputees report feeling a phantom limb almost immediately after amputation of an arm or a leg. . . . The phantom limb is usually described as having a tingling feeling and a definite shape that resembles the real limb before amputation. It is reported to move through space in much the same way as the normal limb would move when the person walks, sits down, or stretches out on a bed. At first, the phantom limb feels perfectly normal in size and shape – so much that the amputee may reach out for objects with the phantom hand, or try to get out of bed by stepping onto the floor with the phantom leg. As time passes, however, the phantom limb begins to change shape. The arm or leg becomes less distinct and may fade away altogether, so that the phantom hand or foot seems to be hanging in mid-air. Sometimes the limb is slowly 'telescoped' into the stump until only the hand or foot remain at the stump tip.

In addition to such tingling and kinaesthetic sensations, amputees report a variety of other 'projected' sensations including pins-and-needles, itching, sweating, warmth or coldness and heaviness in their phantom limbs (Melzack, 1973; Craig, 1978).

Projected auditory sensations

We tend to think of the entities and events we perceive outside our bodies as *physical* and *observer-independent*. Sounds, for example, are usually thought of as physical events out in space that must be distinguished from experiences *of* sound 'in the mind or brain'. Acoustic energy (in the form of air molecule

Box 6.2 Where are your tactile sensations?

Notice the way this book feels hard when you press it with your fingers. The experienced hardness is subjectively located in the region of the stimulated tactile receptors at the point of contact between your fingers and the book. But the proximal neural causes of such sensations are located in the region of the somatosensory cortex. Hardness and solidity are commonly thought of as physical rather than psychological properties by virtue of the fact that they *represent* aspects of the physical world. Nevertheless the hardness we *experience* at the point of contact between the fingers and the book is as much a product of brain processing as is an experience of pain. So, how does the sensation of hardness get back down to the fingers?

Now press the tip of a pencil against the table on which the book sits. The table feels hard *at the point where it is pressed*. But there are no sensory organs located at the pencil tip! In interpreting the shear force exerted on the skin by the pencil (when the pencil presses on the table), the brain habitually refers the origin of the felt resistance to the point of contact between the table and pencil tip – an everyday, illusory projection of tactile sensations beyond the surface of the skin. In this instance, closer attention to the phenomenology of the tactile sensations weakens the illusory projection of tactile sensations to the pencil tip (on close inspection they appear to be at the point of contact between the pencil and the skin). But note that no amount of attention alters the impression that the tactile sensations are located at the surface of the fingers rather than on or in the somatosensory cortex.

vibration) does, of course, have an independent existence. When a tree falls in the forest such energy is produced whether or not there is anyone to hear. But, without anyone to hear, there can be no perceived sound. The brain detects the pattern of air molecule vibration at the eardrums, along with cues regarding the source of such vibration provided by slight differences in intensity, phase, and modulations of the acoustic energy provided by the pinnae of the ears. Just as the brain translates damage to the skin into pain in the skin, or translates deformation of the skin (caused by pressure) into a feeling of 'hardness' of the object that the skin touches, the brain reflexively projects resulting auditory sensations to the judged location of their origin. And these auditory sensations *become* the sounds we experience in three-dimensional phenomenal space.

Notice again the basic similarities in these causal sequences. An entity or event that we can describe in physical terms (as a form of energy, mechanical deformation of the skin, etc.), once detected, identified and modelled by the mind/brain, is translated into an entity or event as-experienced, subjectively located in the place where the modelled entity or event is judged to be. Note that whether we regard such experienced phenomena to be 'physical' or 'mental' depends on *what* we judge them to be experiences *of* rather than on *where* the subjective locations of the phenomena are experienced to be. Pain, for example, is typically thought of as mental and hardness is typically thought of as a property of something physical. Subjectively, however, pains and sensations of hardness can be located in the *same place*. If one increases the pressure of the point of a pencil against one's own fingertip, the feeling of hardness of the pencil against one's skin gradually transforms into an experienced pain. We think of the felt hardness as representing a physical property of the pencil because the sensation tells us something about *it*. By contrast, we judge the pain to be 'mental' or 'psychological' because it represents something taking place within ourselves.[12] Yet, *both* experienced phenomena are skin sensations at the fingertip. And in neither case is there some *second* experience *of* the fingertip sensation 'in the mind or brain'.

The implausibility of trying to distinguish 'conscious experiences' from 'physical phenomena' in terms of what is experienced to be 'in the head' as opposed to 'out in the world' is clearly demonstrated by studies of sound localisation that manipulate subjective location, without otherwise altering the perceived sound. One can produce similar manipulations using conventional hi-fi equipment. A symphony orchestra played through stereo speakers, for example, appears to be distributed in the space outside one's body. Being out in space, we conventionally regard such music as a 'physical' phenomenon. But, if the same music, from the same source, is played through stereo headphones the instruments can appear to be distributed around the space inside one's head! Given our dualist heritage, it is tempting to regard these experienced sounds as being 'mental'. They appear, after all, to be roughly in the same place as verbal thoughts. And, as with the verbal thoughts discussed above, it seems absurd to suppose that *in addition to* the music subjectively located inside one's head, there is an experience *of* the music 'inside the mind or brain'.

But it seems equally absurd to suppose that if one switches back from headphones to stereo speakers, an additional conscious percept *of* music appears in the mind or brain at the precise moment that the music switches from being subjectively 'in the head' to being out in the world. Nor does it seem plausible to suggest that the perceived music is somehow *transformed* from being a 'conscious experience' to being 'physical' as it moves from its subjective location in the head to the external world – for, apart from its changed location, it undergoes no other change in its perceived properties.

Studies of 'inside the head locatedness' suggest a far simpler explanation. For example, Laws (1972) investigated the acoustic differences between white noise presented through headphones (which is perceived to be inside the head) and white noise presented through a speaker at a distance of 3 metres (which is perceived to be out in the world), using probe microphones positioned at the entrance to the auditory canals. This revealed spectral differences, produced largely by the pinnae of the ears, between the white noise presented either through the speaker or through the headphones. Ingeniously, Laws then constructed an electrical 'equalising' circuit to simulate these spectral differences and inserted this into the headphone circuit. With the headphones 'unequalised', white noise appeared to be inside the head irrespective of loudness. With the headphones 'equalised', the white noise not only appeared to be outside the head but also appeared to become more distant as its loudness decreased.

Again, it seems absurd to suggest that switching in an 'equalising' circuit transforms a 'conscious experience' into something 'physical' (or vice versa). Rather, the experiment establishes that spectral distortions produced by the pinnae (or their absence) inform the mind/brain whether or not the source of sound lies beyond the pinnae (cf. Blauert, 1983). The phenomenal model of the sound source produced by the mind/brain (the sound as-perceived) is correspondingly located in the head or beyond the pinnae. What we hear and where we hear it result from a reflexive interaction of input acoustic energy with the mind/brain's perceptual processing.

In short, whether we choose to *regard* what we hear as being 'mental' or 'physical' depends largely on our direction of interest. If we are interested in the event in the world (the acoustic energy) that the perceived sound *represents*,[13] and in how that event relates to other events in the external world, then we tend to think of it as 'physical'. If we are more interested in the phenomenology *as such*, for example in how acoustic energy produces certain perceived effects in *ourselves*, then we tend to regard the sound as a 'conscious experience'. As neutral monists such as James, Mach and Russell realised, our judgement about what is mental or physical, in such instances, depends largely on the network of relationships on which we focus (see Chapter 3). Whatever we decide about the (physical or mental) status of such a perceived event, its actual phenomenology remains the same.[14]

Events as perceived versus events as described by physics

It is important to stress that the analysis above applies only to the *phenomenology* of 'physical' versus 'mental' events. Indeed, having blurred the boundaries between 'mental' and 'physical' phenomenology, it becomes important to *sharpen* the distinction between the everyday 'physical' events that we *experience* and these same events *as described by physics* (or other sciences). According to the analysis above, the events we experience result from an interaction of input energies and events with modelling processes in the mind/brain – and the consequent experiences *represent* what is going on in the world, body, or mind/brain itself (in ways appropriate, no doubt, to biological evolution). Modern science, however, has developed representations of the world (in its laws, equations and other descriptions) that are, at times, very different from the everyday world as-experienced (witness quantum mechanics, and relativity theory).[15] Events as-experienced and events as-described by physics can, of course, be related to each other through the study of psychophysics – and in this way we can learn something about the *manner* in which the events we experience represent the world which science describes.[16] I return to this, and related issues, in Chapter 8.

Projected visual worlds

The classical distinction between the 'physical' and the 'mental' in terms of what is 'in the external world' rather than 'in the mind or brain' seems clearest in the domain of vision. Visually perceived objects extended in the three-dimensional space around our bodies seem to be very different, for example, from experienced visual images of those objects. If such visual images exemplify the 'contents of consciousness', then how could objects as-seen do likewise? The analysis presented below does not seek to minimise these differences in how objects and images are experienced, for, in all probability, they represent discontinuities that from the point of view of human interaction with the world are both important and real. But, the fact that seen objects are experienced to be different from visual images does not alter the fact that both objects and images are *experienced* – and that their phenomenology results from mental modelling in the mind/brain.

The dependence of visual images on mental modelling is easy to accept. Subjectively, their generation seems to require mental effort and, phenomenally, they seem to be (roughly) located 'in the mind or brain'. By contrast, the phenomenology of the objects we see appears to require no generative, mental effort on our part. The perceived objects seem to exist in their own right, and they seem to be out in the world, quite separate from the mind/brain. Nevertheless, the evidence for mental modelling in the *construction* of objects as-seen, including their seen location in three-dimensional space, is compelling.

It is well known, for example, that as an object recedes, its perceived size decreases far less than its optical projection on the retina would suggest (the phenomenon of 'size constancy'). Perceived size varies not only with the size of the projected retinal image but also with judged distance – and the judged distance of an object is itself influenced by cues provided by binocular disparity, ocular convergence, textural gradients, the interposition of other objects, motion parallax and so on. Indeed, three-dimensional phenomenal space can itself be shown to be, in part, a 'construct' of the mind/brain.

One demonstration of such constructive processing is the experience of three-dimensional depth which results from the mind/brain's interpretation of visual cues suitably arranged on a two-dimensional surface. As shown in Figure 6.4, the artist Peter Cresswell (1998) achieves quite a strong sense of depth through the use of 'radial perspective'. Try inspecting his painting monocularly, through a reduction tube (a rolled up piece of paper), taking care to avoid the edges of the painting. This enhances the experience of depth

Figure 6.4 How two-dimensional cues can achieve quite a strong sense of depth
        through the use of radial perspective (painting by Peter Cresswell, from
        M. Velmans (1998) 'Physical, psychological and virtual realities', in J.
        Wood (ed.) *The Virtual Embodied*. London: Routledge).

(as the reduction tube eliminates the conflicting cues provided by binocular
vision and by the edge of the painting which indicate that it is really on a
two-dimensional surface).

Stereoscopic pictures of the kind shown in Figure 6.5 create an even more
powerful effect. If one focuses one's eyes *behind* the picture (following the
instructions in the figure caption) a three-dimensional scene should form.
Once formed, one can inspect different objects in the picture without
destroying the three-dimensional effect. Normally, the construction of visual
depth occurs preconsciously, and the processing occurs too quickly for there
to be any indication that construction is involved. Stereoscopic pictures are
particularly interesting in that the full experience of depth emerges *gradually*,
becoming fully formed only as one continues to inspect the picture. In such
instances, one can experience different stages of the construction of a
three-dimensional visual scene (with accompanying changes in perceptual
projection) online, while that construction is taking place.

I have reviewed the evidence for functional similarities in the processes
that construct visual images and visual, phenomenal worlds in Velmans
(1990a) (see also review by Ganis *et al.*, 2004), so I will not recount
this evidence here. Suffice it to say that the phenomenal differences between
images, perceived objects and hallucinations are not always clear. Eidetic

Figure 6.5 A stereoscopic picture of 'snowflakes'. To experience the picture in depth, bring the picture up to your nose and look *through* it, so that the picture is completely blurred. Now leaving your eyes relaxed and looking through the picture, gradually move the picture away to a distance of a foot or more, and a three-dimensional scene should form. Notice that once an experienced three-dimensional scene is formed, it is possible to inspect different parts of it without losing the experience of depth. This is an example of 'perceptual projection' in action, demonstrating the brain's ability to create an experience of depth, in spite of the fact that the cues are arranged on a two-dimensional surface. Originally published by Dragon's World, London.

images, for example, resemble perceived objects in that, subjectively, they appear to have location and extension in three-dimensional space. Eideticers typically report such images to be projected onto surfaces in front of their eyes and as being quite different from visual memories, which they report as being 'inside their heads'. Further, when they describe such images they describe *what they see* as opposed to *what they have seen* (Leask *et al.*, 1969; Haber, 1979).

Such abilities, when they occur, are usually found in children. However, Spanos *et al.* (1973) report that 1 to 2 per cent of adults appear to have the ability to hallucinate an object in a room when asked to do so without the object being present. Very occasionally, a hallucination is so powerful that it is taken to be more 'real' than a perceived object that actually exists. The neurologist Peter Brugger (1994), for example, reports a clinical case history of a young man of 17 suffering from epilepsy caused by a lesion in his left temporal lobe. He was being treated with anti-convulsant drugs to control the condition and was scheduled for surgery when he experienced a 'heautoscopic' episode (a visual hallucination of his body combined with an out-of-body experience) which was disturbing in the extreme:

> The heautoscopic episode, which is of special interest to the topic of this report, occurred shortly before admission. The patient stopped his phenytoin medication, drank several glasses of beer, stayed in bed the whole of the next day, and in the evening he was found mumbling and confused below an almost completely destroyed large bush just under the window of his room on the third floor. At the local hospital, thoracic and pelvic contusions were noted. . . . The patient gave the following account of the episode: on the respective morning he got up with a dizzy feeling. Turning around, he found himself still lying in bed. He became angry about 'this guy who I knew was myself and who would not get up and thus risked being late for work'. He tried to wake the body in bed first by shouting at it; then by trying to shake it and then repeatedly jumping on his alter ego in the bed. The lying body showed no reaction. Only then did the patient begin to be puzzled about his double existence and become more and more scared by the fact that he could no longer tell which of the two he really was. Several times his body awareness switched from the one standing upright to the one still lying in bed; when in the lying bed mode he felt quite awake but completely paralysed and scared by the figure of himself bending over and beating him. His only intention was to become one person again and, looking out of the window (from where he could still see his body lying in bed), he suddenly decided to jump out 'in order to stop the intolerable feeling of being divided in two'. At the same time, he hoped that 'this really desperate action would frighten the one in bed and thus urge him to merge with me again'. The next thing he remembers is waking up in pain in the hospital.
>
> (Brugger, 1994, pp. 838–839)

In short, this patient mistakenly judged the hallucinated body on the bed to be his real one and tried to get rid of his real body (which he judged to be the hallucination) in order to become unified again – a powerful example of the constructed nature of the body as-experienced.

Projected virtual realities

Virtual realities provide an added 'existence proof' for the operation of perceptual projection. In virtual reality (VR) one *appears* to interact with a virtual world outside one's body although there is no *actual* (corresponding) world there. So, in this situation, there is no danger of confusing the appearance of the virtual world with an actual world that one sees. Yet, objects in a VR world appear to have three-dimensional location and extension. Virtual objects can also be given what appear to be classical 'physical' properties such as 'hardness'; for example, the observer may wear a gauntlet on her hand which is programmed to resist closing around a visually perceived, virtual object, making the latter feel 'solid'. In truth, however, there is nothing solid there.

These virtual appearances do not fit easily into either a dualist or a reductionist understanding of consciousness, as, in spite of being nothing more than *seemings*, they do not seem to be 'in the mind or brain'. But in the reflexive model they are easy to explain. In the manner shown in Figure 6.6, when visual input from screens in VR headsets is appropriately co-ordinated with head and body movements, it provides information which resembles that arriving from actual objects in the world. The mind/brain models this information in the normal way, and constructs what it normally constructs given such input – a perceived, phenomenal world located and extended in three-dimensional space.

The world as-perceived is *part of* the contents of consciousness

Some initial principles that follow from the analysis above should now be clear. Within the reflexive model the physical world as-perceived is *part of* the contents of consciousness. In its phenomenology, the contents of consciousness

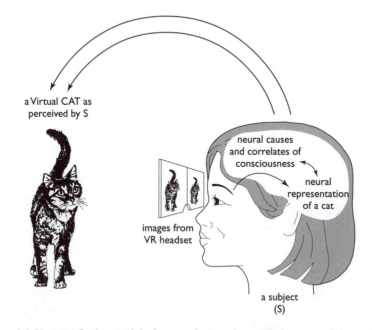

Figure 6.6 How a reflexive model of perception can be applied to an understanding of virtual reality (adapted from M. Velmans (1998) 'Physical, psychological and virtual realities', in J. Wood (ed.) *The Virtual Embodied*. London: Routledge).

do not appear to be in some separate place or space 'in the mind or brain'. Indeed, in terms of phenomenology no clear separation exists between what we normally think of as the 'physical world', the 'phenomenal world', the 'world as-perceived', and our 'experiences of the world'. This does not mean, of course, that these terms have exactly the same *meaning* in all contexts. The term 'physical world' for example is ambiguous: in everyday life we commonly use the term to describe the world as perceived, but in science the term usually refers to the world as described by physics (e.g. quantum mechanics, relativity theory, etc.), which may differ in major ways from the world as normally perceived. The 'world as experienced' also has a different emphasis from 'experiences of the world' in that these phrases focus our attention in different ways. The first phrase places what is *observed* in the foreground, which, in the reflexive model, is the initiating stimulus. If we are interested primarily in what is going on in the world, this is appropriate. The second phrase draws our attention to the results of perceptual processing in the *observer*, that is, to the resulting experience. If we are interested primarily in what is going on for the subject, this is appropriate. But this does not alter the fact that when we look at an object in the world, we experience only an object in the world, whichever way that experience is conceived.

The everyday physical world as-perceived does have to be distinguished from the more abstract world described by *physics* (and other sciences). That is, the physical world as-perceived is just one (biologically useful) representation of the world that science describes. But, with our eyes open, what we normally call the 'physical world' just *is* what we experience, and there is no *additional* experience *of* the world 'in the mind or brain'. This, I suggest, is simple common sense.

If it turns out that experiences are *really* how they seem to be, this conclusion would be devastating for classical dualism, as it challenges the very basis on which Descartes splits the world. Inner experiences such as *thoughts* might have the character of *res cogitans* (thinking stuff without location and extension in space). However, body experiences (pains, tactile and proprioceptive experiences) and external experiences (sounds, visual objects and events as-perceived) have location and extension in three-dimensional phenomenal space, making them part of *res extensa*. The analysis also places a heavy, added burden on reductionism, as it *expands* what needs to be reduced. Not just ephemeral thoughts, so-called percepts 'in the mind' and the like must be reduced to states or functions of the brain, but the *entire phenomenal world*. In Chapters 3 to 5 I have listed some of the conventional problems of reductionism. In Chapter 9, I go on to argue that observed phenomena in science just *are* aspects of the phenomenal world, as experienced by scientists. If one adopts such an expanded view of consciousness, reduction of these observed phenomena to states of the brain becomes absurd.

Redrawing the boundaries of phenomenal consciousness

We have some more work to do to secure these arguments. However, if there is no *phenomenological* separation of objects as-seen from experiences *of* them, the reasons why I believe presuppositions 4, 8, 9 and 10 (Box 6.1) to be false should be apparent. It is implicit in 4 that the objects we see around us are separate and distinct from experiences *of* those objects 'in the mind', and this provides the basis for claims about *phenomenological differences* between perceived objects and experiences (8, 9 and 10). There may be neural causes and correlates of conscious experience in the brain, but on the basis of all available first- and third-person evidence, no additional *phenomenal experiences* of objects 'in the mind or brain' exist. This undermines the very basis of the dualist versus reductionist debate.

Descartes splits the universe into *res cogitans* and *res extensa*, and identifies *res cogitans* with consciousness. Materialist reductionism tries to heal this split by demonstrating *res cogitans* to be nothing more than a bit of *res extensa* (a bit of the brain). Yet, if we examine what we *actually* experience it becomes obvious that much of it does not appear to be like *res cogitans*. Some phenomena that we experience (pains, tactile, auditory and visual phenomena) appear to have a clear location and extension beyond or within our bodies in spite of the fact that others do not (thoughts, some images, feelings, and so on). If so, Descartes' separation of *res cogitans* from *res extensa* does not separate what is 'in consciousness' from what is not.[17] The mind/brain models energies and events into experienced phenomena that have many different 'qualia', and, together, these experienced phenomena form the contents of consciousness. These *include* phenomena that have experienced location and extension that we are accustomed to think of as 'physical'. If so, there never was an unbridgeable divide separating 'physical phenomena' from the 'contents of consciousness'. Physical objects and events as-perceived are *part of* the contents of consciousness.

Notes

1 Varela (1996) gives a useful map of the relative importance of phenomenology in different, contemporary approaches to consciousness.
2 Figure 6.1 is deliberately oversimplified, as its only purpose is to illustrate the dualist separation of the objects we see in the external world from perceptual processing in brains and the consequent experiences of those objects. In particular, the figure does not make explicit, (a) the distinction between objects as seen and objects themselves, and (b) the distinction between what can, in principle, be seen from E's perspective and what can only be inferred. The same applies to the contrasting models in Figures 6.2 and 6.3. Strictly speaking, (a) it is not the cat *as seen by E* that is the source of the light reflectances from its surfaces but the *cat itself*, and (b) while E can see the cat, measure the light reflected from its surface (with appropriate instruments), see the subject, and examine the processes that take place in S's brain (again, with appropriate instruments), E can only infer the nature of S's experience on the basis of what S reports (see the more detailed analysis of these relationships in Chapter 9). I mention this as some commentators

on my analysis have agonised over these (unstated) features of the 'cat diagrams', sometimes interpreting them accurately (e.g. Hoche, 2007), but sometimes mixing accuracy with inaccuracy (e.g. Van de Laar, 2003; Voerman, 2003). As Van de Laar rightly points out, it is always the *cat itself* that one is looking at although it is a phenomenal cat that one sees, which makes the phenomenal cat the *observation* and the cat itself the *observed*. In everyday life we blur these distinctions for the reason that we habitually *treat* phenomenal objects to *be* the observed objects for the reason that this is how those objects appear to us. I will clarify these distinctions in Chapter 7, when they become important to the issues under discussion.

3 Rather than reduce electricity to magnetism or vice versa, modern physics treats these as complementary aspects of electromagnetism. That is, it introduces a broader ontology that encompasses both phenomena. Later, I will argue that a similarly broadened ontology may be required to make sense of the relationship between consciousness and brain.

4 For the purposes of this example we are concerned only with the phenomenology of visual experiences, not with feelings about the cat, thoughts about the cat and so on.

5 In this situation there is (numerically) one cat-itself, but two views of it, resulting in the phenomenal cat experienced by S to be out-there in S's phenomenal world and the phenomenal cat experienced by E to be out-there in E's phenomenal world. We return to a more detailed analysis of how the ontology of entities in the world relates to the ontology of phenomenal objects in Chapters 7 and 8.

6 The view that experiences are really 'in the head or brain' irrespective of where they seem to be is a form of 'phenomenological internalism', while the view that some experiences really are out in the world where they seem to be is a form of 'phenomenological externalism'. According to the reflexive model (and the broader *reflexive monism* that I develop in Part III of this book), experiences really are roughly where they seem to be. While this commits the model to phenomenological externalism for experiences that seem to be external to the head or brain, there is no doctrinal commitment to externalism as such; some sensations seem to be on the surface of the skin and others really do seem to be 'in the head' (for example tactile sensations in the mouth). The location of experiences is an empirical matter that is determined by their phenomenology. The claim that experiences 'are *roughly* where they seem to be' also commits RM to a form of realism about conscious appearances but not to naïve realism. In order to make sense of this, the relation of phenomenal location to *measured* location and to various descriptions of space given by physics has to be examined with care, and we return to this in detail in Chapter 7.

7 For James, 'representative' theories are those that propose the existence of some inner mental image which represents the physical room 'in the mind'.

8 A similar dual-aspect theory of information was later advocated by Chalmers (1996) in his defence of 'naturalistic dualism'. We will return to these similarities and differences in Chapter 14.

9 Holography was first proposed as a model of neural organisation and space perception by Pribram (1971, 1974, 1979). Pribram (2004) develops the model further, and, interestingly, links its consequences specifically to the reflexive monism developed in the first edition of this book.

10 The position of the image relative to the plate, for example, changes slightly as the observer moves around the plate. Nevertheless, the image is sufficiently clear for the observer to (roughly) measure its width and how far it projects in front of the plate (e.g. with a ruler).

11 In this sense, phenomenal location is *observer-relative*, an issue to which we return in Chapter 7.

12 We also base such distinctions on the allegedly public vs. private, or objective

vs. subjective, nature of the perceived phenomena. We will re-examine these distinctions in Chapter 9.

13 In Velmans (1990a) I introduced 'general representationalism' – the view that *all* experiences are intentional. That is, inner experiences, bodily experiences and experienced external phenomena represent entities or events (from a first-person perspective) which can, in principle, be given alternative (scientific) representations, viewed from a third-person perspective. A similar argument relating to this point was later developed by the philosopher Michael Tye (1995), but unlike Tye, I do not regard this to be the royal route to physicalism. Tye combines his representationalism with a form of direct realism – the view that phenomenal properties are actually physical properties that exist, in the form that they are experienced, in the world (see discussion of Tye's view in Chapter 7). In modern philosophy of mind 'representationalism' is sometimes described as holding this combination of views (see discussion in Seager and Bourget, 2007). Within psychology and cognitive science, however, representationalism is far more commonly combined with 'indirect' or 'critical' realism – the view that phenomenal properties and internal neural representations represent events and entities other than themselves but only do so imperfectly in ways determined by the contingencies of evolution. It is this latter form of representationalism that reflexive monism adopts (see Chapter 8).

14 This dual (mental or physical) status is given to some, but not all perceived entities and events. Depending on the context, perceived sounds, visually experienced objects or properties of objects, and some bodily sensations (felt hardness etc.) can be thought of either as 'physical phenomena' or as 'experiences'. By contrast, the phenomenology of thoughts and other 'inner experiences' seems to have a purely 'mental' status. As noted below, these experienced differences are likely to represent important functional differences (in the represented events). But this does not alter the fact that both 'physical' and 'mental' phenomena are *experienced*.

15 To avoid ambiguity, I reserve the term 'a physical phenomenon' for physical events *as-experienced* (or physical events *as-observed*), and use the term 'events as-described by physics' (or other sciences) to refer to the more abstract representations of the same events given within physics (or other sciences).

16 Laws (1972), for example, found that the perceived distance of white noise produced by a speaker at a distance of 25 cm depended not on the distance of the speaker but on perceived loudness of the noise, receding from under 1 metre (on average) at 8 sones, to just over 2 metres (on average) at 1 sone. When the speaker was placed 3 metres away, the average perceived distance of the white noise it produced was similarly dependent on loudness. That is, for a given loudness, the perceived distance of a sound was only slightly further away than that produced by the speaker at 25 cm (a noise of 8 sones had a perceived distance of just over 1 metre, etc.). Under these circumstances, therefore, the *experienced* distance of the sound relates only in a very approximate fashion to the *measured* distance of the source that produces it (see Blauert, 1983, for a review). Generally speaking, at scales of size and distance appropriate to everyday human engagement with the world, perceived size and distance reflect measured size and distance more accurately than this.

17 This is a category error (although one of a very different kind from that claimed by Ryle, 1949).

7 The nature and location of experiences

There is a great deal more to be said about the consequences of the reflexive model introduced in Chapter 6. But, before going any further, it might be useful to secure the simple points I have already made by reviewing some common confusions about the model and some competing ways of making sense of the same data. Let us begin with some confusions.

1 Isn't it odd to talk about pain being 'in' a finger?

According to the psychologist Tony Marcel, there is something distinctly odd about the claim that a pain experience is literally 'in' a finger, or some other body part: 'Let me give an example: I have a pain in my finger at the moment, my finger is on the table, is the pain on the table?' (Marcel, 1993 – in discussion following Velmans, 1993a, p. 98).

Ned Block has made the same point, arguing that predicates like 'in' have different meanings when applied to mental as opposed to physical events – leading one to suspect their usage when applied to mental events. Consider, for example, the following argument:

> The pain is in my fingertip.
> The fingertip is in my mouth.
> Therefore, the pain is in my mouth.

According to Block,

> The argument is valid for the 'in' of spatial enclosure . . . since 'in' in this sense is transitive. But suppose that the two premises are true in their *ordinary* meanings . . . Their conclusion obviously does not follow, so we must conclude that 'in' is not used in the spatial enclosure sense in all three statements. It certainly seems plausible that 'in' as applied to locating pains differs in meaning systematically from the standard spatial enclosure sense.
>
> (Block, 1983, p. 517)

The aim of such examples, of course, is to throw doubt on the notion that the pain is really 'in' the finger at all. In fact, however, the odd consequences of using the predicate 'in' in these cases have nothing to do with the 'mental' nature of pain. The same oddities occur if one replaces the pain with its physical cause – say a cut in the finger. If the cut is in the finger and the finger is on the table is the cut on the table? No. The cut finger is on the table, but the cut remains in the finger. Similarly, if we suck the finger, the cut finger is in the mouth, but the cut is not in the mouth. It should be obvious from these counterexamples that the seemingly odd, intransitive nature of pain location has nothing to do with any misconceived attempt to locate pain experiences in the body. Rather, it is a consequence of the mundane fact that a cut is a *property* of the (affected) body surface or part that the resulting pain *represents*. That is, the cut and the pain 'attach' to the finger and not to surfaces on which it rests or the enclosures in which it is placed.

In any case, no such difficulties attach to phenomenal cats and to most other entities and events that we experience. Say, for example, that we place the perceived cat in Figure 6.3 in a room. Is the phenomenal cat in a phenomenal room? Yes. Is the phenomenal room in a phenomenal house? Yes. Is the phenomenal cat in a phenomenal house? Yes. And so on.

2 Doesn't the reflexive model confuse the vehicle–content distinction?

According to Marcel the suggestion that pain is really in the finger confuses the content of experience with its vehicle (that which carries the experience). In the case of the pain in the finger, part of the vehicle (the physical finger) is out there in the world (it carries the initiating cause of the pain). Additionally, 'The content of your experience may refer to what is in the world. But the experience itself is not in the world. The experience (as a vehicle) is in your head' (Marcel, 1993 – discussion following Velmans, 1993a, p. 98).

McGinn (1997 – personal communication) argues for the same distinction. The phenomenology of pain and many other experiences may seem to have spatial location and extension, but in so far as consciousness is anywhere, it is (as a vehicle) really 'in the head' (where the causes of the experiences are). As McGinn notes elsewhere,

> there are some mental events that do permit a precise location, and that is based on something *like* immediate perception. Thus I feel a pain to be *in* my hand, and that is indeed exactly where it is. Isn't this just like seeing the physical injury to my hand that produces the pain? Well, it is true enough that the pain presents itself as being in my hand, but there are familiar reasons for not taking this at face value. Without my brain no such pain would be felt, and the same pain can be produced by stimulating my brain and leaving my hand alone (I might not even have a hand). Such facts incline us to say, reasonably enough, that the pain is *really* in

my brain, if anywhere, and only appears to be in my hand (a sort of locational illusion takes place). That is, causal criteria yield a different location for the pain from phenomenal criteria.

(McGinn, 1995, p. 152)

McGinn concludes from this that 'consciousness does not slot smoothly into the ordinary spatial world' (ibid., p. 153) and that Descartes was right to think of mental phenomena as essentially non-spatial in character (in which case we are left with the problem of how something non-spatial can emerge from something spatial like the brain).[1]

In contrast, I have argued in Chapter 3 that we should not confuse ante-cedent *causes* with resulting *phenomenology*. While the proximal (neural) causes and correlates of pains and other tactile experiences are in the brain, these need to be distinguished from their *effects* (the *experiences themselves*). At the same time, it is a brute fact about consciousness that examination of the brain from the outside can *only* reveal its physical causes and correlates. It can *never* reveal the experiences themselves. One would never guess, from inspection of the brain alone, that its 'owner' has an inner conscious life, within an experienced body embedded in a surrounding phenomenal world. But, from the subject's perspective, the existence of this rich phenomenology is undeniable and much of its appearance can be readily described. Given that very few of these appearances resemble brain states, it is difficult to imagine what science *could* discover to demonstrate that such phenomenal worlds are *ontologically identical* to states of the brain.

In short, I entirely agree that it is important to distinguish conscious *con-tents* from the *vehicle* which causes or 'carries' them. Indeed, I have repeatedly stressed this point in distinguishing causes (in mind/brain interactions with the surrounding world) from experienced effects (see Chapters 3, 10 and 11). Contrary to Marcel and McGinn, however, this is one of many reasons why one should *reject* the claim that a pain in the finger is really in the brain.

Why should one draw the opposite conclusion to Marcel and McGinn? Let me reiterate that most of the facts are not in dispute. We all agree that the initiating cause of a pain in the finger is (typically) in the finger, for example in the form of a cut, and that the proximal neural causes of the pain in the finger are to be found in the brain. We agree that, viewed from a subjective, first-person perspective, the phenomenal pain is in the finger, and that the phenomenology (usually) represents something actually going on in the finger. We also agree that it is useful to distinguish the phenomenal contents of consciousness from their causes both in the world and in the mind/brain, and that these causes are, in a sense, the vehicle or 'carrier' of conscious experiences.

What I dispute is Marcel's suggestion that, in addition to the phenomenal consciousness that we experience and its causes in the world and brain, there is some *consciousness as a vehicle* in the brain which is supposed to be the 'real' consciousness (see quote above). In fact, given the absence of either first- or third-person evidence for such a 'consciousness as a vehicle', it is difficult to understand what the basis might be for this claim. As I have repeatedly noted, when we examine what we experience in different sense modalities from a first-person perspective we find no *added* experience in the mind/brain accompanying the phenomena that we experience (whether those experienced phenomena are in the world, in the body, or inner experiences – see Chapter 6). Indeed, if one strips phenomenal content away from phenomenal consciousness, there is no phenomenal consciousness left![2]

The fact that the everyday phenomenal world is not consciously duplicated 'in the head' (viewed from a first-person perspective) does not of course detract from the argument that there must be a vehicle or *carrier* of conscious experiences. Within consciousness studies the nature of that vehicle is a central, interdisciplinary topic of research. Viewed from the third-person perspective of neuropsychology and cognitive psychology, that vehicle is a brain embedded in a body interacting with a surrounding world. It is widely assumed that some brain processes provide the necessary and sufficient neural conditions for conscious experiences (and may be thought of as antecedent neural 'causes' of those experiences) while other brain processes co-occur with conscious experiences (and may be thought of as their neural 'correlates'). Brain processes that participate in the causal chain which *precedes* a given conscious experience are, of course, nonconscious (or, at best, preconscious). And brain processes that correlate with a given experience are just that – neural *correlates*. They are accompanied by conscious experiences, and along with the entire mind/brain/body/world system of which they are a part they can be thought of as 'carriers' of conscious experiences. But they remain brain states. They are not, in any obvious sense, 'consciousness as a vehicle'.

In short, under normal conditions, first-person consciousness is just *phenomenal consciousness* and its phenomenology reveals no added 'consciousness as a vehicle'. Viewed from a third-person perspective, the carriers of first-person experience appear to be brain processes embedded in a wider mind/brain system, and inspection, once again, reveals no 'consciousness as a vehicle'. Given that one does not require this theoretical fiction to make sense of the way consciousness relates to the brain and physical world, the reflexive model gets rid of it.

3   Doesn't the reflexive model confuse experiences of objects with the objects themselves?

The notion that the three-dimensional phenomenal world is *part of* conscious experience rather than *separate from* it has distinguished precedents in philosophy and psychology (including Kant, James, Whitehead, and Russell). However, in current debates it is far more common to assume that the 'physical' objects that we see in the world are distinct from experiences *of* those objects 'in the mind or brain'. Few would doubt that there really is a physical world surrounding our bodies. But, on first glance, many would doubt that it makes sense to claim that experiences are somehow out-there where the objects are perceived to be. Yet, the reflexive model simply follows the contours of what we actually experience. When we look at a cat, for example, *a cat in the world* is all that we see. When asked to describe our visual experience, there is nothing to describe other than what we see. The notion that there is some other experience *of* a cat 'in the mind/brain' is, in my view, an unwarranted *inference* about what we experience, based on an implicit, dualist vision of the world.

This shift is simple, but radical – and it is important to examine this position in its own terms to be clear about what is being claimed. Given the common assumption that the objects we see are quite separate from our experiences of those objects, it is not surprising that, on first exposure to this position, some theorists believe that I have made an elementary mistake. For example, following a brief introduction to the reflexive model, Thomas Nagel and Stevan Harnad wondered whether I had just confused the *experience* with the object that it is an experience *of* (the 'intentional object' – see discussions following Velmans, 1993a, pp. 92–93).

Let me stress again that in suggesting an object as-experienced to be one and the same as an experience *of* an object, I am making a claim solely about their *phenomenology* (when one looks at an object, the only visual experience one has *of* the object is the object as-seen out in the world). That said, the reflexive model accepts that, for many explanatory purposes, it is useful to distinguish the *observer* and the *observation* from the *observed object itself*. For example, in cases of exteroception of the kind shown in Figure 6.3, the *object itself* is the source of the stimuli that initiate visual processing. These stimuli interact with the perceptual and cognitive systems of the observer to produce the observation, an object a*s-seen*. Barring hallucinations, this perceived object (a phenomenal cat in three-dimensional space) *represents* something that actually exists beyond the body surface. But it does not represent it fully, as it is *in itself*.

In short, it is really the *cat itself* that S is looking at in Figure 6.3, although it is a phenomenal cat that she sees. The cat might, for example, appear black, fat and furry (whether viewed by S or E), but, at any given moment, it can only be seen from a given angle of view and there are only a few macrocosmic aspects of its surface detail that are represented in normal vision. With the aid of physical instruments (microscopes, X-rays, ultrasound, infrared, fMRI, etc.) many additional details of the entity may become observable. Other properties may be describable only through mathematics (for example, at the level of quantum mechanics). But neither physical instruments nor mathematics enable one to observe 'what it is like to be' that cat. In short, the phenomenal cat that S and E see out in space is just one partial, approximate, representation of the thing itself.[3]

Consequently, the reflexive model does not confuse experiences with what they are experiences of. In supporting the common-sense notion that the phenomenal world just *is* what we experience, it eliminates added experiences *of* objects in the mind or brain (on the grounds that these are theoretical fictions). But it retains the view that experienced objects and events are just representations of objects and events *in themselves*.

Some deeper questions

In terms of their *phenomenology* the 'physical world', the 'phenomenal world', the 'world as experienced', and our 'experiences of the world' are one and the same. However, as noted in Chapter 6, one insight does not make a theory, and this observation about the phenomenology of the 'physical world' raises three immediate questions:

1   Given that the proximal neural causes and correlates of experiences are inside the brain, how can one *explain* the fact that most visually experienced objects and events seem to be outside the brain?
2   Are these experienced (phenomenal) objects and events really where they seem to be?
3   What is the ontological status of the phenomenal world?

How can one explain that some experiences seem to be outside the brain?

In recent years, the seemingly external, three-dimensional nature of the visual world has been a point of departure for three competing theories of how conscious experiences relate to the physical world: 'transparency' theory, 'biological naturalism', and reflexive monism. The contrasts between these are particularly illuminating in that they highlight the main (current) explanatory options and their consequences in a relatively clear way.[4]

Transparency theory

According to Tye (1995, 2007) perceptual experiences are *transparent* and visual perception is rather like peering through a pane of glass:

> suppose that you have just entered a friend's country house for the first time and you are standing in the living room, looking out at a courtyard filled with flowers. It seems to you that the room is open, that you can walk straight out into the courtyard. You try to do so and, alas, you bang hard into a sheet of glass, which extends from ceiling to floor and separates the courtyard from the room. You bang into the glass because you do not see it. You are not aware of it; nor are you aware of any of its qualities. No matter how hard you peer, you cannot discern the glass. It is transparent to you. You see right through it to the flowers beyond. You are aware of the flowers, not by being aware of the glass, but by being aware of the facing surfaces of the flowers. And in being aware

of these surfaces, you are also aware of a myriad of qualities that seem to you to belong to these surfaces. You may not be able to name or describe these qualities but they look to you to qualify the surfaces. You experience them as being qualities of the surfaces. None of the qualities of which you are directly aware in seeing the various surfaces look to you to be qualities of your experience. You do not experience any of these qualities as qualities of your experience. For example, if redness is one of the qualities and roundness another, you do not experience your experience as red or round. . . . Visual experiences, according to many philosophers, are like such sheets of glass. Peer as hard as you like via introspection, focus your attention in any way you please, and you will only come across surfaces, volumes, films, and their apparent qualities. Visual experiences thus are transparent to their subjects (Moore 1922). We are not introspectively aware of our visual experiences any more than we are perceptually aware of transparent sheets of glass. If we try to focus on our experiences, we see right through them to the world outside. By being aware of the qualities apparently possessed by surfaces, volumes, etc., we become aware that we are undergoing visual experiences. But we are not aware of the experiences themselves.

(Tye, 2007, p. 30)

Tye rightly notes that, in normal perception, we feel that we experience the world, and that it doesn't really make sense to say that one 'experiences one's experiences'. We *have* experiences or, to use Tye's words, we undergo them, but 'experiencing one's experiences' does seem to involve an unnecessary (and non-existent) regression.

There are nevertheless two obvious problems with this analysis.

Tye is a physicalist and adopts the view that experiences are nothing more than representations in the brain that are 'transparent'. Consequently, on his account, when we 'introspect' our experiences, we 'see right through' perceptual representations in the brain to see the colours, smells and other qualities that actually exist in the world.[5] While this has a certain force as a metaphor, it is difficult to see how this translates into a viable theory. How can one 'see right through' one's brain states? Who is it that does the looking? For dualists, that 'someone' would presumably be a disembodied mind. But for physicalists that 'someone' would itself have to be a state of the brain that somehow sees through some other state of the brain. Either way, this sounds suspiciously like an added, inner perceiver (or homunculus) – a suggestion that is routinely dismissed in scientific and philosophical theories of conscious perception (a) on the grounds that there is no evidence for such a homunculus, and (b) on the grounds that even if there were, all the problems of perception would simply regress to the homunculus (so it has little explanatory value).

Tye does not deny that we do have experiences of colour, smell and so on;

so, if these are *not* properties or qualities of experience as such (as Tye insists), they must be properties of the world, as there is nothing else left of which they could be properties – a form of 'direct realism'. Although this view has some currency amongst direct-realist, physicalist philosophers for the reason that they need it to make their version of physicalism work as a theory of consciousness, it is routinely dismissed by scientists.

Why? As van der Heijden *et al.* (1997) note in their commentary on a similar position adopted by Block (1995), such a view simply does not take the natural sciences seriously.

> That there are colours in the external world is a naive idea, unsupported by physics, biology, or psychology. Ultimately, it presupposes that the representation (the perceived colour) is represented (as a perceived colour). A perceptual system performs its proper function when it *distinguishes* the relevant things in the outer world. For vision, the information about these relevant things is contained in the structure and composition of the light reflected by the outer world that enters the eyes. For distinguishing the relevant things in the external world, a unique and consistent representation of the corresponding distinctions in the light is all that is required.
>
> (van der Heijden *et al.*, 1997, p. 158)

However, according to Block (1997), van der Heijden *et al.* are

> wildly, unbelievably wrong. They say that we should give up the idea that a rose or anything else is ever red. The only redness, they say, is mental redness. But why not hold instead that roses are red . . . rejecting colors in the mind? Why not construe talk of red in the mind as a misleading way of expressing the fact that P-conscious states[6] represent the world as being red? And a representation of red need not itself be red (like the occurrences of the word 'red' here).
>
> (p. 165)

Of course Block is right that neural representations of red roses need not themselves be coloured. But few claim that they are. What *is* claimed is that once a normal, human visual system is activated in an appropriate way, a visual experience of a red colour will result, *irrespective* of whether that colour corresponds to a physical property out in the world. Penfield and Rassmussen (1950), for example, demonstrated that direct microelectrode stimulation of the visual system resulted in visual experiences, stimulation of the temporal lobe in auditory experiences, stimulation of the somatosensory system in tactile experiences, and so on. Given that such visual, auditory, and tactile qualia can exist *in the absence of* the external physical properties that they normally represent, it is not easy to see how they can be *reduced* to such physical properties.

Tye nevertheless tries to argue that qualia such as colour do reduce in this way, basing his case partly on how things appear to us, and partly on evidence that perceived qualia really do correspond quite well to properties measured by physics. As Tye (1995) notes,

> Certainly we do not experience colors as perceiver-relative. When, for example, a ripe tomato looks red to me, I experience redness all over the facing surface of the tomato. Each perceptible part of the surface looks red to me. None of these parts, in looking red look to me to have a perceiver-relative property. I do not experience any part of the surface as producing a certain sort of response in me or anyone else. On the contrary, I surely experience redness as intrinsic to it, just as I experience the shape of the surface as intrinsic to it.
>
> (p. 145)

Given that we experience such colours as not being perceiver-relative, he regards the view that they *are* perceiver-relative as 'just not credible' (p. 145).

Given that physicalism routinely denies the reliability of appearances as a guide to what experiences are really like,[7] Tye rests his case on shaky ground. There are many obvious counterexamples. The colours of surfaces may seem to be observer-independent, but the colours of after-images do not. For example, if one stares at a red spot for a few minutes, one will experience a green after-image that projects onto any surface that the eye fixates. The apparent size of the after-image also increases as the judged distance of the surface increases. So, if apparent, observer-dependence is to be the criterion of what is 'mental', after-images are surely mental. The observer-dependence of colour attached to surfaces in the world also becomes evident once the visual system no longer functions in a normal way. In cases of red–green colour blindness, for example, red can no longer be distinguished from green – and in cases of achromatopsia the entire world appears in shades of grey. More fundamentally, the reason that surfaces just appear coloured (without any conscious contribution on our part) is due to the fact that visual processing operates *preconsciously*. That is, once structured visual scenes appear in conscious experience, the binding of colour with shape, movement and so on has already taken place (Singer, 2007). Finally, it is important to note that variations in *how* things are experienced cannot be used to decide *whether or not* things are aspects of experience.

Tye's second main argument relies on evidence that in some circumstances the qualia–physical property correspondence may be relatively invariant. Colours remain fairly similar for example when viewed outdoors, indoors (illuminated by incandescent lamps), or through sunglasses. Tye asks,

> Why should this be? Surely the most straightforward answer is that the human visual system has, as one of its functions, to detect the real, objective colors of surfaces. Somehow, the visual system manages to

ascertain what colors objects really have, even though the only information immediately available to it concerns wavelengths.

(Tye, 1995, p. 146)

After a review of some of the relevant evidence, Tye concludes that,

Colors are objective, physical features of objects and surfaces. Our visual
systems have evolved to detect a range of these features, but those to
which we are particularly sensitive are indirectly dependent on facts about
us. In particular there are three types of receptor in the retina, each of
which responds to a particular waveband of light, and the spectral reflectances of surfaces at those wavebands (that is, their disposition to reflect
a certain percentage of incident light within each of the three bands)
together determine the colors we see. So the colors themselves may be
identified with ordered triples of spectral reflectances. An account of the
same general sort may be given for smells, tastes, sounds, and so on.

(Tye, 1995, p. 150)

Tye is right to point out that the way perceived colour maps onto given
patterns of light reflectance may be more invariant than is sometimes
thought. After all, it makes evolutionary sense for our perceptual systems
to pick out physical invariances when they occur and to translate these into
relatively invariant experiences. However, even a *perfect correlation* between
perceived qualia and events described by physics would not establish their
ontological identity. Causation, correlation, and ontological identity are
very different relationships, as we have seen in Chapter 3. Indeed, physical
descriptions as such do nothing to explain why one pattern of light reflectances should be perceived as 'red', and another as 'green'. Nor do physical
descriptions explain the rather arbitrary way the visual system translates electromagnetic energies with wavelengths ordered on a *ratio scale* into colour
categories ordered on a *nominal scale*. For example, wavelengths of 700 nm
are longer than wavelengths of 400 nm (by a ratio of 7:4). However, while red
is *different* from violet it is not *longer* than it. If our experiences simply
'mirrored' the world, we would expect the relationships between properties
described by physics to be more faithfully preserved in the way such relationships are experienced. To this one must add the many differences in the way
given physical properties can be experienced both within and between species
(see Chapter 8 for a review). As van der Heijden *et al.* (1997) note, the view
that perceived qualia exist in the world in a way that is free of such biological
influences simply does not take the natural sciences seriously.

Biological naturalism versus reflexive monism

Although biological naturalism (BN) and reflexive monism (RM) offer very
different ways of understanding the relationship of consciousness to the

brain and physical world, they share many background assumptions and explanatory features. Consequently, to sharpen the issues in contention, I will discuss them in tandem.

Unlike transparency theorists who view colour, spatial extension and so on as observer-independent properties of the *world*, BN and RM both accept that *experiences themselves* have qualities. These qualities usually *represent* aspects of the world in useful ways developed over the course of biological evolution, but are not necessarily qualities of the *world itself*. Rather, if we take seriously the many alternative representations of the world offered by physics and other sciences, our everyday experiences must only be rough and ready representations of what is really going on[8] – a standard view in science variously known as 'indirect realism' or 'critical realism', with a lineage dating back to Newton, Galileo, and Locke.

In short, both BN and RM adopt a form of *appearance–reality* distinction which accepts that the appearances of the world only indirectly represent (and sometimes misrepresent) the nature of the world itself. For the purposes of the following discussion I will call this 'the world appearance–reality distinction'.

In the form defended by Lehar (2003) and Revonsuo (1995, 2006), BN, like RM, also accepts that spatial extension is fundamental to visual experience, and that the three-dimensional phenomenal world *appears* to be outside the brain. However, BN is a form of physicalism. Consequently, unlike RM, Lehar and Revonsuo also insist that this three-dimensional phenomenal world can be nothing more than a brain state that must be inside the brain. To reconcile this difference between how the phenomenal world *appears* and how it *really is*, they suggest that the visual phenomenal world is in fact a form of virtual reality. One's experienced body with its surrounding experienced world is part of this virtual reality – and, despite appearances, this entire virtual world really only exists inside one's brain.

In claiming conscious experiences that seem to be outside the brain to be nothing more than brain states located in the brain, BN therefore goes on to adopt a *second* appearance–reality distinction applied not to the contrast between the appearances and nature of the *world*, but to the appearances and nature of the *appearances themselves*. Let us call this 'the appearance appearance–reality distinction'.

It is on this issue that BN and RM part company. RM accepts the world appearance–reality distinction, but rejects the appearance appearance–reality distinction. According to RM conscious appearances really are (roughly) how they seem to be.[9]

The appearance appearance–reality distinction is, of course, entirely congenial to those reductionist and eliminativist philosophers who wish to question the nature or even the existence of conscious appearances. However, BN (like RM) claims to be a *nonreductionist* theory, which raises the tricky issue of how one can both argue that conscious appearances are really very different from how they appear to be, *and* that one is being nonreductive about conscious appearances.

John Searle, for example, was one of the first to grapple with this issue. As he noted,

> Common sense tells us that our pains are located in physical space within our bodies, that for example, a pain in the foot is literally in the physical space of the foot. But we now know that is false. The brain forms a body image, and pains like all bodily sensations, are parts of the body image. The pain in the foot is literally in the physical space in the brain.
>
> (Searle, 1992, p. 63)

At the same time, Searle wishes to defend the reality of conscious appearances. Indeed, later in the same book, he concludes that, 'consciousness consists in the appearances themselves. *Where appearance is concerned we cannot make the appearance–reality distinction because the appearance is the reality*' (Searle, 1992, p. 121; my italics).

Lehar (2003, 2006) develops the same point. He does not deny that the phenomenal world *appears* to be out-there in space. On the contrary, 'The inescapable conclusion is that visual experience is spatially structured. To deny the spatial aspect of experience is to deny the single most characteristic property of that experience, or what makes visual experience what it is' (Lehar, 2006). Nor does he have any doubt that such experiences are real.[10] On the contrary,

> the eliminative hypothesis turns epistemology *on its head* and asks us to doubt the existence of the one and only thing that we can be absolutely certain to exist, and that is our own experience. . . . Even in the case of dreams and hallucinations, I can be absolutely certain that I am having an experience, and *I can be absolutely certain that that experience has the properties I experience it to have. To claim that conscious experience is any different than it is experienced to be, is a contradiction in terms!*
>
> (Lehar, 2006; my italics)

This illustrates the acute problem that apparent, external spatial location poses for biological naturalism: if biological naturalism is true, experiences are states of the brain, which are necessarily in the brain. However, if 'the appearance is the reality', and if 'I can be absolutely certain that experience has the properties that I experience it to have', then if the pain appears to be in the foot, it really is in the foot, and if the phenomenal world appears to be out there beyond the body surface then it really is out there beyond the body surface.[11] Either biological naturalism is true, or the appearance is the reality. One can't have both.

What science has discovered about the location of experiences

Let us weigh the alternatives. Has science discovered that (despite appearances) pains really are in the brain as Searle suggests? It is true of course that

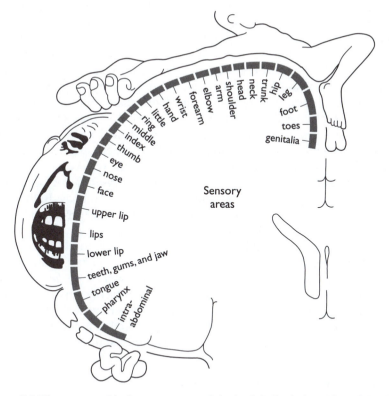

Figure 7.1 The topographical arrangement of the brain's 'body image' on the soma-
tosensory cortex From Penfield and Rassmussen THE CEREBRAL
CORTEX OF MAN. Copyright © 1950 Gale, a part of Cengage Learning,
Inc. Reproduced by permission. www.cengage.com/permissions.

science has discovered *representations* of the body in the brain, for example,
a tactile mapping of the body surface distributed over the somatosensory
cortex (SSC) – see Figure 7.1. The area of SSC devoted to different body
regions is determined by the number of tactile receptors in those regions. In
SSC, for example, the lips occupy more space than the torso. It has also been
found that regions of the body that are adjacent in phenomenal space may
not be adjacent in SSC. For example, we feel our face to be connected to our
head and neck, but in SSC, the tactile map of the face is spatially separated
from the map of the head and neck by maps of the fingers, arm and shoulder.
Thus, the topographical arrangement of the brain's 'body image' is very
different from the body as-perceived.

Given this, how does the 'body image' in the brain *relate* to the body as-
perceived? According to Searle, science has discovered tactile sensations in
the body to literally *be* in the brain. However, no scientist has observed actual
body sensations to be in the brain, and no scientist ever will, for the simple
reason that, viewed from an external observer's perspective, the body *as*

experienced by the subject cannot be observed; one cannot *directly* observe another person's experience. Science has nevertheless investigated the *relationship* of the body image (in SSC) to tactile experiences. Penfield and Rassmussen (1950), for example, exposed areas of cortex as they prepared to remove cortical lesions that were responsible for focal epilepsy. To avoid surgical damage to areas essential to normal functioning, they first explored the functions of these areas by lightly stimulating them with a microelectrode and noting the subject's consequent experiences. As expected, stimulation of the somatosensory cortex produced reports of tactile experiences. However, these feelings of numbness, tingling and so on were subjectively located *in different regions of the body, not in the brain.* In sum, science has discovered that neural excitation of somatosensory cortex *causes* tactile sensations, which are subjectively located in different regions of the body. Rather than being scientific evidence for BN, this effect is precisely the 'perceptual projection' that the reflexive model describes.[12]

In sum, science has found *no* evidence of tactile sensations in the brain. Direct microelectrode stimulation of somatosensory cortex *causes* tactile sensations that are *subjectively located in different regions of the body.* That is exactly what the reflexive model describes. But if tactile sensations cannot be found in the brain, viewed *either* from the experimenter's third-person perspective *or* from the subject's first-person perspective, how can one justify the BN claim that these are nothing more than brain states?

The scientific status of perceptual projection

Unlike BN, RM remains faithful to both the scientific evidence and everyday experience. However, it still has to explain how phenomenal objects and events get to be 'out-there' in the phenomenal world. The reflexive model of perception in Figure 6.3 shows, in schematic form, how reflexive monism works in human visual perception. As will be evident from the arrows at the top of Figure 6.3 leading from the subject's brain to the perceived cat, the reflexive model posits a form of *perceptual projection* that completes the reflexive process. However, it is important to be clear about what is meant by 'perceptual projection' in order to convey its precise role in the model. Crucially, perceptual projection refers to *an empirically observable effect* – for example, to the fact that this print seems to be out here on this page and not in your brain. In short, perceptual projection is an effect that requires explanation; perceptual projection is not itself an explanation. We know that preconscious processes within the brain, interacting with events in the external world, produce consciously experienced events, which may be subjectively located and extended in the phenomenal space beyond the brain, but we don't really know how this is done. We also know that this effect is subjective, psychological, and viewable only from a first-person perspective. Nothing physical is projected from the brain.[13]

How can one investigate this effect scientifically? There is convincing evidence that the experience of depth is, in part, a construction of the mind/ brain, for example in cases of depth perception arising from cues arranged on two-dimensional surfaces in stereoscopic pictures, 3D cinemas, holograms, and virtual realities – and I have reviewed scientific evidence for perceptual projection in various other sense modalities in Chapter 6, and in more detail in Velmans (1990a). One can also study underlying processes such as the perception of distance and location in space – standard topics in the psychology of perception that one can find in any introductory psychology textbook. One can study the cues, or information, in the light that contribute to depth perception (Hershenson, 1998); one can study the neural structures that support it (e.g. Goodale and Milner, 2004; Goodale, 2007); and one can study the various instances where depth perception breaks down (Robertson, 2004). One can also study how the judged metrics of phenomenal space relate to physical measurements of space (e.g. Lehar, 2003) and how both of these relate to neural state space. Given that neural state space is (by definition) in the brain, and that phenomenal state space is (according to RM) mostly outside the brain, an understanding of how neural state space relates to phenomenal state space would also provide a *topology* of perceptual projection.

In short, accepting 'perceptual projection' as a ubiquitous, but poorly understood perceptual effect does not place it beyond science. Rather, it draws attention to the need to investigate it more deeply. Accepting that the phenomenal world is *part of* conscious experience also encourages an expanded study of how perceptual processes in the brain combine to support such an integrated, three-dimensional experience (a point on which RM and BN fully agree). A fuller understanding of perceptual projection also offers a more unified understanding of a wide range of phenomena experienced to have both location and extension, including phenomena as diverse as lucid dreams, hallucinations, eidetic imagery, the creation of virtual realities, the construction of a body image, and the normal perception of events in three-dimensional space. Accepting perceptual projection as a normal effect (when perceptual processes form representations of events in the world) also makes it easier to understand what happens in artificial or pathological situations. For example, three-dimensional virtual worlds can be understood to arise from artificial stimulation of the same projective processes that create normal, phenomenal worlds. Hallucinations can be understood to result from mental models that erroneously project information that has an internal rather than an external origin (consequent on a breakdown of the usually reliable modelling of internal versus external events). And projection, transference and counter-transference of the kinds that arise in therapeutic interactions can be understood as similar internal/external confusions where information about one's own feelings, thoughts or past experiences are bound into one's projected experience of another human being. As the processes that achieve 'binding' and 'projection' operate *preconsciously*, one literally experiences others to manifest the traits and qualities which in reality are one's own.

There is however an important caveat. While such studies all contribute to our understanding of perceptual projection viewed as a psychological effect, they do not fully *explain* how proximal neural causes within the brain support visually experienced events that seem to be outside the brain. For this, we require an added explanatory model – and no adequate explanatory model currently exists.[14] As we have seen in Chapter 6, holograms and virtual realities provide tempting analogies. There are, for example, many tempting similarities between projection holograms and projected visual experiences. However, there is little convincing evidence (as yet) that there is literally a 'neural projection hologram' in the brain. While virtual realities do not completely explain perceptual projection either, they provide added ways of studying its operation, thereby further illuminating the processes underlying perceptual projection.

Critical differences between biological naturalism and reflexive monism

Given that both BN and RM accept that visual perception has spatial characteristics, and given that RM views perceptual projection as a *psychological effect*, it should be clear that scientific investigations of the spatial nature of perception and perceptual projection can inform *both* theories. Let us turn, therefore, to the critical issues that divide them.

Driven by its physicalist philosophy, BN is forced to argue that conscious appearances are really nothing more than brain states that are, by definition, in the brain. On this view not only are conscious appearances not what they appear to be, but they are also not where they appear to be. Given that defenders of BN also wish to claim that 'where appearance is concerned we cannot make the appearance–reality distinction because the appearance is the reality' (Searle) and that 'I can be absolutely certain that that experience has the properties I experience it to have' (Lehar), this produces a serious internal inconsistency, as we have seen. Either the appearance–reality distinction applies to conscious appearances, or it doesn't. One can't have both. The insistence that the apparent location of experiences has no bearing on their actual location also makes this aspect of BN unfalsifiable.

In contrast, I suggest that RM is an internally consistent, 'common-sense' position that closely follows the contours of everyday experience, which accepts that conscious appearances really are (roughly) how they seem. It is consistently realist about experiences without being naïvely realist about experiences. RM also fully accepts the findings of science regarding the evidence for perceptual projection and its causes, along with the evidence for other neural causes and correlates of conscious experience in the brain. In sum, RM understanding of conscious phenomenology conforms closely to *all* the first- and third-person evidence, giving it greater 'ecological validity' than BN which requires one to discount those aspects of the first-person evidence that relate to apparent spatial location and extension ('ecological validity' is a standard test of a psychological theory that assesses how well it applies to real-life situations). Perhaps, given the current physicalist zeitgeist, these differences between BN and RM are not decisive. However, these differences have some further, surprising consequences – and it is in terms of these consequences that the theories can be judged.

Is the entire phenomenal world inside the brain?

Like RM, BN (as developed by Lehar, Revonsuo and Gray) takes it as self-evident that the three-dimensional phenomenal world extends to one's perceptual horizons and the perceived dome of the sky. However, unlike RM, BN claims that this entire phenomenal world is just a virtual reality located inside the brain. This leads to a surprising conclusion. As Lehar (2003) rightly points out, if the phenomenal world is inside the brain, the real skull must be *outside* the phenomenal world (the former and the latter are logically equivalent).

Let me be clear. If one accepts that:

(a) The phenomenal world extends to the experienced horizon and dome of the sky.
(b) The phenomenal world is literally inside the brain.

It follows that:

(c) The real skull (as opposed to the phenomenal skull) is beyond the experienced horizon and dome of the sky.

While Lehar (2003), Revonsuo (2006) and Gray (2004) accept that this conclusion is entailed by (a) combined with (b), Lehar admits that this consequence of biological naturalism is 'incredible'. And, rather than abandoning the view that the phenomenal world is in the brain, Lehar, Revonsuo and Gray accept this consequence. As Searle once wryly commented (on a different theory), 'It is rather as if someone got the result 2+2=7 and said "Well maybe 2 plus 2 does equal 7." '[15]

Note that the difference between RM and BN on this issue also has very different consequences for how one thinks about the nature of the real skull and brain. RM adopts critical realism – the conventional view that, although our experiences do not give us a full representation of how things really are, they normally provide useful approximations. As a first approximation, brains are what one finds inside the skulls that we feel sitting on the tops of our necks, that one can find pictures of in neurophysiological textbooks, and that are occasionally to be seen pickled in jars. Although I accept that these 'skulls' and 'brains' are really phenomenal or experienced skulls and brains, these mental models are roughly accurate. Consequently, the location and extension of the phenomenal and real skull and brain closely correspond.

Lehar also accepts that phenomenal skulls and brains are mental models of real ones, but BN forces him to claim that the real skull is beyond the experienced dome of the sky. If so, our assumption that the real brain is more or less where it seems to be (inside the experienced skull) must be a massive, communally shared delusion! The alternative is that the BN understanding of conscious phenomenology is wrong. Not only is the notion of a skull beyond the experienced universe unfalsifiable (it would always be beyond any phenomena that one could actually experience), but it is also hard to know in what sense something that *surrounds* the experienced universe could, in any ordinary sense, be a 'skull' (it certainly isn't the skull that we can feel on top of our necks). Nor is it easy to grasp in what sense something that *contains* the experienced universe is a 'brain' (it certainly isn't the brain that one can perceive inside the skulls on top of our necks).[16]

In my view, this casts an entirely different light on the so-called 'scientific' status of biological naturalism and the so-called 'unscientific' claims of the reflexive model. Put your hands on your head. Is that the real skull that you feel, located more or less where it seems to be? If that makes sense, the reflexive model makes sense. Or is that just a phenomenal skull inside your brain, with your real skull beyond the dome of the phenomenal sky? If the latter seems absurd, biological naturalism is absurd. Choose for yourself.

The importance of this issue cannot be overemphasised, as an entire worldview depends on it. Following the best traditions of intellectual honesty, the 'incredible' consequence of biological naturalism (the 'skull beyond the sky') has been pointed out by one of its staunchest defenders (Lehar) and this consequence is accepted by other respected defenders of BN (Revonsuo and Gray). But no position can survive a *reductio ad absurdum*. So, if the 'skull beyond the sky' is absurd, some other assumption underlying BN needs to be changed – perhaps in the direction that RM suggests.

Is the phenomenal world really where it seems to be?

The reflexive model fits in with common sense. But, to understand how experienced objects and events might *really* be (roughly) where they are experienced to be, we have to look more closely at the way that phenomenal space relates to 'real' space. No one doubts that physical bodies can have real extension and location in space. Dualists and reductionists nevertheless find it hard to accept that experiences can have a real, as opposed to a 'seeming', location and extension. They do not doubt, for example, that a physical foot has a real location and extension in space, but, for them, a pain in the foot can't really be in the foot, as they are committed to the view that it is either nowhere or in the brain. For them, location in phenomenal space is not location in real space.

According to reflexive monism, however, this ignores the fact that, in everyday life, we take the phenomenal world to *be* the physical world. It also ignores the pivotal role of phenomenal space in forming our very understanding of space, and, with it, our understanding of location and extension in measured or 'real' space.

What we normally think of as the 'physical foot' for example is actually the *phenomenal foot* (the foot as seen, felt and so on). That does not stop us from pointing to it, measuring its location and extension and so on. If so, at least some phenomenal objects can be measured. While a pain in the foot might not be measurable with the same precision, few would doubt that we could specify its rough location and extension (and differentiate it for example from a pain in the back).

What we normally think of as 'space' also refers, at least in the initial instance, to the phenomenal space that we experience through which we appear to move. Our intuitive understanding of spatial location and extension, for example, derives in the first instance from the way objects and events appear to be arranged relative to each other in phenomenal space (closer, further, behind, in front, left, right, bigger, smaller and so on). We are also accustomed to making size and distance estimates based on such appearances. This print for example appears to be out here in front of my face, and THIS PRINT appears to be bigger than this print. However, we recognise that these ordinal judgements are only rough and ready ones, so when we wish to establish 'real' location, distance, size or some other spatial attribute, we usually resort to some form of *measurement* that quantifies the dimensions of interest using an arbitrary but agreed metric (feet, metres, etc.), relative to some agreed frame of reference (for example a Euclidian frame of reference with an agreed zero point from which measurement begins). The correspondence or lack of correspondence between phenomenal space and measured space is assessed in the same way, by comparing distance judgements with distance measurements in psychology experiments. For example, I can estimate the distance of this phenomenal print from my nose, but I can also place one end of a measuring tape on the tip of my nose (point zero) and the other end on this print to determine its real distance.

Such comparisons allow one to give a broad specification of how well phenomenal space corresponds to or maps onto measured space. There are of course alternative representations of space suggested by physics (four-dimensional space-time, the eleven-dimensional space of string theory, etc.) and non-Euclidian geometries (e.g. Riemann geometry). However, a comparison of phenomenal to measured (Euclidian) space is all that we need to decide whether a pain in my foot or this perceived print on this page is, or is not, really in my brain. According to the reflexive model, phenomenal space provides a natural representation, shaped by evolution, of the distance and location of objects viewed from the perspective of the embodied observer, which models real distance and location quite well at close distances, where accuracy is important for effective interaction with the world. My estimate that this page is about 0.5 metres from my nose, for example, is not far off. However, phenomenal appearances and our consequent distance judgements quickly lose accuracy as distances increase. For example, the dome of the night sky provides the outer boundary of the phenomenal world, but gives a completely misleading representation of distances in stellar space.

Note that, although we can use measuring instruments to correct unaided judgements of apparent distance, size and so on, measuring tapes and related instruments themselves appear to us as phenomenal objects, and *measurement operations appear to us as operations that we are carrying out on phenomenal objects in phenomenal space*. In short, even our understanding of 'real' or measured location is underpinned by our experience of phenomenal location. And crucially, whether I make distance judgements about this perceived print and judge it to be around 0.5 metres in front of my face, or measure it to find that it is only 0.42 metres, *does not alter the phenomenon that I am judging or measuring*. The distance of the print that I am judging or measuring is the distance of this perceived print out here on this visible page, and not the distance of some other (non-existent) 'experience of print' in my brain.

Observer-dependent versus observer-independent existence and location

There is however a complication. According to RM, in normal veridical perception, experienced phenomena are projected onto objects and events themselves. Consequently, in everyday life, we usually behave as naïve realists, and treat the objects and events we perceive as if they were the objects and events themselves. This produces a potential ambiguity that, in the analysis of phenomenal location and distance above, can lead to confusion – for example, a confusion of the *experienced* object (the 'intentional object') with the object itself. One might accept, for example, that when measuring or judging the distance of this print on this page, one can measure the distance of the *print itself* or *page itself*, while rejecting the suggestion that this amounts to measuring the distance of the *phenomenal* print or page – or that one is, in any sense, measuring the distance of an *experience*.

The *observer-dependence* of experienced phenomena adds a further complication. In so far as the appearance of phenomena depends on the perceptual-cognitive systems and supplementary observation arrangements employed by an observer, experienced phenomena have an observer-dependent existence. It follows that their phenomenal properties, including their phenomenal location and distance, are likewise observer-dependent. By contrast, according to the critical realism that RM adopts, things themselves can exist at a given location whether they are observed or not.[17] Consequently, the apparent location and distance of the phenomenal print are observer-dependent, while the print itself has a location that is, in a sense, observer-independent.[18] Given all this, in what sense can one claim the apparent location and distance of experienced phenomena to be 'real'?

Virtual realities provide a convenient way to sort out these relationships for the reason that in VR we can remove the tight linkage of projected, phenomenal objects onto objects themselves. At the time of writing, some of the most convincing virtual realities are provided by 3D cinemas that use polarised spectacles to direct different views of a visual scene to the left and right eyes, thereby employing retinal disparity to create the impression of virtual objects distributed in a three-dimensional virtual space. So-called '4D' cinemas which mix virtual with real effects are even more convincing. A virtual arrow flying past one's right ear can, for example, be accompanied by a real rush of air past one's ear (which is actually generated by the seat in front).

One can employ the same mix of real and virtual objects to measure the distance of virtual objects – thereby *literally measuring the distance of an experience*. For example, in the film *Bugs*, a virtual spider appears to come down a thread suspended from the ceiling of the theatre to spin a web positioned about a foot in front of one's face. To measure the distance of the virtual spider from one's face, all one has to do is to line up one end of a measuring tape with the spider and place the other end on the tip of one's nose. As the virtual spider has no solidity, this measurement can, of course, only be a rough one, as one has to judge the alignment of the end of the tape with that of the spider. But that does not make quantification of apparent distance impossible. Similar comparisons of visual appearances with reference-measuring objects are commonly made to quantify visual illusions in psychology experiments.

Note that although the distance of the virtual spider from one's face is real in the sense that it is (roughly) measurable, both the existence of the virtual spider and its location are observer-dependent. It is obvious, for example, if the entire audience closed their eyes for a moment, that no virtual spiders would exist (in any sense) during that moment. It is also important to note that the location of each virtual spider, perceived by each member of the audience, is observer-relative to that member of the audience. Each virtual spider will appear about a foot in front of each observer's face, irrespective of how the observers are positioned relative to each other, and the apparent distance of the virtual spider from a given observer will be affected in only a minor way if that observer moves around the room.

A virtual reality thought experiment

Suppose now that we replace the virtual spider with a real spider that spins its web about a foot in front of one's face, and, for the purpose of this thought experiment, suppose that the virtual spider and real spider are visually identical. In this situation, the initiating causes of the observer's perceptual processing are different. In the virtual case, processing was based on information arriving at the visual system generated by the cinema screen combined with the polarised spectacles, while in this case it is initiated by the pattern of light reflectances from the surface of the spider itself. What is perceived is nevertheless the same – and, as before, one can line up one end of a measuring tape with the real spider and place the other end on the tip of one's nose to measure its distance from one's face.

While the existence of the spider in this instance is observer-independent in the sense that it will continue to exist and spin its web whether it is observed

or not, its *appearance* remains observer-dependent. Indeed there is no difference in this situation between the appearance of the real spider and that of
the virtual spider. Likewise, although the real spider can be said to have an
observer-independent location relative to other objects in the world (it has
a location relative to other objects whether it is observed or not),[19] each
observation of its location can only be based on where it is *seen* to be, and is
likewise observer-dependent. Indeed, if one uses the measuring tape in the
way described above, the very same measurement operations can be applied,
with the same result, to the real spider and the virtual spider.

And here's the point: the virtual reality thought experiment demonstrates
that the very same measurement operations can be applied to real and virtual
objects to determine their location – in spite of the fact that in the case of a
virtual object, one is unambiguously measuring the location of an *experience*.
It goes without saying that the existence and properties of such experiences
are observer-dependent, as are the phenomenal properties of objects themselves. Nevertheless, in cases of veridical perception we habitually base our
initial judgements about the nature of objects themselves on their observed
phenomenal properties, and consequently judge their measured location
(based on appearances) to be an observer-independent property of the object
itself. Nor do we have any doubts that objects themselves are really out-there
beyond the body surface.

Given this, are phenomenal objects *also* really out-there beyond the body
surface? It depends on what one means by 'really'. If one means, 'do they
have an observer-independent existence out-there in the world?', then of
course they don't. But, if one means that they have a *measurable* distance and
location out there in the world, then they really do. Is there any empirical
evidence to the contrary? No. Such phenomenal objects do not appear to be,
and certainly can't be measured to be, located in the brain.[20]

Is the phenomenal world physical or psychological?

Let us turn, finally, to the ontology of the phenomenal world (in RM), which
has also, at times, been puzzling to its critics. For example, in a recent online
commentary on RM, Voerman (2003) asks,

> If there really is a phenomenal cat 'out there', on the table, in *addition to*
> the noumenal cat, then what kind of material is there on my table out
> of which the phenomenal cat is composed, and *how did it get there? Of*
> course, Velmans would not give a straight answer to this question,
> because he would not want to agree that there is *material* 'out there' in
> addition to the material out of which the noumenal table and cat are
> composed. For that would make him a substance dualist, and he wants
> to be a monist.

And Van de Laar (2003)[21] is puzzled by a similar issue,

Should we take projection seriously and interpret Velmans as saying that the brain is in fact projecting 'stuff' onto the things themselves? This would amount to a world that contains the individual things themselves and further is smeared all over by projected phenomenal experiences belonging to all kinds of different creatures like for example Homo sapiens.[22]

Scientific investigations of how experiences get to be 'out-there' (the investigation of mechanisms underlying perceptual projection) have already been discussed above. However, the question of *what it is* that gets projected is a further, legitimate question. Conventionally, we think of the manifest universe as consisting of autonomously existing material objects that are observer-independent along with our conscious experiences of those objects that are observer-dependent. How does that address the questions raised by Voerman and Van de Laar above? The situation is shown in microcosm in Figure 6.3, where there is just one material cat out there in the world – the 'noumenal' cat which exists whether the subject perceives it or not. When the subject or the external observer looks at the noumenal cat, it is a phenomenal cat that they see. So we have a cat itself (the noumenal cat) whose existence and nature are observer-independent, and a seen (phenomenal) cat that *represents* the noumenal cat, whose existence and nature are observer-dependent. In everyday life we usually think of the cat we see as a 'physical cat' and, for the purposes of everyday life, we usually treat it as being the cat itself rather than a representation of the cat itself. But this does not double the number of *actual* cats, nor does it 'smear' any additional phenomenal cats all over the noumenal cat. Rather, the one, noumenal cat has as many numerically distinct appearances as there are views of it by individual observers.

Although it would be misleading to think of the phenomenal cat as composed of 'physical material', it does have an ontology, which can initially be described in terms of its properties – and in the case of phenomenal cats, its properties are its *experienced* properties. It looks fat and furry, it feels sleek, warm and solid, it is seen to have a particular location and extension in phenomenal space and so on. Note again that in everyday life we habitually *treat* properties such as fat, furry, sleek, warm, solid, seen location and extension as 'physical' properties of the cat itself – indeed, according to physicalist philosophers such as Tye and Block, such properties *really are* properties of the cat itself (see critique of transparency theory above). However, according to RM these are only biologically evolved *representations* of the cat itself that physics would describe in different ways. Its warmth, for example, might be described in terms of the Brownian motion of its surface molecules, its solidity in terms of its internal molecular bindings, its apparent location and extension in terms of its measured location and extension relative to some reference frame, and so on. As before, each phenomenal property is 'psychological' in the sense that it is an experienced property produced by preconscious interaction of the cat itself with the observer's perceptual-cognitive systems. But, conventionally, we also treat it as 'physical' for the reason that it represents something about the actual (noumenal) cat that physics would describe in a related, but often very different way.[23]

How the phenomenal world relates to processing in the mind/brain

Given that the phenomenal cat is in fact a psychological (mental) representation (of something that exists out there in the world), we can further clarify its ontology by examining its relation to the processes that support it within the mind/brain. Here RM tells a conventional story. It assumes that each phenomenal feature of the cat has a distinct neural correlate that encodes the same information (about the cat itself). From the perspective of an external observer, this correlate will appear as a form of neural encoding (in neural state space), while from the subject's perspective the same information (about the cat itself) appears in the form of a phenomenal cat located and extended in phenomenal space. Consequently, representations in the mind/brain have two (mental and physical) aspects, whose apparent form is dependent on the perspective from which they are viewed.[24]

Given its intimate links to the brain, does it follow that the phenomenal world is *nothing more than a state of the brain*, as biological naturalism and other forms of physicalism suggest? No. Within RM the brain is simply what the human mind looks like when it is viewed from an external (third-person) perspective, and neither the observations of external observers nor those of subjects have a privileged status. Suppose, for example, that I ask you to look at a cat out in the world while I examine the physical correlates of what you see in your brain (in the way shown in Figure 6.3). In terms of their *phenomenology*, my observations of your brain states are just my visual experiences of your brain states. While I examine your brain I simply report what I see (whether or not I am aided by sophisticated equipment), and while you are looking at the cat you simply report what you see. In this situation, we both experience something out in the world that we would describe as 'physical'. You have a visual experience of a cat, located beyond your body, out in the world. I have a visual experience of the physical correlates of your experience (the cat that you see) beyond my body, in your brain.

What you see is a phenomenal cat – a visual representation containing information about the shape, size, location, colour and texture of an entity that currently exists out in the world beyond your body surface. What I see is the same information encoded in the physical correlates of what you experience in your brain. That is, the information structure of what you and I observe is identical, but it is displayed or 'formatted' in very different ways. From your point of view, the only information you have (about the entity in the world) is the phenomenal cat you experience. From my point of view, the only information you have (about the entity in the world) is the information I can see encoded in your brain. The way your information (about the entity in the world) is displayed appears to be very different to you and me for the reason that the 'observational arrangements' by which we access that information are entirely different. From my external, third-person perspective I can only access the information encoded in your neural correlates by means of my visual or other exteroceptive systems, aided by appropriate equipment. Because you *embody* the information encoded in your neural correlates and it is already at the interface of your consciousness and brain, it displays 'naturally' in the form of the cat that you experience.[25]

You experience a cat, rather than your neural encodings of the cat, for the reason that it is the information *about the world* (encoded in your neural correlates) that is manifest in your experience rather than the embodying format or the physical attributes of the neural states themselves.[26] I observe/experience the neural encodings of the cat in your brain (rather than the cat) for the simple reason that my visual attention is focused on your brain, not the cat. If I wanted to experience what you experience, I would have to shift my attention (and gaze) away from your brain to the cat.[27]

From my 'external observer's perspective', can I assume that what you experience is really nothing more than the physical correlates that I can observe? From my external perspective, do I know what is going on in your mind/brain/consciousness better than you do? Not really. I know something about your mental states that you do not know (their physical embodiment). But you know something about them that I do not know (their manifestation in experience). Such first- and third-person accounts of mind are *complementary and mutually irreducible*. We need your first-person story and my third-person story for a complete account of what is going on.

The suggestion that the mind has physical and phenomenal aspects that are only knowable from respectively third- and first-person perspectives combines the ontological dual-aspect monism of RM with a form of *epistemological dualism*. The suggestion that these third- and first-person ways of knowing the mind are complementary and mutually irreducible adds a further *psychological complementarity* principle. We return to all these issues in Part III of this book.[28]

Notes

1 For McGinn (1995) this emergence of something non-spatial from something spatial reveals a deep mystery about the nature of space which may be beyond our powers of comprehension (p. 163). I have argued the opposite: as noted in Chapter 6, the operation of perceptual projection has been and is a rich topic for scientific research that is entirely within our powers of comprehension (even if we don't as yet know exactly what is going on).

2 Note that various Eastern philosophies refer to a state of 'pure' content-less consciousness (accessible via meditative techniques) that forms a ground state within which the play of phenomenal experiences takes place. However this should not be confused with Marcel's suggestion that a given experience such as a pain in the finger is (as a vehicle) 'in your head'. Within Eastern philosophies, states of pure consciousness are not thought to have attributes such as 'location in the head'. We return to this issue in Chapter 13, where I explore the possibility that the

'nature of mind' is, in a deeper sense, the 'carrier' of conscious experience – and that the nature of mind can only be inferred from the nature of *both* conscious experiences and their neural correlates, encompassing them both.

3 I have borrowed Immanuel Kant's term, the 'thing itself', but unlike Kant I will argue that the thing itself is knowable, albeit imperfectly – see Chapter 8.

4 The current intellectual landscape is however somewhat more complicated. 'Biological naturalism' could be thought of as a broad heading to describe all theories that view conscious experiences as brain states (see, for example, Searle, 2007), but this term is used here in the narrower sense adopted by Lehar (2003) to describe a group of physicalist theories that deal specifically with the spatial nature of the phenomenal world (see also Revonsuo, 2006, and Gray, 2004). These theories are particularly interesting in that, like reflexive monism, they fully accept the rich phenomenology of conscious experience while nevertheless claiming to be *nonreductive* forms of physicalism. As will become apparent later in this book, 'reflexive monism' is a broad position with many consequences (alongside 'dualism', 'physicalism' and so on); however, on the issue under discussion it can be viewed as a form of 'projectivism' (see, for example, Boghossian and Velleman, 1989; Wright 2003); it could also be classified as a form of 'radical externalism' (a term recently introduced by Honderich, 2006). Recent 'enactive' theories of the mind can also be said to be 'externalist'. However, such theories deal largely with the distributed nature of the causes of perception, rather than the external nature of the resulting conscious phenomenology, and so I do not consider them in detail here (but see discussion in Velmans, 2007a).

5 Notice that Metzinger (2003) also uses the term 'transparency' to describe the fact that we are not aware of inner representations as being representations; rather we seem to 'look through' our inner representations directly onto the world (see Chapter 5). However, in Metzinger's analysis this is what *makes* the inner representations conscious – the representations are not literally transparent media that give access to physical properties that exist in the world as such. In adopting this latter view, Tye's position resembles naïve realism – which, in its older, classical version, amounts to the view that we 'look through the windows of our own eyes to see the world as it really is'.

6 P-conscious states are states of phenomenal consciousness, contrasted in Block's analysis with A-conscious states, which provide information access.

7 For example, physicalism routinely claims that conscious qualia, *contra* appearances, are just states of the brain.

8 To be more precise, while human perceptual representations are normally useful, they are species-specific, approximate, and incomplete. Being representations, they can also, at times, be misrepresentations of what is really going on (in cases of misperception, illusion, hallucination and so on). A detailed analysis of how the dimensions of experience relate to the dimensions of the physical world as measured by physical instruments is given in Chapter 8.

9 In rejecting the appearance appearance–reality distinction, RM is committed to a form of realism about appearances, but not to naïve realism about appearances – and I have added the qualifier 'roughly' to take account of the fact that our descriptions and understanding of our own phenomenology are revisable depending on many factors: how we attend to that phenomenology, what descriptive systems or measurement systems are available, how well experienced distance and location correspond to measured distance and location, and so on. Consequently our beliefs about our conscious experiences are revisable, but they are not, under normal circumstances, *completely wrong*. We might for example erroneously believe that we would *always* notice major changes in the areas of the visual field to which we attend, although experiments on change blindness show this to be false. On the other hand, we are not usually wrong about our ability to *see* (unless

we suffer from anosagnosia) or, in ordinary circumstances, about *what* we can see, hear, feel, and so on (unless there is clear evidence to the contrary). There are extensive areas of psychological research (perception, attention, psychophysics, etc.) devoted to the study of such issues, and RM adopts a form of *critical phenomenology* that is typical in such research – see discussion in Chapter 9 and in Velmans, 2007c).

10 Lehar would claim to be a 'nonreductive physicalist', but is nevertheless reductive in the sense that he insists that, *contra* appearances, conscious experiences are nothing more than brain states. However he is not an eliminativist for the reason that he believes that these conscious brain states are real.

11 Strictly speaking, of course, what we normally think of as 'the foot' is actually the experienced (phenomenal) foot, and what we think of as 'the body surface' is, likewise, the experienced (phenomenal) body surface. One might argue therefore that relations such as a pain being 'in' a foot, or the external world being 'beyond' the body surface, only obtain *within* this world of appearances. I will return to this issue in the discussion of how phenomenal space relates to physical space below.

12 Given that direct cortical somatosensory stimulation bypasses normal sensory input channels, this projective effect is a surprising empirical finding, and consequently a valid empirical test of BN versus RM on this point. If the apparent external location of many experiences is a kind of illusion or hallucination as BN suggests (see later discussion), it might be possible, under suitable experimental conditions, to experience such phenomena as they really are and the findings could have turned out differently. For example, in the study of 'inside-the-head-locatedness' discussed in Chapter 6, Laws (1972) found that he could manipulate whether sounds presented through earphones were experienced to be inside the head or out in the world, by switching in an electrical equalising circuit that reproduced the spectral differences produced in external auditory stimuli by the pinnae of the ears. Being an empirically based theory, RM fully accepts that the location of the experienced sound in such experiments can be either 'inside the head' or 'out in the world', depending on the state of the headphones and how the acoustic cues that they provide are interpreted by the auditory system. By contrast, BN either has to accept that some experiences are outside the brain, which is inconsistent with them being nothing more than brain states, or it has to insist that experienced sounds (and all other experienced phenomena) are really in the brain *whatever the phenomenal evidence* – making this aspect of BN unfalsifiable.

13 As noted in Chapter 6, I am *not* suggesting that there are rays emitted from the eyes that light up the world. However, contrary to what Van de Laar (2003) suggests, the fact that perceptual projection is not 'physical' in this sense does not make it just 'metaphorical', or, as Lehar (2003, 2006) suggests, 'ghostly' or 'spiritual'. Psychological effects are real and investigable by science. A more detailed discussion of this confused understanding of RM in Lehar and Van de Laar is given in Velmans (2008a).

14 Transparency theory is not viable as an explanatory model for the reasons discussed above, while biological naturalism simply tries to explain the effect away by denying that perceptual projection is a real effect. But viewing perceptual projection as an illusion does nothing to explain how that illusion comes about. If the entire phenomenal world (including both one's experienced skull and its visually experienced surround) is part of a virtual reality that is literally located inside the real skull and brain, then experiences might not actually be outside the brain. However, that does not alter the way that they *seem* to be – and this manoeuvre gets one no closer to explaining why things seem to be the way that they do. While BN rightly makes the point that what we normally think of as the 'skull' is just a

virtual skull (a skull as experienced), not to be confused with the real one, the virtual external world still appears to be outside the virtual skull. So within BN the problem of out-thereness simply regresses to relationships *within* the virtual model (to relationships between the virtual skull and virtual surrounding world, supposedly located inside the brain).

The absence of an adequate explanatory model for how neural causes and correlates inside the brain support conscious experiences outside the brain does not rule out the possibility of such a model any more than the current absence of adequate models rules out their possibility in other areas of science. Nor is a spatial separation of neural cause from experienced effect an impediment to theory development. The existence of non-local connectedness is not peculiar to brain states and projected experiences. Physics for example accepts that there are various forms of non-local causation, such as gravity, non-locality in quantum mechanics, and electromagnetism (for example in the way electrical current in a wire produces a magnetic field outside the wire).

15 Searle's comment was actually made in a *New York Times* book review of Chalmers (1996) regarding the consequences of his view that anything that functions is conscious solely by virtue of the fact that it functions (see Chapter 14). Given this 'incredible' consequence of BN, it seems appropriate to apply the same comment to a position that Searle might wish to defend himself (Searle (2007) is undoubtedly a 'biological naturalist' but I only suggest that he *might* want to defend this position as, at the time of writing, he has not, to my knowledge, directly addressed this consequence of BN).

16 Readers with a particular interest in this debate should refer to the more detailed treatment of it given in Velmans (2008a). Note that RM also postulates a global 'envelope' that contains the experienced universe. However, as will become apparent in Part III of this book, within RM, reflexive observer–observed interactions and their consequent experiences all take place within the psychophysical *universe itself*, rather than in some 'real skull' beyond the dome of the experienced sky.

17 I refer here only to macroscopic things such as tables, chairs and cats that can be adequately described (for most purposes) by classical physics, and, for the purposes of this discussion, I will ignore quantum mechanical events where the observer independence of observed events is much in dispute.

18 As before, we are concerned here only with macroscopic nearby objects (ignoring both quantum mechanics and relativistic effects). Actual location can of course only be assigned within some standardised measurement system that has an agreed zero point from which measurement begins. So, in this sense, an assigned location cannot be observer-independent even for these objects. However, this is tangential to the issue under discussion. What matters here is that we can treat the location of *objects themselves* as observer-independent in the sense that they *have* a location whether they are being observed at any given moment or not.

19 While both the apparent and actual distance of the spider from the observer will change if the observer moves away from or towards the spider, its location in relation to other immobile objects in the room will remain the same.

20 Note that transparency theorists who argue that phenomenal properties are just physical properties of objects themselves are thereby committed to the view that such properties have both an observer-independent existence and a real location out-there in the world. So, while they disagree with RM about the ontology of phenomenal properties, they agree that such properties have a genuine location out-there in the world that can be determined by measurement. However, virtual objects that are visually indistinguishable from real ones are a serious problem for this position, as their phenomenal properties appear to exist in spite of the fact that the virtual objects are nothing more than appearances. Conversely, biological naturalism, like RM, accepts that phenomenal properties are observer-dependent,

but rejects measured location of phenomenal objects as a criterion of their 'real' location as this would require BN to abandon the doctrine that phenomenal objects are really in the brain. As noted above, this doctrine has the absurd consequence that the real skull is beyond all the objects we could ever see (the skull beyond the visible universe), and, rather than abandoning their philosophical position, biological naturalists accept this consequence. However, the rejection of measured location as a criterion of actual location produces a further, serious problem for BN. Given that the normal method of determining location is to *measure* it, on what grounds, other than doctrinal ones, can one justify the rejection of measurement as a way of determining the locations of phenomenal objects, particularly where these correspond to the locations of the objects themselves?

21 Voerman (2003) and Van de Laar (2003, 2007) have both published detailed online commentaries on RM which do not appear to have been published in peer-reviewed journals. Unfortunately these both contain many confusions about RM that I cannot address here as they would take us too far afield. However, some of the questions they raise are good ones, and exemplify common confusions that I am pleased to have the opportunity to address.

22 Voerman (2003) also writes, 'Sometimes, Velmans says that the cat experience is out there, but that this is "phenomenally speaking". What could that mean? If it means that the experience is *not* there *noumenally speaking*, then where is it, noumenally speaking?' In order not to lose sight of the issue under discussion (is the phenomenal cat in the brain or out there where it seems to be?), and given that physics offers a number of competing models for what Voerman refers to as 'noumenal space', I have restricted my analysis to how phenomenal space relates to measured Euclidian space in the ways outlined above. If a phenomenon can be measured to be at a given location, we can for these purposes regard that as its 'real' location.

23 That perceived phenomena can be thought of as either 'physical' or 'psychological' *depending on the relationships under consideration* has been recognised for well over 100 years – for example in the work of neutral monists such as Mach, James, and Russell, as we have seen in Chapter 3.

24 This is a form of dual-aspect monism, expressed in this instance as a dual-aspect theory of information. Note too that this dual-aspect nature of mind provides a way of making sense of James's observation 'that what is evidently one reality should be in two places at once, both in outer space and in a person's mind'. The external phenomenal world appears to exist in what we normally think of as the external space surrounding our bodies, but it is nevertheless a mental representation (of the world itself) and it is, in this sense, 'in the mind'. According to dual-aspect monism, the *information* displayed in such spatially extended phenomenal representations is also encoded in the brain (the mind as it appears when viewed from the outside) – providing another sense in which the same reality seems to be in two places at once. We will have more to say about the dual-aspect nature of mind in Chapter 13.

25 RM assumes that it is simply a 'natural' empirical fact about the world that certain physical events in the brain (the correlates of consciousness) are accompanied by experiences. In short, this relationship follows some natural law, however mysterious this presently seems. Studies of perceptual projection (see above) and, more generally, the entire field of neuropsychology with its search for the neural correlates of consciousness (the NCC) are directly or indirectly devoted to discovering such natural laws.

26 This is a rather simpler version of 'transparency theory' that makes no reductive assumptions about the qualia of experience being nothing more than physical properties (either in the world or in the brain).

27 See the thought experiment on 'Changing Places' and the extensive discussion of subjectivity, intersubjectivity and objectivity in Chapter 9.
28 An introduction to 'psychological complementarity' is also given in Velmans, 1991a, section 9.3; Velmans, 1991b, sections 8 and 9; and Velmans, 1993b, 1996c. An extensive discussion of how this can be applied to understanding the causal interactions of consciousness and brain is given in Chapter 13 and in Velmans, 2003a.

8 Experienced worlds, the world described by physics, and the thing itself

According to Descartes, only the physical world (*res extensa*) has spatial extension. The contents of consciousness are composed of a nonmaterial thinking stuff (*res cogitans*) which has no location or extension in space. But, if the analysis presented in Chapter 6 is correct, this misdescribes the phenomenology of everyday conscious experiences. Whereas thoughts and some feelings and images may have qualia of the kind that Descartes describes, most experienced events do not. Tactile sensations, pains, and kinaesthetic sensations generally have a location and extension within the body or on the body surface. The sounds we hear and the many objects we see are generally experienced to be out in three-dimensional space. Taken together, our experiences comprise entire three-dimensional, phenomenal worlds, produced by a reflexive interaction of represented events (external or internal to our bodies) with our own perceptual and cognitive processes. Looked at in this way, what we normally think of as being the 'physical world' is *part of* what we experience. It is not *apart from* it. And there is no mysterious, *additional* experience *of* the world 'in the mind or brain'. If so, physical objects as-perceived are *not* quite distinct from our percepts *of* those objects, contrary to common belief.

Chapter 7 investigated some immediate questions that arise from looking at conscious phenomenology in this reflexive way. Given that the phenomenal world is a mental model of external, body and inner events, is it really 'out-there' where it seems to be? If so, how does it get out there, given that its proximal neural causes and correlates are in the brain? And what is the *relationship* of this phenomenal world to the processes that support it in the mind/brain? To complete our introduction to the reflexive model we now need to consider how the phenomenal world relates to other available models of the world and to the world itself (or *thing itself*). Once again, we can ask three obvious questions:

> **Question 1**: Even if one accepts that what we commonly refer to as the 'physical world' is just the world we experience, this clearly remains very different from the world described by modern physics (the world of quantum mechanics, relativity theory, grand unified theory and so

on). So how does the phenomenal, 'physical world' relate to the world described by physics?

Question 2: It is commonly taken for granted that the contents of consciousness are observer-dependent, while physical objects as-perceived are observer-independent (Box 6.1, claim 5). However, if physical objects as-perceived are actually aspects of what we experience, they *cannot* be observer-independent (see for example the discussion of observer-dependent versus observer-independent existence and location in Chapter 7). On first glance, this might seem to commit us to Berkelian Idealism. If the perceived physical world is part of what we experience, then if we don't experience it, it doesn't exist. Yet, this conflicts with our natural intuitions, bolstered by a wealth of circumstantial evidence, that the external physical world has a 'real' existence that is independent of our experience. Material objects, for example, seem far more solid and substantial than the 'inner' events that we normally think of as exemplifying experiences, such as thoughts, images, and dreams. So, what are the consequences of the model for the *realism versus idealism* debate?

Question 3: In dualist and reductionist models of the world it is easy to see what experiences of the external world are supposed to represent: percepts *of* objects 'in the mind or brain' represent the objects we see out in the world. But if experiences *of* objects and objects *as-perceived* are phenomenologically identical, then what could experiences *of* objects *represent*? One may ask the same question about the experienced body and about 'inner' experiences.

I will address each of these questions in turn.

Question 1: How perceived physical worlds relate to the world described by physics

The 'experiential materials' from which the everyday physical world is constructed are drawn from a very limited number of sources – five, to be precise. The world we perceive consists of what we see, what we hear, what we touch, what we taste and what we smell. Each modality of experience is consequent on the activation of specific neuronal pathways in the peripheral and central nervous systems. Activation of the optic nerve and visual system is experienced as 'light' whether they are stimulated by implanted microelectrodes, by excessive rubbing of the eyes or by impacting photons triggering molecular changes in the photo-pigments of retinal cells. Likewise activation of the auditory nerve and its projection areas is experienced as 'sound' whether produced by direct electrical stimulation, or normally, by air disturbances causing the bending of hair receptors in the inner ear. Sensory systems are committed to specific modalities of experience. It is not possible to produce experiences of 'light' by stimulating the auditory nerve or experiences of 'sound' by stimulating the optic nerve. Nor can 'touch' fibres produce some other sensation such as 'taste' or 'smell'.[1]

From another point of view, afferent neurons are the living strands that connect our brains to the surrounding world. The sense organs at their tips convert a small selection of the energies surrounding our bodies into electro-chemical changes that activate the neurons to which they attach. Photo-sensors in the eye respond to electromagnetic energies radiated, reflected and refracted by entities in the external world. Mechanoreceptors in the inner ear respond to minute disturbances produced by such entities in the surrounding air. Sensors in the skin monitor conditions at the interface of our bodies and the environment, responding to mechanical deformations and thermal changes on the skin surface. Receptors in the nasal cavity and those embed-ded in the tongue monitor aspects of the chemistry of substances we inhale and ingest. In so doing, these sense organs decide which events are to be experienced as light, which as sound, which as touch and so on – and the systems to which they attach decide the manner in which detected energies are translated into different forms of experience. For our purposes we do not need to review the extensive literature on how this is done.[2] A few, basic exam-ples will suffice to illustrate how the world described by physics is translated, by our biology, into a world as-experienced.

Translating electromagnetic energy into experienced light

Photoreceptive cells in the eye have extraordinary sensitivity. As the neuro-psychologist Richard Gregory notes,

> We cannot with the unaided eye see individual quanta of light, but the receptors in the retina are so sensitive that they can be stimulated by a single quantum, though several (five to eight) are required to give the experience of a flash of light. The individual receptors of the retina are as sensitive as it is possible for any light detector to be, since a quantum is the smallest amount of radiant energy which can exist. It is rather sad that the transparent media of the eye do not quite match this develop-ment of absolute perfection. Only about ten per cent of the light reaching the eye gets to the receptors, the rest being lost by absorption and scatter-ing within the eye before the retina is reached. In spite of this loss, it would be possible under ideal conditions to see a single candle placed seventeen miles away.
>
> (Gregory, 1966, p. 19)

The range of stimulus intensities that the eye can handle is also impressively wide. The largest stimulus is estimated to be around 10,000,000,000 times the size of the smallest detectable stimulus. On the other hand, the range of electromagnetic frequencies that our eyes are able to detect is very limited. Visible light occupies only a very small bandwidth of the electromagnetic spectrum, from around 730 nanometers (seen as red) to around 370 nano-meters (seen as violet). Beyond the sensitivity of our eyes are radio waves, radar waves, microwaves, infrared, ultra-violet, X-rays and Gamma rays. As Gregory puts it, 'Looked at in this way, we are almost blind' (ibid., p. 18).

Energies that are detected are translated into events as-experienced in ways that bear only a remote resemblance to the simple descriptions of those energies given by physics. For example, as a first approximation, the relation between the intensity of a white light and its perceived brightness is described by a simple power function (Stevens, 1966). However, brightness also depends on frequency. Colours in the middle of the visible spectrum appear brighter than those at the ends. A hundred-watt light bulb painted yellow, for example, appears brighter than one painted blue or red. The relative brightness of different colours also varies from night to day. In daylight, when the eye is light-adapted, reds appear brighter than blues. When the eye is dark-adapted, blues appear brighter than reds (the 'Purkinje shift'). Perceived brightness also varies with the intensity of the light in the surrounding area. The darker the surrounding area, the brighter the inner area appears ('brightness contrast').

Turning mechanical energy into experienced sound

Like the eye, the ear has extraordinary sensitivity. The smallest disturbance in the air that can be heard as a sound produces a pressure at the eardrum of around 0.0002 dynes/cm^2 (at a frequency of 1 kHz). The movement this produces in the eardrum is minute – around the diameter of a hydrogen atom (Green, 1976). The range of stimulus intensities that the ear can handle is even more impressive than the eye. The largest stimulus (around 140 decibels at the threshold of pain) is about 100,000,000,000,000 times greater than the smallest detectable stimulus. As with the eye, the range of frequencies that the ear can detect is very limited. The signals produced by animals and insects for the purposes of communication and navigation, for example, vary in frequency from around 200 Hz to 200,000 Hz, but our ears are tuned to detect only those in the lower frequencies – from around 200 Hz to 20,000 Hz.

Even for simple dimensions of experience such as the loudness of a sound, the mapping of events as experienced onto the same events as described by physics is a complex one. As with light, the mapping of intensity of sound (at a given frequency) into perceived loudness follows a power function. For example, to double judged loudness one has to increase sound intensity by a factor of ten (by around 10 decibels). A common way of putting this is that it takes ten violins to sound twice as loud as one violin. Perceived loudness of a pure tone of a given intensity also varies with frequency, increasing in loudness as frequency increases from 1 kHz to 4 kHz, and decreasing in loudness from 4 kHz to 10 kHz.

Colour and pitch

Changes in the frequency of electromagnetic waves are translated by the visual system into changes in colour, and changes in the frequency of pressure waves in the air are translated into changes in pitch. The differences between seen colour and heard pitch are obvious. But there are also subtler differences in the way sensory and perceptual systems translate such frequency changes into dimensions of experience. As the frequency of pressure variation at the eardrum increases, the perceived pitch also tends to increase and these perceived changes can be ranked on an ordinal scale that preserves order relations (lower versus higher pitch). By contrast, if the frequency of the electromagnetic waves detected by the eye increases, the perceived colour changes from deep red, through orange, yellow, green and blue to violet. But it does not make sense to speak of violet being a 'higher' colour than deep red. Rather, the colour spectrum has the properties of a nominal scale, where perceived changes can be categorised and named, but not ranked (into lower versus higher).

It is also worth noting that *detectable* changes in the loudness and pitch of sound or the brightness and colour of light are complex transforms of the measurable changes in their intensity and frequency. For the dimensions of loudness and brightness, the minimal difference in stimulus intensity that is just noticeable is, as a first approximation, described by *Weber's Law*, i.e. by the equation $\delta I/I = C$ (where I is the intensity of the stimulus, δI is the change in intensity which is just noticeable, and C is a constant for a given dimension of experience).[3] This states that the minimal detectable change in intensity is a constant proportion of the intensity to be changed (if the intensity increases the change in intensity required to produce a just noticeable difference also increases). In the case of brightness C is roughly 1/100, whereas for loudness C is roughly 1/5. Thus, adding one candle to one hundred other candles in a darkened room may just make a noticeable difference to brightness, but adding the noise of one machine to the noise of a hundred similar machines makes no difference to perceived loudness at all (one would need to add around twenty machines to make a difference).

The change in sound frequency required to produce a just noticeable change in perceived pitch, on the other hand, follows a somewhat different pattern. Below 1 kHz, the minimal discriminable change in frequency is roughly constant; every time the frequency changes by about 3 Hz one can hear a change in pitch. Above 1 kHz, Weber's Law seems to apply – the greater the frequency, the greater the change in frequency needs to be before it is heard as a change in pitch. For visible light, the change in frequency required to produce a just noticeable difference in the hue of a colour is described by a W-shaped curve – a very different relationship again.

How sensory systems translate energies into experiences

Our sensory systems provide us with dimensions of experience which model the energies surrounding our bodies. However, even for simple dimensions of experience such as brightness, loudness, pitch and colour, the mapping of what is experienced onto what physics describes is a complex one. Our eyes, ears and other sense organs are not general-purpose sound level meters, frequency analysers and so on. They are energy detectors of a very specialised kind. The perceptual processes that operate on their output, furthermore, do so in a very specialised way. Needless to say, when more complex aspects of perception are taken into account, such as the effects of adaptation, context, and expectation (based on prior experience), the relation of what is perceived to the simple measurements that meter readings provide becomes even more remote. Studies with sensory-impaired individuals and experiments with systems that alter the normal translation of energies described by physics into events as experienced also make it clear that there is considerable *variation* in the phenomenal worlds that can, potentially, be experienced by humans.

Experienced worlds with bits missing

To those with red–green colour blindness, traffic lights do not change colour as they change from 'stop' to 'go'. Only a change in the relative brightness of the top and bottom lights is seen. For the sensorineural deaf with hearing only in the low frequency ranges (say below 1 kHz), many environmental sounds, and sounds of speech, cannot be heard. Gas does not 'hiss', the rain does not 'spatter', doorbells do not 'ring', and the words sue, shoe, chew, zoo and true all sound like 'ooh'. Amoore (1977) has listed seventy-six 'anosmias' – specific smells to which one may be 'blind'. There are those who cannot smell the odour of cloves, those who cannot smell mint, others who cannot smell garlic, and so on. Some individuals live in a world that has no pain. Those who suffer from this congenital insensitivity provide convincing testimony about the value of pain:

> Many of these people sustain extensive burns, bruises and lacerations during childhood, frequently bite deep into the tongue while chewing food, and learn only with difficulty to avoid inflicting severe wounds on themselves. The failure to feel pain after a ruptured appendix, which is normally accompanied by severe abdominal pain, led to near death in one such man. Another man walked on a leg with a cracked bone until it broke completely.
>
> (Melzak, 1973, p. 15)

The world of the congenitally blind

As the severity of the impairment increases, the experienced change in what is taken to be the 'normal' world may be profound. Not only are there experiential elements missing, but the functions of impaired senses may also be taken over by remaining ones. Once this happens, the world that is manifest in perception, imagery or imagination, or symbolised in experienced thoughts, may be of a very different kind. For example, objects in the form that we know them do not exist for the congenitally blind. Their objects have no visible shape or colour in perception, memory, or imagination. Objects are known largely in terms of how they feel, and, to some extent, in terms of how they sound. Studies of echolocation used by blind individuals reveal that the size, distance, form, density and texture of objects can be known in varying degrees of accuracy in terms of the sound echoes reflected from their surfaces. Some gifted individuals are even able to use this ability to ride bicycles and skate in busy streets, play ball games and even go on hiking trips over rough, unfamiliar terrain.[4] Not surprisingly, if vision is suddenly restored by a cataract operation or by a corneal graft, such individuals may at first find it impossible to identify even simple shapes such as triangles and squares by sight alone, although by touch they identify these with ease. Visual identification may also be very difficult to learn. Von Senden (1932), in a review of such cases, noted that one patient was trained to discriminate a triangle from a square over a period of thirteen days but still could not 'report their form without counting corners one after the other'. Even if patients do learn to identify an object promptly, seemingly trivial changes in the nature of the object may destroy recognition. For example, Hebb reported that,

> The patient who had learned to name a ring showed no recognition of a slightly different ring; having learned to name a square, made of white cardboard, could not name it when its color was changed to yellow by turning the cardboard over; and so on.
>
> (Hebb, 1949, p. 28)

What kind of world is it that the blind inhabit? Sheila Hocken, who has made the journey both into and out of blindness, describes it with eloquence:

> I had no idea that I could not see normally until I was about seven. I lived among vague images and colours that were blurred, as if a gauze was over them. But I thought that was how everybody else saw the world. My sight gradually became worse and worse until by my late teens, I could just about distinguish light from dark, but that was all. Even in my dreams the people had no faces. They were shapes in a fog. From my earliest recollection, waking or dreaming, the fog had always been there,

and it slowly closed in until it became impenetrable and even the blurred shapes finally disappeared.

(Hocken, 1977, p. 1)

Her memories of her childhood contained no images of her mother and father, 'except in terms of touch and sound'; she remembered the house she lived in 'by the smell of bread baking and pies cooking, and the warmth and sound of a coal fire crackling and hissing in the grate. But no more' (ibid., p. 2).

Her blindness resulted from congenital cataracts with attendant retinal deterioration. However, when at the age of 30 an operation was performed to restore the transparency of the lens, her visual world was born anew:

> What happened then – the only way I can describe the sensation – is that I was suddenly hit, physically struck by brilliance, and through my entire body. It flooded my whole being with a shock-wave, this utterly unimaginable, incandescent brightness: there was white in front of me, a dazzling white that I could hardly bear to take in, and a vivid blue that I had never thought possible. It was fantastic, marvellous, incredible. It was like the beginning of the world.

(ibid., p. 148)

After a few days she leaves the hospital and is amazed by the way the world that now surrounds her differs from the one that she has previously taken for granted as being 'real'. She is surprised, for example, by the trees:

> Of course I knew there were trees. I'd always been aware of them, and could hear them when the wind blew. But I have never imagined so many, or that they were everywhere, growing out of pavements, in gardens and, as we drove through the countryside towards Nottingham, more and more of them, all different shapes. I could not get over the shapes, some round, some tall, and all in varying, breathtaking shades of green.

(ibid., p. 160)

Like von Senden's patients she initially found it difficult to relate some of the images she could see to her prior 'reality' which depended on touch. At the greengrocers, for example,

> There was something on the counter that I could not, try as I would, put a name to. I could see some red, and green, and a shape. That was all it meant to me. It would not fit any description I could think of. Then I touched it. I realized I was seeing leaves and flowers. It was a plant. I could not understand why I had not immediately known what it was.

(ibid., p. 168)

For her, a childhood 'reality' constructed from what is felt and heard, that she can smell and taste but cannot see, has now been reconstructed and must be re-*cognised* in a visual form.

The world of the deaf

To those who previously had hearing, the loss of auditory sensation is traumatic and, in some ways, surprising in its effects. As D.A. Ramsdell points out, sound not only serves to communicate our verbal thoughts, it also forms an auditory background to all of daily living:

> we react to such sounds as the tick of a clock, the distant roar of traffic, vague echoes of people moving in other rooms in the house, without being aware that we do hear them. These incidental noises maintain our feeling of being part of a living world and contribute to our sense of being alive. We are not conscious of the important role which these background sounds play in our comfortable merging of ourselves with the life around us, because we are not aware that we hear them. Nor is the deaf man aware that he has lost these sounds; he only knows that he feels as if the world were dead.
>
> (Ramsdell, 1947, p. 395)

The English politician Jack Ashley describes his final loss of hearing with sadness:

> I was cut off from mankind, surrounded by an impenetrable barrier. I could see people clearly, but they belonged to a different world – a world of talk, of music and laughter. I could hardly believe I would never hear again. I tried pressing a radio to the side of my head in a vain attempt to make contact; when I turned the volume to full pitch I could only feel a delicate vibration as the set trembled. It was undeniable confirmation that although sound existed it was not for me. That fragile wisp of hearing had maintained for me a slender contact with reality, a hint of that background of sound which, to a normal person, is so familiar as to be unnoticed. Without it, life was eerie; people appeared suddenly at my side, doors banged noiselessly, dogs barked soundlessly and heavy traffic glided silently past me. Friends chatted gaily in total silence. The greatest deprivation was being unable to hear the human voice. Casual conversation – the common currency of everyday life – repartee or even a passing joke were things of the past. . . . I was struggling like a newly caught bird in a foolproof cage.
>
> (Ashley, 1973, p. 135)

Deafness is isolating. Fortunately, for those who are born deaf, the deep sense of loss is absent. And pre-school profoundly deaf children develop concepts and solve problems just as normal hearing children do.[5] However, lacking phonemic imagery, they do not experience their thoughts in the form of 'inner speech'.[6] Rather, they 'symbolise' their thoughts to themselves in hand signs, hand symbols and, to some extent, in facial or bodily expressions. Not only is their world a silent one – but the thoughts they come to have about it are imaged in a visual, tactile or kinaesthetic form rather than inwardly 'heard'.

Artificial worlds for the sensory impaired

It should be clear from the above that not all human beings inhabit similar phenomenal worlds. Naturally occurring sensory impairments can produce radical external and internal experienced differences. With the application of a little technology, further variations are possible. In principle, for example, it is possible to develop forms of echolocation or sonar for the blind that exploit the reflective properties of ultrasound (Ashmead *et al.*, 1998; Bousbia-Salah and Fezari, 2007). Alternatively, by converting light arrays into vibration patterns on the skin of the back, it may be possible for the blind to 'feel' objects at a distance (Bach-y-Rita, 1972). For those who have residual hearing only in the low frequencies, it is possible to lower the frequency of otherwise inaudible high frequency speech and environmental sounds thereby mapping them onto the residual hearing range (Velmans *et al.*, 1988; Rees and Velmans, 1993; Lenhart, 2007). If no residual hearing exists, it may be beneficial to transform auditory signals into patterns of microelectrode stimulation applied directly to the inner ear or auditory nerve using cochlear implants (Lenarz, 1997; Loizou, 1998, 2006). Such transforms of acoustic energy may produce usable auditory experiences that are quite different from the sounds we normally hear. Other techniques map speech sounds into some other sense modality, for example into visual displays or into vibro-tactile signals applied to the fingers and to other regions of the skin. While such altered mappings of events as-described by physics into events as-perceived have met with varying degrees of success in the rehabilitation of the blind and the deaf, they are clearly not just exercises in metaphysics. The possibility of translating physical energies into non-normal phenomenal worlds is within current technological means.

Artificial worlds – the goggle people

Even where sensory systems operate normally, the way information detected by the sense organs is translated into a 'normal' experienced world is not entirely rigid. The objects that we see around us appear to be the right way up. But the images projected on the retina are inverted. This is somewhat odd. In 1897, the American psychologist G.M. Stratton decided to put matters right. He built an inverting telescope, attached this to a pair of spectacle frames, and became the first human being to have his retinal image the right way up.

Not surprisingly, the world at first seemed illusory and unreal. However, after wearing the system for a few days, individual objects and even whole visual scenes occasionally appeared to be 'upright'. On the third and fourth days this tendency increased and on the fifth his new 'reality' seemed almost normal. Although, on close examination, objects still seemed inverted, Stratton could walk about the house with ease. On the evening of the seventh day he was sufficiently accustomed to his novel world to appreciate the beauty of his evening walk. On the eighth day he removed the spectacles and was intrigued to find that,

> the scene had a strange familiarity. The visual arrangement was immediately recognised as the old one of pre-experimental days; yet the reversal of everything from the order to which I had grown accustomed during the last week, gave the scene a surprising, bewildering air which lasted several hours. It was hardly the feeling, though, that things were upside down.[7]

Theodor Erismann of the University of Innsbruck was interested in a different arrangement. He devised a pair of goggles that transposed left and right. Amazingly after several weeks of wearing the goggles one of Erismann's subjects became so at home in his transposed world that he was able to drive a motorcycle through Innsbruck with his goggles on! Ivo Kohler and his colleagues have investigated distortions of the visual field that are even more extreme. In one arrangement with prism goggles, when the head is turned to the right objects appear broader and when the head is turned to the left objects appear narrower, producing a 'concertina effect'. Further, if the head is moved up and down, objects seem to slant first one way and then the other (a 'rocking-chair' effect). In the words of one subject it is 'as if the world were made of rubber'. After several weeks of wearing the goggles, however, even this world appears relatively normal. And,

> If, after weeks or months, the subject is allowed to remove his goggles, the adaption continues to operate when he views the normal world. The result is an apparent squeezing of images when he glances one way and an expansion when he glances the other way. It is as if he were looking for the first time through prisms that have an orientation exactly opposite to those he has been wearing for so long. Moreover, all the other distortions, such as the rocking-chair effect, to which his eyes have slowly become adapted now appear in reverse when the goggles are removed. These after effects in their turn diminish in strength over a period of days, and the subject finally sees the stable world he used to know.
>
> (Kohler, 1962, p. 67)

In these visual adaptation experiments, the way physical entities and events are experienced is grossly altered in orientation or shape and, sometimes, in both. Yet, these distorted realities are ones to which we can adapt. Motor responses gradually adjust to the altered visual input to restore successful interaction with the world and, within a period of weeks, these new realities come to be accepted as normal. Given this evidence, it would seem that *what we take to be 'normal perceived reality' has more to do with what enables successful interaction with the world than with any immutable, one-to-one mapping of the events described by physics into events-as-perceived.*[8]

Nonhuman perceived worlds

There is also an extensive literature on the many different ways that the energies described by physics are perceived by nonhuman animals. For example, our eyes are structured to detect electromagnetic wavelengths from around 370 to 730 nm but wavelengths in the ultra-violet region (below 370 nm) are too short to see. The multifaceted eye of the bee, in contrast, is sensitive to wavelengths from 300 to 650 nm. Within this range, it can discriminate between ultra-violet lights of many different frequencies, but it cannot detect those longer waves (from 650 to 730 nm) that we perceive as 'red' (Von Frisch, 1971).

To some extent we can *feel* electromagnetic waves that are too long to see. Wavelengths from around 750 nm to 3×10^{-4} m (from the infrared to the microwave region) are capable of inducing those special oscillatory frequencies in molecules that we perceive as 'heat'. However, pit vipers such as the American rattlesnake have far greater heat sensitivity. A temperature change of around one-tenth of a degree centigrade is required to trigger heat-sensitive receptors embedded in the human skin. But, in shallow pits between the nostril and the eyes, the rattlesnake has sensors that can respond to changes in temperature of one-thousandth of a degree (Mattison, 1998).

Our ears are tuned to detect pressure variations in the air with frequencies in the 200 Hz to 20,000 Hz range. Compared to the ears of many other animals and insects this band of frequencies is both low on the frequency axis and relatively narrow in bandwidth. Smaller whales and dolphins, for example, can detect frequencies that range from around 750 Hz to around 170,000 Hz (Sales and Pye, 1974).

Amongst the sensory fibres mediating taste in the cat, some have been found (in the chorda tympani) that are sensitive to acid alone ('sour' fibres?), some that are sensitive to quinine alone ('bitter' fibres?), and some that are sensitive to salt. Unusually, there is also a type of fibre especially sensitive to distilled water (see Moncrieff, 1967). To our tongues, water has no distinctive taste; it is not sweet or sour or salty or bitter – but perhaps it does have a distinct taste to the domestic cat. In humans, taste is also intimately related to our sense of smell (food tastes bland if one has a blocked nose). We can also use smell to monitor our surroundings. But, compared to the bloodhound and the silkmoth, our nasal receptors are blunt instruments. The male silkmoth Bombyx, for example, has large feathery antennae that enable it to smell a female up to several kilometres away.[9]

In sum, human sense modalities appear tuned to detect ranges of events that may overlap with, but are not identical to those detected by other animals. Indeed, there are forms of energy to which other creatures have exquisite sensitivity that our sense organs, unaided, cannot detect at all. Various species of fish have sensors to detect the electric fields that they themselves produce. They are also able to detect the minute distortions formed in these fields by objects that have different conductivity to the surrounding water, and they use this information to locate and identify such objects. For example, the elephant-nosed fish (the mormyrid *Gymnarchus Niloticus*) has sensors able to detect gradients in field potential of only 0.03 microvolts per cm, or current densities of 0.04 microamps per square cm. Although it lives in heavily mudded African waters and is almost blind, it uses this fine sensitivity to manoeuvre in and out of obstacles with precision and pursue the smaller fish it eats (Guo and Kawasaki, 1997; Lissman, 1963). There is also behavioural evidence that animals as varied as termites, ponds nails, wasps, and homing pigeons can detect weak magnetic fields with magnitudes approaching that of the earth's magnetic field (slightly less than one gauss) (Droscher, 1971; Mouritsen and Ritz, 2005; Wiltschko and Wiltschko, 1995).

What the frog's eye tells the frog's brain

As with humans, the experienced worlds that nonhuman animals inhabit are likely to be influenced not just by the range of energies that their sense organs detect, but also by the perceptual and cognitive processes that operate on that information. Many creatures, for example, have eyes, but this is not to say that they see what we see. In a now classical study, Lettvin *et al.* (1959) discovered that the 'frog's eye tells the frog's brain' just four things. Some fibres in the frog's optic nerve responded only to a difference in brightness of two portions of the visual field ('sustained contrast detectors'). Some fibres responded only to moving edges ('moving edge detectors'). Other fibres responded only to the presence of small moving spots ('net convexity detectors'). And some fibres responded only to an overall dimming of the field. Each of the four fibre types projects onto a different layer of the superior colliculus. Consequently, the retinal image is represented four times in the frog's central nervous system, each representational layer being responsive to one of four, distinct, stimulus features.

Accordingly, Lettvin *et al.* suggested that the frog sees just four things essential to its survival. A sudden dimming of the light or a moving edge may indicate a predator and is likely to initiate an escape response. Sustained differences in brightness may allow the frog to separate water from land and lily pad. The moving spots that trigger the 'convexity detectors' subtend an angle at the eye of around 1 degree, which closely corresponds to the image projected by a moving fly at tongue's length. In this regard, what the frog does not respond to is equally suggestive. A frog may seem hypnotised by an approaching snake. But if the snake does not dim the light and presents no clearly moving edge, the frog simply may not see it. Stationary spots trigger no responses in the frog's optic nerve so, if it is surrounded by dead flies, the frog will starve.

Nor do the differences between 'human reality' and the worlds of other animals end with the world as-perceived. Like humans, other animals may know more than they immediately perceive. In varying degrees they learn, solve problems and encode what they have learnt in their representational systems. To varying degrees they can also communicate with others of their species and enter into social relationships. Needless to say, the variations amongst species are immense and form much of the subject matter of zoology and comparative psychology. We need not dwell on the details. It is enough to note that the worlds of other sentient creatures are dependent on *all* their capacities, sensory, perceptual, cognitive, affective and social (see Bekoff and Jamieson, 1996; Dawkins, 1998; Panksepp, 2005, 2007).

What is it like to be a bee?

We cannot be absolutely certain that other humans have experiences, let alone that nonhuman animals have experiences (the problem of 'other minds'). But on the basis of evolutionary theory, it seems reasonable to assume that forms of consciousness evolve along with the biological forms that embody them. But what is it that the bee sees? Is there a colour more 'ultra' than violet? If there is, we cannot visualise it. And what do the moth and dolphin hear? If there is a pitch 500 times higher than middle C (500×261.63 Hz) we cannot imagine it. And if water is not sweet or sour, salty or bitter to the cat, then what could its taste be like? Although we can extrapolate to some extent from what we can perceive, whatever conclusions we may draw are little more than speculative.

Once one considers nonhuman sense modalities, even the possibility of imaginative extrapolation disappears. The 'experiental materials' from which the external world perceived by humans is constructed are drawn from the products of human exteroceptive sense modalities. But, what is it like to experience an electrical field? If the elephant-nosed fish perceives distortions in its own electrical field it is likely to do so in a sense modality different from any we possess. This may also be true of the sensed changes in magnetic field experienced by the pond snail, homing pigeon, and wasp.

A peculiarly human world

How does the phenomenal, 'physical world' relate to the world described by physics? The data from physics, sensory physiology, perception and psychophysics make it clear that the perceived world 'models' only a selection of the events and energies described by physics. There are electromagnetic energies of many kinds that permeate space and even penetrate our bodies, to which our eyes (and other sense organs) are blind. There are signals produced by animals and insects to which our ears are deaf. Each sensory system has its own limits of resolution. Changes in light intensity of less than around 5 per cent, or in sound intensity of less than around 20 per cent are not perceived as changes. A change in sound frequency from 1000 Hz to 1005 Hz produces a just noticeable rise in pitch, but not a change from 4000 Hz to 4005 Hz. A change in electromagnetic wavelength from 480 to 481 nanometers will produce a noticeable change in hue, but not a change from 550 to 551 nanometers. Our sense of smell and taste monitor, but tell us little of the chemistry of the substances we inhale and ingest. Sensation and perception are limited in their spatial resolution to detect events of a size and distance that are relevant to normal human action and survival – beyond this we need microscopes and telescopes. Our sensory systems are also structured to detect events of a given duration. Light bulbs, for example, actually flash fifty times per second (the frequency of the a.c. mains voltage). However, this 'flicker frequency' is faster than the visual system can resolve which makes the light seem continuous. By contrast, the movement of a flower out of the earth is too slow to see, so one needs time-lapse photography to 'see' the movement.

The data from comparative psychology and zoology suggest that the 'physical reality' perceived by humans is only one of many possible perceived realities. The precise mix of sensory, perceptual, cognitive, affective and social capacities in each species is unique. As we have seen, human sensory and perceptual systems perform broadly similar functions to those of other animals. But the sensitivity of sense organs, the range of energies to which they are tuned, and the way information detected by the sensors is subject to perceptual processing vary considerably from species to species. Consequently, the 'physical reality' that we *perceive* is actually a peculiarly *human* world.

Recall, too, that according to the arguments presented in Chapter 6, this peculiarly human reality just *is* the world of earth and tree, sea and stone that we normally think of as the 'physical world' external to our bodies. It is not some additional percept *of* the world located 'inside the mind or brain'. If one grants that similar perceptual, projective processes operate in at least some nonhuman animals, then the worlds that they experience just *are* the worlds that they perceive surrounding their own bodies. Other animals do not have an atrophied, distorted experience 'inside their heads' of the world that we take for granted as 'real'. What we perceive does not form a reference point for their perspective, any more than what they perceive forms a reference point for our perspective. Rather, they construct phenomenal worlds out of the energies and events surrounding their bodies in their own nonhuman ways. In this respect, their worlds co-exist with and are genuine alternatives to ours.

> The mind, in short, works on the data it receives very much as a sculptor works on his block of stone. In a sense the statue stood there from

eternity. But there were a thousand different ones beside it, and the sculptor alone is to thank for having extricated this one from the rest. Just so the world of each of us, howsoever different our several views of it may be, all lay embedded in the primordial chaos of sensations, which gave the mere matter to the thought of us indifferently. We may, if we like, by our reasonings unwind things back to that black and jointless continuity of space and moving clouds of swarming atoms which science calls the real world. But all the while the world we feel and live in will be that which our ancestors and we, by slowly cumulative strokes of choice, have extricated out of this, like sculptors, by simply rejecting portions of the given stuff. Other sculptors, other statues from the same stone! Other minds, other worlds from the same monotonous and inexpressive chaos! My world is but one in a million alike embedded, alike real to those who may abstract them. How different must be the worlds in the consciousness of ant, cuttle-fish, or crab!

(James, 1890, Vol. 1, pp. 288–289)

Question 2: What are the implications of the reflexive model for realism versus idealism? [10]

According to the above:

- In terms of their *phenomenology* the perceived 'physical world' and percepts *of* the physical world are one and the same (there is no *additional* experience of the world 'in the mind or brain').
- The perceived 'physical world' is just a representation (produced by perceptual and cognitive processing) of some more fundamental reality which natural science might describe in very different ways.
- The perceived 'physical world' that we take for granted is a peculiarly human world. Given their different sensory and perceptual systems, other animals are likely to experience different 'worlds'. To some extent this applies also to humans with major sensory impairments (such as the congenitally blind or deaf).

If so, the following conclusions seem inescapable: if our perceptual processes do *not* operate, then it is not just some ephemeral set of 'mental' events that disappears; it is the world we experience surrounding our bodies that, for us, ceases to exist. This world may still, of course, exist for other human beings. There might also be nonhuman worlds as experienced by nonhuman animals. However, if there *were* no human beings and there were no other creatures with perceptual processes similar to human beings, then the world *as we perceive it* would literally cease to be. In this sense, the reflexive model commits one to *idealism* – that the existence of the world *as perceived by us* depends on the existence of and operation of our own perceptual processing.

It does not follow, however, that if there were no human or similar sentient creatures, the world *itself* would cease to be, and it is here that we part company with Berkeley's version of idealism. As noted above, the world as-perceived may be thought of as a representation of a more fundamental reality which physics, for example, would describe in a very different way. We have every reason to believe that such a reality existed prior to the appearance of humans and would continue to exist after their departure. Even if there were *no* sentient creatures to perceive that reality, the universe might exist, although it would not be *experienced* to exist. In this sense, the reflexive model is committed to *realism*.

This is *not*, however, a realism of the conventional kind. If the world as-perceived (by humans) is, in essence, a *representation* (of a more fundamental reality), then the familiar world that we experience would *not* be here if we were gone. Without a sense of touch or an ability to feel weight, there would be no hard-felt and heavy-felt objects. Without eyes there would be no appearance of movement or light. And the chatter of birds and clap of thundercloud become silence if there is no one to hear.

In this way, the reflexive model combines elements of *both* realism and idealism, but they apply to different things. While the world we experience is a representation that depends for its existence on human perceptual processing, the reality so represented does not.

Don't objects have colours whether or not anyone sees them?

As far as I can judge, the above account of how observer-dependent, per-ceived phenomena represent an independently existing 'reality' which natural science might describe in other ways is consistent both with science and with common sense. However the observer-dependence of qualia such as colour, smell, taste and so on has been strongly resisted by some physicalist philosophers of mind. Their resistance is a consequence of their commitment to physicalism. If qualia such as 'redness' are, in their essence, observer-dependent experiences, then it is not easy to reduce such qualia to 'objective' states of the brain, no matter how brain states are construed (see Chapters 3 and 4). Armstrong (1968), for example, acknowledges that unless one can exclude phenomenal properties such as 'redness' from perception he would have to abandon his entire reductive programme, which claims perception to be nothing more than the capacity to make certain discriminations (see Chapter 4, note 3). The same would be true of Dennett's analysis of colour perception discussed in Chapter 5. But 'redness' undeniably exists, so Armstrong is forced into the view that redness is an *observer-independent*, physical property of certain physical objects (having excluded such qualia from perception there is nowhere else for them to go). In short, for Armstrong, objects are 'red' whether or not there is anyone to perceive them.[11]

Tye (1995, 2007) develops a very similar argument, as we have seen in Chapter 7. However, according to the analysis presented above, colour appears only once light waves (in the visible waveband) have been translated by the visual system into colour experiences. That is, objects are only red if (a) they reflect light with the appropriate wavelengths (around 700 nm) and (b) the visual system translates that electromagnetic energy into a red colour experience. Of these two conditions, (b) is the more important. That is, the visual system can produce a colour experience without being innervated by light in the 700 nm region (for example in dreams, vivid imagery, and hallucinations). But, without visual systems of the appropriate kind, light waves of 700 nm have no colour at all (colour as such is not an electromagnetic property).

Question 3: What does the world as-experienced represent?

There is nothing particularly mysterious about the experienced world being a *representation* that is somewhat different from the world described by physics. Perceptual processes are likely to have developed in response to evolutionary pressures, and select, attend to, and interpret information in accordance with human adaptive needs. Consequently, they only need to model a subset of the available information. At the same time our perceptual models must be useful, otherwise it is unlikely that human beings would have survived. Given this, it seems reasonable to assume that the experienced world produced by perceptual processing is a partial, approximate but nonetheless useful representation of what is 'really there'.

The view that our percepts represent 'reality' in a partial, approximate way is sometimes known as 'indirect realism' or 'critical realism'. This position allows that useful knowledge of the world is provided by observations (observed phenomena), but it also allows that representations of the world provided by theories, causal laws and so on can sometimes be more accurate, more general, and quite different from the world as perceived. Tacitly or explicitly, a form of critical realism is adopted in much of science – and I develop a form of it below. As the present text focuses on *Understanding Consciousness*, I will not dwell in any depth on the classical debates surrounding this, and other, competing epistemologies. But we cannot avoid epistemological issues completely, for the reason that consciousness as such, and the phenomena of which we are conscious, play an important role in knowledge. Becoming conscious of something *is* a way to know it (see Chapter 13). The phenomena of which we are conscious also provide data for our theories, whether in science or everyday life (see Chapter 9). In any case, the critical realist position outlined above requires some justification. It claims that our percepts and concepts represent 'reality' in a partial, approximate way. But what is this 'reality'? And, if there is such a reality, how can we possibly *know* that our percepts or our theories represent it?

Needless to say, these are classical epistemological problems, shared to varying degrees by all representational theories of knowledge. As we have seen in Chapter 3, such problems are particularly acute in the sceptical empiricist philosophy of John Locke (1690). According to Locke sensations 'in the mind' are as close to the real world as one can get. Concepts, theories and so on relate to the world only in so far as they reduce to or can be seen to derive from sensations. However the qualities of sensations vary in their representational accuracy. Primary qualities of sensation such as 'extension', 'figure' (shape), 'solidity' and 'motion' represent qualities that actually inhere in the material world. Secondary qualities such as light, sound and heat are produced in the mind by the motions of material particles, but do not represent what the particles themselves are like. This resembles contemporary views about how sensations relate to the world described by physics (light is produced by photons, sound by the vibrations of air molecules, heat by molecular Brownian motion, etc.). But, given his own theory of knowledge, it is not easy to see how Locke arrives at this view. If sensations are as close to the real world as one can get, how can Locke judge the *resemblance* of sensations to the 'real world' which lies beyond them? And what justifies Locke's implicit belief that the world is 'really' composed of 'insensate corpuscles' (the atoms of seventeenth-century physics) which are quite *unlike* sensations?

What do theories represent?

The obvious way around the problem posed by Locke's sceptical empiricism is to allow the possibility that human cognitive processes can sometimes provide representations of the world which are more accurate than those provided by sensations – a view taken to extremes in the rationalism of the ancient Greeks. In modern physics, such a view is implicit in the belief that a grand unified theory that somehow combined relativity with quantum mechanics would literally be a theory of everything. As the physicist Stephen Hawking puts it,

> if we do discover a complete theory, it should in time be understandable in broad principle by everyone, not just a few scientists. Then we shall all, philosophers, scientists and just ordinary people, be able to take part in the discussion of the question of why it is that we and the universe exist. If we find the answer to that, it would be the ultimate triumph of human reason – for then we would know the mind of god.
>
> (Hawking, 1988, p. 193)

However, many scientists take a more cautious view. The astrophysicist John Gribbin, for example, notes that we have different models of the atom. But none of them can claim to represent its 'true' nature to the exclusion of the others. Rather, their 'goodness of fit' depends on their domain of application:

> The point is that we do not know what an atom is 'really'; we cannot ever know what an atom is 'really.' We can only know what an atom is like. By probing it in certain ways, we find that, under certain circumstances, it is

'like' a billiard ball. Probe it another way and we find it is 'like' the Solar System. Ask a third set of questions, and the answer we get is it is like a positively charged nucleus surrounded by a cloud of electrons. These are all images that we carry over from the everyday world to build up a picture of what an atom 'is.' We construct a model, or an image; but then, all too often, we forget what we have done, and confuse the image with reality.

(Gribbin, 1995, p. 186)

Nor can one escape the tentative nature of our concepts and theories about the world by expressing them in the precise language of mathematics. As Albert Einstein put it, 'As far as the laws of mathematics refer to reality, they are not certain; and as far as they are certain they do not refer to reality.'[12] Rather,

Physical concepts are free creations of the human mind, and are not, however it may seem, uniquely determined by the external world. In our endeavour to understand reality we are somewhat like a man trying to understand the mechanism of a closed watch. He sees the face and the moving hands, even hears its ticking, but he has no way of opening the case. If he is ingenious he may form some picture of a mechanism which could be responsible for all the things he observes, but he may never be quite sure his picture is the only one which could explain his observations. He will never be able to compare his picture with the real mechanism and he cannot even imagine the possibility of the meaning of such a comparison.

(Einstein and Infeld, 1938, p. 31)

In this more cautious view, scientific theories no longer claim to represent absolute truth. Rather, their value is judged in terms of their ability to explain, control and predict observable phenomena. The acquisition of scientific knowledge involves an ongoing dynamic between observed phenomena, theories about the nature of such phenomena, and an implicit underlying reality that grounds both. Scientific progress is at once data-driven and concept-driven. Karl Popper notes that, 'in the history of science it is always the theory and not the experiment, always the idea and not the observation that opens the way to new knowledge'. On the other hand, 'it is always the experiment which saves us from following a track that leads nowhere, which helps us out of the rut, and which challenges us to find a new way' (Popper, 1959, p. 268).[13] In his view, scientific theories are 'best conjectures' (on the basis of currently available data) that are eternally open to refutation. What is taken to be 'scientific reality' at any given time also depends on the questions one is inclined to ask. Prevailing theories influence the observations that we seek. They suggest which measurements are trivial and which of fundamental interest. When theories change, decisions relating to these issues also change. For reasons such as these,

The empirical basis of objective science has nothing 'absolute' about it. Science does not rest upon solid bedrock. The bold structure of its theories rises, as it were, above a swamp. It is like a building erected on piles. The piles are driven down from above into the swamp, but not down to any natural or 'given' base; and if we stop driving the piles deeper, it is not because we have reached firm ground. We simply stop when we are satisfied that the piles are firm enough to carry the structure, at least for the time being.

(Popper, 1959, p. 111)

The status of observed phenomena, theories, and the thing itself

This cautious stance regarding the observer-relative nature of observations and the conjectural status of any given scientific theory is consistent with the critical realist epistemology that I adopt in this book. It is also implicit in my analysis of how consciousness relates to knowledge (in Chapters 13 and 14). In essence, this epistemology involves three interacting elements: observed phenomena, theories, and an implicit 'reality' (or thing itself) that observed phenomena and theories represent. In broad terms, I assume the status of these elements to be as follows.

Observed phenomena

Observed phenomena are entities or events that observers experience. They result from an interaction of an observer with an observed (a thing itself), and they are concept-driven as well as data-driven. Consequently, they are not objective in the sense of being 'observer-free'.

There are many differences between the phenomenal world (the world as-perceived) and the world described by natural science. So, unless one is prepared to reject natural science, one must reject the view that the world simply is as it appears to be.[14] Observed phenomena cannot fully or exclusively represent, or be, 'what is real'. Rather, sensory and perceptual systems translate the energies and events they detect into neural representations of those energies in different ways in different animal species, producing 'mental models' of the world appropriate to each form of life. Human 'mental models' form one, small subset amongst many.

Evolutionary pressures have ensured that our mental models and their phenomenal accompaniments are normally useful to our form of life. Observed/ experienced phenomena form the basis of our physical and social interactions, and they provide the point of departure and the place of testing for our theories. But their utility and accuracy are not guaranteed. Like all forms of representation, experienced phenomena can misrepresent actual states of affairs (for example, in illusions and hallucinations). However, for the purposes of everyday life, what we experience usually corresponds in some useful way to what is 'actually there'. Judged in terms of utility, the phenomenal world is not an illusion. Observed phenomena are partial, approximate, species-specific, but useful representations of the thing itself.[15]

Theories

Theories are abstractions that are overtly symbolised in our experience in the form of natural language, mathematics or other symbol systems (such as the flow diagrams used in functional modelling and systems analysis).[16] They are based on observed phenomena and tested against them, but their representational content is not reducible to the content of the phenomena on which they are based. They are general rather than particular and provide representations of patterns *exemplified* by observed phenomena, including the categories they exemplify and the causal sequences into which they enter, thereby enabling explanation, prediction and control.

In so far as theories symbolise patterns which are general rather than particular, they can represent aspects of what the world is like which are, potentially, universal (as in causal laws and grand unified theories). However, being conjectural and refutable they are not certain. Nor can any one theory be a *complete* theory of everything for the simple reason that there are just too many things to explain at many different levels of organisation (physical, biological, psychological, social, anthropological and so on). Consequently, each theory has a domain of application or 'range of convenience', and the utility of any given theory can only be assessed in the light of the *purposes* for which it is to be used.[17] Like experienced/observed phenomena, theories may provide useful representations of what the world is like, but they are not the 'thing itself'.

The 'thing itself'

According to the above, both experienced phenomena and theories are representations. However, this does not make sense unless there is something there to represent. Unless representations are *of* something, they are not representations.[18] But *what* are they representations of? Could they just represent each other? No. Observed phenomena may *exemplify* theories, but it does not make sense to say that they 'represent' theories. Rather, they represent (in our experience) what the world itself 'is like'. Conversely, theories about the world do not just represent experienced phenomena (contrary to what the sceptical empiricists believed). While *descriptions* of particular phenomena may be said to represent those phenomena, theories *about* phenomena provide representations of their causes, their consequences and other inferred patterns in the world that they exemplify. In so far as theories abstract general truths or even universals from particulars they too attempt to represent what the world 'is like'. This implies that there is a 'reality' which is like something. I use the term the 'thing itself' to refer to this implicit reality.

The thing itself may also be thought of as a 'reference fixer' required to make sense of the fact that we can have multiple experiences, concepts or theories of the *same thing*. How this page looks for example depends on whether one views it in darkness or light, with unaided vision, a microscope or an electron microscope. One can think about it as ink on paper, as English text, a treatise on the 'thing itself', etc. Which is it 'really'? *It* is as much one thing as it is the other, and many other things besides. But it does not make sense to suggest that *It* changes, as our experiences of it or our theories about it change.[19] Nor does it make sense to suppose that there is *nothing there* other than the experiences or thoughts we have about it (unless one is willing to accept all the consequences of Berkelian Idealism). The critical realism I adopt assumes instead that there really is something there *to experience* or *to think about* whether we perceive it, have thoughts about it, or not.

Can one know anything about the thing itself?

It should be apparent that my initial reasons for using the term the 'thing itself' are mundane. Representations have to be of something other than themselves, and there has to be some *thing* which underlies the various views, concepts, or theories we have of it. This contrasts sharply with the status of the 'thing itself' in the work of Immanuel Kant who invented the term (*ding an sich*). According to Kant, the thing itself is *unknowable*. This has produced understandable caution in making any reference to it in post-Kantian theories of knowledge – for how could anything be both unknowable and an object of knowledge?

Kant argued (as I have done) that the everyday 'physical world' consists of *phenomena*. That is, 'External objects (bodies) . . . are mere appearances, and are, therefore, nothing but a species of my representations' (Kant, 1781, p. 346). The 'thing itself' is a transcendental reality that lies behind and brings about what we perceive. But, how it does so, 'is a question which no human being can possibly answer. This gap in our knowledge can never be filled' (ibid., p. 359). And, because our 'representations' are all that we experience, he concludes that, of the thing itself, 'we can have no knowledge whatsoever . . .' and 'we shall never acquire any concept' (ibid., p. 360).

I do not wish to skate over the fundamental problems raised by Kant's analysis of how the mind's own nature constrains what it can know. Kant is surely right to point out that we cannot have knowledge of 'reality' in a way that is free of the limitations of our own perceptual and cognitive systems.[20] We cannot make observations that are 'objective' in the sense of being observer-free, or have knowledge that is unconstrained by the way that our cognitive processes operate. Our knowledge is filtered through and conditioned by the sensory, perceptual and cognitive systems we use to acquire that knowledge. Given this, we cannot assume that our representations provide *observer-free knowledge of the world as it is in itself*.

Nor is empirical, representational knowledge *certain* knowledge. As Einstein observed, understanding 'reality' is like trying to understand the mechanism of a closed watch. One sees the face and the moving hands, and even hears its ticking. But there is no way of opening the case. For representational knowledge it is easy to see why this is so. Whether the representations be in humans, nonhuman animals or machines, a representational system can only have (access to) its own representations of that which it represents. Consequently, a system's representations define the limits of its current knowledge. Lacking any other access to some ultimate reality or 'thing itself', there is no way that a representational system can be *certain* that its representations are accurate or complete.[21]

Uncertainty appears to be *intrinsic* to representational knowledge. Kant's view that the thing itself is *unknowable* is nevertheless extreme. Partial, species-specific, uncertain knowledge of what the world 'is like' is still knowledge. Although it is logically possible that the world we experience is entirely illusory (along with the concepts and theories we have about it), the circumstantial evidence against this is immense. We necessarily base our interactions with the world on the experiences, concepts and theories we have of it, and these representations enable us to interact with it quite well. Kant's extreme position is in any case self-defeating. If we can know nothing about the 'real' world, then no genuine knowledge *of any kind* is possible whether in philosophy or science – in which case one cannot *know* that the thing itself is unknowable, or anything else.

Interpreted in Kant's way, a theory of knowledge grounded in a 'thing itself' is also internally inconsistent. If the appearances of the external world are *not* representations of the thing itself, then these appearances cannot really be *representations*, as there is nothing else for them to be representations of. Conversely, if they *are* representations of the thing itself, the latter cannot be unknowable.[22] Similarly, if we can 'never acquire any concept' about what the world is really like, then our concepts and theories cannot be about anything 'real'. Conversely, if these do provide a measure of knowledge about how things really are, then it cannot be true that of the thing itself 'we can have no knowledge whatsoever'.[23]

Little wonder that even those who accept the limitations of scientific knowledge generally believe it to be about something 'real'. In the extracts above, for example, Gribbin implies that there is something 'real' which we call an 'atom', even if we can only know what an atom 'is like'. Einstein implies there is a 'closed watch' even if we can only hear its ticking. And Popper accepts that there is something into which we drive the piles that support the edifice of knowledge even if that 'something' is more like a swamp than solid rock. I adopt a similar 'critical realism' here.

Critical realism in the reflexive model

In dualism and reductionism, percepts *of* objects 'in the mind or brain' *represent* the objects we see out in the world. But if experiences *of* objects and objects as-perceived are phenomenologically identical, this does not make sense. Given this, what do experiences *of* objects *represent*? And what do experiences of the body and 'inner' experiences represent? The reflexive model makes the conventional assumption that causal sequences in normal perception are initiated by *real things* in the external world, body or brain.[24] Barring illusions and hallucinations our consequent experiences *represent* those things. Our concepts and theories provide alternative representations of those things. However, neither our experiences nor our concepts and theories are the things themselves. In the reflexive model, things themselves are the true objects of knowledge.

Although this position is neo-Kantian in some respects, the role that the 'thing itself' plays is very different. Rather than the thing itself (the 'real' nature of the world) being unknowable, one cannot make sense of knowledge without it, even if we can only know this 'reality' in an incomplete, uncertain, species-specific way. Conversely, if the thing itself cannot be known, then we can know nothing, for the thing itself *is all there is to know*.[25]

Notes

1 A given modality of experience may be associated with experience in other modalities, for example, in cases of synaesthesia. However, in such cases, the specific cortical projection areas supporting each associated modality are simultaneously activated (Cytowic, 1995).

2 In addition to the exteroceptive systems there are of course interoceptive systems which monitor body equilibrium, the position and movement of the limbs (kinaesthesis) and the condition of the body's internal organs (see for example Boff *et al.*, 1986).

3 This relation holds only in intermediate ranges of detectable loudness and brightness.

4 See extensive review by Kish (2002). See also the remarkable online video report on Ben Underwood, 'Extraordinary people – the boy who sees without eyes', at www.youtube.com/watch?v=qLziFMF4DHA

5 In the deaf child, the unconscious cognitive processes may operate normally. Only the modality of 'symbolisation' and, therefore, of communication is different. In intellectual development it is the ability to symbolise and not the modality which is crucial. Accordingly, it is found that deaf children born of deaf parents tend to be more intellectually advanced than those with normal hearing parents. The reason for this is that deaf parents tend to communicate with their deaf children more effectively (using visual signs and symbols) than untrained, normal-hearing parents do. Prior to formal language instruction, deaf children of hearing parents may also develop an individual, gestural language with many of the properties of normal language (for example, signs and sign combinations at morphemic and syntactic levels of organisation – Feldman *et al.*, 1978).

6 An inability to communicate with others verbally does not rule out the possibility that some inner speech exists, albeit of an atrophied kind, particularly if the child has some residual hearing – see Conrad (1979) for a discussion.

7 See Stratton (1897) or a review of this and later work in Kohler (1962) and Gregory (1966). Kohler (1962) also gives an account of Erismann's experiment (below).

8 This theme has recently been developed in some depth in 'enactive' theories of perception and cognition. See, for example, Clark (1997) and Noë (2002, 2004, 2007).

9 The chemical 'bombykol' can be detected by the silkmoth in concentrations of about 200 molecules/cm^3 (Schneider, 1974). In contrast, butyl mercaptan which has a foul, putrid odour and is one of the most potent olfactory stimulants for man, requires concentrations of around 10^7 molecules/cm^3 for detection.

10 The following analysis was first presented in Velmans (1990a).

11 Armstrong, of course, tries to translate perception into discrimination. So, in Armstrong's terms, redness exists as a physical property whether or not there is anyone to make appropriate discriminations.

12 From 'Geometry and Experience', an expanded form of an address to the Prussian Academy of Sciences, Berlin, 27 January, 1921, cited by Margenau (1970).

13 There are many other examples of such perceptual-cognitive interactions that have been revealed by psychological research. Babies of around 8 months, for example, realise that objects do not really disappear when a blanket is thrown over them. This suggests that prelinguistic concepts are used to correct the perceptual evidence in the development of 'object constancy' in the sensory-motor representations of the developing child.

14 The term 'naïve realism' is usually applied to the view that we perceive the world as it 'really is'.

15 In classical Eastern philosophy the phenomenal world is often said to be an illusion or 'maya'. However, there are two distinct views about how this is to be interpreted, even in Eastern thought. In the philosophy of Shankara, for example, the phenomenal world is entirely an illusion (in no sense 'real'). In other writings such as those of Aurobindo, the phenomenal world is thought of as illusory in the sense that it is a only a projection of what is 'real', filtered through human sensory and perceptual systems. As far as I can judge, the view I develop here is consistent with the second position (but not the first).

16 It is important to distinguish the overt symbolic forms of concepts and theories from their covert forms of encoding in the brain. How concepts and theories are represented in the brain (in some neural language – sometimes referred to as 'mentalese') is not, at present, fully known.

17 For the purposes of physics, a theory which unifies quantum mechanics with relativity theory will provide a representation of the fundamental forces in the universe which is far more general than any representation of the world provided by the unaided visual system. On the other hand, a grand unified theory of everything will not assist one to walk across the road without being hit by a bus.

18 This applies even if the representations are of some hypothetical entity or event, rather than an actual one. It also applies to self-knowledge, where knowledge of the self needs to be distinguished from the 'self itself' (self-knowledge, like other forms of knowledge, may be partial and inaccurate).

19 For the moment, I am ignoring 'observer effects' at the limits of measurement in quantum mechanics, or in the use of introspective methods in consciousness studies, where the act of observation can disturb the observed.

20 We can of course *extend* the capacities of our perceptual and cognitive systems, by training or with the aid of technology. However, extending the range of our perceptual and cognitive systems does not free them of all constraints.

21 This point is supplementary to the classical philosophical distinction between (uncertain) contingent truth and (certain) necessary truth. Scientific knowledge can only be gained by empirical investigation because it is contingent on how the world happens to be (when it could be otherwise). Necessary truths are certain because they are true in any possible universe, so they do not require any empirical investigation.

22 Illusory phenomena might not represent anything real (other than the workings of the mind itself), in which case one could think of them as mental constructions which do not represent what they seem to represent. But if they are representations

of the world they must tell us *something* about what the world is 'really' like, or they are *not* representations of the world.

23 There is also a deeper point that I will develop later in this book. According to the reflexive monism developed in Part III, human life, experience and the very means by which we come to know the world and ourselves are embodied in and embedded in a supporting universe. The forms of perceptual and cognitive knowledge available to humans are as much expressions of the universe as human life itself and its sustaining surround. Rather than being 'cut off' from the thing itself, the human knower and the means of knowledge available are a particular manifestation of the thing itself – and it is this that makes a limited knowledge of it possible. Note that even if we could only know something about the phenomena that are present in our own experiences, we would know something about the *manifest* nature of the thing itself (i.e. about the way that it manifests in human life). One might then still argue that the *unmanifest* thing itself is entirely unknowable. However, even here there is a case to be made for a limited form of knowledge. For example, physics currently assumes that on the basis of observed phenomena (such as the expansion of the universe) it may even be possible to infer something about the properties of unmanifest nature (for example about the properties of 'dark matter') or about other universes (for example in 'multiverse' theories). The critical realism adopted by reflexive monism allows all these possibilities, at least in principle, viewing them as attempts to explore ever more deeply into the nature of the thing itself.

24 I use the neutral term 'thing' as convenient shorthand here, but leave open the question of whether a given object of knowledge is better thought of as a thing, event, or process.

25 Readers with a particular interest in this issue should also read the critique of this aspect of reflexive monism given by Hoche (2007) and the reply in Velmans (2007b). Hoche compares RM with both Kant and Husserl and argues in favour of a Husserlian 'noematic' approach that defends the importance of phenomenology (as I do) but avoids reference to a thing itself. In my reply, I argue that avoiding reference to a knowable reality behind appearances leads to more complex explanations of how knowledge is possible, with less explanatory value and counterintuitive conclusions – and that the critical realism adopted by reflexive monism appears more useful (than a purely noematic approach), as well as being consistent with science and common sense. We return to some of these issues in the discussion of reflexive monism in Chapters 12 and 14.

9 Subjective, intersubjective and objective science

The reflexive model introduced in Chapters 6 and 7 differs from conventional models of perception on one, fundamental point. In terms of *phenomenology* objects and events *as-perceived* and percepts *of* those objects and events are one and the same. Chapter 8 examined how this insight can be incorporated into a critical realist theory of knowledge. In the present chapter we examine some of the consequences for a science of consciousness.

Public, objective, physical science

Following the implicit, dualist separation of objects as-perceived from percepts of objects, illustrated in Figures 6.1 and 6.2, it is generally taken for granted within psychology and philosophy that percepts of objects (and other contents of consciousness) are *private, subjective*, and *observer-dependent* (their existence depends on the mind of the observer). This is commonly thought to impede their investigation. By contrast, the physical objects we see around us are *public, objective*, and *observer-independent*, that is they exist independently of the mind of the observer (see for example presuppositions 5, 6 and 7 in Box 6.1). In the words of the philosopher Curt Ducasse,

> In the case of the things called 'physical,' the patent characteristic common to and peculiar to them, which determined their being all denoted by one and the same name, was simply that all of them were, or were capable of being, *perceptually public* – the same tree, the same thunderclap, the same wind, the same dog, the same man, etc., can be perceived by every member of the human public suitably located in space and in time. To be material or physical, then, *basically* means to be, or to be capable of being, perceptually public.
>
> (Ducasse, 1960, p. 85)

Given its grounding in publicly observable events, many also believe that physical science can provide *objective knowledge*. That there is something to explore which can be known in a public, objective way is supported by the fact that the edifice of science is constructed by different individuals at different times and in different geographical locations. As the philosopher of science Alan Chalmers notes,

> The theoretical structure that is modern physics is so complex that it clearly cannot be identified with the beliefs of any one group of physicists. Many scientists contribute in their separate ways with their separate skills to the growth and articulation of physics, just as many workers combine their efforts in the construction of a cathedral. And just as a happy steeplejack may be blissfully unaware of some of the implications of some ominous discovery made by labourers digging near the cathedral's foundations, so a lofty theoretician may be unaware of some new experimental finding for the theory on which he works. In either case, a relationship may objectively exist between parts of the structure independently of any individual awareness of that relationship.
>
> (Chalmers, 1992, p. 116)

In his book *Objective Knowledge*, the philosopher of science Karl Popper makes the added claim that the logical content of books, and the world of scientific problems, theories and arguments, form a kind of 'third world' of objective knowledge,[1] and

> knowledge in this objective sense is totally independent of anybody's claim to know; it is also independent of anybody's belief, or disposition to assert, or assert, or to act. Knowledge in the objective sense is knowledge without a knower; it is knowledge without a knowing subject.
>
> (Popper, 1972, p. 109)

Public, objective psychological science

Given the success of physical science, along with its promise of 'objective knowledge', it is not surprising that much of psychology tried to mould itself in its image, particularly in the behaviourist period (see Chapter 4). This attempt to 'objectify' both the contents and methods of psychology extended even to areas that dealt directly with subjective experience, such as psychophysics. Psychophysics tries to discover the precise ways in which the stimuli described by physics are mapped into experiences *of* those stimuli. Physical descriptions of the stimuli can be obtained using standard scientific techniques (instruments that measure intensity, frequency and so on), but these techniques do not allow one to access (let alone measure) conscious experiences. To avoid a return to 'experimental introspectionism' twentieth-century psychologists consequently tried to translate conscious experiences into externally observable, quantifiable responses (to 'operationalise' conscious experiences). In some writings this was combined with an attempt to *redefine* conscious experiences (of subjects) in terms of the operations used to measure them – and, for consistency, this redefinition also had to apply to the experiences of the experimenters. The psychophysicist S.S. Stevens argued, for example, that

> The study of sensation divests itself of many tangles, provided the distinction between the experimenter and experimentee is carefully preserved. . . . Of course, a given experimenter may use himself as a 'subject' or as an 'observer', but he ought properly to treat his own responses and reactions as he would treat those of another observer. . . . Under this view, the meaning of sensations rests in a set of operations involving an observer, a set of stimuli and a repertoire of responses. Sensations are reactions of organisms to energetic configurations in the environment. The study of sensations becomes a science when we undertake to probe their causes, categorise their occurrences, and quantify their magnitudes.
>
> (Stevens, 1966, p. 218)

According to Stevens, such operationalism makes psychological science like physical science. For example,

> We know the temperature of a body only through that body's behaviour which we note by studying the effects the body produces on other systems. It is much the same with sensation; the magnitude of an observer's sensations may be discovered by a systematic study of what the observer does in a controlled experiment in which he operates on other systems. . . . He may, for instance, adjust the *loudness* in his ears to match the *apparent intensity of various amplitudes of vibration* applied to his fingertips and thereby tell us the relative rates of growth of loudness and the sense of vibration.
>
> (ibid., p. 225; my italics)

Or, in the case of visual sensations,

> Perhaps the easiest way to elicit the relevant behaviour from an observer is to stimulate his eye, say, with a variety of different light intensities, and to ask him to assign a number proportional to the *apparent magnitude of each brightness as he sees it*.
>
> (ibid., p. 225; my italics)

In terms of methodology, it is clear what such translations of private, subjective states into public, objective measures achieve. Requiring a subject to adjust the growth of loudness in his ears to match the apparent intensity of vibration applied to his fingertips enables his judgements of heard loudness and felt intensity of vibration to be expressed in terms of the settings of two dials which control the intensity of the auditory and tactile stimuli. This both 'externalises' his subjective judgements and expresses them in the form of numbers on two scales.

But the difficulties of *removing* conscious experiences from psychophysics or of *redefining* them in this operational way should be clear from Stevens's inability to describe what subjects are required to do in a way that avoids reference to what they experience. In the auditory/tactile matching task the subject is required to match the intensity of *what he hears* to the intensity of *what he feels*, a procedure which can hardly be said to have removed his experience from the experiment. When quantifying the relative brightness of lights of different intensities, the subject is asked to assign a number proportional to the apparent magnitude of each brightness *as he sees it* – which makes it difficult to pretend that the subject is doing anything other than reporting on his visual experience (albeit by assigning a number rather than giving a verbal description). Given this, Stevens's contention that the 'meaning of sensation rests in a set of operations involving an observer, a set of stimuli and a repertoire of responses' (i.e. a set of operations that avoids reference to what a subject experiences) seems more an attempt to assimilate the study of sensations to a behaviourist preconception of psychological science, than an attempt to describe what subjects in perception experiments actually do.

However, that leaves us with a problem. If physical science relies on public, objective data, how can one establish a 'science of consciousness' which relies, at least in part, on subjective experiences? Dualists such as Descartes believed this problem to be insoluble (the nature of consciousness, in his view, is a matter for theologians). Reductionists have tried to deal with consciousness by eliminating it or reducing it to something 'objective' such as behaviour or a state or function of the brain. Yet, neither dualism nor reductionism gives an accurate description of what many subjects and experimenters actually do. In psychological science there are many areas of research which record or try to manipulate subjective experiences *as-such*, for example in the study of sensation, perception, dreams, imagery, emotion, thinking and so on. In some cases, thousands of experiments have been devoted to the study of just one aspect of these broad research areas. For example, the PsychInfo database currently lists over 16,500 articles on illusions, which are impossible to describe without some reference to what subjects experience. Even more impressive, the Medline database lists over 160,000 publications on pain and its alleviation. That is, pain has been the focus of extensive medical research, in spite of it being a paradigm case of a private, subjective, mental event within philosophy of mind. While there are many ways to measure the subjective experience of pain,[2] at the present time no valid 'objective' measure of pain experience (in terms of a physiological index) exists.

In sum, modern science does not exclude or eliminate conscious experiences from study, nor does it always replace their study with measures of behaviour or activities in the brain. So, how are we to make sense of this extensive study of private, subjective experiences within a supposedly, public, objective science?[3]

A closer examination of physical and psychological phenomena

I want to suggest that the problems posed by a 'science of consciousness' are largely artefactual, arising from the misconceived, dualist, split of the world into public, objective 'physical phenomena' versus private, subjective 'psychological phenomena' introduced in Chapters 6 and 7. This separation of physical phenomena from psychological phenomena is illustrated in a simple way by the separation of physical objects (in the world) from percepts *of* those objects (in the mind or brain) shown in Figures 6.1 and 6.2.

To see how this works out in a psychophysical experiment, let us replace the cat in Figure 6.1 with a simple stimulus of the kind used in these experiments, such as the light shown in Figure 9.1.

Following usual procedures, the subject (S) is asked to focus on the light and report on or respond to what she experiences, while the experimenter (E) controls the stimulus and tries to observe what is going on in the subject's brain. E has observational access to the stimulus and to S's brain states, but has no access to what S experiences. In principle, other experimenters can

Figure 9.1 A dualist model of a perception experiment, showing a clear separation between an 'objective' stimulus light out in the world (observed by an external observer) and a 'subjective' experience of a light in the mind or brain of the subject.

also observe the stimulus and S's brain states. Consequently, what E has access to is thought of as 'public' and 'objective'. However, E does not have access to S's experiences, making them 'private' and 'subjective' and a problem for science, in the ways noted above. This apparently radical difference in the *epistemic status* of the data accessible to E and S is enshrined in the words commonly used to describe what they perceive. That is, E makes *observations*, whereas S merely has *subjective experiences*.

Although this way of looking at things is adequate as a working model for many studies, it actually misdescribes the phenomenology of consciousness – and, consequently, misconstrues the problems posed by a science of consciousness. According to the model in Figure 9.2, when S attends to the

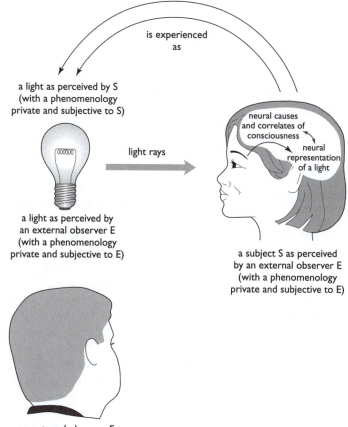

Figure 9.2 A reflexive model of what E and S actually observe in a perception experiment, which suggests that in terms of their phenomenology there is no actual difference in the subjective vs. objective status of the light 'experienced' by the subject and the light 'observed' by the external observer.

light in a room she does not have an experience *of* a light 'in her head or brain' – with its attendant problems for science. She just sees a light in a room (see Chapter 6). Indeed, what the subject experiences is very similar to what the experimenter experiences when he gazes at the light (she just sees the light from a different angle), in spite of the different terms they use to describe what they perceive (a 'physical stimulus' versus a 'sensation of light'). If so, there can be no actual difference in the subjective versus objective status of the light *phenomenology* 'experienced' by S and 'observed' by E. One can easily grasp the essential similarities between S's 'experiences' and E's 'observations' from the fact that *the roles of S and E are interchangeable*.

A thought experiment: 'changing places'

What makes one human being a 'subject' and another an 'experimenter'? Their different roles are defined largely by *differences in their interests* in the experiment, reflected in differences in what they are required to do. In Figure 9.2, the subject is required to focus only on her *own* experiences (of the light), which she needs to respond to or report on in an appropriate way. The experimenter is interested primarily in the *subject's* experiences, and in how these depend on the light stimulus or brain states that he can 'observe'.

But the roles of E and S are interchangeable. To exchange roles, *S and E merely have to turn their heads*, so that E focuses exclusively on the light and describes what he experiences, while S focuses her attention not just on the light (which she now thinks of as a 'stimulus') but also on events that she can observe in E's brain, and on E's reports of what he experiences. In this situation, E becomes the 'subject' and S becomes the 'experimenter'. Following current conventions, S would now be entitled to think of her observations (of the light and E's brain) as 'public and objective' and to regard E's experiences of the light as 'private and subjective'.

However, this outcome is absurd, as the phenomenology of the light remains the same, viewed from the perspective of either S or E, whether it is *thought of* as an 'observed stimulus' or as an 'experience'. Nothing has changed in the character of the light that E and S can observe other than the focus of their interest. That is, in terms of *phenomenology* there is no difference between 'observed phenomena' and 'experiences'.[4]

But which is it? If the phenomenology of the light remains the same whether it is thought of as a 'stimulus' or as an 'experience', is the phenomenon *private and subjective* or is it *public and objective*? These are subtle matters that we need to examine with care.

There is a sense in which all experienced phenomena are private and subjective

In dualism, 'experiences' are private and subjective, while 'physical phenomena' are public and objective, as noted above. However, according to the reflexive model there is no *phenomenal* difference between physical phenomena and our experiences *of* them. When we turn our attention to the external world, physical phenomena just *are* what we experience. If so, there is a sense in which physical phenomena are 'private and subjective' just like the other things we experience. For example, I cannot experience your phenomenal mountain or your phenomenal tree. I only have access to my own phenomenal mountain and tree. Similarly, I only have access to my own phenomenal light stimulus and my own observations of its physical properties (in terms of meter readings of its intensity, frequency, and so on). That is, w*e each live in our own private, phenomenal world.* Few, I suspect, would disagree.

If we each live in our own private, phenomenal world then each 'observation' is, in a sense, private. This was evident to the father of operationalism, the physicist P.W. Bridgman (1936), who concluded that, in the final analysis, 'science is only my private science'. However, this is clearly not the whole story. When an entity or event is placed beyond the body surface (as the entities and events studied by physics usually are), it can be perceived by any member of the public suitably located in space and time. Under these circumstances such entities or events are 'public' in the sense that there is *public access* to the observed entity or event *itself*.

Public access to the stimulus itself

While we normally think of the phenomena that we perceive as being 'physical', this distinction between the phenomena perceived by any given observer and the stimulus entity or event *itself* is important. Being appearances, perceived phenomena *represent* things themselves, but are not identical to them (see Chapter 8). The light perceived by E and S, for example, can be described in terms of its perceived brightness and colour. But, in terms of physics, the stimulus is better described as electromagnetism with a given mix of energies and frequencies. As with all visually observed phenomena, the phenomenal light only *becomes* a phenomenal light once the stimulus interacts with an appropriately structured visual system – and the result of this observed–observer interaction is an *experienced* light which is private to the observer in the way described above. However, if the stimulus itself is beyond the body surface and has an independent existence, it remains there *to be* observed whether it is observed (at a given moment) or not. That is why the stimulus itself is *publicly accessible* in spite of the fact that each observation/experience of it is private to a given observer.

Public in the sense of similar private experiences

To the extent that observed entities and events are subject to similar perceptual and cognitive processing in different human beings, it is also reasonable to assume a degree of *commonality* in the way such things are experienced. While each experience remains private, it may be a private experience that others share. For example, unless observers are suffering from red/green colour blindness, we normally take it for granted that they perceive electromagnetic stimuli with a wavelength of 700 nm as red and those with a wavelength of 500 nm as green. Given the privacy of light phenomenology there is no way to be certain that others experience 'red' and 'green' as we do ourselves (the classical problem of 'other minds'). But in normal life, and in the practice of science, we adopt the working assumption that the same stimulus, observed by similar observers, will produce similar observations or experiences. Thus, while *experienced* entities and events (phenomena) remain private to each observer, if their perceptual, cognitive and other observing apparatus is similar, we assume that their experiences (of a given stimulus) are similar. Consequently, experienced phenomena may be 'public' in the special sense that other observers have similar or shared experiences.

In sum:

- There is only *private* access to individual observed or experienced *phenomena*.
- There can be *public* access to the entities and events which serve as the stimuli for such phenomena (the entities and events which the phenomena represent). This applies, for example, to the entities and events studied by physics.
- If the perceptual, cognitive and other observing apparatus of different observers is similar, we assume that their experiences (of a given stimulus) are similar. In this special sense, experienced phenomena may be *public* in so far as they are *similar or shared private experiences*.

From subjectivity to intersubjectivity

This reanalysis of private versus public phenomena also provides a natural way to think about the relation between *subjectivity* and *intersubjectivity*. Each (private) observation or experience is necessarily *subjective*, in that it is always the observation or experience of a *given* observer, viewed and described from his or her individual perspective. However, once that experience is shared with another observer it can become *inter*-subjective. That is, through the sharing of a similar experience, subjective views and descriptions of that experience potentially converge, enabling intersubjective agreement about what has been experienced.

How different observers establish intersubjectivity through negotiating agreed descriptions of shared experiences is a complex process that we do not need to examine here. Suffice it to say that it involves far more than shared experience. One also needs a shared language, shared cognitive structures, a shared worldview or scientific paradigm, shared training and expertise and so on. To the extent that an experience or observation can be *generally* shared (by a community of observers), it can form part of the database of a communal science.

Dispassionate objectivity versus observer-free objectivity

The terms 'objectivity' and 'intersubjectivity' are often used interchangeably in philosophy of science (for example in Popper's writings). But note that, so far, this analysis of intersubjectivity avoids any reference to 'objectivity' in spite of the fact that it deals with a standard *physical* phenomenon (an observed light). Intersubjectivity of the kind described above requires the *presence* of subjectivity rather than its *absence*.

It goes without saying that, in science, descriptions of what one experiences need to be 'objective' in the sense of being dispassionate, accurate, truthful and so on. But it is important to distinguish 'being objective' in this conventional sense from the claim that, in science, observations or the 'object-ive' knowledge derived from them can provide data or knowledge that is, somehow, *observer-free*.

As Popper (1972) notes, knowledge that is codified into books and other artefacts has an existence that is, in one sense, observer-free. That is, the *books* exist in our libraries after their writers are long dead and their readers absent, and they form a repository of knowledge that can influence future social and technological development in ways which extend well beyond that envisaged by their original authors. However, the *knowledge itself* is not observer-free. Rather, it is valuable precisely because it encodes individual or collective experience. Nor, strictly speaking, is the print in books 'knowledge'. As Searle (1997) points out, words and other symbolic forms are intrinsically just ink marks on a page (see Chapter 5). They only become *symbols*, let alone convey meaning, to creatures that know how to interpret and understand them. But then the knowledge is in the knowing agent, not in the book. If so, the autonomous existence of books (and other media) provides no basis for 'objective knowledge' of the kind that Popper describes, that is, knowledge 'that is totally independent of anybody's claim to know', 'knowledge without a knower', and 'knowledge without a knowing subject' (see quote above). On the contrary, without knowing subjects, there is no knowledge *of any kind* (whether objective or not).

Neither observer-free objectivity nor social relativism

This grounding of science in intersubjectivity rather than some observer-free objectivity places scientific knowledge back where it belongs, in individual researchers and scientific communities. Individuals, interacting with their communities, establish intersubjectively shared, consensus realities. Different social and scientific communities may, of course, hold very different views about the nature of the world, and investigate it in ways determined by very different paradigms. The grounding of science in intersubjectivity therefore introduces a measure of social relativism. But it does not, in my view, open the way to an unfettered social relativism.

Knowledge may exist only in the knower (or a community of knowers), but *it is constrained by the nature of that which is known*. Consequently, the reflexive model adopts a form of critical (or indirect) realism. It assumes that experiences are experiences *of* entities and events (in the external world, body or mind/brain itself) and that these experiences are representations of those entities and events. This allows that there are many different ways of experiencing a given entity or event (from different perspectives and distances, with attention directed to different properties, and so on), but it also accepts that, for given purposes, representations can differ in their accuracy or utility. In the visual system, for example, there are clear differences between 'veridical' percepts, illusions and hallucinations, which can be tested by physical interaction with the world. In a similar way, there are many ways of construing or theorising about the nature of observed entities and events appropriate to the purposes of different social and intellectual communities. But this does not prevent an assessment of the relative merits of different theories, for example in terms of their ability to explain, predict or control observed events, that is, in terms of their ability to *fulfil* the purposes for which they are to be used.

Science provides an interesting, special case of communal knowledge for the reason that its procedures are, potentially, transportable to different cultures. Chalmers (1990) notes, for example, that science has developed many techniques for circumventing the idiosyncrasies of human perception, involving standardised procedures for translating data into meter readings, computer printouts and so on. Consequently, anyone following the same procedures should get the same results. In this way, he claims, 'observations become objectified'.

Once again, however, we need to be careful about the use of the term 'objectified'. The standardisation of procedures, and the development of instruments that provide precise measurement, greatly facilitates the process by which scientists reach intersubjective agreement, settle disagreement and establish repeatability. But, without *conscious scientists* to interpret them, meter readings, computer printouts and the like are not really 'observations'. Intrinsically, they are no more meaningful than uninterpreted ink marks on a page. That is, the standardisation of procedures and consequent repeatability of observable phenomena does not provide an objectivity that, somehow, strips away the experiences of observers. It does not provide 'observer-free observations' or 'knowledge without a knowing subject'.[5]

Four kinds of scientific objectivity

Reflexive monism nevertheless supports a more nuanced understanding of 'scientific objectivity'. It accepts that:

1 Science can be 'objective' in the sense of 'intersubjective'.
2 Descriptions of observations or experiences (observation statements) can be 'objective' in the sense of being dispassionate, accurate, truthful and so on.

3   Scientific method can be 'objective' in the sense that it follows well specified, repeatable procedures (perhaps using standardised measuring instruments).

However, one cannot make observations without engaging the experiences and cognitions of a conscious subject (unobserved meter readings are not 'observations'). If so:

4   Science *cannot* be 'objective' in the sense of being *observer-free*.

Intra-subjective and inter-subjective repeatability

According to the reflexive model, there is no phenomenal difference between *observations* and *experiences*. Each observation results from an interaction of an observer with an observed. Consequently, each observation is observer-dependent and numerically unique.[6] This applies even to observations made by the same observer, of the same entity or event, under the same observation conditions, *at different times* – although under these circumstances the observer may have no doubt that he/she is making *repeated* observations of the same entity or event.[7]

If the conditions of observation are sufficiently standardised (e.g. using meter readings, computer printouts and so on) the observation may be repeatable within a community of (suitably trained) observers, in which case intersubjectivity can be established by *collective agreement*. Once again, however, it is important to note that different observers cannot have a numerically *identical* experience. Even if they observe the same event, at the same location, at the same time, they each have their own, unique experience. *Inter*-subjective repeatability resembles *intra*-subjective repeatability in that it merely requires observations to be sufficiently similar to be taken for 'tokens' of the same 'type'.[8] This applies particularly to observations in science, where repeatability typically requires intersubjective agreement amongst scientists observing similar events at *different* times and in *different* geographical locations.

Consequences of the above analysis for a science of consciousness

The analysis has, so far, focused on physical events. But the same analysis can be applied to the investigation of events that are usually thought of as 'mental' or 'psychological'. Although the methodologies appropriate to the study of physical and mental phenomena may be very different, the same *epistemic* criteria apply to their scientific investigation. Physical phenomena and mental (psychological) phenomena are just different kinds of phenomena which observers experience (whether they are experimenters or subjects).

This closure of psychological with physical phenomena is self-evident in

Figure 9.3 In what way does the central line tilt?

situations where the same phenomenon can be thought of as either 'physical' or 'psychological' depending on one's interest in it. At first glance, for example, a visual illusion of the kind shown in Figure 9.3 might seem to present difficulties, for the reason that physical and psychological descriptions of this phenomenon conflict.

Physically, the figure consists entirely of squares, separated by a horizontal line. But subjectively, the line seems to tilt down to the left, and the squares don't seem to be entirely square. However, these physical and psychological descriptions result from two different observation procedures. To obtain the physical description, an experimenter E can place a straight edge against the central line, thereby obscuring the cues responsible for the illusion and providing a fixed reference against which the curvature and orientation of the line can be judged. To confirm that the line is actually straight and horizontal, other experimenters ($E_{1 \text{ to } n}$) can repeat this procedure. In so far as they each observe the line to be straight and horizontal under these conditions, their observations are public, intersubjective and repeatable.

But, the fact that the line *appears* to be bent and to tilt to the left (once the straight edge is removed) is similarly public, intersubjective and repeatable (amongst subjects $S_{1 \text{ to } n}$). Consequently, the illusion can be investigated using relatively conventional scientific procedures, in spite of the fact that the *illusion* is unambiguously *mental*. One can, for example, simply move the straight edge to just below the figure and orient it so that it seems parallel to the central line (sloped down to the left) – thereby obtaining a measure of the angle of the illusion. Similar criteria apply to the study of other mental events. $S_{1 \text{ to } n}$ might, for example, all report that a given increase in light intensity produces a just noticeable difference in brightness, an experience/observation that is intersubjective and repeatable. Alternatively, $S_{1 \text{ to } n}$ might all report that a given anaesthetic removes pain, or that if they stare at a red light spot, a green after-image appears, making such phenomena similarly public, intersubjective, and repeatable.

The empirical method

In sum, it is possible to give a non-dualist account of the empirical method, that is, a non-dualist account of what scientists actually do when they test their theories, establish intersubjectivity, repeatability and so on which accepts that, in terms of *phenomenology*, the phenomena that scientists 'observe' and the phenomena that scientists 'experience' are one and the same. While this forces one to re-examine the sense in which observed phenomena are 'public and objective' rather than 'private and subjective', the crucial *role* of observations in theory test and development remains the same.

The above analysis also retains a number of senses in which observations can be made 'objective'. That is, observations can be 'objective' in the sense of *intersubjective*, and the observers can 'be objective' in the sense of being dispassionate, accurate and truthful. Procedures can also 'be objectified' in the sense of being standardised and explicit. No observations, however, can be objective in the sense of being *observer-free*. Looked at in this way, there is no unbridgeable, epistemic gap that separates physical phenomena from psychological phenomena.

In short, once the *empirical method* is stripped of its dualist trappings, it applies as much to the science of consciousness as it does to the science of physics in that it adheres to the following principle:

> If observers $E_{1 \, to \, n}$ (or subjects $S_{1 \, to \, n}$) carry out procedures $P_{1 \, to \, n}$ under observation conditions $C_{1 \, to \, n}$ they should observe (or experience) result R

(assuming that $E_{1 \, to \, n}$ and $S_{1 \, to \, n}$ have similar perceptual and cognitive systems, that $P_{1 \, to \, n}$ are the procedures which constitute the experiment or investigation, and that $C_{1 \, to \, n}$ include *all* relevant background conditions, including those internal to the observer, such as their attentiveness, the paradigm within which they are trained to make observations and so on).[9]

Or, to put it more simply:

> *If you carry out these procedures you should observe or experience these results.* [10]

Complicating factors: some brief notes about methodology

It goes without saying that the empirical method, formulated in this way, provides only basic, *epistemic* conditions for the study of consciousness. One also requires *methodologies* appropriate to the subject matter – and the methodologies required to study conscious appearances are generally very different from those used in physics. There are many ways in which the phenomena we usually think of as physical or psychological differ from each other and amongst themselves (in terms of their relative permanence, stability, measurability, controllability, describability, complexity, variability, dependence on the observational arrangements, and so on). Even where the *same* phenomenon is the subject of both psychological and physical investigation (as might be the case with the light in Figure 9.2 above), the *interests* of psychologists and physicists differ, requiring different investigative techniques. A physicist, for example, is typically interested in the nature of the light as-such, characterised for example in terms of the quantum mechanical properties of its constituent photons. Psychologists are more interested in how such physical energies are translated by the visual system into phenomenal appearances, for example in the ability of the visual system to translate changes in light intensity and frequency into discriminable changes in brightness and colour. These differences in interests or in the phenomena themselves can greatly complicate systematic study and it is not my intention to minimise these difficulties. Unlike entities and events *themselves*, one cannot hook measuring instruments up to conscious appearances. For example, an instrument that measures the intensity of the light in Figure 9.2 (in lumens) cannot measure its experienced brightness. Given this, one needs some method of systematising subjective judgements and consequent reports, for example, by recording minimal, discriminable differences in brightness, in the ways typically used in psychophysical experiments.[11]

The need to translate observations into observation reports also occurs, of course, in natural science, although, here, reports are often made precise through the use of measuring instruments (which can be hooked up to the observed entities and events themselves). In some cases, a mental phenomenon can also be 'measured', in spite of the fact that the only observer with access to that phenomenon is the subject. It is standard practice, for example, to measure the size of a visual illusion by requiring subjects to adjust the dimensions or orientation of an external, comparison stimulus so that it matches the dimensions or orientation of the illusion (see, for example, the discussion above of the illusion in Figure 9.3).

That said, not all phenomena of interest to consciousness studies are easy to measure or even to communicate in an unambiguous way. Some experiences are difficult to translate into words, and therefore into subjective reports. Images, for example, generally lack the clarity, vividness and relative permanence of events as-experienced out in the world, which may make them difficult to describe with accuracy and precision. Consequently, indirect measures of imagery such as its effects on memory, learning, perception and so on are common in imagery research. Difficulties may also arise because one does not have a vocabulary adequate to communicate some experience unambiguously. Most human beings know what it is to love or to be angry but the many nuances of such experiences are more difficult to describe (the differences in the feeling of the love of wild places, love of one's child, love of one's lover, love of the truth, love of life, compassionate love, and so on). Investigators typically deal with such situations by developing new typologies and descriptive systems (as with the typologies developed for the chemical sense modalities, taste and smell). The way experiences are categorised into types and the extent to which given categories are differentiated in ordinary language are also, in part, culture-specific. English, for example, has a highly differentiated colour terminology (consequent on the development of pigments and dyes), whereas the language of the Dani tribesmen of New Guinea has only two colour terms ('mola' for warm, light colours, and 'mili' for dark, cold ones). In such situations, investigators can bypass linguistic

differences by using nonverbal responses, measuring, say, colour discrimination or memory by requiring subjects to visually match target colours with
comparison colours on a colour chart.

These brief points about methodological problems and some of the ways
that they are commonly addressed will be familiar to those trained in psychological research. Psychology and its sister disciplines have developed many
different methodologies for investigating sensation, perception, emotion,
thinking, and many other areas that deal directly or indirectly with how
phenomena are experienced. But there is much more to be said about this
subject and much to be done. Consequently, new methodologies for investigating phenomenal consciousness are once more a focus of scientific interest
(see readings in Jack and Roepstorff, 2003, 2004; Pope and Singer, 1978;
Varela and Shear, 1999; Velmans, 2000). It has to be said that the methodological problems are sometimes complex and the solutions sometimes controversial – for example in the use of introspective and phenomenological
methods where subjects become the primary investigators of themselves (see,
for example, Ericsson, 2003; Güzeldere and Nahmias, 2000; Hurlburt and
Akhter, 2006; Petitmengin, 2006; Schooler and Schreiber, 2004; Shear, 2007;
Shear and Jevning, 1999; Stevens, 2000; Varela, 1999; Vermersch, 1999). But
this does not alter the fact that the *phenomena* of consciousness provide
data that are potentially public, intersubjective and repeatable. Consequently,
the need to use and develop methodologies appropriate to the study of
such phenomena does not place them beyond science. Rather, it is part of
science.

Complicating factors: symmetries and asymmetries of access

The methodological differences between natural science and consciousness
science arise partly from differences in the questions of interest, partly from
differences amongst some of the phenomena studied, and partly from systematic differences in the typical *relation* of the observer to that which is
observed. For experimental purposes, the entities and events studied by physics are located *external* to the observers. Placed this way, such entities and
events afford *public access* (see above) and different observers establish intersubjectivity, repeatability and so on by using similar exteroceptive systems
and equipment to observe them. E and S in Figure 9.2, for example, might
observe the light via their visual systems, supplemented by similar instruments that measure its intensity, frequency and other physical properties.
When S and E (and any other observer suitably placed in space and time) use
similar means to access information about a given entity or event we may say
that they have *symmetrical access* to the observed (in this case, to the stimulus
light itself). If the event of interest is located on the surface of or within S's
body, or within S's brain, as would be the case in the study of physiology or
neurophysiology, it remains external to E. Thus placed, it can still afford
public, symmetrical access to a community of other, suitably placed external

observers ($E_{1 \text{ to } n}$). Consequently, such events can be investigated by the same 'external' means employed in other areas of natural science.

In the study of consciousness, however, what the *subject* observes or experiences is of primary interest and, if one compares the information *about* S available *to* S with the information *about* S available *to* E (and other external observers), various forms of *asymmetry* arise. If the event of interest is located on the surface of or within S's body, she may be able to observe or experience that event through interoceptive as well as exteroceptive systems. For example, if she stabs her finger with a pin, she might be able not only to see the pin go in, but also to experience a pain in her finger consequent on skin damage. Under these circumstances, she has two sources of information about the event taking place in her skin, while E retains only exteroceptive (visual) information about this event, as before. Likewise, if one stimulates S's brain with a microelectrode, she might, like E, be able to observe the electrical stimulation (with an 'autocerebroscope').[12] But, in addition, she might be able to experience the effects of such stimulation in the form of a consequent visual, auditory, tactile or other experience (see discussion of Penfield and Rassmussen, 1950, ch. 3). In such situations, observers E and S have *asymmetrical access* to the observed.

Crucially, E and S (and any other observers) have *asymmetrical access* to each other's *experiences* of an observed (asymmetrical access to each other's observed phenomena). That is, they know what it is like to have their own experiences, but they can only access the experiences of others indirectly via their verbal descriptions or nonverbal behaviour. This applies to *all* observed phenomena – for example, it applies even if the observed is a simple physical stimulus, such as the light in Figure 9.2. As E does not have direct access to S's experience of the light and vice versa, there is no way for E and S to be *certain* that they have a similar experience (whatever they might claim). E might nevertheless *infer* that S's experience is similar to his own on the assumption that S has similar perceptual apparatus, operating under similar observation arrangements, and on the basis of S's similar observation reports. S normally makes similar assumptions about E. It is important to note that this has not impeded the development of physics and other natural sciences, which simply ignore the problem of 'other minds' (uncertainty about what other observers actually experience). They just take it for granted that if *observation reports* are the same, then the corresponding *observations* are the same. The success of natural science testifies to the pragmatic value of this approach.

Given this, it seems justifiable to apply the same pragmatic criteria to the observations of subjects in studies of consciousness (i.e. to their 'subjective reports'). If, given a standard stimulus and standardised observation conditions, different subjects give similar reports of what they experience, then (barring any evidence to the contrary) it is reasonable to assume that they have similar experiences (see also Baars and McGovern, 1996; Velmans, 1999b). Ironically, psychologists have often agonised over the merits of observation reports *when produced by subjects*, although, like other scientists, they take them for granted *when produced by experimenters*, on the grounds that the observations of subjects are 'private and subjective', while those of experimenters are 'public and objective'. As experimenters do not have access to each other's experiences any more than they have access to the experiences of subjects, this is a fallacy, as we have seen. Provided that the observation conditions are sufficiently standardised, the observations reported by subjects can be made public, intersubjective and repeatable amongst a community of subjects in much the same way that observations can be made public, intersubjective and repeatable amongst a community of experimenters. This provides an epistemic basis for a science of consciousness that includes its phenomenology.

In sum, asymmetries of access complicate, but do not prevent, the investigation of experience. In Figure 9.2, E has access, in principle, to the events and processes in S's visual system, but not to S's experience. While S focuses exclusively on the light, she has access to her experience, but not to the antecedent processing in her visual system. Under these circumstances, the information available to S *complements* the information available to E. To obtain a complete account of visual perception one needs to utilise *both* sources of information.

Complicating factors: how to distinguish a physical cause of experience from a perceptual effect

Asymmetries of access to each other's conscious states are a fundamental given of how we are situated in the world, and their consequences need to be understood if we are to unravel the puzzles surrounding consciousness. In exteroception, it seems entirely natural to think of physical stimuli *causing* our perceptions *of* them.[13] The resulting percepts, in turn, *represent* their causal antecedents. This only makes sense if physical stimuli are, in some sense, *distinguishable* from our experiences of them – and in classical dualist thought, the separation of physical stimuli from experiences *of* them is clear. The light in Figure 9.1, for example, is out in the world, while the experience *of* the light is thought to be 'in the subject's mind'. From the perspective of an external observer E, the light is the initiating stimulus that causes the experience of the light in the subject's mind, while the experience of the light (in her mind) *represents* the initiating stimulus. Materialist reductionists give a similar analysis, with the caveat that the experience of light is really a state of S's brain. Dualists and reductionists also accept that E can *observe* the stimulus light and the events in the subject's brain, but E does not have direct access to S's subjective experience. E can only make *inferences about* the existence and nature of S's experience on the basis of her subjective reports (although reductionists doubt the accuracy of such reports).

The reflexive model agrees with these other models that physical stimuli can *cause* our perceptions *of* them, and that the resulting experiences can *represent* their causal antecedents.[14] It also accepts that E can *observe* the stimulus light (and events in the subject's brain) and can only make *inferences about* the existence and nature of S's experience. But it rejects the dualist claim that, in addition to the light that S can see in the world, there is some separate experience of the light 'in S's mind'. When S focuses on the light, there is a *neural* representation of the stimulus formed in S's brain (as reductionists assume). Viewed from S's perspective, there is also a nonreducible *experience* of the light that represents the initiating stimulus (as dualists assume). But dualism gives a misleading understanding of the phenomenology of this experience. While S focuses on the light in the world, all she experiences is a light in the world in the way shown in Figure 9.2. In this, there is little difference between the light experienced by S and the light observed by E, although E thinks of the light that he observes as the physical *cause* of the light that S experiences.

At first glance, this might seem to present a paradox for the reflexive model. If, in terms of their phenomenology, there is little difference between the light in the world that E 'observes' and the light in the world that S 'experiences', how can the former be a 'physical cause' and the latter a 'perceptual effect'?

To resolve this paradox one has to bear in mind, once again, that E and S play different *roles* in a typical experiment. While E acts as an 'external observer' his interest is focused on S's perceptual processing and consequent experience – and while S acts as a subject she is interested only in her own experience. One also has to bear in mind that different information about S's perceptual processing and experience is accessible to S and E. As noted above, this allows two, complementary accounts of what is going on: an account of the causal sequence in S's perception viewed from the perspective of E (in terms of the information accessible to E), and an account of the causal sequence in S's perception viewed from the perspective of S (in terms of the information accessible to S).

Perception viewed from the perspectives of the external observer and the subject

The external observer can *observe* the causes of a subject's experiences but can only *infer* the existence of the experiences themselves. For example, in Figure 9.2, E can observe the stimulus light that he takes to be the 'physical cause' of S's experiences. In principle, E can also observe the events in S's visual system, for example the formation of retinal images, and the consequent neural activity in her optic nerve and brain. However, E can only infer the existence of S's experience of the light, on the grounds that he can see the light himself, that the subject claims to do likewise, that the subject has a similar visual system to his own, and so on.

By contrast, the subject can *observe* (and report on) what she experiences,[15] but can only *infer* the antecedent causes of what she experiences. While she attends to the light that she experiences, she can observe no light stimulus that is antecedent to what she experiences; nor can she observe her own retinal images, or the neural activity in her own optic nerve and brain. She can nevertheless infer that such processes operate (prior to her experience) on the grounds that she could observe those processes operating in others (if she were to adopt the role of an external observer) and, given similar visual systems, what applies to others must apply to herself.

In short, whether we *regard* a phenomenal light in the world as an 'experience' or a 'physical cause' of an experience depends entirely on whether we adopt the role of the subject or the external observer (see also the thought experiment on 'changing places' above). If we take the role of the subject, the light we can see out in the world is a 'perceptual effect' of our current perceptual processing. If we adopt the role of an external observer, we regard the same light we can see as the initiating cause of perceptual processing in someone else.

Note that dualists and reductionists give a very different analysis of this situation. For them, the perceptual effect (the experience of the light) is not the light one can see in the world at all, but something else, somewhere else 'in the mind or brain'. Consequently, the light in the world that one can see is the *physical cause* of perception whether one views it from the perspective of the external observer or the subject. This might seem to be a more straightforward analysis as one does not have to deal with how things look from the perspective of an external observer versus a subject, with symmetries and asymmetries of access, and so on. However, these classical positions have a highly counterintuitive consequence:

Adopting the perspective of an external observer towards oneself

Imagine that you are an external observer interested in a subject's perceptual processing and that, in the ways shown in Figures 9.1 and 9.2, you are interested in how they experience a light that is positioned directly in front of them in the external world. In this situation it makes sense to think of the external light as the *initiating cause* of the perceptual processing that produces the subject's experience – and, on this, the dualist, reductionist and reflexive models agree.

But suppose now that you reflect on your *own* experience of the stimulus light. In this situation, is the stimulus that you can see the 'physical cause' of your own experience or the 'perceptual effect'?

As noted above, dualists and reductionists ignore asymmetries of access between external observer and subject. Consequently, if you are either a dualist or a reductionist, when you consider your own perception you will probably not think twice about adopting the role of an external observer towards yourself. The light that you can see is the cause of S's experience, so it must be the cause of your own experience. Given that the light that you can see is the physical cause of your own experience, the perceptual effect must be something else, somewhere else (in your own mind or brain). This cause–

effect relationship is just as it was for S. You can *observe* the cause of your own experience, but you can only *infer* the existence and nature of the perceptual effect (the experience itself).

The alert reader will have noticed that something went desperately wrong in the last sentence (just above). This consequence of dualism and reductionism is highly counterintuitive. It goes without saying that you can only have indirect, inferential access to the experiences of *others*, but the suggestion that you only have indirect, inferential access to your *own* experience is absurd. If this were true you could not know that you were in love or in pain simply by feeling them, and you could not know what it is like to see, hear, smell or taste simply by having such experiences. Like the experiences of others, you would have to work out what you were experiencing on the basis of observed external or internal stimuli, brain states and your own subjective reports!

But if you do accept that you have direct access to your *own* experiences, and not to its antecedent causes, then your conviction that you can directly observe the *cause* of your own experience needs to be reversed. The light that you can see in the world is the *effect* of your own (recently completed) perceptual processing – and it is the antecedent cause of what you (currently) experience that needs to be *inferred*.

Why is this important? Because it undermines the very basis of dualism, and, with it, the basis for the dualist–reductionist debate. If the light that one experiences out in the world *is* the 'perceptual effect' (to which one has direct access) then there would seem to be no grounds for inferring the existence of some *added* experience *of* a light 'in the mind'. The only obvious escape for dualism is to *resist* the claim that there is no phenomenal difference between observed lights and (visual) experiences *of* them. But this is an empirical matter, not a philosophical matter. One only has to look.[16]

The reflexive model gives a very different analysis. At the point that you, the external observer, reflect on your own experience you adopt the role of the 'subject' (see above). Like S you can *observe* (and report on) what you experience, but you can only *infer* the antecedent causes (the existence of antecedent stimulation, retinal images, and neural activity in your own optic nerve and brain). Consequently, the light that you can see is the experienced *effect* of your own perceptual processing. Once you see it, the processes that enable you to see it have already operated. If you switch back to being an external observer of someone else, you quite rightly *regard* the light that you can see as the cause of what S experiences (it is, after all, your own perceptual representation of the stimulus that causes S's perceptual processing). However, whether you *think* of the light as the 'perceptual effect' (of your own processing) or the 'cause' (of S's processing), its *phenomenology* remains the same.

Can the study of experiences be a science?

There are many other consequences of the above analysis that we have not, as yet, addressed. For example, asymmetries of access and the complementary information available to a subject and an external observer also help to explain one of the great paradoxes of consciousness – that it both *must* and *can't* have a causal role in the activities of the brain (see Chapters 4, 10 and 13).

But it is worth pausing for a moment to reflect on the consequences of the analysis so far for a science of consciousness. Classical dualism *separates* consciousness from the surrounding physical world, leaving our conscious nature isolated from it 'in the mind'. This underlies the conventional view that the contents of consciousness are private and subjective, in contrast to physical phenomena (such as the objects we perceive) which are public and objective (presuppositions 6 and 7 in Box 6.1).

According to the reflexive model, there is no actual conscious experience/ physical phenomenon separation. For everyday purposes, it is useful to think of the phenomena we observe as the 'physical causes' of what other people experience. However, once we have observed such physical phenomena, they are *already* aspects of what we ourselves experience. That is, physical phenomena are *part of* what we experience rather than *apart from* it. There is a sense therefore in which physical phenomena are private and subjective in the ways conventionally attributed to 'mental' events.

But this does not prevent either the development of a science of physics or the development of a science of consciousness. Observations arise from an interaction of a given observer with a given observed and, under appropriate conditions, the observed *events and entities themselves* may be publicly accessible; alternatively, they may be reproducible at different times and geographical locations. Under these circumstances, observations (or experienced phenomena) may become repeatable within a community of observers, in which case they become 'public' in the sense of being *shared* private experiences, and 'objective' in the sense of *intersubjective*.

While the role of observation (the empirical method) remains central in this reanalysis of science, it removes the *pretence* that observations have nothing to do with the conscious experiences of observers. Within psychology, for example, it challenges the convention that the observations of an external observer are always 'objective' while the experiences of a subject are always 'subjective'. Either E or S can make observations that are objective in the sense of being intersubjective, dispassionate and truthful, or in a way that follows well specified procedures. But neither E nor S can make observations that are objective in the sense of having nothing to do with what they experience. Both E and S observe or experience phenomenal worlds, which arise from a reflexive interaction of attended-to entities and events with their perceptual processes. *What* E or S observes depends entirely on their focus of attention. $E_{1 \text{ to } n}$ might be able to observe what E observes, making his observations public, intersubjective and repeatable. Equally, $S_{1\,to\,n}$ might be able to observe what S observes, making her observations public, intersubjective and repeatable.

Critical phenomenology

The analysis above supports a form of *critical phenomenology* (CP) – a common-sense, natural, but nonreductive approach to the study of mind. This adopts the conventional view that human experiences have causes and correlates in the external world, body and brain that can be investigated by a range of *third-person methods* commonly used in cognitive science, neuroscience and related sciences. However CP recognises that third-person methods do *not* provide direct access to subjects' experiences, and that the causes and correlates of conscious experiences are not the experiences themselves (see Chapters 3, 4 and 5). Subjects do, however, have access to their own experiences, on which they can report. Consequently, third-person methods have to be supplemented by *first-person methods* that guide subjects to attend to aspects of their conscious experience that are of interest to experimenters (or to the subjects themselves).[17]

Why call this approach '*critical* phenomenology' rather than just 'phenomenology'? First, to dissociate it from the classical, European versions of phenomenology (in the tradition of Husserl, Merleau-Ponty, etc.) in which third-person methods and third-person science have a minor (and sometimes suspect) role (see Gallagher, 2007). Instead, critical phenomenology adopts a form of 'psychological complementarity principle' in which first-person descriptions of experience and third-person descriptions of correlated brain states provide accounts of what is going on in the mind that are complementary and mutually irreducible. A complete account of mind requires both (see above). Second, while CP takes subjective experiences to be real, it remains cautious about the veridical nature of phenomenal reports in that it assumes neither first- nor third-person reports of phenomena to be incorrigible, complete, or unrevisable – and it remains open about how such reports should be interpreted within any given body of theory.

CP is also open to the possibility that first-person investigations can be improved by the development of more refined first-person investigative methods, just as third-person investigations can be improved by the development of more refined third-person methods. CP also takes it as read that first- and third-person investigations of the mind can be used conjointly, either providing triangulating evidence for each other, or in other instances to inform each other. Third-person observations of brain and behaviour for example can sometimes inform and perhaps alter interpretations of first-person experiences (very subtle differences in first-person experience for example can sometimes be shown to have quite distinct, correlated differences in accompanying neural activity in the brain). Likewise, first-person accounts of subjective experience can inform third-person accounts of what is going on in the brain – indeed, without such first-person accounts, it would be impossible to discover the neural correlates of given conscious experiences. In adopting the view that subjective conscious experiences are real, but our descriptions and understanding of them revisable, CP exemplifies the *critical realism* outlined in Chapter 8.

Finally, CP is *reflexive*, taking it for granted that *experimenters* have first-person experiences and can describe those experiences much as their subjects do. And crucially, experimenters' *third-person reports of others* are based, in the first instance, on their *own first-person experiences* in the ways shown above.

Can the study of experiences be a science? If this analysis is correct, the 'phenomena' observed by experimenters are as much a part of the world that they experience as are the 'subjective experiences' of subjects. If so, the *whole* of science may be thought of as an attempt to make sense of the phenomena that we observe or experience.[18]

Notes

1 In Popper's scheme, the physical world is the first world, the psychological world (conscious experience) is the second world, and the world of objective knowledge recorded in books and other artefacts is the third world.

2 Standard measuring instruments include verbal rating scales, numerical rating scales, visual analogue scales, and questionnaires such as the McGill Pain Questionnaire (Melzack, 1975, 1987).

3 There are, of course, extensive investigations of neurophysiological indices of conscious experiences of many differing kinds (e.g. using PET scans, fMRI, microelectrode implantation, and so on – see Rees and Frith, 2007). But one still needs to study experiences themselves in order to discover how such neuro-physiological activities relate to them.

4 While I make no phenomenal distinction between observations and experiences, I accept the usual distinction between observations and observation statements (observation statements are descriptions of observations, which in these terms are also descriptions of experiences).

5 Whether science has an observer-free 'objectivity' or an entirely socially relative 'intersubjectivity' has been extensively debated in philosophy and sociology of science (see, for example, Chalmers, 1990). My brief discussion of this issue is intended merely to illustrate how intersubjective knowledge, constrained by that which it is knowledge of, might provide a plausible, middle-way between these polarised positions.

6 At any given moment in time t_1, a given observer S can have only one, particular experience/observation O_1.

7 If, at times $t_{1 \text{ to } n}$ S makes observations $O_{1 \text{ to } n}$ of a given entity or event X under fixed observation conditions C, and observations $O_{1 \text{ to } n}$ are indistinguishable (in terms of the parameters which are relevant to the purposes of the observation), then O is said to be repeatable. Under these circumstances, $O_{1 \text{ to } n}$ can also be said to be 'token' observations of the same 'type'.

8 Intersubjective agreement is, of course, greatly simplified if the observation is a number on a digital counter. For example, my observation of the number 4.13 can safely be assumed to be similar to your observation of the number 4.13 obtained from a similar counter under similar experimental conditions, even though my

observation at time and location t_1l_1 is unique to me, and your observation at t_2l_2 is unique to you.

9   The values of subscript n can differ, of course, for E, S, P and C respectively.

10 These principles for an *Intersubjective Science* were introduced in Velmans (1999a). Richardson (2000) has suggested ways in which these principles may be applied to establishing intersubjectivity in clinical or therapeutic situations.

11 To clarify the epistemic issues, I have so far focused only on very simple cases of conscious experience (simple visual percepts, pains and so on) which are relatively easy to study and control. Under normal conditions, for example, visual perception appears to be so tightly guided by the information picked up by the retina that the resulting experience gives every appearance of being a 'direct perception' of what is out-there in the world. Consequently, given similar stimuli, presented under similar viewing conditions, with similar expectations, experimental instructions and so on, different subjects are likely to agree that they see the same thing. By contrast, experienced thoughts, emotions and images are largely determined by endogenous factors, and even when they are influenced by events in the external world, they generally represent some inner response *to* external events, rather than representing the events themselves. This makes them heavily dependent on individual differences in heredity, personal history, momentary fluctuations in attention and interest, and on other endogenous factors, making them less easy to reproduce under controlled conditions. Other experiences may be rare or even unique to the individuals involved. While these factors complicate investigation they do not prevent it. Psychologists simply include such complicating factors within their research – investigating the effects of heredity, learning, and attention on thinking and emotion, making use of single case studies where needed and so on. In some studies investigators harness subjects' ability to control their own experience. A common method of studying imagery for example is to ask subjects to generate a given image, and then to perform some task that reveals something about its nature or use. When a given experience is very difficult to reproduce at will, it can be investigated when it occurs naturally, as in studies of dreaming during REM sleep. As in natural science, the accuracy of reports can become suspect when stimuli or experiences are near the limits of detectability, for example, when a weak signal is embedded in noise – in which case estimation procedures have to be developed, such as those suggested by signal detection theory. One also has to be mindful of the well known effects of the act of observation on the nature of the observed. Such 'experimenter effects' have been extensively investigated in psychology (along with the means by which they can be minimised), but they can be particularly powerful when the observer *is* the observed, for example, when a subject studies (rather than simply reports on) her own conscious experience. In such cases one has to attempt either to limit such influences (cf. Ericsson, 2003; Ericsson and Simon, 1984; Hurlburt and Akhter, 2006; Petitmengin, 2006) or to harness them, for example in situations where focused self-observation is intended to transform conscious states rather than to describe them (see, for example, discussion in Shear, 2007).

12 A hypothetical machine for viewing activity in one's own brain, for example, via a TV monitor attached to sensors which detect electrical, magnetic or other activity.

13 Endogenous, cognitively driven processes also contribute to what is experienced, but this does not affect the causal status of the external stimulus. In forms of exteroception that allow exploration of what is perceived through bodily movements, there may also be dynamic, preconscious sensory-motor forms of exploration of what is perceived of the kind stressed by 'enactive' theories of perception. In normal exteroception, external stimuli may nevertheless be regarded as 'initiating causes' of what is experienced.

14 As noted in Chapter 8, such experiences ultimately represent the stimuli *themselves*

(in a way that is biologically appropriate to the perceiver); but, following more usual conventions, they could also be said to be the subject's phenomenal representations of the stimuli observed by the experimenter. These accounts of what the experience represents do not conflict. They differ only in their 'level of analysis'.

15 S can observe her own experiences in the sense that S has direct (non-inferential) access to them. That is, they provide a form of data about which she can make reports. This entails no regression to some additional, inner observer or homunculus, and it entails no commitment to those reports being incorrigible.

16 In terms of *phenomenology*, the light you observe and the light you experience are one and the same (see Chapter 6). I do not, of course, wish to deny that there may be other experiences consequent on seeing the light such as thoughts about the light, feelings, images and so on. However, these are additional to visual experiences of the light as-such. I only claim visual experiences of the light as-such to be phenomenally indistinguishable from the observed light out in the world.

17 It will be apparent to those familiar with the consciousness studies literature that this even-handed, nonreductive approach to first- and third-person methods distinguishes CP from more behaviourally oriented approaches such as Dennett's *heterophenomenology* which tries to restrict the science of consciousness to third-person methods. Dennett's heterophenomenology is intimately related to his computational functionalist analysis of mind, in that it tries to develop an investigative method that is consistent with consciousness itself being nothing more than given forms of brain functioning, specifiable in entirely third-person terms, in spite of how it may seem. As I have given an extensive critique of Dennett's computational functionalism in Chapter 5, I will not consider his heterophenomenology in any detail here. Readers with a particular interest in how critical phenomenology compares with heterophenomenology may find my online dialogue with Dennett in Velmans (2001) entertaining, and should refer to the more detailed arguments presented in Dennett (2003) and Velmans (2007c).

18 See also an interesting essay developing a very similar theme from the joint perspectives of neurophenomenology and quantum mechanics by the philosopher Michel Bitbol (2008), and an insightful analysis given from the perspective of European phenomenology by Dan Zahavi (2007).

10 How consciousness relates to information processing in the brain

In Chapters 2 to 5, I have summarised the case against both dualist and reductionist accounts of the *nature* of consciousness. Chapters 6 and 7 provide an alternative, 'common-sense' analysis of conscious phenomenology that does not require it to be anything other than it *seems*. According to the reflexive model I develop, phenomenal consciousness neither is mysterious in the sense of *res cogitans*, nor does it reduce to a state or function of the brain. That said, there is little doubt that the phenomenology of human consciousness relates closely to the activities in human brains. Some activities in the visual system have causal effects on consequent visual experiences; some activities in the somatosensory system appear to cause tactile experiences, and so on. Other activities appear to correlate with (co-occur with) experiences. According to many theorists, once experiences appear, they in turn have causal effects on, and functions in, subsequent brain activity. In the present chapter we examine these relationships with care.

Where to start

The activities in brains can be specified at many levels of analysis, ranging from the microcosmic events specified by quantum mechanics to the macro-cosmic action of large neuronal populations and the integrated activity of the entire brain. As I am concerned with how ordinary experiences relate to mental processes of the kind traditionally studied in cognitive psychology, the discussion which follows largely relates subjective experience to mental activities specified in traditional, *macro-functional* terms (in terms of human information processing, neural network systems and so on). Quantum mechanical effects might turn out to be important and the nature of embodying neurophysiology is undoubtedly important, but we do not need to enter into the details of these for now. The puzzle of how conscious experiences relate to the everyday mental processes that we think of as being conscious (thinking, reading, speaking and so on) turns out to be mysterious enough.

As noted in Chapter 4, early psychological speculations about the relationship of consciousness to human information processing can be traced back to the writings of William James (1890), who associated consciousness with selective attention and primary memory. Until the late 1960s, the precise nature of this 'association' between consciousness and information processing remained ambiguous. Theories were not clear, for example, about whether focal attentive processing *caused* consciousness, *correlated* with consciousness, or was *identical* to consciousness. However, in the early 1970s, with the ascendance of cognitive psychology, a number of theorists began to *redefine* consciousness in information processing terms, thereby finessing such questions. Posner and Warren (1972), for example, defined a conscious process as one that makes use of a limited capacity central processing system; Bjork (1975) referred to this central processor as a kind of 'executive consciousness', and so on. Similar redefinitions recur in more recent writings, for example in Mandler's (1997) treatment of the central processor as a form of executive consciousness, Baddeley's (2001) association of consciousness with the central executive component of working memory, and Baars's (1988, 2007) identification of consciousness with information in a 'global workspace'.

The relationship of consciousness to information processing is a foundational issue both for psychology and for philosophy of mind. If consciousness really is nothing more than a form of information processing, then psychologists can investigate the nature of consciousness by investigating the nature of such processing using traditional third-person methods, and not worry about how conscious *phenomenology* relates to information processing accounts of mind. Similarly, philosophers do not need to agonise over the ontological nature of 'qualia' or about how experiences and neurons can have causal interactions. If experiences just *are* forms of information processing in the brain, then their nature and causal interactions with other, nonconscious forms of processing present no philosophical mysteries.

Unfortunately, nature does not always fit conveniently into the conceptual boxes we have prepared for her. As I have noted in Chapter 3, it is a fallacy to conflate *causation, correlation* and *ontological identity*. Attentional processing might, for example, cause or correlate with conscious experience without *being* conscious experience. A redefinition of phenomenal consciousness in terms of attentional or other processing is justified only if nothing essential to the nature of phenomenal consciousness is lost in the redefinition. But, arguably, the very heart of phenomenal consciousness is lost. Exact knowledge of the brain's 'limited capacity central processor' or 'executive monitor' would tell us something important about how the brain functions, but nothing about what it is like to have a given experience. This is true for humans, but it becomes particularly obvious once we imagine such processing being instantiated in a silicon brain. *We* know what it is like to have conscious states from our own first-person, subjective experience and we have good reasons for inferring the existence of similar states and experiences in other humans (on the basis of what they tell us, shared heredity, education and so on). With silicon brains, however, there is no way to know on the basis of their *information processing alone* whether the same functioning is accompanied by (a) the same experience, (b) a distinct 'silicon experience', or (c) no experience at all.

If so, functionalist redefinitions of experience in terms of information processing must leave something out. I have examined the many other problems of such functionalist reductionism in Chapters 4 and 5. In the present chapter I assume that conscious phenomenology provides first-person psychological data that does not need to be redefined to be investigated, an assumption shared by many workers involved in consciousness research (and one that I have justified in Chapter 9). From this starting point, we can examine how such phenomenology can be *related* to information processing without redefining it or reducing it to that processing.

The analysis that follows briefly summarises and updates the extensive treatment of these issues that originally appeared in *Behavioral and Brain Sciences* in Velmans (1991a), forty published commentaries, and my replies in Velmans (1991b, 1993b, 1996c).[1] Broadly speaking, psychologists who have examined the relationship of consciousness to human information processing experimentally have focused on three questions:

1   When (in time) does consciousness appear in human information processing?
2   Where (in the sequence of operations) does consciousness appear in human information processing?
3   How does conscious processing differ from preconscious and unconscious processing?

Many psychologists have assumed that answers to these questions will reveal the adaptive function of consciousness in the activities of the brain.

How long does it take to become conscious of something?

Subjectively, we seem to be immediately aware of what we attend to. However, experiments on the timing of conscious awareness by the neurophysiologist Benjamin Libet suggest that consciousness of input does not arise until at least 200 milliseconds (ms) after stimuli arrive at the cortical surface (see Libet, 1996, for a review). Libet *et al.* (1979), for example, found that direct microelectrode stimulation of the somatosensory cortex required a pulse train of at least 200 ms duration before any conscious awareness of the stimulus was reported (pulse trains 10 per cent shorter than this were not subjectively experienced). Libet *et al.* also found that tactile stimuli applied to a finger were masked (prevented from entering consciousness) by microelectrode stimulation of the somatosensory cortex applied up to 200 ms after the arrival of the tactile stimuli. On the grounds that one cannot prevent a stimulus from entering consciousness *after* it has done so, they concluded that at least 200 ms of processing time are required to produce neural conditions adequate to support consciousness. The reason we do not experience any mismatch between experienced and actual stimulus arrival time appears to be that the brain records the actual time of arrival of the stimulus at the cortical surface. The brain then enters this into the representations of input that it constructs (in spite of the fact that the representations themselves take about 200 ms to construct).

What is the basis for this claim? Libet (1996) reviews evidence that the brain records the time of tactile stimulus arrival with a 'time marker' in the form of an early evoked potential at the somatosensory cortical surface. However microelectrode stimuli applied directly to cortical areas such as the medial lemniscus (LM) do not produce such early evoked potentials. By contrasting the subjective timing of stimuli with and without such time markers Libet found that the former but not the latter are subjectively referred 'backwards in time' (to the time of occurrence of the marker). For example, tactile stimuli applied 100 ms *after* the LM cortical stimuli appeared, subjectively, to *precede* them (by around 100 ms). Consequently such tactile stimuli do not appear to be subjectively delayed (by 200 ms – see Figure 10.1).

These surprising findings and conclusions about 'subjective referral' have

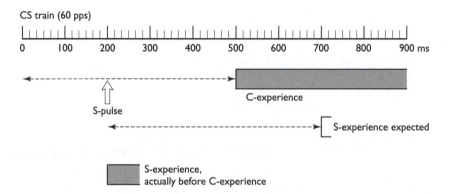

Figure 10.1 Referral backwards in time an experiment in which the subjective arrival time of a stimulus applied to the skin is compared with that of a train of electrical stimuli applied directly to the somatosensory cortex (at a rate of 60 per second). Under the conditions of the experiment the cortical stimuli need to be applied for around 500 ms before they produce neural conditions able to support a conscious experience (a C-experience). There is evidence that a similar time delay of around 500 ms is required for a threshold stimulus applied to the skin (the S-pulse) to result in a conscious experience. So if the latter is applied 200 ms after the cortical stimulus, it should be experienced as occurring after the cortical stimulus. However, in this experiment the skin stimulus was experienced as occurring before the cortical stimulus. According to Libet *et al.* (1979), a skin stimulus produces an early negative-going potential on arrival at the cortical surface which acts as a 'time marker' for its time of arrival, and the brain subjectively refers experienced time of arrival 'backwards in time' to this time marker. Electrical stimuli applied directly to the somatosensory cortex produce no equivalent time marker, so they are not referred backwards in time. Hence the skin stumulus seems to precede the cortical stimuli (figure adapted from Libet *et al.* (1979). *Brain*, 102: 199 by permission of Oxford University Press).

not gone unchallenged.[2] However, the suggestion that consciousness of input is preceded by a period of preconscious processing is broadly supported by cognitive research (Merikle, 2007), and a common estimate of preconscious processing time is in the order of 250 ms (see, for example, Neeley, 1977; Posner and Snyder, 1975). In information processing terms there is much to do before one can identify a stimulus. For example, stimuli must be transformed into neural code, analysed, and matched to memory traces before they can be identified. Complex stimuli such as sentences also require syntactic and semantic analysis and an interpretation of meaning in the light of prior verbal context, current physical context, and accumulated 'global knowledge' of the world. Actual inputs also need to be compared with predicted inputs to determine whether they are unexpected and require focal attention (Gray, 1995). Such processing requires time. It makes evolutionary sense for mental models of stimulus arrival time to compensate for the processing time required to make those stimuli conscious.

To understand Libet's results and conclusions it is important to distinguish information about the time of occurrence, location and extension of *events in the world* from the temporal and spatial properties of the *neural representations* which encode information about such events. Subjective experiences and their neural correlates 'model' the represented events, not themselves.[3] As noted in Chapters 6 and 7, similar principles apply to the subjective experience of space. In visual perception, the location and extension of objects in the world is encoded in the brain, which is dramatically illustrated when brain damage causes a loss of depth perception. Two cases have been reported, for example, in which brain-damaged patients saw the world and the people in it as perfectly flat. Consequently, 'the most corpulent individual might be a moving cardboard figure, for his body is represented in outline only' (cited in Crick, 1994, p. 167). In normal vision, however, objects are subjectively experienced as having depth, extension, and a location *out in the world*, rather than being 'in the head or brain' (in the region of their neural encoding). For reasons that will be evident from Chapters 6 and 7, I have termed this phenomenon 'perceptual projection' (rather than adopting Libet's term 'subjective referral'), but the effect is analogous to events being subjectively experienced as occurring when they actually arrive at the cortex, rather than at the time when neural representations of their arrival time are fully formed. That is, both effects are cases of 'subjective referral' (the former in space, the latter in time).[4]

At what stage of analysis do stimuli become conscious?

If Libet is right, it takes some 200 ms or so before input stimuli become conscious. But what happens (in functional terms) to *make* a stimulus conscious? As we have seen in Chapter 4, there has been extensive theory and experiment devoted to the differences between preconscious and conscious processing, much of it influenced by the seminal writings of William James.

As James observed, we select what we attend to and we are consciously aware of what we select, but we are not aware of unattended information (for example, you are not aware of the feel of your tongue inside your mouth – until I mention it and your attention switches). So, conscious phenomenology must relate closely to information that has been selected for *focal attention*. This is convincingly demonstrated by the phenomenon of *inattentional blindness*. For example, in their now famous demonstration, 'Gorillas in our midst', Simons and Chabris (1999) filmed two teams of students throwing a ball to other members of their team. One team was dressed in white T-shirts, the other team in black, and observers were asked to count the number of passes made within either the white or the black team. While this is going on, a woman dressed in a gorilla suit walks into shot, moves to centre stage, faces the camera, beats her chest, and walks slowly off again. Amazingly, when asked about it afterwards, roughly 50 per cent of observers fail to notice the gorilla, demonstrating that we do not consciously see what we do not attend to *even when we are directing our gaze at it.*[5]

Returning to another theme from William James, the contents of consciousness also seem to form a kind of 'psychological present' which is immediately accessible for report. This contrasts with our 'psychological past' which forms a kind of unconscious context for our psychological present and which must be accessed differently, through recall or recognition. This suggests a functional distinction in mental processing between a temporary short-term (working, or primary) memory system which holds information relating to the psychological present, and a relatively long-term (secondary) memory which encodes learnt information relating to past experience and various forms of knowledge derived from it.

The precise way in which such systems operate and relate to each other has been and continues to be the subject of extensive psychological research (particularly in investigations of preconscious versus conscious perception, attention, automatic versus controlled processing, and memory). Given our present focus on *consciousness* we do not need to enter into the many, ongoing controversies about the details of such processing. We do, however, need to focus on how processes accompanied by consciousness differ from processes that are not accompanied by consciousness. For this we need to take stock of what happens in the brain *before* consciousness arises and of how functioning changes once it does. Below, I present a brief sketch of some typical findings and the controversies that accompany them.[6]

The extent of preconscious analysis

The transition from preconscious to conscious processing and the differences between these are well illustrated by the 'cocktail party situation' which, in the 1950s, became a primary focus of research. At a cocktail party, the conversation one attends to enters consciousness, while the competing conversations seem to form a relatively undifferentiated background noise. Given this, attended information must be analysed in a different way from non-attended information. At the same time, if someone mentions one's name across the room, one's attention is likely to switch, suggesting that, to some extent, even non-attended messages are analysed – but to what extent?

Initial investigations of this by Cherry (1953) and Broadbent (1958) used a shadowing task in which subjects were required to attend to and repeat a message presented through earphones to one ear, while another message was simultaneously presented to the other, non-attended ear. After the task, subjects were required to report what they could remember of the non-attended message. Early findings indicated that subjects could not report the identity or meaning of stimuli on non-attended channels, although they could report certain physical features, for example whether the stimuli were spoken by a male or female voice, whether they were speech rather than a pure tone, and so on. On the basis of such findings Broadbent (1958) proposed an 'early selection' model of attention in which all input stimuli receive a physical analysis in an automatic, parallel, pre-attentive fashion. However only those stimuli that are selected for more detailed focal attention receive an analysis for meaning, update long-term memory and enter consciousness.

One interesting consequence of these early findings is their support for the suggestion that consciousness might be necessary for the *analysis of meaning* – a recurring theme in both psychological and philosophical writings. Conversely, psychological experiments which have managed to *dissociate* semantics and consciousness have consequences for both psychological and philosophical debates. In the 1970s, for example, various experiments demonstrated that the meaning of non-attended stimuli can influence the attended message or otherwise affect the hearer, in the absence of any conscious awareness of the non-attended stimuli or subsequent recall (cf. Dixon, 1981). Corteen and Wood (1972), for example, found that changes in galvanic skin response (GSR) which accompanied target words conditioned to electric shocks continued when those target words appeared in the non-attended ear, although subjects were unable to identify the words themselves. This occurred also with words which were *semantically related* to the conditioned word (but not with unrelated words). Various replications of Corteen and Wood's study also indicated that their results were reliable (see review in Velmans, 1991a).

Such effects *might*, of course, be explainable in other ways. According to Holender (1986), subjects in such studies might switch their attention momentarily to the non-selected ear and then forget they had done so. Dawson and Schell (1982), for example, found that if subjects were told beforehand that they would be required to name the conditioned word in the non-selected ear, they could sometimes (but not always) do so. According to Holender (1986), this suggests that subjects had been momentarily aware of the non-selected, conditioned words in the earlier studies – a possibility admitted by Corteen (1986). If so, one cannot be certain that these studies demonstrate meaning analysis without conscious awareness.[7]

However, focal-attentive switching cannot account for the evidence of preconscious semantic analysis (in non-selected channels) found by Groeger (1984a, 1984b, 1988). Groeger demonstrated that words in a non-attended ear could bias the meanings of attended-to words, and, crucially, he found that the effects of non-attended words were different if they were *above threshold* (consciously detectable) versus *below threshold*. For example, in one experiment subjects were asked to complete the sentence 'She looked ____ in her new coat' with one of two completion words, 'smug' or 'cosy'. Simultaneous with the attended sentence the word 'snug' was presented to the non-selected ear (a) above threshold, or (b) below it. With 'snug' presented above threshold, subjects tended to choose 'smug', which could be explained by subjects becoming momentarily aware of the physical form of the cue. With 'snug' presented below threshold, subjects tended to choose 'cosy', indicating semantic analysis of the cue word without accompanying awareness.

One cannot assume from these findings that semantic analysis of non-selected messages always takes place in dichotic listening studies, and it is often difficult to be certain that subjects have no awareness of stimuli presented to the non-selected ear. Overall, however, such studies have produced diverse evidence of semantic analysis of non-selected words, under conditions where subjects claim to have no awareness of those words and are unable to report them afterwards.[8] This suggests that under some circumstances a preliminary analysis for meaning can take place outside the focus of attention, without *reportable* consciousness.

Such findings have been used to support a 'late selection' model (Deutsch and Deutsch, 1963; Norman, 1969) in which all familiar input stimuli are identified and given a simple meaning analysis. This makes evolutionary sense. As Norman pointed out, unless one does analyse the meaning and significance of input stimuli on non-attended channels it would be difficult to judge whether they are important enough to switch one's focal attention to them. If so, the analysis of meaning (of simple familiar stimuli) may not always require focal attention, or entry of the stimuli into consciousness.[9]

How does pre-attentive processing differ from attentional processing?

On the basis of experimental findings in the early 1970s, Posner and Snyder (1975) extended this late-selection model into a two-process model in which pre-attentive, preconscious processing is thought of as a fast, automatic, spreading activation in the central nervous system. This activates not only memory traces of a given input stimulus but also related traces that share some of its features. For example, reading the word 'DOCTOR' also activates or 'primes' semantically related features in the word 'NURSE', making the latter easier to recognise (Meyer *et al.*, 1975). However, this process has no effect on unrelated traces (for example, 'DOCTOR' does not prime 'BREAD'). This would also explain the finding that non-attended words which are semantically related to those associated with electric shocks affect

GSR, but not unrelated words (see discussion of Corteen and Wood, 1972, above). By contrast, attentional processing occurs only after such spreading activation, it is relatively slow and serial in nature, and it cannot operate without intention and awareness. This process not only activates the traces of related stimuli but also *inhibits* the activation of unrelated stimuli (making them harder to recognise).[10]

However, focal-attentive processing is likely to involve far more than simple activation and inhibition. La Berge (1981) and Kahneman and Treisman (1984) for example pointed out that different *forms* of attention may have to be devoted to different stages of input analysis. Processing resources may be devoted to the identification of physical features if one is searching for a target input stimulus, but other resources may be required to integrate the set of features at the location found by the search. In addition, if any consequent action is to follow input analysis, its results need to be disseminated to other processing modules (see also Baars, 1988, 2007; Baars and McGovern, 1996). According to Posner *et al.* (1997) this would require orienting to sensory stimuli, executing control (including target detection and response selection), and maintaining an alert state.

While the details of focal-attentive processing are still under active research,[11] there appears to be some consensus within the experimental litera-ture that input stimuli in different channels are pre-attentively analysed in a fast, parallel, automatic, preconscious fashion, with little mutual interference, up to the point where each stimulus is matched to its previous traces in long-term memory, enabling a simple analysis of its meaning or significance.[12] Whether non-attended processing can extend to more complex analyses is uncertain. Underwood (1977) for example found that placing the non-attended words in a sentence context did not influence the effect of non-attended words on attended words in a shadowing task. This suggested that without attention there may only be limited integration of words into sen-tences. Greenwald (1992) called this apparent upper limit on the complexity of pre-attentive, preconscious processing the 'two-word challenge'.[13]

It would be misleading to suggest that all the evidence relating to pre-attentive and focal-attentive processing fits into this relatively neat picture.[14] Nevertheless, the transition from processing single, familiar words to process-ing more complex or novel input stimuli such as phrases and sentences is often thought to mark the transition from pre-attentive to focal-attentive processing. The latter is thought to be more flexible, relatively slow, serial, voluntary, limited in capacity, and conscious. Given this, few cognitive theorists would disagree with William James that there is a close *association* between attention and consciousness.

The functional correlates of consciousness

It should be evident that the processes which govern how attentional resources are allocated are themselves *preconscious*. That is, once we become consciously aware of some input (e.g. someone talking about us on the other side of the room), it has *already* been selected for attentive processing. This is true for both early-selection and late-selection models of attention (these differ only in terms of *how extensively* input is analysed before selection takes place). Indeed, there is a self-contradiction implicit in the claim that consciousness selects what enters *itself*. Consciousness cannot *consciously* select what enters itself, for the reason that the selected information would *already* have to be in consciousness for such a selection to take place.[15] Such caveats aside, we can still ask, 'What is it *about* attentional processing that relates most closely to consciousness?'

Clues about the functional correlates of consciousness are offered by situations where attentional processing is partially *dissociated* from consciousness, for example where subjects focus their attention on an input stimulus but consciousness of the stimulus does *not* arise. It seems reasonable to assume in such situations that some aspects of attentional processing are operating but other aspects (associated with consciousness) are not. A classic example occurs in 'blindsight' produced by striate cortex lesions (Weiskrantz, 1986, 1997, 2007). Blindsighted subjects can direct their attention to an input stimulus, identify some of its properties and make appropriate identification responses, but are unable to experience the stimulus to which they attend. Such subjects, however, need to be *forced* to make decisions about stimuli that they believe they cannot see, indicating that information about the stimulus is not readily available to all parts of their information processing system. Marcel (1986) also found that blindsighted patients make no attempt to grasp a glass of water in their blind field even when thirsty, suggesting that information about the input remains dissociated from systems serving voluntary control (see also Danckert *et al.*, 2002).[16]

Partial dissociations also occur in implicit learning and memory studies. Here, information about stimuli or the relationships between them which is not present to consciousness at the time of learning (according to subjective reports) may update long-term memory and influence performance, although it is not available for explicit recognition and recall (Gardiner, 1996; Berry and Dienes, 1993; Reber, 1993, 1997; Schacter, 1992). Although some of these studies have been challenged on methodological grounds (Shanks and St John, 1994) there is a sense in which the existence of implicit learning and memory in advance of any explicit knowledge of *what* has been learnt is obvious. As the psychologist Arthur Reber puts it:

> What do psychologists think is going on when a child acquires a natural language or becomes socialised and inculcated with the mores of society? With language development the case is quite clear. Formal instruction is essentially irrelevant, explicit processes are absent, learning is essentially unintentional, individual differences in the basic skill are minimal, language users have virtually no access to the rules of their language, and the end product of the acquisition is a rich, complex, and abstract

representation that mirrors that of the structure of the linguistic corpus. A similar picture is easily painted for the processes of socialization and acculturation.

(Reber, 1997, p. 139)

Another dissociation of attention from consciousness and memory occurs in hypnotic analgesia, where patients are induced to direct their attention away from the painful stimulus. However, during hypnosis the patient may be told that a *hidden observer* will continue to monitor everything that is happening although the *patient* will experience no pain (Hilgard, 1986). In subsequent surgery, the awake patient may report no experience of pain and this may be accompanied by an absence of physiological indices of pain along with reduced bleeding and salivation (Oakley and Eames, 1985). This indicates that information about the painful input is not generally available to other parts of the system. But the hidden observer continues to attend to the pain and to enter information about it into memory. After surgery, with the subject still under hypnosis, one can ask to speak to the 'hidden observer', in which case it gives a vivid report of the pain it has experienced.

What such findings demonstrate is that partial dissociations of attentional processing from consciousness result in different forms of information 'encapsulation'. Subjects have knowledge, but they do not 'know that they know'.[17] As Kahneman and Treisman (1984) suggest, the dissemination of currently processed information to other information processing modules may be one of the functions of focal-attentive processing, enabling greater resources to be devoted to the input and allowing the system as a whole to respond to input at the focus of attention in a coherent, global way. This would account for the greater flexibility and sophistication of 'conscious', focal-attentive processing (compared to 'preconscious', pre-attentive processing). When information dissemination is disrupted, disruption of consciousness (of that information) also occurs. This would suggest that input analysis becomes conscious around the time that its products are being *disseminated* – a late-arising stage of focal-attentive processing.

Other conditions for consciousness, specifiable in information processing terms, also need to be met. For example, for complex information to be usefully disseminated it needs to be sufficiently well integrated to support consequent processing along with an integrated conscious experience (the 'binding problem'). Nevertheless, in the sequence of attentional processes, the information dissemination stage appears central. Through an extensive review of the contrasts between conscious and nonconscious processes, Baars (1988, 2007) and Baars and McGovern (1996) come to similar conclusions (via a different route), although the term they use for 'information dissemination' is 'broadcasting'.

What is the nature of the association between consciousness and information integration/dissemination?

Many psychologists have explicitly or tacitly assumed that 'preconscious' processing is identical to 'pre-attentive' processing, whereas 'conscious' processing is identical to 'focal-attentive' processing (e.g. Baars, 1991; Mandler, 1975, 1985, 1991; Merikle and Joordens, 1997; Miller, 1962). However, as we have seen in Chapter 4, psychological views about the precise nature of the consciousness/processing relationship have been ambiguous. For example, Miller (1962), one of the clearest, early writers on this subject, sometimes claimed that 'the selective function of consciousness and the limited span of attention are complementary ways of talking about one and the same thing' and that consciousness is a 'process or group of processes'. But Miller also claimed that 'no activity of mind is ever conscious'. So, which is it to be?

As Kahneman and Treisman (1984) observed, the question of how attentional resources are allocated is in principle distinguishable from the question of what is or is not conscious. A *close association* of consciousness with focal attention does not establish their *ontological identity* (see Chapter 3). In Velmans (1991a) I argued that consciousness *results* from focal-attentive processing but is not identical to it. To be more specific, consciousness relates closely to the information integration/dissemination stage of focal-attentive processing (see above), but the terms 'consciousness' and 'focal-attentive processing' remain dissociable in their normal meaning and usage. Conscious *phenomenology* and information processing also remain dissociable in terms of the methods used to investigate them. Thus,

> in its ordinary usage 'consciousness' refers to something other than 'focal-attentive processing.' It refers primarily to 'awareness,' whereas 'focal-attentive processing' refers to a functional subdivision within an information-processing model of the brain. Focal-attentive processing is thought to be a *necessary condition* for conscious awareness. Operationally, however, they are distinct (Nissen and Bullemer, 1987; Kahneman and Treisman, 1984). Conscious contents are typically investigated by the use of *subjective reports* (of subjective experience) – usually verbal reports, although various other means of communicating experience exist (Ericsson and Simon, 1984; Pope and Singer, 1978). By contrast, human information processing and functional divisions within such processing are typically inferred from performance measures such as reaction time, error score, and so forth.
>
> (Velmans, 1991a, p. 665)

In his commentary on this position, Mandler (1991) accepted that the mechanisms of selection and choice which determine what we attend to are preconscious and that, under normal conditions, attentional processing results in conscious experience.[18] He also agreed that, '*information processing is not conscious, but its products are*' (p. 688; my italics).

At the same time, Mandler (1975, 1997) claims a central role for consciousness in information processing. For example, he treats the central processor as a kind of 'executive consciousness' with the properties of seriality, limited capacity, and relative slowness, with a range of functions which 'permit the organism to react reflectively instead of automatically', allow 'more adaptive transactions between the organism and the environment', and permit 'a focusing on the most important and species relevant aspects of the environment' (see Chapter 4).[19]

So, once again, we need to ask, 'is consciousness a *form* of information processing or a *product* of it?' (the dilemma faced by Miller, 1962, discussed above).

Baars (1991), commenting on the same (1991a) target article, objected to my distinction between focal attention and consciousness. According to him, awareness and focal attention 'covary so perfectly, we routinely infer in our everyday life that they reflect a single underlying reality'. My target article, he claimed, is just one of a series of misguided attempts (by philosophers, psychologists, and neuroscientists) to deny the 'common-sense and scientifically useful idea that reports of conscious experience, focal-attention, and wakefulness reflect an internal but nevertheless knowable aspect of our nervous system', and to 'demonstrate that consciousness cannot be associated with all of its obvious correlates – in this case with "focal attention" ' (p. 669).

In my reply (Velmans, 1991b) I pointed out that my text had placed great stress on the close *association* of consciousness with focal attention (consciousness *results* from focal-attentive processing). I merely denied their *ontological identity* (causes are not ontologically identical to their effects). Nor does an account of human information processing in itself (magically) yield an account of phenomenal consciousness. Worse, *redefinitions* of consciousness in terms of focal attention effectively collapse the phenomena observed from a subject's first-person perspective to phenomena observed or inferred from an external observer's third-person perspective, thereby removing the subject's experience from science. All that remains is an entirely mechanistic account of mind (in terms of information processing) which neither requires nor provides any understanding of how subjective experiences contribute to mental life.

To add to the confusion, Baars agreed that subjective experience should be somehow included in scientific theory. As he noted,

> denial of first-person conscious experience in other people may lead to a profound kind of dehumanization. It comes down to saying that other people are not capable of joy or suffering, that in fact, as far as the outside observer is concerned, we are not to see others as they see themselves. *The consequence of this prohibition against the first-person perspective is a kind of mechanization of other people.* Psychology under the thumb of behaviorism did indeed display this kind of dehumanizing, mechanistic thinking. It is only when we acknowledge the reality of

conscious experience in the minds of others, that we can recognize their full humanity.

(Baars, 1991, p. 670; my italics)

However, Baars overlooked the fact that replacing subjective experience with third-person accounts of information processing is equally dehumanising and mechanistic. For him, a third-person account of consciousness in terms of information in a global workspace *is* an account of subjective experience – that is, it is an account of consciousness *as such* (Baars, 1994, 2007). The difficulties of incorporating *first-person*, phenomenal consciousness within a *third-person* account of information processing in this way are well illustrated by Baars's subsequent attempts to grapple with this issue. In contrast to his (1991) claim that awareness and focal attention 'covary so perfectly, we routinely infer in our everyday life that they reflect a single underlying reality', Baars (1997a) is at pains to *dissociate* consciousness from focal attention (for reasons very similar to the ones I gave in 1991). As he then pointed out, in ordinary usage these terms have different meanings. For example:

> English makes a clear distinction between 'looking' and 'seeing', 'listening' and 'hearing', and 'touching' and 'feeling'. The first word of each pair describes a way of *gaining access to* a conscious perceptual experience (looking, listening, touching), while the second refers to the resulting experience itself (seeing, hearing, feeling). We use the first verb of each pair in order to gain access to the second. We *look* in order to *see*; *listen* in order to *hear*, and *touch* in order to *feel*. The distinction is between selecting an experience and being conscious of the selected event. In everyday language, the first word of each pair involves attention; the second involves consciousness.

(p. 364)

Baars goes on to argue that attention and consciousness can also be dissociated operationally. For example,

> Attentional operations include instructions to attend and disattend, effortful control of attention against competing input, and experimental manipulations of attentional selection priorities. . . . In contrast, our most obvious index of consciousness involves people *describing their experiences* in some verifiable way, under conditions that maximise accuracy.[20]

(ibid., p. 364; my italics)

However, rather than rejecting the ontological identification of consciousness with information processing (as I did in Velmans, 1991a), Baars then goes on to identify consciousness with *a slightly later stage* of information processing (as does Mandler, 1997), in terms that once again have very little to do with people's descriptions of what they experience. Attention now becomes the 'gatekeeper' for the global workspace and, as before, the contents of the global workspace are equated with consciousness. Thus, 'attention creates access to consciousness', but 'consciousness is needed to create access to unconscious processing resources', and 'we can create access to any part of the brain using consciousness' (Baars, 1997b, p. 296; see also Baars *et al.*, 1997). In short, consciousness carries out the many functions which require global access to unconscious processing resources such as system-wide integration and dissemination of information, the formation of new links between unconscious processors, and so on (see Chapter 4). Unfortunately, in his *summary* of his 1997b position, Baars once again shifts his position (to one different from that outlined in the body of his paper), now stressing that, 'In the view presented here, *global access* may be a necessary condition for consciousness; but in the nature of science we simply do not know at this time what would be the truly *sufficient* conditions' (p. 308).

If global access is a necessary (but not sufficient) condition for consciousness, then global access is *causally antecedent* to consciousness. However, if consciousness *creates* global access, then consciousness is causally antecedent to global access. Like Miller and Mandler, Baars tries to have it both ways. Such confusions illustrate the need to analyse the relation of conscious phenomenology to its associated information processing with care.

Preconscious analysis of complex messages in the attended channel

Theories of consciousness that give it selective functions (in attentional processing), or identify it with a 'central processor', 'central executive', or 'global workspace', treat it as a distinct, functional module which clearly does something useful in the activities of brain. For example, if nothing happens without consciousness other than the identification of simple, familiar stimuli, then consciousness must be necessary for the analysis of complex, novel stimulus combinations which occur, for example, in reading or the perception of connected speech. This would be consistent with the evidence that preconscious analysis (in non-attended channels) may be limited to the meanings of individual words (see Kihlstrom, 1996; Greenwald, 1992; Underwood, 1991). If this widely held view is correct, *preconscious* analysis of complex, novel information should be impossible. According to Greenwald (1992), even the preconscious analysis of *two connected words* poses 'a challenge' (see above). Perhaps this is so for non-attended input. However, the evidence for *preconscious* analysis of complex, novel messages in *attended* input is clear.

In psychological tasks, the 'attended' channel is operationally defined by combining instructions to subjects to attend in a given way with appropriate forms of stimulus presentation. For example, the subject might be asked to focus on material in one ear rather than the other, or to fixate a particular point on a screen, and then the stimulus is presented to the point of focus. In the sense that subjects can choose whether or not to follow instructions, their attention may be said to be voluntary, controlled and conscious. It has to be borne in mind, however, that most models of attentional processing assume that input stimuli receive some initial, preconscious analysis (preliminary attention) *whether or not* they are in the attended channel. This applies to both early-selection models (e.g. Broadbent, 1958) and late-selection models (e.g. the 'two-process' model of Posner and Snyder, 1975, discussed above). Stimuli in the attended channel differ in that they are normally selected for further 'focal-attentive processing' and it is only when this happens that they enter consciousness. In principle, therefore, it might be possible for input in an attended channel to be given a preliminary, preconscious analysis *without* being subject to 'conscious' focal-attentive analysis, as in the case of blindsight discussed above.

Suppose, however, that focal-attentive analysis is *not* disrupted in any way. In what sense, under these circumstances, is the analysis of complex stimuli 'voluntary, controlled and conscious'?

How conscious is conscious speech perception and conscious reading?

Marslen-Wilson (1984) reviewed evidence that the analysis of words in attended-to connected speech is both 'data-driven' and 'cognitively driven', combining knowledge of the stimulus with knowledge of its context. For example, in Grosjean's (1980) word recognition task, successively longer initial fragments of a word were presented. If the words were presented in isolation, subjects required fragments of 333 ms (on average) to identify them (total word length was in excess of 400 ms). But if the words were presented in normal verbal contexts, a fragment of 199 ms (on average) was sufficient to identify them. In a related experiment, Marslen-Wilson and Tyler (1980) found that the average reaction time to detect target words (in context) was 273 ms although their mean length was 370 ms. Once one takes into account the 75 milliseconds or so required to make a response (the time to press a button) this again suggests a word identification time of around 200 ms.

Now, a word fragment of 200 ms is large enough to contain just the first two phonemes and, according to Marslen-Wilson (1984), these convey useful information. Assuming that one has a 'mental dictionary' of around 20,000 American-English words, knowledge of the first phoneme reduces the set of possible words to a median of 1,033, knowledge of the first two phonemes reduces the set size to a median of 87, and so on (Kucera and Francis, 1967). In this way, sensory analysis (a largely 'data-driven' process) contributes to word identification. After two phonemes, however, a large number of possible words remain (a median of 87). Hence subjects who can identify the word on the basis of the first two phonemes must use their knowledge of the context to decide which of the remaining words is the correct one (a 'cognitively driven' process).

On the basis of this and other evidence Marslen-Wilson (1984) concluded that to cope with a complex acoustic waveform developing over time the speech processing system moves the analysis of the sensory signal as rapidly as possible to a domain where all possible sources of information (semantic as well as phonemic) can be brought to bear on its further analysis and interpretation. Such 'online interactive analysis' has considerable sophistication and flexibility.

These findings and conclusions have a surprising consequence. The stimuli to be identified in these experiments are in the attended channel. Yet if words (in context) are identified within 200 ms, this confluence of data-driven and cognitively driven processing *cannot be conscious*, for according to the evidence reviewed earlier (Libet *et al.*, 1979; Posner and Snyder, 1975; Neeley, 1977), consciousness of a given stimulus does not arise until at least 200 ms *after* the stimulus arrives at the cortical projection areas, that is, after the identification of a word (in context) has been achieved!

In these experiments spoken words in the attended channel are therefore analysed in preconscious fashion. Rather than consciousness *entering into* input analysis of well known stimuli, consciousness of those stimuli appears to *follow* sophisticated, preconscious analysis and identification. If this is the case, consciousness cannot be *necessary* for the analysis and identification of such stimuli even when they occur in novel, complex combinations. This conclusion may seem counterintuitive. It is, however, easy to show how it applies to everyday situations. For example, *reading* is universally thought of as a *complex, conscious* process. But how conscious is it? (See Box 10.1.)

In spite of their complexity, the processes that enable reading operate preconsciously. Note too that the analysis of well known stimuli proceeds in a largely involuntary fashion, whether or not the stimuli are in the attended channel. Even if one 'consciously attends' to a given stimulus, it may be difficult to prevent certain analyses from being carried out. In this sense, the analysis is automatic. This point was demonstrated by Stroop (1935), who observed that subjects instructed to name the colour in which a word is printed found the task far more difficult if the word was itself a colour name, but of a different colour. For example, subjects presented with the word 'red' printed in orange cannot restrict their analysis to the colour of the print (orange) because they cannot prevent themselves from reading the word ('red').

On the basis of this and other evidence, Kahneman (1973) concluded that 'subjects cannot prevent the perceptual analysis of irrelevant attributes of an attended object'. Even if a stimulus is consciously attended to, what is analysed may not be under conscious voluntary control. However, an 'involuntary' process is not necessarily 'inflexible' (see discussion of speech perception above). Nor need it be 'effortless'. For example, studies of the Stroop effect indicate that while input analysis may be automatic in the sense of 'involuntary', it nevertheless draws on limited processing resources,

---

Box 10.1 How conscious is conscious reading?

Try silently reading the following sentence and note what you experience:

> *If we don't increase the dustmen's wages, they will refuse to take the refuse.*

Note that on its first occurrence in your phonemic imagery or 'covert speech', the word 'refuse' was (silently) pronounced with the stress on the second syllable (re*fuse*), while on its second occurrence the stress was on the first syllable (*refuse*). But how and when did this allocation of stress patterns take place? Clearly, the syntactic and semantic analysis required to determine the appropriate meanings of the word 'refuse' must have taken place prior to the allocation of the stress patterns; and this, in turn, must have taken place *prior* to the phonemic images entering awareness.

Note too, that while reading, one is not conscious of any of the visual processing or pattern recognition that is required to identify individual words, or of any syntactic or semantic analysis being applied to the sentence. Nor is one aware of the processing responsible for the resulting covert speech (with the appropriate stress patterns on the word 'refuse').

The same may be said of the paragraph you are now reading, or of the entire text of this chapter. You are conscious *of* what is written, but not conscious of the complex input analysis involved. Nor are you aware of *consciously* carrying out any system-wide integration and dissemination of information, or of forming new links between unconscious processors. Rather, information that enters consciousness has *already been integrated* and appears to be *generally available* to the system as a whole.

---

thereby slowing a subject's ability to name the colour in which a colour name (of a different colour) is written (Kahneman and Treisman, 1984).

Automatic, flexible, preconscious analysis of attended-to input

Conventionally, 'preconscious' analysis is thought to be automatic (in the sense of being involuntary), and restricted to simple, familiar stimuli whose long-term memory traces are accessed in data-driven fashion. The terms 'preconscious analysis', 'pre-attentive analysis', or 'preconscious pre-attentive analysis' are often used interchangeably. 'Conscious' analysis or 'focal-attentive' analysis is thought to be voluntary and flexible (involving cognitively driven as well as data-driven processing) and, again, the terms 'conscious analysis', 'focal-attentive analysis', or 'conscious focal-attentive analysis' are often treated as if they are synonymous.

The evidence reviewed above suggests that this rigid linkage of the 'pre-conscious' versus 'conscious' processing distinction to the difference between 'pre-attentive' and 'focal-attentive' processing requires re-examination. Stimuli in attended channels are subject to a far more sophisticated analysis than stimuli in non-attended channels. But, if the meanings of attended-to phrases and sentences can be analysed *before they enter consciousness*, this attentional analysis cannot be conscious. Conversely, preconscious analysis in *attended* channels cannot be restricted to simple, familiar words. Reading and the on-line analysis of speech are amongst the most sophisticated of human pattern recognition tasks, involving both cognitively driven and data-driven processing. If the input analysis of text and speech operates preconsciously, then preconscious, attentional analysis might be automatic (in the sense of being involuntary) but it cannot be inflexible.

To put the point another way, by the time perceived text or speech enters consciousness the analysis of words in context (including both semantic and syntactic analysis) *has already been achieved*. If so, consciousness (of the input) arises *too late* to affect the processing with which it is most closely associated. Reading and speech perception of attended-to messages are universally thought of as 'conscious processes'. Yet, the processes that enable reading and speech perception are, strictly speaking, *preconscious*.

It is important to note that, while consciousness of input does not come too late for processing that *follows* input analysis, we are not (introspectively) aware of carrying out the operations typically specified in cognitive models of such processing. For example we are not aware of consciously integrating and disseminating information throughout our own brains and, normally, we do not think of such processing as being conscious. This leaves functionalist reductionism on the horns of a dilemma. If consciousness *does* carry out such functions, in the way Baars (1997a, 1997b) suggests, it must do so *unconsciously* – which doesn't make sense.

I am not just being difficult. Cognitive psychology has made considerable progress in locating those aspects of information processing most closely *associated* with consciousness. But deep problems follow from the reductionist *identification* of consciousness with information processing, which has become common in functionalist analyses of experience.

One cannot, of course, extrapolate from two examples (speech perception and silent reading) to the whole of human information processing. However, the particular problems introduced here generalise to other information processing accounts of psychological functions that are typically thought of as 'conscious'. As I have analysed these in depth in Velmans (1991a, 1991b, 1993b, 1996c), I will give just a few, illustrative examples.

How conscious is volition?

The discussion above focuses on input analysis and some of its consequences (information integration and dissemination). However this is only the first stage of human information processing. Once input has been identified, one has to choose what to do. As Carr and Bacharach (1976) note, *input* selection must be distinguished from *task* selection. So, even if input analysis and selection are preconscious, task selection might be conscious. This suggestion dates back to the classical dualist-interactionism of Plato and Descartes. The bodily senses might act on the conscious mind to produce experiences, but perhaps the conscious mind can also act on the body, through the exercise of free will.

However, one of the most surprising findings of modern neuroscience is that even a 'conscious voluntary choice' may have preconscious neural antecedents. It has been known for some time that voluntary acts are preceded by a slow negative shift in electrical potential (recorded at the scalp), known as the 'readiness potential', and that this shift can precede the act by up to one second or more (Kornhuber and Deeke, 1965).

In itself, this says nothing about the relation of the readiness potential to conscious volition, that is, to the *experienced wish* to perform an act. To address this, Libet (1985) developed a procedure which enabled subjects to note the instant they experienced a wish to perform a specified act (a simple flexion of the wrist or fingers) by relating the onset of the experienced wish to the spatial position of a revolving spot on a cathode ray oscilloscope, which swept the periphery of the face like the sweep-second hand of a clock.[21] Recorded in this way, the readiness potential preceded the voluntary act by around 550 ms and *also preceded the experienced wish* (to flex the wrist or fingers) by around 350 ms (for spontaneous acts involving no preplanning).

In a replication of Libet's findings, Haggard and Eimer (1999) used the same methodology. However they varied whether subjects had to use their left or right hand to respond, in order to allow calculation of the lateralised readiness potential (LRP). This is obtained by measuring the activity over the primary motor cortex and subtracting activity from the hemisphere on the same side as the response hand from activity of the hemisphere on the opposite side to the response hand. As the left hemisphere controls the right hand and vice versa, this provides a marker of motor preparation for a particular hand movement in a given hemisphere, rather than the more general preparedness indexed by RP. As was the case with RP, LRP occurred before the conscious wish to act, although in this case by around 100 ms. That is, LRP onset was about 300 ms prior to onset of motor activity (measured on an electromyogram), with the wish to act occurring around 200 ms prior to this activity. Haggard and Eimer also found that LRP onsets that were earlier than average tended to be followed by wishes to act that were earlier than average while later LRP onsets were followed by later wishes, suggesting a direct relationship between wishes and LRP. However, no such relationship obtained between wishes and RP. Consequently, while they supported Libet's conclusion that the brain prepares for action prior to both the wish to act and the act itself, they argued that LRP rather than RP is a more direct index of the brain's preparations.[22]

This suggests that, like the act itself, the experienced wish (to flex one's wrist) may be one output from the (prior) cerebral processes that actually select a given response. If so, conscious volition may be no more necessary for such a (preconscious) choice than the consciousness of a stimulus is necessary for its preconscious analysis. Rather than solving the problem (posed by input analysis) of what consciousness does in the brain, such findings exacerbate the problem – with clear implications for our understanding of conscious free will.

As Libet observed, the experienced wish *follows* the readiness potential, but *precedes* the motor act itself by around 200 ms, and this might provide enough time to consciously *veto* the wish before executing the act (the same applies to LRP). In a manner reminiscent of the interplay between the libidinous desires arising from Freud's unconscious *id* and the control exercised by the conscious *ego*, Libet consequently suggested that the *initiation* of the voluntary act and the accompanying wish are developed preconsciously, but consciousness can then act as a form of censor which decides whether or not to carry out the act. In short, maybe we don't have conscious free will, but perhaps we do have conscious free won't!

While this is an interesting possibility, it does invite an obvious question. If the wish to perform an act is developed preconsciously, why doesn't the decision to censor the act have its own preconscious antecedents?[23] Libet (1996) argues that it *might* not need to do so as voluntary control imposes a change on a wish that is already conscious. Yet, it seems very odd that a wish to do something has preconscious antecedents while a wish not to do something does not. Preconscious influences on a decision *not* to respond are, of course, tricky to investigate as, if they are successful, the subject does not respond. EEG measures can nevertheless be used to distinguish response inhibition from response activation. Karrer *et al.* (1978) and Konttinen and Lyytinen (1993), for example, found that *refraining* from irrelevant movements is associated with a slow *positive-going* readiness potential.

A readiness to respond, inhibited by a decision not to respond, can also be directly investigated in psychology experiments using various go/no-go tasks – for example, where subjects are asked to fix their attention on a screen where one of two target stimuli will appear. One target stimulus cues the subject to press a button as quickly as possible (go), while the other stimulus cues the subject not to respond (no-go). Behavioural measures in the no-go condition remain a problem, of course, as the subject does not do anything. The brain nevertheless responds differently under the two conditions. Response inhibition in this situation is thought to be associated with the 'no-go N2', a negative-going potential measured over frontally placed electrodes occurring about 200 ms after stimulus onset, arising from cognitive control processes in the anterior cingulate cortex (Falkenstein *et al.*, 1999; Nieuwenhuis *et al.*, 2003). In a series of experiments designed to investigate preconscious influences on a decision *not* to respond, Hughes (2008) found that the onset of this N2 on no-go trials could be influenced by masked (unconscious) primes presented 100 ms before the conscious target stimuli. In particular, a masked prime that cued a no-go response led to a significantly earlier no-go N2 than a masked prime that cued a go response, demonstrating preconscious priming of a decision not to respond (Hughes *et al.*, in press). In short, even a decision *not* to respond can be initiated preconsciously.

Is consciousness necessary for carrying out voluntary acts?

Choosing whether or not to do something is, of course, different from actu-ally doing it, and in the psychological literature consciousness is often thought to be necessary for *carrying out* voluntary acts (unless they are very well practised). This is particularly true if the acts are complex, novel, or require monitoring. Consider for example the degree of focused attention and complex muscle adjustments required to play a successful game of tennis. But there is a problem. If consciousness of what is happening does not arise until at least 200 ms after stimuli arrive at the cortex, conscious awareness is simply too slow for such adjustments to be conscious. This has been a matter of considerable interest to sports psychologists. In his review of their findings John McCrone (1999) notes,

> An easy example to study was the return of serve in tennis. Facing a fast serve, players have barely 400 milliseconds in which to see whether the ball is headed for their forehand or backhand, and then to make any late adjustments for unexpected skids or jumps of the ball off the court surface. Given that simply turning the shoulders and lifting the racket back occupies a third of a second, and that it takes about half a second to reach wide for a ball, anticipation has to have a role. Even if awareness were actually instant, it would not be fast enough to get a player across the court in time.
>
> (p. 145)

So, in what way is anticipation involved?

> Tests were carried out in which novice and professional players were shown film clips of a person serving. The film was stopped at different stages of the server's actions and subjects were then asked to guess whether the ball was going to land on their forehand, backhand, or smack down the middle. Neither the novices or experts had any trouble predicting where the ball would go after seeing just 120 milliseconds of flight. . . . But the significant finding was that professionals were able to guess the direction of the serve with fair accuracy if the film was halted

forty milliseconds before the ball was struck. The seasoned players were gleaning hints from the way the server was shaping up during the ball toss, and not having to wait to sample the actual flight of the ball.

(ibid., p. 145)

Bruce Abernathy (1981), a sports psychologist at the University of Queensland, found similar evidence of anticipation in cricketers and badminton players. Films of cricket batsmen showed that they were stepping forward in anticipation of a short-pitched delivery about 100 ms before the bowler released the ball, and that top badminton players were picking up a lot of information from the way an opponent's chest and shoulders begin to move a full 170 ms before the shuttlecock is struck. It is tempting to conclude that the players were consciously anticipating how to respond. But,

> Frustratingly for the sports psychologists, who obviously wanted to be able to teach the secrets of good anticipation, none of the top players could explain what it was they were actually looking at to get their clues. When questioned, they said that they did not feel that they were watching anything in particular. Indeed, most said they had not even been aware they were making guesses ahead of time. They believed they had simply been concentrating hard and making sure they watched the ball right on to their bat or racket, so were conscious of the shots pretty much as they happened.
>
> (ibid., p. 146)

There are also many claims about the role of consciousness in processes that *intervene between* input analysis and overt behaviour, for example in learning, memory, thinking, problem solving, and planning. However, in most instances where we are conscious *of* what we do we are not conscious of *how* we do it, which provides reason to doubt the causal influence of consciousness on such processing. As Miller (1962) noted, we have no awareness whatsoever of the processes which enable one to remember something (e.g. to recall one's mother's maiden name – see Chapter 4), nor are we aware of how we are able to encode new information in long-term memory. Baars (1988) makes the same observation about learning. As he notes,

> To learn *anything* new we merely pay attention to it. Learning occurs 'magically' – we merely allow ourselves to interact consciously with algebra, with language, or with a perceptual puzzle . . . and somehow, without detailed conscious intervention, we acquire the relevant knowledge and skill. But we know that learning cannot be a simple, unitary process in its details . . . all forms of learning involve specialized components of knowledge and acquisition strategies.
>
> (Baars, 1988, p. 214)

In Velmans (1991a) I reviewed evidence that, under appropriate circumstances, many of these processes can operate (to a limited extent) *without* consciousness – again calling into question the *necessity* of consciousness for those functions. For example, at first glance, it seems unlikely that subjects might be able to discriminate between stimuli without being conscious of them, but this can happen in blindsight. It also seems hard to believe that something can be remembered without first being experienced, yet this seems to happen in hypnotic analgesia, where the 'hidden observer' remembers the pain of an operation which the subject claimed, at the time, not to experience. In actual practice, however, one cannot completely dissociate consciousness from functioning. If consciousness is absent then some aspect of functioning is also likely to be absent. In blindsight and hypnotic analgesia, for example, information available to one part of the system may not have been disseminated to other parts of the system (so 'broadcasting' is absent).[24]

To close in on the relationship of consciousness to functioning it is therefore particularly important to focus on normal functioning, on cases where consciousness is *present*. Here, there are some real surprises as we have seen – for example, the fact that consciousness arrives *too late* to influence input analysis in reading, and the emergence of a preconscious 'readiness potential' to carry out an act roughly 350 ms in advance of the conscious wish to carry out that act. It is just as surprising that a similar relationship of consciousness to functioning applies to the production of overt speech *and even covert thoughts*.

What is conscious about the production of overt speech and verbal thoughts?

Speech production, like reading, is one of the most complex tasks humans are able to perform. Yet, one has no awareness whatsoever of the motor commands issued from the central nervous system that travel down efferent fibres to innervate the muscles, nor of the complex motor programming that enables muscular co-ordination and control. In speech, for example, the tongue may make as many as twelve adjustments of shape per second – adjustments which need to be precisely co-ordinated with other rapid, dynamic changes within the articulatory system. According to Lenneberg (1967), within one minute of discourse as many as 10,000–15,000 neuromuscular events occur. Yet only the *results* of this activity (the overt speech itself) normally enter consciousness.

Preconscious speech control might of course be the result of *prior* conscious activity. For example, Popper (1972) and Mandler (1975) suggest that consciousness is necessary for short- and long-term planning, particularly where one needs to create some novel plan or novel output response. In the case of speech production, for example, planning *what* to say might be conscious, particularly if one is expressing some new idea, or expressing some old idea in a novel way.

Conveniently, the planning and execution of speech have been subject to considerable experimental examination. Speech production is commonly thought to involve hierarchically arranged, semantic, syntactic, and motor control systems in which communicative intentions are translated into overt speech in a largely top-down fashion.[25] As noted above, articulatory control (motor programming and execution) is largely preconscious. According to Bock (1982), syntactic planning by skilled speakers is also relatively automatic and outside conscious voluntary control. Planning *what* to say and translating nonverbal conceptual content into linguistic forms, however, require effort. But to what extent is such planning conscious? Let us see.

A number of theorists have observed that periods of conceptual, semantic and syntactic planning are characterised by gaps in the otherwise relatively continuous stream of speech (Goldman-Eisler, 1968; Boomer, 1970). The neurologist John Hughlings Jackson, for example, suggested that the amount of planning required depends on whether the speech is 'new' speech or 'old' speech. Old speech (well known phrases etc.) requires little planning and is relatively continuous. New speech (saying things in a new way) requires planning and is characterised by hesitation pauses. Fodor *et al.* (1974) point out that breathing pauses also occur (gaps in the speech stream caused by the intake of breath). However, breathing pauses do not generally coincide with hesitation pauses.

Breathing pauses nearly always occur at the beginnings and ends of major linguistic constituents (such as clauses and sentences). So these appear to be co-ordinated with the syntactic organisation of such constituents into a clausal or sentential structure. By contrast, hesitation pauses tend to occur within clauses and sentences and appear to be associated with the formulation of ideas, deciding which words best express one's meaning, and so on.

If this analysis is correct, conscious planning of *what* to say should be evident during hesitation pauses – and a little examination of what one experiences during a hesitation pause should settle the matter. Try it. During a hesitation pause one might experience a certain sense of effort (perhaps the effort to put something in an appropriate way). But nothing is revealed of the *processes* which formulate ideas, translate these into a form suitable for expression in language, search for and retrieve words from memory, or assess which words are most appropriate. In short, no more is revealed of conceptual or semantic planning in hesitation pauses than is revealed of syntactic planning in breathing pauses. The fact that a process demands processing *effort* does not ensure that it is *conscious*. Indeed, there is a sense in which one is only conscious of what one wants to say *after one has said it*!

It is particularly surprising that the same may be said of *conscious verbal thoughts*. That is, the same situation applies if one formulates one's thoughts into 'covert speech' through the use of phonemic imagery, prior to its overt expression (Box 10.2).

In short, whether we consider conscious forms of input analysis (speech perception and reading), information transformation (verbal thinking) or

---

Box 10.2 How conscious is conscious thought?

Decide how well you have followed the argument so far, and simply note what thoughts come to mind. Once something comes to mind, read on.

You might have thought something like 'I'm with it so far', 'I'm not sure about some of this', or even 'I disagree with this' – but for the purpose of this exercise it doesn't matter. All that matters is that once a verbal thought comes to mind it will be manifest in the form of inner speech (phonemic imagery).

Now ask yourself, 'Where did that thought come from?'

Although you might be able to give reasons for whatever judgement you made after the fact, you have little or no introspective access to the *detailed processes* that gave rise to the immediate thought, that is, to the processes that somehow analysed the meaning of the question, accessed your global memory system, somehow made the judgement about how well the arguments presented here fit in with your current understanding of the topic, and then expressed that judgement in the form of a verbal thought. Once one *has* a conscious verbal thought, manifested in experience in the form of phonemic imagery, the complex cognitive processes required to generate that thought, including the meaning it expresses, the choice of grammar and words, and the processing required to encode these into phonemic imagery *have already operated*. In short, the conscious aspects of covert speech and overt speech have a similar relation to the processes that produce them. In neither case are the complex antecedent processes available to introspection.

---

output (speech production), the conscious experience that we normally associate with such processing *follows* the processing to which it relates. Given this, in what *sense* are these 'conscious processes' conscious?

Unravelling the three senses in which a process may be 'conscious'

According to Velmans (1991a), the psychological and philosophical literature confounds three distinct senses in which a process might be said to be 'conscious'. It might be conscious:

(a) in the sense that one is conscious *of* the process;
(b) in the sense that the operation of the process is *accompanied* by consciousness (of its *results*);
(c) in the sense that consciousness *enters into* or *causally influences* the process.

We do not have introspective access to how the preconscious cognitive processes that enable thinking produce individual, conscious thoughts in the form of 'inner speech'. However, the content of such thoughts and the sequence in which they appear do give some insight into the way the cognitive processes (of which they are manifestations) operate over time in problem solving, thinking, planning and so on.[26] Consequently such cognitive processes are partly conscious in sense (a), but only in so far as their detailed operation is made explicit in conscious thoughts, thereby becoming accessible to introspection.

Many psychological processes are conscious in sense (b), but not in sense (a) – that is, we are not conscious of how the processes operate, but we are conscious of their *results*. This applies to perception in all sense modalities. When consciously reading this sentence for example you become aware of the printed text on the page, accompanied, perhaps, by inner speech (phonemic imagery) and a feeling of understanding (or not), but you have no introspective access to the processes which enable you to read. Nor does one have introspective access to the *details* of most other forms of cognitive functioning, for example to the detailed operations which enable 'conscious' learning, remembering, engaging in conversations with others and so on.

The extent to which such processes might, under suitable conditions, *become* accessible to introspection, making them partly conscious in sense (a) as well as in sense (b), is an open, empirical question. The construction of three-dimensional depth in visual perception, for example, normally operates too quickly to be noticeable. However, if one stares through the two-dimensional stereoscopic picture shown in Figure 6.5, the construction of depth operates sufficiently slowly to experience the change from two dimensions to three dimensions. As with planning and problem solving, close attention to and reflection on other forms of processing may yield introspective insights into their nature. The linguist Noam Chomsky, for example, developed his theories of 'language competence' by formalising his own intuitions about the nature of grammar.[27] It is also possible, in some instances, to develop special techniques for making otherwise nonconscious or preconscious processes partly conscious in sense (a), for example through the use of biofeedback, or through the development of training in appropriate phenomenological methods.[28]

Crucially, having an experience that gives some introspective access to a given process, or having the results of that process manifest in an experience, says nothing about whether that experience *carries out* that process. That is, whether a process is 'conscious' in sense (a) or (b) needs to be distinguished from whether it is conscious in sense (c). Indeed, it is not easy to envisage how the experience that makes a process conscious in sense (a) or (b) *could* make it conscious in sense (c). Consciousness *of* a physical process does not make consciousness responsible for the operation of that process (watching a kettle does not determine when it comes to the boil). So, how could consciousness *of* a mental process carry out the functions of that process?[29] Alternatively, if conscious experience *results* from a mental process it arrives *too late* to carry out the functions of that process.

The 'Causal Paradox'

I believe that we cannot resolve the conceptual muddle surrounding the causal interactions of consciousness and brain unless we recognise the very different senses in which mental processing has been claimed to be 'conscious'. Once we accept that a process might be conscious in senses (a) and/or (b) without being conscious in sense (c) we can finally face up to the question of what, if anything, consciousness does. Functionalist theories which simply *redefine* consciousness to be a form of processing such as focal attention, information in a 'limited capacity channel', a 'global workspace', etc., confound these subtle relationships, thereby begging the question about the functional role of phenomenal consciousness in the economy of the mind.[30]

Yet, once we do face up to this problem in a non-question-begging way, we are left with a paradox. If one examines human information processing purely *from a third-person perspective*, that is, from the perspective of an external observer, consciousness does not seem to be necessary for any form of processing. The operation of minds and brains seems to be explainable entirely in functional or physical terms that make no reference to what we experience. For example, once the processing within a system required to perform a given function is sufficiently well specified in procedural terms, one does not have to add an 'inner conscious life' to make the system work. In principle, the same function operating to the same specification could be accomplished by a nonconscious machine. Likewise if one inspects the operation of the brain from the outside, no subjective experience can be observed at work. Nor does one need to appeal to the existence of subjective experience to account for the neural activity that one *can* observe.

The experimental and introspective evidence summarised above regarding how phenomenal consciousness *actually* relates to so-called 'conscious processing' in humans deepens this puzzle. The detailed operations of most processes that we think of as 'conscious' are not available to introspection. And, if one examines the *timing* of the experiences which do accompany 'conscious processing' (in reading, speaking, thinking and so on), the experiences seem to come *too late* to affect such processing. Given this, something *else* must be going on in the brain at the time that experiences arise. What is common to the complex processes that enable one to read, think, speak and so on is that they operate, and 'become conscious', only if they are at the focus of attention. Consequently, a number of cognitive theories have associated consciousness with late-arising aspects of focal-attentive processing such as information integration and dissemination (of what *has been* read, spoken or thought, etc.) – or, as Baars puts it, with entry of information into a 'global workspace'. However, this still does not solve the puzzle of what phenomenal consciousness does. Conscious experience of given information may *correlate* with integration and dissemination of that information throughout the brain, entry into a 'global workspace' and so on, but, given that we have no conscious experience of carrying out such operations in our own brains, nor any conscious knowledge about *how* such operations are carried out, it is difficult to envisage *any* sense in which these operations are *carried out* by consciousness.

When I first presented a similar analysis in Velmans (1991a), I concluded that, *viewed from a third-person perspective*, consciousness appears to be epiphenomenal. Certain kinds of processing in the brain (the late-arising aspects of focal attention) appear to cause or correlate with the conscious experiences reported by subjects. But conscious experiences do not, in turn, seem to cause or carry out the processes that one can observe or infer from an external observer's point of view. As my review had considered all the main phases of information processing (in more detail than the analysis above) I suggested that this conclusion applies to *all* forms of human information processing (when viewed from a third-person perspective).

If one accepts that one cannot dismiss the *existence* of consciousness (that experiences provide psychological *data*), this conclusion is devastating for functionalism. If consciousness does not *have* a function that is specifiable in third-person information processing terms, how can it *be* a function that is specifiable in those terms? This conclusion is also damaging for physicalism – unless one is prepared to accept that consciousness is a physical state of the brain that plays no causal role in the brain's activities.

Given this, it is hardly surprising that my original analysis met with considerable opposition. Accounts of functioning in cognitive psychology are, traditionally, third-person accounts. Consequently, many commentators on my target article took it for granted that if consciousness does not have a function that can be specified in third-person information processing terms, then it has no function at all. In spite of my repeated denials, some also accused me of being an epiphenomenalist. Why do I reject epiphenomenalism? Because I do not believe that one can give an exhaustive account of the nature or function of consciousness from a third-person perspective.

Viewed from a *first-person perspective*, it seems absurd to deny the role of consciousness in mental life. If one examines one's own psychological functioning, consciousness appears necessary for the analysis of novel or complex stimuli, choosing what to attend to or do, and most forms of learning and memory. It also seems necessary for most novel or complex cognitive transformations and output. How, after all, could one think, plan, be creative, give a lecture or write a paper if one were not conscious? Given this, it is hardly surprising that over the last thirty-five years or so, phenomenal consciousness has been thought to play an important role in every major phase of human information processing, ranging from input (the analysis of novel or complex stimuli, selective attention) and storage (working memory, learning), to transformation (thinking, problem solving, planning, creativity) and output (speech, writing, novel or complex adaptive adjustments to the environment).

As David Bakan has argued, we rightly take the causal efficacy of conscious mental states for granted in everyday, practical life:

> Do practical men believe that mental states affect physical conditions? Do practical men concern themselves with mental states, or do they just regard them as epiphenomenal? Judges concern themselves with the mental state of the accused. They are interested in whether there was an intention to murder or not. A United States Supreme Court decision on discrimination ruled that disproportionality itself could not be taken as discrimination. The court ruled there had to be evidence of intention to discriminate. Lawyers are concerned with the mental states of judges and juries. Politicians concern themselves with the mental states of their constituents and others. Military commanders are particularly concerned with the mental states of those against whom they are warring, as well as the mental states of those on whom they spy. The mental events in the minds of Einstein, Fermi, Szilard, and other physicists, in connection with atomic energy, were of no small moment with respect to the physical world. Deceivers are very concerned with the mental states of those whom they deceive and vice versa. Lenders are concerned with the mental states of those who borrow. Salesmen and advertising agents are concerned with the mental states of potential and actual customers. Everybody has an interest in the mental states of motor vehicle operators.
>
> (Bakan, 1980, p. 127)

In short, consciousness presents a *Causal Paradox* (Velmans, 1991b, p. 716). Viewed from a first-person perspective consciousness appears to be necessary for most forms of complex or novel processing. But, viewed from a third-person perspective consciousness does not appear to be necessary for any form of processing. I submit that it does not make sense to reject either perspective. An adequate theory of consciousness needs to resolve the Causal Paradox in a way that violates *neither* our intuitions about our own experiences, *nor* the findings of science.[31]

Elaborating on the different senses in which a process may 'be conscious' provides a place to start, but does not get us very far. However, if we combine this with an accurate account of the phenomenology of conscious experiences (Chapter 6), an understanding of the relation of consciousness to *knowledge* (Chapter 8) and an understanding of asymmetries of access to each other's mental states (Chapter 9) we can resolve the Causal Paradox (see Chapter 13). We also arrive at a different view about the nature and function of consciousness.

Notes

1 A critique of functionalist reductionism which had many similarities to my *Behavioral and Brain Sciences* papers later appeared in the work of the philosopher David Chalmers (1995). See commentary by Velmans (1995a) for a comparison of these similarities as well as some critical differences. This critique was further expanded by Chalmers (1996). Although functionalism continues to be defended in modern writings (see, for example, Baars, 2007; Van Gulick, 2007), the problems with functionalist reductionism raised by these earlier critiques have not (to my knowledge) been overcome.

2 See for example the open peer review accompanying Libet (1985), the commentaries accompanying Libet (2002) and the reply by Libet (2003a).

3 This is true even for meta-representations (representations of representations) such as thoughts about what one perceives, thoughts about thoughts and so on. In such cases the (second order) representations are *of* (first order) representations, not of the (second order) meta-representations themselves (and so on).

4 I am grateful to Ben Libet for bringing this to my attention (see comments by Libet accompanying Velmans, 1993a).

5 Equally surprising, studies of *change blindness* such as Simons and Levin (1998) demonstrate that, under some circumstances, we do not notice *major changes* in what we are gazing at unless fast transitions capture our attention, or we happen to be focusing our attention on the precise features that change. See Eysenck and Keane (2005), ch. 5, and Noë (2007) for useful introductions to recent studies in this area and the conclusions that may be drawn from them.

6 A more detailed account is given in Velmans (1991a, 1999b). Kihlstrom (1996), Goodale (2007), Goodale and Milner (2004), Shiffrin (1997), Merikle (2007), Merikle and Joordens (1997) and the whole of *Consciousness and Cognition* 6(2/3), 1997, also provide useful surveys of different facets of preconscious perceptual processing. See also contrasting views outlined in Holender (1986).

7 In fact, Dawson and Schell's procedure required subjects to *divide* their attention between the selected and non-selected ear, and is not therefore comparable to earlier studies where subjects were simply asked to shadow the message in the attended ear. Their finding nevertheless highlights the difficulty of assessing the awareness of non-selected words in dichotic listening studies.

8 See Dixon (1981), Kihlstrom (1996), Merikle (2007), Merikle and Daneman (1998), and Velmans (1991a) for reviews of the evidence. For a defence of the use of subjective reports in such studies see Velmans (1999b).

9 Recent experimental findings indicate that the depth of input analysis that takes place prior to focal attention varies with the processing load. More demanding forms of input cannot be processed to the same depth before a selection needs to be made (cf. Lavie, 2007). In real-life situations it would nevertheless be advantageous to have enough information about input for an adaptive selection to be made, so, when circumstances permit, it seems reasonable to suggest that sufficient analysis takes place for this to happen.

10 Evidence for this complex theory was gathered by Neeley (1977). Evidence for the preconscious, parallel activation of traces which share features with an input stimulus, followed by selection of the most pertinent traces (and inhibition of non-pertinent traces), has also been found in studies of speech perception (Pynte *et al.*, 1984; Swinney, 1979, 1982). Support also comes from studies of visual masking – a procedure where visual stimuli are prevented from reaching consciousness by the presentation of a subsequent visual stimulus or 'mask' (Marcel, 1980; Greenwald *et al.*, 1989).

11 See, for example, Lavie (2007), Pashler (1999), Styles (1997) and the whole of *Consciousness and Cognition* 6(2/3), 1997.

12 See, for example, the discussion in Chapter 4 of Norman's (1969) model in Figure 4.3.

13 In a study which investigated the effects of visual, masked primes on the speed at which subjects could evaluate visually presented target words as 'positive' or 'negative', Greenwald and Liu (1985) also found that single, subliminal words primed evaluatively congruent meanings, but two-word phrases did not. That is, a negative prime speeded the subject's response to a negative target, but not to a positive target (and vice versa). As one would expect from single-word priming, a two-word prime such as 'enemy loses' speeded the response to negative targets, in spite of the fact that the phrase as a whole is evaluatively positive.

14 For example, Treisman (1964) found that subjects bilingual in English and French recognised the meanings of French translations in the non-attended ear of English prose passages in the attended ear that they were required to shadow. Lackner and Garrett (1973) also found evidence that ambiguous, attended-to sentences which subjects were required to paraphrase were disambiguated by phrases (embedded in sentences) in the non-attended ear. This appears to meet the 'two-word challenge' (but see Underwood, 1991, and Velmans, 1991a, 1991b, for a discussion). There is also a strong case to be made for the *preconscious* analysis of complex meanings in *attended* channels (Velmans, 1991a), as we will see below.

15 See 'A conundrum' in Box 4.3, and the critique of Dretske's position in Velmans (1991b).

16 Campion *et al.* (1983) have argued that blindsight findings may be artefactual; it may be, for example, that the striate is not completely damaged in patients exhibiting some residual visual functioning. Weiskrantz (1988) agrees that, prior to post-mortem, one cannot rule this out. However, he points out that this possibility is far-fetched in blindsight cases where complete unilateral hemispheric decortication obtains (Perenin and Jeannerod, 1978). Campion *et al.* also suggest that residual vision might have arisen from stray light originating from the stimulus and diffused onto intact regions of the visual field, to produce a subtle form of stimulation of which the subjects remained unaware. Weiskrantz (1986, 1988, 2007) reviews various sources of evidence against this. For example, one naturally occurring control for stray light was provided by the optic disk of subject D.B., which fell within his blind hemifield. Within the optic disc, nerve fibres penetrate the retina and no receptors exist. In this region, therefore, the eye is truly blind. Accordingly, when a spot of light (suitably adjusted for intensity and contrast) was projected onto D.B.'s optic disc, he could not see it and his ability to guess whether or not it was present remained at chance. Hence, the spot could not have been a source of stray light; when it was directed to the blind hemifield just adjacent to his optic disc D.B. still maintained he could not see it, but his ability to guess whether or not it was present was very good. This provided clear evidence that 'blindsight' is not an artefact (further methodological issues are discussed in Weiskrantz, 1997).

17 This link of consciousness to 'knowing that one knows' (from Velmans, 1991a) was also later suggested by Reber (1997).

18 Mandler (1997) also states that 'attentional processing produces conscious contents'. However, his position remains ambiguous. For reasons that are not specified, Mandler (1997) also claims that 'conscious content does not presuppose prior attention' (p. 484, note 9).

19 In the psychological literature these properties are typically associated with focal-attentive processing. Consequently, I have included Mandler (1975, 1991) amongst those theorists that treat consciousness as identical to aspects of focal-attentive processing (above). However, Mandler (1991) admits that consciousness and focal-attentive processing are not co-extensive, and Mandler (1997) is similarly ambiguous (see note 18 above).

20 Baars also cites evidence of neurophysiological dissociations between attention and consciousness based on Posner's work on a 'visual attention network' in which cortical regions supporting orienting, selection of input, maintenance of an alert state, switching attention, and executive control over selective functions are distinguished from those supporting consciousness. Shiffrin (1997) also gives a detailed review of dissociations between consciousness and attentional processing.

21 Libet established the accuracy and reliability of this method of establishing a 'clock time' for the onset of a conscious experience, by requiring subjects to judge the clock time of a felt, tactile stimulus (applied to the hand) with a known onset time. They found judged onset to be around 50 ms earlier than actual onset, with a standard error of ± 20 ms

22 There have been many commentaries on and disputes about both Libet's data and his interpretation of that data, for example the peer commentary accompanying his 1985 *Behavioral and Brain Sciences* target article, a special edition of *Consciousness and Cognition* (2002; issue 11) along with Libet's (2003a) reply, and readings in Pockett *et al.* (2006). Recent, extensive reviews of the literature nevertheless continue to support these broad conclusions (see Banks and Pockett, 2007; Hughes, 2008).

23 See Danto (1985) and Velmans (1991b). See also the debate on this issue between Libet (2003b) and Velmans (2003b).

24 In blindsight there is also reason to believe that spared (implicit) visual information is different in kind and mediated by circuitry that is neuroanatomically distinct from the information and circuitry which serves conscious visual experience (see Köhler and Moscovitch, 1997, for a useful discussion of the issues).

25 According to Bock (1982), speech production is arranged in six, relatively distinct 'arenas'. There is a referential arena in which some nonlinguistic coding of thought is transformed into a format that can be used by the linguistic system, a semantic arena in which the propositional relations formed within the referential arena are meshed with lexical concepts, a syntactic arena responsible for structuring lexical items into conventional surface grammatical forms, a phonological arena in which lexical items are mapped onto phonological representations, a phonetic arena that translates phonological codes into codes suitable for entry into motor programmes (e.g. target vocal-tract configurations), and a motor assembly arena responsible for the actual compiling and running of the motor programmes. See also Dell (1986).

26 Newell *et al.* (1960) derived broad design principles of their computer 'General Problem Solver' from such introspective information.

27 Where 'language competence' is the intuitive knowledge of language structure which underlies language performance. The 'psychological reality' of such linguistic intuitions has been extensively researched and debated. However few students of language would deny that at least some useful insights have been gained by examining such intuitions (see Chomsky, 1968, for a defence of this introspective approach).

28 See, for example, the investigation of preconscious processes conducive to the development of intuitive insight by Petitmengin-Peugeot (1999), a detailed account of method in Petitmengin (2006), and the combination of phenomenological and neurophysiological approaches to investigating the nature of experienced time in Varela (1999).

29 I do not wish to deny that introspective attention to a given process may be instrumental in altering that process, particularly in introspection, where the observer is very closely coupled to the observed. Indeed, this can be a serious methodological problem for phenomenological investigations (see, for example, readings in Jack and Roepstorff, 2003, 2004; Hartelius, 2007; Shear, 2007). However, this does not affect the point that consciousness of a process needs to

be distinguished from the process itself, or the point that one can be conscious of a process without consciousness carrying out that process.

30 At the time of writing, these different senses in which a process may be said to be conscious continue to be largely ignored in psychological and philosophical theory, in spite of the obvious need to distinguish between them when claiming the functions of some process to be the functions of phenomenal consciousness. Yet it would seem that these distinctions are fairly self-evident once attention is drawn to them; only one of the forty published commentaries on Velmans (1991a) made any attempt to challenge them (see Glicksohn, 1993, and my reply in Velmans, 1993b); nor have I come across any subsequent critique of these fundamental distinctions in the consciousness studies literature.

31 This paradox is not generally addressed (or even acknowledged) by current, functionialist theories of consciousness, but one cannot escape it by ignoring it. It is evident for example in the self-contradictory positions forced on major psychological theories in this area such as that of Miller (1962), Mandler (1975, 1991, 1997) and Baars (1988, 1997a, 1997b), as we have seen above. While a few theorists have recognised this paradox and tried to resolve it in third-person terms, notably Gray (1995) and Rakover (1996), their suggestions do not deal adequately with the problems outlined above (see the discussion of these positions in Velmans, 1995b, 1996c).

11 The neural causes and correlates of consciousness

A quick sketch of the territory

There is little doubt that, viewed purely from a third-person perspective, the *proximal* causes of human consciousness are to be found in the brain. Direct micro-stimulation of the occipital lobe for example is sufficient to cause an experience of simple visual forms, stimulation of the temporal lobes, auditory experiences, stimulation of the somatosensory cortex, tactile experiences, and so on (Penfield and Rassmussen, 1950; Lee *et al.*, 2000). Causal processes within the brain are of course embedded within a supporting body and surrounding universe – and there is something deeply mysterious about how activities in brain cells could possibly 'produce' conscious experiences. We will return to both of these issues later on. However, provided that we restrict ourselves to thinking of a 'cause' in terms of necessary and sufficient neural conditions for a conscious effect to occur, we can place the broader issues 'on hold' for the moment, and get on with the business of trying to specify these proximal, neural conditions.

Note to begin with that the conditions for the *existence* of consciousness (of any kind) in human brains can be usefully distinguished from the added conditions required to support particular *forms* of human experience. For example, activities in the brain stem that control the sleep–wake cycle, the disruptions that produce coma or other global disorders of consciousness, and the effects of anaesthesia can be usefully distinguished from the added activities in mid-brain systems responsible for motivation and emotion that give experiences their affective tone. These effects of mid-brain activities may, in turn, be distinguished from the activities of neocortical systems that are primarily responsible for the variety of sensory experiences and experiences associated with higher cognitive functions such as the inner speech accompanying thinking, remembering and so on. Ultimately, of course, these activities interconnect, mutually influencing each other within the highly interconnected brain.

Following current conventions, the conditions for the existence of consciousness or of its many forms can be specified in either functional or structural terms. Knowledge of the brain's functions inferred, say, from experimental psychology can be very useful in the search for neural structures that support such functions. We have examined some of these functionally specified conditions for consciousness in Chapter 10. In brief, the evidence suggests that consciousness takes time to develop once a stimulus arrives at the brain – perhaps 200 ms or so (according to Libet, 1996). What *makes* a stimulus conscious? As William James observed, we select what we attend to and we are consciously aware of what we select, but we are not aware of unattended information. If so, conscious phenomenology must relate closely to information that has been selected for *focal attention*. The contents of consciousness also seem to form a kind of 'psychological present' which is immediately accessible for report, that contrasts with our 'psychological past' which has to be remembered through recall or recognition. This suggests a functional distinction in mental processing between a temporary short-term (working, or primary) memory system that holds information relating to current experience, and a relatively long-term (secondary) memory that holds information relating to past experience.

What is it *about* attentional processing that relates most closely to consciousness? Clues are offered by situations where attentional processing is partially *dissociated* from consciousness, for example where subjects focus their attention on an input stimulus but consciousness of the stimulus does *not* arise. Examples include blindsight, implicit learning and memory, and the 'hidden observer' in hypnotic analgesia. Common to these conditions are different forms of information 'encapsulation'. Subjects have knowledge (of visual input, of regularities in previously presented stimuli, of the painfulness of a surgical procedure) but they do not 'know that they know'. As Kahneman and Treisman (1984) suggest, the *dissemination* of currently processed information to other information processing modules may be one of the functions of focal-attentive processing, enabling greater resources to be devoted to the input and allowing the system as a whole to respond to input at the focus of attention in a coherent, global way. This would account for the greater flexibility and sophistication of 'conscious', focal-attentive processing (compared with 'preconscious', pre-attentive processing). When information dissemination is disrupted, disruption of consciousness (of that information) also occurs. This would suggest that input analysis becomes conscious around the time that its products are being *disseminated* – a late-arising stage of focal-attentive processing. Other conditions for consciousness, specifiable in information processing terms, also need to be met. The constituent features of conscious experience are usually well integrated. For example, under normal viewing conditions we do not experience the colour and movement of individual objects as separate features in spite of the fact that the brain processes colour and movement information in geographically distinct areas of the visual system. Consequently information integration or 'binding' of such features must take place before such integrated experiences arise.

Additional clues

Additional clues about the neural conditions for human consciousness are provided by studies of the sleep–wake cycle (cf. Hobson, 2007) and the global disorders of consciousness arising from severe brain injuries such as coma and vegetative states (cf. Schiff, 2007). The complex organisation of conscious states can also be investigated through the many neurological syndromes that produce dissociations of consciousness or disorders of consciousness, for example the divisions in consciousness that accompany commissurotomy, an operation to relieve focal epilepsy that severs the primary bundle of nerve fibres connecting the left and right cortical hemispheres. According to Sperry (1984) this reveals a distinct left and right hemisphere consciousness – a disturbing possibility that has been extensively debated over three decades (cf. Colvin and Gazzaniga, 2007; Sperry, 1984; Zaidel *et al.*, 2003).

Insights into the ways that brain chemistry affects both the existence of consciousness and its many forms can also be gained from studies of anaesthetics (cf. Kihlstrom and Cork, 2007) and of the way that psychoactive drugs exert their effects by mimicking (agonism) or blocking (antagonism) the activity of normally occurring substances used by neurons to communicate with one another (cf. Julien, 2004; Pace-Schott and Hobson, 2007).

Needless to say, all the areas above have been the subject of highly active research programmes over many decades in studies of attention and memory, psychophysics, perception, neurophysiology, neuropsychology, neurochemistry, psychopharmacology, cognitive neuropsychology and so on. Much has been learnt about the structures in the human brain that support both the existence and content of human experience.

As the present work deals primarily with the fundamental puzzles of consciousness, rather than the fine details of its neural embodiment, I will not attempt to review the encyclopaedic research literature that deals with these issues. Conveniently, many excellent reviews already exist.[1] To make sense of how brain states might cause or correlate with conscious experiences we only have to know what such a causal story *would be like*. In particular, we need to separate the empirical problems from the conceptual ones.

The rough shape of a neural, causal story

What might an account of the neural causes of consciousness be like? As noted in Chapter 1, global changes in consciousness occur when one is awake, in dream sleep, in deep sleep, in coma and so on. But the change from being awake to being asleep does not correspond to being conscious versus nonconscious. When asleep one can have conscious dreams, and when awake there are many stimuli arriving at sensory surfaces of which one is not conscious. At the very least, therefore, any neural causal story will have to include mechanisms which regulate the sleep/awake cycle and the mechanisms which regulate attention.

The sleep–wake cycle[2]

In adult humans, changes in conscious state over the sleep–wake cycle are stereotyped, moving through four stages of brain activation in four or five cycles each night. When one initially goes to sleep, awareness of the outside world is lost, although one may still have visual imagery and associated thoughts. This loss of awareness is associated with a slowing of the EEG which is referred to as Stage I sleep. As activation levels in the brain continue to fall, this is followed by Stage II, indexed by a change in the EEG known as the sleep spindle which reflects independent oscillation of the thalamo-cortical system. As these oscillations progressively block the thalamo-cortical transmission of both external and internal signals within the brain (in NREM Stage II)[3] reportable conscious experience disappears. With further loss of activation, the Stage II spindles are joined by slow high voltage waves. The point at which these occupy over half the EEG record is known as NREM Stage III, and the point at which they dominate the entire record is known as NREM Stage IV. Arousal from this stage is difficult, often requiring repeated stimulation. However, brain activation levels with these stages show periods of major fluctuation. Aserinsky and Kleitman (1953), for example, found that EEG throughout these stages was periodically activated to near waking levels and that these periods were associated with rapid eye movements (REM). When aroused from these REM states, subjects often reported hallucinoid dreaming (Dement and Kleitman, 1957). Over the course of the night there is also a tendency for deactivated periods in Stages I to IV to become shorter, and periods of REM to become longer and more intense. In his review of the evidence, Hobson (2007) concludes that dreaming 'is our conscious experience of brain activation during sleep' (p. 105).

There is also something surprising going on that Hobson summarises in the following way:

> As the activation level is falling resulting in the sequence of sleep Stages I to IV, muscle tone continues to abate passively and the rolling eye movements cease. In Stage IV, the brain is maximally deactivated and responsiveness to external stimuli is at its lowest point. Consciousness, if it is present at all, is limited to low-level, non-progressive thought. It is important to note three points about these facts. The first is that since consciousness rides on the crest of the brain activation process, even slight dips in activation level lead to lapses in waking vigilance. The second is that even in the depths of Stage IV NREM sleep when consciousness is largely obliterated, the brain remains highly active and is still capable of processing its own information. From PET and single neurone studies, it can safely be concluded that the brain remains about 80% active in the depths of sleep.[4]

These conclusions not only emphasize the graded and state dependent nature of consciousness. They also indicate how small a fraction of brain activation is devoted to consciousness and that most brain activity is *not* associated with consciousness. . . . It is evident that consciousness requires a very specific set of neurophysiological conditions for its occurrence.

(Hobson, 2007, p. 103)

What are these conditions? The reticular activating system (RAS) in the brain stem is clearly involved, as it is known to regulate waking and sleep. However, according to the neurophysiologist Stuart Dimond, the RAS is not where consciousness 'resides'. Rather,

The interpretation which is nowadays generally placed on the participation of the subcortical centres is that of the essentially subservient role of waking and alerting without at the same time implying that the machinery of consciousness must reside at the waking centre, any more than military decisions are made by the batman who wakes the officer for duty each morning. In other words, the work of the subcortical centres is to provide the necessary conditions for consciousness, at least in its full wakeful sense, but it is still reasonable to assume that consciousness as we describe it here, as the running span of subjective experience, is essentially something of cortical origin and something essentially under cortical control. The role of the subcortical systems, therefore, according to our view, is essentially to provide an activating loop stretching upwards from the subcortical region to the cortex for the purpose of alerting and waking the cortical centres that deal with the phenomena of subjective experience.

(Dimond, 1980, p. 422)

Coma versus locked-in syndrome

Thirty years later, with a greater understanding of affect, there are reasons to doubt the 'cortical origin' of subjective experience – an issue to which we return below. However the activating role of the RAS is not in doubt. Mid-brain structures such as the thalamus that act as relay centres for communication within the brain are also of major importance. As noted above, disruption of this function by the independent oscillations of the thalamo-cortical systems that accompany Stage II NREM sleep is accompanied by a loss of consciousness. Damage to the thalamus and its associated structures also produces global disorders of consciousness. Castaigne *et al.* (1981) for example reviewed the injuries revealed by autopsies of acute coma patients and found that they nearly all had damage to intralaminar nuclei (ILN) of the thalamus. As Schiff (2007) points out in his own review of the evidence, even small lesions to such intralaminar nuclei can produce coma from which patients never recover. By contrast, cortical lesions, even as large as hemispherectomies, only abolish *some* contents of consciousness, not consciousness itself (Bogen, 1995; see also Schiff and Plum, 2000).

Lesions to the posterior (back) of the brain stem also produce coma, while lesions to the anterior (front) of the brain stem produce locked-in syndrome. While locked-in syndrome is almost as devastating as coma, the way that it differs from coma is instructive. As Damasio (1999) describes it,

> The motor pathways which convey signals to the skeletal muscles are destroyed, and only one pathway for vertical movement of the eyes is spared, sometimes not completely. The lesions that cause locked-in are placed directly in front of the area whose lesions cause coma or persistent vegetative state, yet locked-in patients have intact consciousness. They cannot move any muscle in their face, limbs, or trunk, and their communication ability is usually limited to vertical movements of the eyes, sometimes one eye only. But they remain awake, alert, and conscious of their mental activity.
>
> (Damasio, 1999, p. 292)

In short, in the human brain, there are some very precisely localised regions, such as the intralaminar thalamic and posterior brain-stem nuclei, that seem to be necessary for consciousness, but intact motor functioning is not necessary for consciousness. Does this make such nuclei the 'centres of consciousness'? Not really. As Gray (2004) observes, lesions to posterior brain stem disrupt not only normal waking behaviour, but all the unconscious mental processing associated with that behaviour (see Chapter 10). So the loss of consciousness may actually result from a loss of this associated activity. And Schiff (2007) makes a similar point about the role of thalamic intralaminar nuclei: conscious behaviour involves sustained attention, working memory and the programming of motor response – activities that involve widely distributed, persistent cerebral activity. Given its strategic position, 'the ILN may facilitate the formation, distribution, maintenance, and dissolution of sustained cerebral activity representing elementary cognitive building blocks for organized behavior during wakefulness' (Schiff, 2007, p. 597). In enabling communication, the relay centres of the thalamus may provide critical links in such extended neural causal chains – and these, in whole or in part, may support consciousness.

Affect

Note too that subcortical structures are not *confined* to such activating, communicative activities. They are also the primary source of ancient *qualities* of consciousness that we probably share with many other animals. For example, affective systems based in the mid-brain limbic system and prefrontal cortex provide motivation and provide the raw feelings associated with lust, caring and nurturing, panic, joy, fear, rage and so on (cf. Panksepp, 1998, 2007). These affective systems profoundly influence the more cognitive, cortically based forms of information processing described above, sometimes dominating them, and in any case permeating them with an affective, feeling tone. A simple demonstration of such subcortical influences is provided by situations where the neocortex is completely removed. Panksepp reports that,

> If one surgically eliminates neocortical influences in very young mammals, especially the 'primitive' ones such as laboratory rats, one consistently obtains adult animals that are outwardly indistinguishable from normal. . . . After neodecortication most instinctual operating systems remain intact, even disinhibited. For instance, once I prepared a set of neonatal decorticated rats and presented fully grown pairs (one decorticate, and one normal) to each of 16 students in a neuroscience practicum. During a lab session devoted to the observation of behavior, the students' task was to identify which animal of each pair was missing approximately a third of their brain. The result was that 12 of 16 students selected the decorticated animals as being normal. This statistically significant mistake apparently emerged because the decorticates readily exhibited their subcortical 'instinctual energies'. They were more active, explored and investigated their environments more vigorously, while the normals were comparatively inactive, and seemingly more timid.
>
> (Panksepp, 2007, p. 121)

Panksepp also points out that,

> In animals, localized electrical stimulation of the brain (ESB) can evoke a series of core instinctual behaviors, and to the best of our ability to evaluate such issues animals are experiencing the stimulation as either desirable or aversive (Panksepp, 1998, 2005). Animals work vigorously to sustain such affective states (i.e., they self-stimulate for the ESB) and they escape and/or avoid stimulation that evokes aversive behavior patterns. They also exhibit conditioned place preference and aversions for environments paired with such stimulation, and exhibit conditioned positive and negative vocalizations when confined in those environments where they experience such ESB (Knutson *et al.*, 2002).
>
> Such effects are concentrated in sub-neocortical paramedian limbic regions, and a few frontal cortical areas where such systems project. Human studies yield the same patterns. One can provoke feelings of anxiety, anger, desire, and many of the social feelings such as sadness, sexual arousal and mirth by stimulating the same brain regions where comparable effects are obtained in other animals (Heath, 1996).
>
> (ibid., p. 121)

When affective changes take place in humans, paramedian limbic cortical and sub-neocortical control centres for affect are also shown to be activity 'hot spots' by brain imaging studies using positron emission topography (PET) (Damasio *et al.*, 2000; Liotti and Panksepp, 2004). In human orgasms, PET studies also indicate activation of mid-brain structures such as periaquaductal gray (PAG) extending to medial frontal cortical regions that are also found to control sexual behaviour in other animals (Holstege *et al.*, 2003). Widespread limbic arousal is also associated with passionate encounters in REM dreams (Braun *et al.*, 1997).

In adult human beings such affective changes are, of course, extensively modulated by more cognitive, neocortical mechanisms (LeDoux, 1998). There are innumerable examples. To take just one, the neuropsychologist Jeffrey Gray suggests,

> Suppose yourself in a seemingly tranquil and innocuous conversation with the Dearly Beloved (as 'significant others' were once, more romantically, called). She (or he, to taste) says something wounding (or rejecting, or arousing your jealousy, also according to taste). At first, you merely notice the offending remark and carry on the conversation as before, perhaps calmly thinking 'I can ignore that', or 'it isn't all that important anyway'. But then – and again it takes some seconds to happen – you start to feel a knot in the stomach, a clenching in the jaws, a clamminess in the hands, a tremulousness in the voice. The wounding remark has after all hit home, it just took you some time to find out.
>
> (Gray, 2004, p. 275)

Equally, however, there is extensive evidence that emotional arousal guides, energises and, at times, drives thinking.[5] In his summary of the evidence, Panskepp (2007) concludes,

> Although this mental background of affective consciousness may become peri-conscious in the 'glare' of intense cognitive processing (like stars fading in the glare of Times Square), it is likely that those higher mental abilities remain critically dependent on the intrinsic, neurobiologically instantiated brain values of our various affective states. . . . Affective pre-adaptations may have provided a solid platform for the emergence of the more sensorial-perceptual forms of consciousness that characterize cognitive life, where rational discourse was eventually possible. . . . It is easier to envision why certain affective experiences have the phenomenological feel that they do than rational cognitive processes. The dynamics of emotional feelings may have more than a passing resemblance to the psychodynamics of instinctual emotional actions. It is possible that such large-scale neurodynamics provide self-referential envelopes that are able to ensnare perceptual cognitive states into various attractor basins. In sum, affective consciousness – a primary process kind of phenomenology

– may have been an essential, and highly conserved, evolutionary platform for the emergence of more cognitively resolved forms of awareness, where much vaster species differences have emerged in the neuro-evolutionary emergence of mind.

(p. 127)

Attention, memory and the global workspace

To become conscious, information has somehow to be 'activated' in the brain. However, merely being active is not sufficient for consciousness, as the bulk of active processing is unconscious. It is also widely accepted that much of this unconscious or preconscious processing is carried out automatically and efficiently by organised groups of neurons or 'modules' that are specialised to carry out very specific tasks. There is extensive evidence from neurological patients that there are many specific areas of the brain where localised lesions result in correspondingly specific malfunctions. Lesions to area V4 and V4a of the visual system for example destroy the ability to see colour, while lesions to area V5 destroy the ability to see movement (we return to this below). Such modular processing can also be carried out simultaneously, with little interference from other modules, in a massively 'parallel' way. However, efficient specialisation comes at the cost of a loss in flexibility, complexity, and an ability to deal with novelty. So, when faced with more demanding tasks, the brain also needs some means of communication amongst and combining its modularised skills to allow all its cognitive resources to be brought to bear. Given the added processing loads and the co-ordination of functions required it is not surprising that the brain has a limited capacity to carry out such tasks. Consequently it has to select what is of sufficient interest or importance to warrant such 'focal-attentive' processing.

Once information is selected for focal-attentive processing it also has to persist long enough for that processing to be carried out (in some form of 'working memory') and to be globally accessible to its more specialised resources. According to 'global workspace' theories of consciousness it is at this stage that the information also becomes conscious (Baars, 1988, 2007; Dehaene and Naccache, 2001).

Theories of how all this might be implemented in the brain have to translate each of these functional stages into some plausible neural story. For example, neural structures that select information for attention have to be appropriately positioned to act as gates for selected input channels as well as having the means to block or inhibit non-selected channels. In order that selected information can serve as the basis for further processing there must be neural mechanisms that enable it to persist for as long as needed to carry out that further processing, for example by employing some version of Hebb's 'reverberatory circuits' that maintain activity over extended periods through the use of feedback loops. In order for information to become globally available there must be some means of distributing or disseminating it throughout the brain, perhaps through long-range neural connections, and there must be some common neural language that enables meaningful communication between widely distributed, specialised, neural systems.

At present, there is no consensus about how the brain actually does all this. There are, for example, competing suggestions about which structures may be central to the operation of attention. As noted earlier, the thalamus, which nestles just below the cortex and maps onto it in a point-to-point fashion, is likely to be a particularly important 'gateway' to consciousness – and Crick (1984), not surprisingly, likened activation ascending from the thalamus to a 'searchlight' of attention that shines out from the thalamus to illuminate corresponding regions of cortex. Crick and Koch (1990) also suggested that thalamo-cortical reverberatory neural circuits provide the physical substrate for the very brief memory required to support short-term memory and an extended conscious present.

However, guided by somewhat different considerations, Posner and Raichle (1993) suggested that visual attention involves *two* attentional 'spotlights'. The first highlights a place in the world on which to focus, and the second selects specific features for analysis. In a world of competing stimuli there may also be mechanisms that actively inhibit the processing of information that is *not* selected for attention (see Chapter 10). Such functions are likely to involve highly complex interactions between different systems in the brain. For example, whenever attention switches from one object to another, it must (a) disengage from the current object, (b) move, and (c) engage with the next object. According to Posner and Raichle the posterior parietal cortex is likely to be central to these functions as damage to this system impairs the performance of any task that requires this particular ability. For example, in 1909 R. Balint described a patient with bilateral parietal lesions who found it very difficult to shift his visual attention. If his attention was directed toward a given object he simply did not notice other objects. When urged, he could identify new objects placed before him, but then completely neglected other objects. This made it very difficult for him to read, as each letter was seen as being a separate object. On the other hand, lesions confined to just the right inferior parietal cortex produce a rather different impairment – an inability to attend to objects in the left visual field (a condition known as 'left-sided unilateral neglect'). As Jeffrey Gray notes in his description of such cases,

> Such patients often behave as if only the right side of their world exists. They may shave only the right side of the face, eat from only the right side of the plate, dress only the right side of the body, read only the right side of the page, and so on. In formal tests, given a straight line to bisect, they mark the middle at a point three-quarters of the way over to the right, as though the left half of the line is missing ... or they copy only the right side of a drawing. Their problems affect all the senses: vision, hearing, touch, proprioception (that is, perception

'from the inside' of the position and state of one's own limbs), even smell.[6]

(Gray, 2004, p. 215)

To interact with objects in the world it is not enough, of course, simply to attend to them. Once one has focused on an object, one still has to select which features to analyse and then respond to what one finds in an appropriate way. This requires one to remember the features of interest long enough to make the right response. According to Posner and Petersen (1990) frontal lobe structures such as the anterior cingulate are likely to be central to these functions. Evidence is again provided by neurology, in this case from patients with frontal lobe damage who are notorious for saying one thing and doing another. Experiments with monkeys provide converging data, for example Fuster (1989) demonstrated that if monkeys are shown objects that they must remember for a short period before they are allowed to make a response, neurons in their frontal cortex continue to fire during the delay. Accordingly, Posner and Petersen suggest that the frontal lobe system operates as an 'executive attentional system' that provides the short-term memory required to link analysis to action. They also, rather boldly, went on to suggest that the information processed in this system forms the contents of consciousness.

However, the neural underpinnings of attention, memory and consciousness are likely to be far more complex. Damage to the frontal lobes is now recognised to be the cause of many impairments of short-term memory in which subjects must remember the temporary location of *visual* stimuli.[7] But other brain regions are known to be crucial for the performance of *verbal* short-term memory tasks. Warrington and Weiskrantz (1978) for example investigated a patient K.F. with a left posterior temporal lobe lesion that resulted in an almost total loss of short-term memory measured by an inability to repeat back verbal stimuli such as digits, letters, words and sentences.

Psychological studies of how selective attention operates also make it clear that many additional processes must be involved in how selection takes place. Input stimuli not only need to be analysed, they also need to be recognised (at least to some extent), before their importance can be assessed, which requires the system to access long-term traces of such stimuli already stored in memory. In order to understand how this is done, we would first have to understand exactly how long-term memory traces are stored and accessed, and how matching of input to those traces takes place. Assessment of importance also requires an *evaluation* of competing stimuli in the light of current events and past experience. We have little knowledge of how the brain carries out such evaluations – but it seems likely that such complex forms of processing involve many widely dispersed, interacting neural systems.

In addition, once information is selected for focal attention and eventually becomes conscious, the neural activities that are most closely associated with consciousness (the neural correlates of consciousness) must, somehow, 'support' the varied 'qualia' of consciousness[8] – how things look, sound, smell, taste, feel and so on. The brain regions known to support such sensory qualia are widely dispersed throughout the neocortex along with mid-brain structures that give those sensations and percepts an affective tone.

Crucially, most theories now accept that the processes which select information for focal attention operate *preconsciously*. Once material enters consciousness, analysis, attempted recognition and selection have *already taken place* (see Chapter 10). In sum, while it remains possible that information processed by the frontal lobe 'executive attentional system' eventually becomes conscious, there are good reasons to doubt that consciousness is somehow *located* in this system any more than it is located in the reticular activating system, or the intralaminar nuclei of the thalamus discussed above.

Currently popular 'global workspace' theories of consciousness accept that selective attention operates prior to consciousness (of what has been selected) and go on to develop the idea that the brain combines highly specialised, local forms of functioning with widely distributed forms of functioning, and that consciousness is associated with these more distributed forms of functioning. Bernard Baars, who introduced the term 'global workspace' in his 1988 book, puts it in the following way:

> The brain shows a distributed style of functioning, in which the detailed work is done by millions of specialized neuronal groupings without instructions from some command centre. By analogy, the human body works cell by cell; unlike an automobile, it has no central engine that does all the work. Each cell is specialized for a specific function according to its DNA, its developmental history, and chemical influences from other tissues. In its own way the human brain shows the same distributed style of organization as the rest of the body.
>
> (Baars, 2007, p. 238)

At the same time, the brain can also operate in a more integrated fashion:

> Global Workspace Theory . . . suggests that the brain has a fleeting integrative capacity that enables access between functions that are otherwise separate. This makes sense in a brain that is viewed as a massive parallel set of highly specialized neuronal processors. In such a system coordination and control may take place by way of such a central information exchange, allowing some specialized processors – such as sensory regions in cortex – to distribute information to the system as a whole. This solution also works in large-scale computer architectures, which show typical 'limited capacity' behavior when information flows by way of a global workspace. A sizable body of evidence suggests that consciousness is the primary agent of such a global access function in humans and other mammals.
>
> (ibid., p. 240)

Whether there is a system in the brain that provides global access, and whether information in this workspace becomes conscious, should not, of course, be confused with whether consciousness *itself* provides global access – and we have already examined many reasons to doubt that 'consciousness is the *primary agent* of such a global access' in Chapters 4 and 10. For the moment, however, we can set this caveat aside and ask what a 'global workspace' might look like in the brain.

How a global workspace might operate in the brain

In line with the suggestions of Crick (1984) and Crick and Koch (1990), Baars and Newman (1994) stressed the strategic location and function of the thalamus and its widespread connections to the cortex. Combined with activating systems in the brain stem, these form what Baars termed an 'exended reticular activating system' (or ERTAS) whose function is to switch various cortical modules on and off (a form of selective attention). Modules that are switched on then participate in the global workspace. Mid-brain structures such as the intralaminar nuclei of the thalamus play a central role in receiving information from and broadcasting information to both cortical and subcortical modules.[9]

Dehaene and Naccache (2001) develop similar ideas in a somewhat different and more detailed way. As they note, individual areas of the cortex not only have long-range connections to the thalamus (through thalamo-cortical 'vertical' projections), they also have long-range connections to each other (through cortico-cortical 'horizontal' or 'tangential' projections). The neocortex is arranged into six vertical layers and the long-range 'tangential' projections mostly originate from the pyramidal cells of layers 2 and 3, which are particularly prominent in regions of the prefrontal and parietal cortex. This combined (horizontal and vertical) system of connections forms the global workspace architecture. Horizontal connections are nearly all reciprocal (if region A sends signals to region B, then region B also sends signals to region A), so cells that fire in such assemblies mutually excite each other, maintaining a pattern of activation in the global workspace. Lateral inhibition to other assemblies ensures that only one can be dominantly active at any one time. Given the important roles of prefrontal and parietal cortex in attention and short-term memory (see above), activation from projections in these areas is thought to provide a further attentional 'amplification' to selected cell assemblies that deal with information at the focus of attention, boosting their ability to maintain their activity in the workspace, thereby forming the contents of working memory and consciousness.

Edelman and Tononi (2000) have also developed a detailed global workspace model involving the thalamus and cortex. However, they suggest a rather different mechanism by which modules compete, communicate, and combine with one another to dominate the workspace. At any given time there will be different patterns of neural activity in different cell assemblies each distributed over a range of brain regions and modules. Each of these has access to the long-range connections that form the workspace, thereby allowing the currently active patterns to interact with each other. Such interactions can either be mutually reinforcing or inhibitory. If they are mutually inhibitory, the activity of the assemblies is weakened. If they are reinforcing they enter into a mutually self-sustaining, larger assembly of cells. Eventually, a super-assembly of self-sustaining cells emerges that carries more complex information than all competing cell assemblies.[10] This dominates the workspace to become what Edelman and Tononi describe as the 'dynamic core', and it is this dominant pattern that becomes conscious. As the dominant pattern of activation changes, so does the associated consciousness.

The brain might, of course, combine specialised, local forms of input processing with more generalised global forms of processing without requiring these to take place at *different places*. Instead, as Singer (2007) suggests, the brain might adopt two, complementary *processing strategies*. If so, modular processing and processing in the 'global workspace' might take place in overlapping regions of the brain. According to Singer,

> The first strategy is thought to rely on individual neurons that are tuned to particular constellations of input activity. Through their selective responses, these neurons establish explicit representations of particular constellations of features. It is commonly held that the specificity of these neurons is brought about by selective convergence of input connections in hierarchically structured feed-forward architectures. This representational strategy allows for rapid processing and is ideally suited for the representation of frequently occurring stereotyped combinations of features; but this strategy is expensive in terms of the number of required neurons and not suited to cope with the virtually infinite diversity of possible feature constellations encountered in real world objects. The second strategy, according to the proposal, consists of the temporary association of large numbers of widely distributed neurons into functionally coherent assemblies which as a whole represent a particular content whereby each of the participating neurons is tuned to one of the elementary features of composite perceptual objects. This representational strategy is more economical with respect to neuron numbers because, as already proposed by Hebb (1949), a particular neuron can, at different times, participate in different assemblies just as a particular feature can be part of many different perceptual objects. Moreover, this representational strategy is more flexible. It allows for the rapid de novo representation of constellations that have never been experienced before because there are virtually no limits to the dynamic association of neurons in ever changing constellations. Thus, for the representation of highly complex and permanently changing contents this second strategy of distributed coding appears to be better suited than the first explicit strategy.

(p. 607)

Singer goes on to suggest that such temporary associations of neurons constitute higher order 'meta-representations' that form the neural substrate of conscious experience. As he notes,

> The meta-representations postulated as substrate for conscious experience have to accommodate contents that are particularly unpredictable and rich in combinatorial complexity. In order to support the unity of consciousness, the computational results of a large number of subsystems have to be bound together in ever changing constellations and at the same rapid pace as the contents of awareness change. It appears then as if the second representational strategy that is based on the formation of dynamic assemblies would be more suitable for the implementation of the meta-representations that support consciousness than the explicit strategy. Further support for this view comes from considerations on the state dependency and the non-locality i.e. the distributed nature of mechanisms supporting conscious experience. If conscious experience depends on the ability to dynamically bind the results of subsystem computations into a unified meta-representation, conditions required for the formation of meta-representations ought to be the same as those required for awareness to occur.
>
> (p. 607)

What are the processes that bind neuronal modules into meta-representations? As we have seen in Chapter 3, one 'binding' process might be mutual entrainment of neuronal oscillations resulting in the synchronous or correlated firing of diverse neuron groups representing currently attended-to objects or events. While this possibility, suggested by Von der Malsburg (1986), remains tentative, evidence for the existence of such binding processes, involving rhythmic frequencies in the 30 to 80 Hz region, is now quite extensive. Such bindings also tend to be associated with conscious rather than unconscious states.[11] Consequently, Singer (2007) concludes that

> consciousness, rather than being associated with the activation of a particular group of neurons in a particular region of the brain, appears to be an emergent property of a particular dynamical state of the distributed cortical network – a state that is characterized by a critical level of precise temporal coherence across a sufficiently large population of distributed neurons.
>
> (p. 613)

Given the complexity of the processes involved, and given that we are only concerned here with the rough 'shape' of a neural story, we do not have to enter into the debate over which of these theories is the most plausible, or into the fine detail of these, and other similar theories.[12] Suffice it to say that, given the mix of specialised and generalised functions undertaken by the brain, a combination of modular functioning with some form of 'global workspace' or its functional equivalent is plausible. It is also consistent with well established psychological theories of attention. There is also extensive evidence that shifting populations of widely distributed cell assemblies enter into momentarily synchronous firing patterns, as one might expect from global workspace theory.

But what is it about neural activity that actually makes it conscious?

It seems safe to say that in the human brain neural *activation* is somehow related to consciousness. However, this bland assertion does not get us very far. At any given moment, the brain is active in many ways and the bulk of this activity takes place without associated consciousness. Even in the deepest stage of NREM sleep (Stage IV), where there is no associated consciousness, brain activity levels may be as high as 80 per cent. Fluctuations in activity levels nevertheless make a difference. In REM dreams, for example, overall activity levels approach those in the waking state.

That said, fluctuations in activity levels on their own do not decide *what* will become conscious as there are many forms of active processing that are simply *inaccessible* to consciousness. As Gray (2004) observes, global workspace models tend to assume that 'the neural basis of consciousness is directly related to executive functions: that is to systems that *manipulate* information. The contrasting intuition . . . is that the neural basis of consciousness lies in systems which directly "*code*" this information – that is, in perceptual systems' (p. 181). The contents of consciousness also appear to relate most closely to the *results* of perceptual processing rather than to the processing itself. When we look around us we consciously experience objects and events located and extended in a three-dimensional visual world, but we have no conscious experience of the complex processes that *enable* us to see. Similarly, when we produce speech, we experience the sounds of our own voices and, perhaps, a sense of how well our description is going, but we have little conscious awareness of the processes that *enable* us to speak. As we have seen in Chapter 10, visual experiences of the external world, auditory experiences of our own voices, internal experiences of the feel of our own bodies, and experiences in other exteroceptive and interoceptive sensory modalities *follow* the information processing that *enables* us to see, to speak and to experience in other ways. While executive functions such as attention, working memory and information dissemination enter into neural causal chains that support conscious experiences along with perceptual functions such as input analysis and pattern recognition, it is the neural representations of stimuli *that have been* analysed and selected for focal attention that appear to correlate most closely with the 'qualia' of conscious experiences. The phenomenology of human consciousness also reveals its contents to be largely composed of (or derived from) materials drawn from a limited range of resources provided by our sensory systems – vision, hearing, touch, smell, taste, and various interoceptive modalities such as bodily pain, pleasure, and so on (see Chapter 8). It seems safe to say therefore that for any given experience there must be activation in neural assemblies in corresponding sensory and or affective regions of the brain.

Essential nodes

As one might expect, normal perception requires activation of those primary areas of cortex onto which input from the sense organs projects. Ress and Heeger (2003), for example, found that visual stimuli that reach consciousness evoke significantly greater activity in the primary visual cortex (V1) than stimuli that do not reach consciousness. Triangulating evidence is provided by studying the conditions under which consciousness does *not* occur. Lesions of V1 for example produce a loss of subjective experience (for example in blindsight), confirming that activation above a given threshold in intact V1 is one, early condition of normal visual experience in the neural causal chain. However, activation of V1 may not be a necessary condition for all forms of visual experience. For example, while visual imagery also activates V1 (Kosslyn and Thomson, 2003), visual dreams and hallucinations do not (Braun *et al.*, 1998; Ffytche *et al.*, 1998). Patients blinded by lesions of V1 can also sometimes experience the motion of high contrast, rapidly moving stimuli (the Riddoch syndrome).

Studies of the visual system also suggest that activation of *very specific* neuronal assemblies is required to support an experience of the specific features of stimuli that are processed by those assemblies (whether this principle applies to all sensory modalities remains to be seen). Activation of V1 is not sufficient to experience features of visual experience such as shape, colour, movement, and so on. Other, specific regions of the visual system also need to be involved. Areas V4 and V4a, for example, are particularly important for the experience of colour, while perception of movement is more dependent on activity in V5 and its satellite regions. Direct or indirect cortical stimulation of such functionally specialised visual areas generally evokes a corresponding visual experience (Rees and Frith, 2007). Conversely, damage to that area removes the ability to experience that feature. For example, damage to the V5 complex produces *cerebral akinetopsia* (an inability to see visual motion), but does not affect colour vision, while damage to the V4 complex produces *achromatopsia*, an inability to see the world in colour, without affecting the ability to see motion (Zeki, 2007). Such findings led Zeki and Bartels (1999) to suggest that the visual system is organised into multiple, functionally distinct, spatially separated, 'essential nodes' each responsible for the perception of a given feature of visual experience.[13]

Is activation of such an essential node *sufficient* for conscious experience of its corresponding feature? According to Zeki (2007) no higher order processing such as 'binding' of features into object representations needs to be involved, making such consciousness of individual features a form of 'micro-consciousness'. However, while no other region of the brain that codes specifically for that feature may be involved, the level and type of activity are also important. As Rees and Frith (2007) point out, for most specialised brain areas, activation has been observed or inferred to occur without any corresponding experience. Unconscious activation is typically weaker or of a different character (for example, not synchronised) than conscious activation. And crucially, such activities do not take place in isolation, but are embedded in and influenced by other activities in the highly interconnected brain. Patients with particular forms of damage to right inferior parietal cortex for example ignore visual stimuli presented to the left side of their visual field ('left-sided unilateral neglect'), as we have seen.

Does information need to be integrated to be conscious?

Whether or not neural 'binding' is required for consciousness of an individual feature, the integration of the features processed by essential nodes is likely to be required for more *integrated* forms of consciousness – and given this, it is not surprising that Crick and Koch (1990) and Singer (2007) have proposed that the synchronous oscillations that integrate the activities of widely dispersed neuronal assemblies are the neural basis of consciousness. Once again, however, there are reasons to be cautious about this view. As noted in Chapter 3, Crick (1994) reported that 40 Hz synchronised oscillations have been found in the visual systems of anaesthetised cats, suggesting that such integrated operation can take place in the absence of normal experience. A dissociation between consciousness and useful, integrated functioning in human auditory cortex indexed by 40 Hz synchronous oscillations was also found by Schwender *et al.* (1994) in a study of auditory processing that produced implicit learning in surgically anaesthetised patients (see Chapter 4). Given this, it may be that synchronous firing enables *integrated functioning* and fosters competition for focal-attentive processing without being sufficient for consciousness – and for reasons such as these, Crick and Koch (2007) now explicitly reject the view that synchronous cortical oscillations are sufficient for consciousness. As they note, synchronised firing may assist a coalition in its competition with other coalitions; however, if the visual input is simple there might be no significant competition and consciousness of an input may occur without it.

Some preliminary conclusions

In the human brain, the antecedent neural causes of conscious experiences need to be distinguished from their proximal, co-temporal neural correlates. The systems and conditions that govern the *existence* of consciousness (for example, the sleep–wake cycle and selective attention) also have to be distinguished from the added conditions required to support its varied *forms*. At any given moment the bulk of processing remains unconscious and only very specific activities appear to be *eligible* for consciousness, such as the end products of interoceptive and exteroceptive perceptual processing that result in inner experiences (such as thoughts and visual images), body sensations (such as pleasure and pain) and a surrounding, phenomenal world extended in three-dimensional space and time. While these contents are indefinitely varied, the basic experiential materials from which they are constructed are drawn from a limited number of sensory resources and their derivatives. The external phenomenal world for example is constructed from what we see, hear, touch, taste and smell, while verbal thoughts and dreams draw on auditory-phonemic and visual imagery. Such sensory qualia appear to be largely cortically based although mid-brain structures play a major role in giving such qualia an affective tone. In the visual system (and perhaps in other systems) there appear to be 'essential nodes' – topographically distinct neural assemblies that are specialised for the processing of individual features of visual input (such as colour, shape and motion). Activation of an essential node appears to be necessary to have an experience of the feature that it processes, which makes such activation a prime candidate for being a neural correlate of that experienced feature. Integrated experiences of objects require integration of their features, and phase-locked neural oscillations (in the 40 Hz region) might be the mechanism which 'binds' such widely distributed feature representations into the integrated neural activity required to support an integrated conscious field. Whether or not this turns out to be correct, it should be apparent that an account of the neural structures and func-tions that govern the sleep cycle, selective attention, and the construction of conscious contents through feature activation and binding would be a well formed theory of the 'neural causes and correlates of consciousness'. Establishing the accuracy of such complex theories is difficult science, but it is *normal* science.

Is there *a specific place in the brain* where conscious experiences are gener-ated? While there are some vital, precisely located, early links in the chain of neural causation that support human consciousness, for example the intrala-minar nuclei of the thalamus where lesions produce irreversible coma, the general answer appears to be no. And while it makes sense to treat those neural activities that code the features of a given conscious experience (for example the 'essential nodes') as the proximal neural correlates of that experience (or NCC), such activities are normally supported by activation and attentional systems elsewhere in the brain. Normal exteroception also involves complex, preconscious interactions with the external world, so, ultimately, in the chain of causation, the entire brain, body and embedding world might be directly or indirectly involved.

Is there *a special kind of neuron* for different modalities of experience (vision versus audition and so on)? Again (on present evidence) the answer seems to be no. Different affective qualia appear to be associated with differ-ent neurotransmitters (pleasure with dopamine, anxiety with noradrenaline, etc.); however, different sensory qualia appear to be linked to the functional organisation of the nodes that process the features associated with those qualia, and to the roles that these functions play within the global economy of the brain.

What is it about neurophysiological activity that *makes* it conscious? In 1976, the neurophysiologist E. Roy John confessed that,

> We do not understand the nature of . . . the physical and chemical inter-actions which produce mental experience. We do not know how big a neuronal system must be before it can sustain the critical reactions, nor whether the critical reactions depend exclusively upon the properties of neurons or only require a particular organisation of energy and matter.
>
> (John, 1976, p. 2)

Over thirty years later, we still don't know. In the human brain, the level of activation appears to be important. However, at any given moment, very little of the brain's activity reaches consciousness, and only some activities, such as the results of perceptual processing, appear to be eligible for consciousness. Those activities in the human brain that are eligible for consciousness also have to *compete* for consciousness – a recurring theme that can be traced back to the dawn of thinking about attentional processes in the writings of William James. Competition is also a common strand in current neuro-psychological theories of consciousness. As Crick and Koch (2007) and Singer (2007) make clear, synchronous firing is likely to be a mechanism by which given neural assemblies enter into *winning coalitions*, and, although their theories differ in detail, Dehaene and Naccache (2001) and Edelman and Tononi (2000) suggest that entry of information into the 'global work-space' and, more specifically, *dominating* the information in the global workspace is what makes neural information conscious.

What is perhaps most surprising about these converging views is that *no special, added ingredient may be required for consciousness*. Neural assemblies that are eligible for consciousness might be more or less active, and they might or might not enter into phase-locked synchronous firing with other assemblies which allow their firing patterns to become integrated and domin-ant. But doing *more* of what they normally do, or doing this in *synchrony* with other neural assemblies, does not fundamentally alter the nature of such neural activities. In short, eligible neural activities that remain unconscious may not be *different in kind* from those which become conscious, any more than the sound of individual voices at a football stadium is different in kind from the concerted singing of the crowd that drowns them out.[14]

Notes

1   For example, good introductory overviews to most of these areas can be found in *The Blackwell Companion to Consciousness* edited by Velmans and Schneider (2007). Gray (2004) provides a thoughtful introduction to the neurophysiological

issues in a way that is sensitive to both the philosophical issues and the empirical research; Zeman (2003) also provides an engaging introduction, and Rose (2006) provide extensive reviews of current neuropsychological research and associated theories of consciousness.

2 This account is based largely on Hobson (2007).

3 NREM or non-rapid eye movement sleep is distinguished from REM or rapid eye movement sleep which is associated with dreaming.

4 The 80 per cent figure is based on cerebral blood flow measures using techniques developed by Kety and Schmidt following the 'Fick Principle' and, as one might expect, the figure varies somewhat with the measure of global activation used. It should be noted too that not all regions of the brain are affected in the same way – for example, in deep sleep mid-brain reticular cells decline in activity by about 50 per cent. The fundamental point nevertheless remains that the brain activity remains considerable even during NREM sleep (Hobson, 2008, personal communication).

5 In recent years the investigation of such influences has become the basis of *affective neuroscience*, a distinct subfield of neuroscience that seeks to provide a balancing influence to the more established, 'cooler' forms of information processing examined by cognitive neuroscience (see, for example, Damasio, 1999; Panksepp, 1998).

6 The 'left side of space' is egocentrically defined (for the reason that it changes position as you move your body or head around). So it is generally accepted that such lesions damage the brain's ability to form a map of egocentric space, which makes it difficult for patients to attend to stimuli that appear in the affected area.

7 For example, using a combination of PET and MRI with human subjects, Petrides *et al.* (1993) found that frontal area 8 was active when subjects had to search for a given pattern in a visual array. But areas 9 and 46 were active if the same eight-pattern array was repeated eight times and subjects were required to point to a different pattern each time (requiring them to keep track of their own history of pointing). See Kolb and Whishaw (2003) for a review.

8 In this context, I am using the term 'support' loosely. We return to a more detailed examination of how the neural correlates of conscious qualia relate to the qualia themselves in Chapter 13.

9 Baars and Newman accept that, given the very large profusion of cells in the cortex in comparison to the relatively few cells in the thalamic nuclei, this would put a very heavy load on the limited capacity of those nuclei, so for this to work the information flow must be compressed in some way. As Rose (2006) notes, this would seem to be a weakness in the model.

10 'Information complexity' is the information shared by all the modules in the system and they suggest that it is this, rather than activation as such, which determines what is conscious (Tononi, 2007).

11 See reviews by Crick and Koch (1990, 1998), Engel and Singer (2001), Gray (1994), and Singer (2007).

12 Readers wishing to study these in detail should consult the cited sources. See also reviews by Zeman (2003), Gray (2004) and Rose (2006).

13 Note that it does not follow that such nodes are essential to *unconscious* processing of the relevant feature. Gray (2004, p. 158) for example reports fMRI experiments which show that conscious experiences of different facial expressions activate different regions of the brain. Fearful expressions light up the amygdala, while disgusted expressions light up the insula. If the faces are presented briefly (30 ms) and then masked to prevent them becoming conscious people can still discriminate the expressions; however neither the amygdala or insula is activated. Instead, unconsciously processed fear and disgust respectively activate the dorsolateral

prefrontal cortex and the putamen. However, the issue remains open. Moutoussis and Zeki (2002) for example used fMRI to compare brain activity when subjects discriminated between faces and houses presented either consciously or unconsciously (masked), and found activity in the same regions in both cases, albeit lowered activity in the unconscious situation.

14 This has some interesting implications for the distribution of consciousness both in the human brain and elsewhere, to which we return in Chapter 14.

Part III
A new synthesis: reflexive monism

12 What consciousness is

To what does the term 'consciousness' refer?

As noted in Chapter 1, when defining the meaning of a term, it is useful, if possible, to begin with an *ostensive definition* – to 'point to' or 'pick out' the *phenomena* to which the term refers and, by implication, what is *excluded*. Normally we point to some *thing* that we observe or experience. The term 'consciousness' however refers to experience itself. Rather than being exemplified by a particular thing that we observe or experience, it is exemplified by *all* the things that we observe or experience.

In everyday life there are two contrasting situations which inform our understanding of this term. We have knowledge of what it is like *to* experience or *to be* conscious (for example, when we are awake) as opposed to not being conscious (for example, when in dreamless sleep). Viewed this way, consciousness refers to one of two potential *states of mind* (conscious versus not conscious). We also understand what it is like to be conscious *of* something (when awake or dreaming) as opposed to not being conscious of that thing. At any given moment, we can be conscious of some phenomena but not others. The phenomena of which we are conscious at any given moment are the *contents of consciousness*.[1]

What the contents of consciousness are like

Theories about the nature of any phenomenon need to start with an accurate description of what it is that they need to explain. A theory of consciousness needs to explain why some states are conscious but others are not conscious. It also needs to explain the different forms that consciousness can take, exemplified by its contents. Most theories of consciousness start with pre-theoretical assumptions about the forms that consciousness can take that have little to do with its actual phenomenology. So they start in the wrong place.

With some notable exceptions (including Kant, Russell, Whitehead, and James), most theories of consciousness are either explicitly dualist or implicitly so (see Chapters 2 to 5). Dualist-interactionism (following

Descartes) is, of course, explicitly dualist: consciousness consists of non-material thinking stuff without location or extension in space. Reactions to dualist-interactionism such as physicalism and functionalism in their eliminativist, reductionist and emergentist forms are implicitly dualist in their acceptance of a dualist vision of what it is that they need to eliminate, reduce or otherwise explain away.

Oddly, these shared presuppositions about what the contents of consciousness are like seem to have little to do with what we actually experience. While some experiences such as thoughts and feelings might seem to have no clear location and extension in space, other sensations and experiences do seem to have a clear physical location and extension. Body sensations, for example, seem to be distributed around the body (if you touch this paper with your fingertips, the tactile sensation seems to be on the skin surface at the point of contact between paper and skin). And the experiences that result from the operation of exteroceptive systems such as vision and audition just *are* the objects and events we see and hear in the surrounding three-dimensional space. Your visual experience of this print on the page, for example, just *is* this seen print on the page (introspection reveals no *added* visual experience *of* print 'in the mind or brain').[2] In short, the contents of consciousness are not some mysterious *duplicate* of the everyday world that we experience. Taken together, the phenomena that we experience *constitute* what we think of as the everyday world. I have developed this theme, with supporting evidence, in Chapters 6 and 7. Given that this view also meets with 'common sense' (in that it does not require the contents of consciousness to be anything other than they *seem*), I will adopt it, as a point of departure, here.

Analysing the contents of consciousness into its component parts

When specifying the nature of phenomena it is useful to ask (a) what they are *composed of*, and (b) what they are *part of* (Wimsatt, 1976). What are their component parts, and what is the greater whole of which they are a part? The same principles can be applied to the contents of consciousness.

As noted above, dualist and reductionist analyses of the composition of conscious phenomena have been driven by pre-theoretical commitments. While Descartes' dualism recognised that experiences come in many varieties, his claim that consciousness is composed of *res cogitans* (thinking stuff) implies that these parts are relatively uniform in that they all have the character of immaterial 'thoughts' which do not have location and extension in space. For materialists, on the other hand, only material stuff exists. Consequently, experiences *have* to be composed of physical stuff such as neurons or neuronal states (or functions), however they might *seem*.

The present analysis is very different. The contents of consciousness encompass all that we are conscious of, aware of, or experience. These contents are immensely rich in complexity and variety and they can be categorised in an indefinitely large number of ways. Nevertheless, the 'experiential materials' from which the contents of human consciousness are constructed are drawn from a limited number of sources, largely defined by the sense modalities. The external phenomenal world for example consists of what we touch, smell, taste, hear and see. Body experiences include additional, intero-ceptive sensations, including kinaesthesis, and bodily pleasure and pain. And inner experiences such as thoughts, memories and so on normally consist of verbal, visual and other forms of imagery. Some experiences derive from a combination of resources. Our body image, for example, combines internal or surface body feelings with aspects of the body that we can see. Emotions can combine bodily sensations with cognitive components. If one analyses this phenomenology into its component parts one obtains minimally discriminable *phenomena* – minimal discriminable differences in brightness, colour, loudness, pitch and so on. I have examined the many different ways in which conscious contents can be analysed in Chapter 8, so I will not repeat this here.

It should be obvious that minimally discriminable phenomena do not all have the non-extended character of *res cogitans*. Discriminable pains, tactile sensations, and kinaesthetic experiences for example have a fairly clear location and extension within the body or on the body surface. And, in terms of their phenomenology, experiences of the external world simply *are* all the phenomena we see, hear or otherwise perceive to be located and extended in the surrounding three-dimensional space. Once they are accurately described, it is also hard to imagine *any* sense in which such experiences could be 'com-posed of' neurons or neural states. One cannot analyse experiences into parts by performing histology on the brain. Given neural states may cause or correlate with given conscious experiences, but causes and correlates are not component parts. If one combines microcosmic neural states together one obtains more complex, macrocosmic neural states. And if one adds all the neurons in the brain together one obtains a whole brain, not a phenomenal world (see Chapter 3).

If this approach to phenomenological analysis is correct, the only proper 'components' of macro-phenomena are *micro-phenomena*. And the proper methods for carrying out such analyses are those used in psychophysics, the psychology of perception, and other disciplines that focus (at least to some extent) on developing descriptive systems for the world as-experienced.

What is the greater whole of which consciousness and its contents are parts?

To understand what consciousness is, it is not enough to 'point to' it or analyse it into parts. It also needs to be *contextualised*. We need to know how it 'fits' into the broader universe of which it is, in turn, a part. For this, we would need to know the causes of consciousness and the functions of consciousness (see Chapter 13). To begin with, however, we need to be clear about what lies *beyond* consciousness, that is, about what exists that the term 'consciousness' excludes.

Dualism and materialism have different opinions on this matter. For substance dualists, consciousness and its contents exist in an immaterial realm that has no location or extension in space. They form one part of a dual universe, the other part being the material world. In this vision, the extended, material world lies beyond the boundaries of consciousness and interacts with it. However, consciousness is not in any sense *contained* by the material world.

For materialists, consciousness and its contents are nothing more than selected states or functions of the brain which have causal interactions with other, nonconscious states or functions of the brain. Viewed this way, consciousness and its contents form only a small part of the physical universe and occupy little space. That is, conscious neural states (or functions) are parts of rather small brains that make up a minute proportion of the material of the earth, which is, in turn, a tiny fragment of an immense, material universe.

According to the present analysis, the contents of normal phenomenal consciousness are neither *beyond* three-dimensional space (as dualists assume) nor contained *within* just a tiny bit of three-dimensional space (as materialists assume). Rather, these contents *define and fill* three-dimensional space as they are *none other* than the everyday world, or universe, as-experienced. What one experiences at a given moment depends, of course, on how one directs one's attention. Conscious contents differ enormously, for example, if one's eyes are open or closed. However, with open eyes, the contents of consciousness stretch to one's visual horizons. They include not just inner and body experiences, but also the external phenomenal world that we conventionally think of as the 'physical world'.

Given this expansion of consciousness to include all that we experience in the various forms that we experience, what do these contents *exclude*? If we are to take natural science seriously, very little of what actually exists in the world is manifest in normal experience. Our eyes and ears for example detect only a small bandwidth of the available electromagnetic and acoustic energies surrounding our bodies, and our chemical senses (smell and taste) convey little of the chemistry of the substances that we inhale and ingest. Sensory systems are also limited in their spatial and temporal resolution to detect events of a size, distance and duration that are relevant to normal human action and survival (to make observations beyond these limits we need telescopes, microscopes, atomic clocks and so on). The perceptual processes that translate the information detected by our sense organs into the perceived 'qualia' that we experience, furthermore, do so in a very specialised, species-specific way. Even three-dimensional phenomenal space existing through time turns out to be an approximation of the universe that modern physics describes. General relativity theory, for example, requires four-dimensional space-time in which the shortest distance between two points is an arc (that follows the curvature of space) not a straight line. There are many other ways in which the physical world we experience differs from the world that physics describes. As these points are entirely conventional and as I have developed this case in depth in Chapter 8, I will not labour the point. The three-dimensional phenomenal world that we think of as the 'physical world' is only a partial, approximate, species-specific model of the greater universe described by physics.

In assessing what the contents of consciousness exclude, it is important to note that we normally perceive entities and events of an intermediate scale. In humans, the phenomenal world is also predominantly visual, and, unaided, our visual systems normally provide information only about exterior surfaces. Beyond what we can normally see, there is an immensely detailed structure *within* the nature of the things as well as a structure that extends beyond our perceptual horizons. The external visual appearance of the human body, for example, yields little information about its macrocosmic internal structure and functioning. Interoception provides some added details about the body's internal condition (the position of limbs, temperature, internal damage, the need for sustenance, sleep and so on), but reveals little of how the body actually works, let alone any details of its microscopic organisation at cellular, molecular, atomic and subatomic levels. Similar limitations apply to our ability to experience the detailed operation of our own minds. As noted in Chapter 10, a few details of mental processing are normally available to introspection, such as the progressive stages in problem solving, long-term planning and so on. However, the bulk of so-called 'conscious mental processing' is not conscious at all. For example, one has little or no conscious awareness of the detailed processing which enables one to read this book.

In sum, the contents of consciousness in a typical awake state *include* the external 'physical world' as-perceived along with various body and inner experiences. But they *exclude* a far greater set of entities, events and processes within the external world, body and mind. Given their close linkage to consciousness, it is of particular significance that the *operations* of the mind/ brain are largely nonconscious. Metaphorically, the contents of consciousness have often been likened to the tip of an iceberg. The bulk of the mind, like the iceberg, remains unseen below the water. The present analysis extends this metaphor. Once one expands consciousness to include the experienced body and surrounding phenomenal world, what is 'above the waterline' is not just the tip of the iceberg but everything that one can experience extending to one's perceptual horizons. What is 'below the waterline' expands correspondingly to include the entire universe of entities, events and processes that, at a given moment, has no representation in what we experience.[3]

In this vision, human consciousness is embedded in and supported by the greater universe (just as the tip of the iceberg is supported by the base and the surrounding sea). The contents of human consciousness are also a natural *expression* or *manifestation* of the embedding universe. In humans, the *proximal* causes of consciousness are to be found in the human brain, but it is a mistake to think of the brain as an isolated system. Its existence as a material system depends totally on its supporting surround, and the contents of consciousness that it, in turn, supports arise from a reflexive interaction of perceptual processing with entities, events and processes in the surrounding world, body and the mind/brain itself.

Perception viewed as a reflexive process

For many purposes it is useful to categorise contents of consciousness according to whether they are (1) experiences of the external world (which seem to have location and extension), (2) experiences of the body (which seem to have location and extension), and (3) 'inner' experiences (thoughts, images, feelings of knowing and so on) which have no clear location and extension in phenomenal space (although they can be loosely said to be 'in the head or brain'). But, whatever the contents, the reflexive pattern of interaction described in Chapter 6 (initiating stimulus ↔ perceptual/cognitive processing → perceived stimulus) remains the same. An initiating stimulus located in the space beyond the body surface interacts with the exteroceptive systems of the observer to produce an entity or event experienced to be out in space beyond the body surface (such as a seen object, or heard sound). An initiating stimulus on the body surface interacts with the interoceptive systems of the observer to produce an experienced sensation in the location of the initiating stimulus on the body surface (such as a touch or pain). An initiating stimulus within the mind/brain itself is translated by endogenous systems into 'inner experiences' which seem to be located in the region of the initiating stimulus (such as a thought or image that seems to be 'in the head or brain'). In this reflexive manner, the contents of consciousness are both *produced by* initiating entities, events and processes (interacting with perceptual and cognitive systems) and *represent* those entities, events and processes.[4] Together, an individual's conscious representations are formed into a phenomenal world extending in three dimensions beyond the perceived body to one's perceptual horizon and the dome of the sky. Overall this may be thought of as a biologically useful model of a universe that is described in a very different way by modern physics.

While a good deal is known about how such phenomenal worlds are 'constructed' (see Chapters 6, 7 and 8) there is something mysterious about the way that information about spatial location and extension encoded in the brain is translated into location and extension as experienced. This psychological effect (which I have termed 'perceptual projection') is nonetheless ubiquitous. It is demonstrated by the way that THIS WORD seems to be out here on this page rather than in the occipital lobes of your brain, and by every other object or event perceived to be in the surrounding phenomenal world. Mysterious though it might seem, there are many ways in which perceptual projection has been (and continues to be) studied by science (see Chapter 7).

Consciousness and virtual reality

Virtual reality systems, in which one *appears* to interact with a (virtual) three-dimensional world in the absence of an *actual* (corresponding) world, provide one of the best demonstrations of perceptual projection in action – and the investigation of virtual realities will no doubt provide useful information about what the necessary and sufficient conditions for perceptual projection might be. Virtual reality also provides a useful metaphor for understanding how the contents of consciousness *relate* to the entities, events and processes that they reflexively 'model'. This is nicely illustrated in a tale told by the Finnish philosopher/psychologist Annti Revonsuo (1995) about a 'Black Planet':

> *The Black Planet.* Imagine that you are going to land into an unexplored planet. When you get out of your space capsule, you are engulfed by an impenetrable darkness and silence. You cannot see anything, hear anything, feel anything. There certainly is an environment somewhere out there, but you are utterly unable to sense it in any way and, consequently, there is no 'organism–environment interaction' to speak of. You feel like you are floating in a sensory-deprivation tank, not able to perceive the position of your body, let alone the environment you are surrounded by. Somehow you manage to return to your mother ship. You examine carefully all the data that was collected from the planet's surface. You find out that actually there is a lot of physical activity going on but of a kind you have never encountered before. Consequently, you were not able to perceive anything. Well, you do not give up – you design a suit that has sensors for the alien radiations and vibrations on the planet, translating them to the sort of physical stimuli that your body is able to handle. Thus, a certain sort of alien radiation is translated, by your goggles, into electromagnetic radiation of the visible wavelengths; the vibrations of the planet's strange atmosphere are translated into vibrations near your ears, and so on. When you return to the planet, you step out into a quite different, spatial and extended world of objects, colors and sounds. Now your brain is able to construct an experienced model of the world which enables you to successfully interact with the world. Of course, the world, in itself, is still silent and dark, but nevertheless, your brain is now clothing it (its model, that is) with properties that do not really exist out there. The phenomenological level of organization is, thus, an illusion created by the brain, but still, a most useful one.
>
> It may not come as a surprise if I now tell you that actually the strange planet is the earth, the spacesuit is our physical body, especially its sense organs; the 'translation' of alien physical signals to familiar ones is the transmutation from physical stimuli to neural firings; and the useful illusion somehow created inside the brain is the thing that we ordinarily call 'reality': the experienced model of the world with the self as the

central actor. 'Reality' is only the 'VR' constrained by current sensory input.[5]

(Revonsuo, 1995, p. 51)

To know what consciousness is we also have to know what it *does*. The story of the Black Planet provides an initial hint. The creation of an experienced, phenomenal world brings a conscious 'light' into an otherwise 'dark' universe. To get a fuller understanding of what consciousness does, we also need to come to terms with the many functions that have been proposed for it in cognitive psychology, and we need to make sense of its causal interactions with the brain (see Chapter 13).

Reflexive monism

The above analysis of what consciousness *is* 'points' at it, analyses it into component parts, and begins to 'fit' it into the wider universe of which it is, in turn, a part. This sketch of how consciousness fits into the wider universe supports a form of nonreductive, *reflexive monism*. Human minds, bodies and brains are embedded in a far greater universe. Individual conscious representations are perspectival. That is, the precise manner in which entities, events and processes are translated into experiences depends on the location in space and time of a given observer, and the exact mix of perceptual, cognitive, affective, social, cultural and historical influences which enter into the 'construction' of a given experience. In this sense, each conscious construction is private, subjective, and unique.[6] Taken together, the contents of consciousness provide a *view* of the wider universe, giving it the appearance of a three-dimensional phenomenal world. This results from a reflexive interaction of entities, events and processes with our perceptual and cognitive systems which, in turn, *represent* those entities, events and processes. However, such conscious representations are not the *thing-itself*.[7]

In this vision, there is *one* universe (the *thing-itself*), with relatively differentiated parts in the form of conscious beings like ourselves, each with a unique, conscious view of the larger universe of which it is a part. In so far as we are parts of the universe that, in turn, experience the larger universe, we participate in a reflexive process whereby the universe experiences itself.[8]

Notes

1 Under normal conditions, conscious states of mind do not occur without phenomenal contents. However, the distinction between consciousness as a state of mind and its phenomenal contents is important for consciousness science. As we have seen in Chapter 11, the conditions necessary for the *existence* of consciousness need to be distinguished from the *added* conditions required to produce its various contents.

2 There are visual and auditory representations along with memory traces of perceived events in the brain, but in normal exteroception there seem to be no visual

or auditory *experiences* in the brain viewed from either a first- or third-person perspective.

3 In conventional reductionist thought, the metaphorical 'border' separating what is 'in consciousness' from what is outside it is drawn vertically. In Figure 6.2, for example, what is in consciousness is 'in the subject's mind or brain' on the right side of the diagram, and this is clearly separated from the 'objective physical world' on the left of the diagram. In this extended iceberg metaphor, the 'border' is drawn horizontally. Everything 'visible' (in consciousness) is above the waterline, including the entire experienced world. What is not conscious is metaphorically 'below' the waterline, including not only a personal unconscious but everything that exists which is not experienced (at a given moment) but which contextualises and grounds those aspects of the world that *are* experienced. I am grateful to the philosopher Marion Goethier for pointing this out (personal communication).

4 Hallucinations, eidetic images, virtual realities, etc. may, of course, not represent actual events in the world. Such experiences are constructed by similar processes to those that are responsible for veridical perception, although in these instances the information has its origins in inner or artificial sources such as memory, VR headsets and so on (see Chapter 7).

5 Revonsuo developed this argument from the 'reflexive model' presented in Velmans (1990a) (and in Velmans, 1993b, I also suggest a link to VR). However, Revonsuo tries to explain the spatially extended nature of visual and other exteroceptive experiences in terms of a form of 'biological naturalism' that claims virtual phenomenal worlds to be states of the brain that are literally in the brain. While the reflexive model accepts that the *information* displayed in the experienced VR reality is encoded in the brain (in the neural correlates of the VR experience), the VR *experience* is not itself in the brain. See the extensive discussion of this issue in Chapter 7.

6 Under appropriate conditions, individual, private experiences/observations can become 'public', and 'intersubjective', thereby contributing to communal, consensual knowledge. As I have discussed these conditions in depth in Chapter 9, I will not repeat the analysis here.

7 As noted in Chapter 8, there may be many other ways of representing the same entities, events and processes – for example, through the more abstract representations of science.

8 In this way, reflexive monism combines ontological monism and epistemological pluralism (there is one thing that can be known in many ways) with the added suggestion that knowledge is, ultimately, reflexive.

13 What consciousness does

What needs to be explained

That brain states have a causal influence on conscious experiences seems undeniable. As Thomas Huxley pointed out in 1874, one has only to stick a pin in oneself to give a sufficient demonstration. But if consciousness is viewed in traditional dualist terms, *how* brain states cause conscious experiences seems inexplicable. Neural causes might have neural and other physical effects, but how could something 'objective' and 'physical' produce a 'subjective experience'?

Nor is it clear how consciousness might influence processing in the brain. We normally take it for granted that we have a conscious mind that controls our voluntary actions, and this view is fundamental to our ethics, politics and legal systems. But *how* the conscious mind exercises its influence is not easy to understand. Viewed from a first-person perspective, consciousness appears to be necessary for most forms of complex or novel processing. But, viewed from a third-person perspective, consciousness does not appear to be necessary for any form of processing as there are no 'gaps' in the chain of neurophysiological events which require the intervention of consciousness to make the brain work. In short, consciousness presents a *Causal Paradox*.

To make matters worse, there are four distinct ways in which body/brain and mind/consciousness might, in principle, enter into causal relationships. There might be physical causes of physical states, physical causes of mental states, mental causes of mental states, and mental causes of physical states. Establishing which forms of causation are effective in *practice* has clear implications for understanding the aetiology and proper treatment of illness and disease.

Within conventional medicine, physical→physical causation is taken for granted. Consequently, the proper treatment for physical disorders is assumed to be some form of physical intervention. Psychiatry takes the efficacy of physical→mental causation for granted, along with the assumption that the proper treatment for psychological disorders may involve psychoactive drugs, neurosurgery and so on. Many forms of psychotherapy take mental→mental causation for granted, and assume that psychological disorders can be alleviated by means of 'talking cures', guided imagery, hypnosis and other forms of mental intervention. Psychosomatic medicine assumes that mental→physical causation can be effective ('psychogenesis'). Consequently, under some circumstances, a physical disorder (for example, hysterical paralysis) may require a mental (psychotherapeutic) intervention. Given the extensive evidence for *all* these causal interactions (cf. Velmans, 1996a), how are we to make sense of them?

How could mental states affect illness and disease?

Although large bodies of research and clinical practice exist for each of these domains, those that assume the causal efficacy of mental states (psychotherapy and psychosomatic medicine) do not fit comfortably into the reductionist, materialist paradigm that currently predominates in Western philosophy and science. For example, according to Churchland (1989) all descriptions of, or theories about, human nature based on conscious experience may be thought of as prescientific forms of 'folk psychology' which are destined to be replaced by some future, advanced neurophysiology. In short, all descriptions of mind or conscious experience will turn out to be descriptions of states of the brain. If so, all claims about mental causation would turn out to be 'prescientific' claims about physical causation – and the clinical consequence might be that psychotherapy would eventually be replaced by some advanced form of physical medicine.

In spite of this materialist trend, clinical and experimental evidence for the causal efficacy of states of consciousness and mind on states of the body has continued to accumulate. For example, Barber (1984) and Sheikh *et al.* (1996) review a large body of evidence that hypnosis, the use of imagery, biofeedback, and meditation may be therapeutic in a variety of medical conditions. Particularly striking (and puzzling) is the evidence that, under certain conditions, such influences extend to autonomic bodily functions including heart rate, blood pressure, vasomotor activity, pupil dilation, electrodermal activity, and immune system functioning.

The most well accepted evidence for the effect of states of mind on medical outcome is undoubtedly the 'placebo effect'. Simply receiving treatment, and having confidence in the therapy or therapist, has *itself* been found to be therapeutic in many clinical situations. As with other instances of apparent mind/body interaction, there are conflicting interpretations of the causal processes involved. For example, Skrabanek and McCormick (1989) claim that placebos can affect *illness* (how people feel) but not *disease* (organic disorders). That is, they accept the possibility of mental→mental causation but not of mental→physical causation. However, Wall (1996) cites evidence that placebo treatments may produce organic changes. Hashish *et al.* (1988), for example, found that use of an impressive ultrasound machine reduced not only pain, but also jaw tightness and swelling after the extraction of wisdom teeth *whether or not the machine was set to produce ultrasound.*

As McMahon and Sheikh (1989) note, the absence of an acceptable *theory* of mind/body interaction within philosophy and science has had a detrimental effect on the acceptance of mental causation in many areas of clinical theory and practice. Conversely, the extensive *evidence* for mental causation within some clinical settings forms part of the database that any adequate theory of mind/consciousness–body/brain relationships needs to explain.

Dualist and reductionist accounts of causal interactions between consciousness and brain

We have examined the many ways that dualism and reductionism try to make sense of consciousness/brain relationships in Chapters 2 to 5 so I will give just a very brief summary here. The main appeal of dualist-interactionism is that it gives a simple, straightforward account of the following facts: (1) Bodies and brains *seem* to be very different from minds and consciousness, so perhaps they *are* very different. (2) There is extensive evidence that the body and brain affect mind and consciousness via the senses (for example that the visual system affects visual experience). There is also extensive evidence that mind and consciousness affect the body and brain (see above). It is plausible therefore to suggest that mind and consciousness *interact* with body and brain.

As far as it goes, nothing could be simpler. However there are a number of large 'explanatory gaps'. Dualism leaves the nature of consciousness a mystery. After all, what *kind* of substance is a 'substance that thinks'? And, if the physical world is causally closed, how could consciousness affect it? In any case, how could entities as different as *res cogitans* and *res extensa* causally influence each other? To Descartes' contemporaries Leibniz and Spinoza, such interactions were inconceivable.

While reductionism has many variants, they all attempt to heal the dualist split by reducing consciousness to a state or function of the brain. If this *ontological reduction* can be successfully achieved, the 'explanatory gaps' above would disappear. Consciousness would be one kind of brain state (or function), unconscious mind would be a different kind of brain state (or function), and the interaction of consciousness with (the rest of) the brain would be entirely a matter for neurophysiological research. Needless to say, no scientific discovery has yet been made which *demonstrates* consciousness to be nothing more than a state of the brain. Reductionist theories consequently focus on the kind of discovery that would *need* to be made to establish their case.

As noted in Chapter 3, conscious experiences are first-person *data* (which we would like to understand more deeply). That is, the claim that conscious experiences are nothing more than brain states (or functions) is a claim about one set of phenomena (our experiences) being nothing more than another set of phenomena (brain states or functions viewed from the perspective of an external observer). It is important to be clear about this, because reductionist arguments frequently rely on false analogies. From our own point of view, experiences are not *hypothetical constructs* which science might discover to be physically *real* (in the way that genes were found to be DNA molecules – as suggested by Crick, 1994). Nor are our own conscious experiences pre-scientific *theories* (or 'folk psychologies') waiting to be replaced by a more advanced physical theory of mind (contrary to Churchland, 1989). Given the extensive differences between the ways that conscious experiences appear (to us) and the ways that brain states appear (to others), the reduction of one to the other is a tall order. Formally, one must establish that, despite appearances, conscious experiences are *ontologically identical* to brain states.

Reductionists typically claim that finding the neural causes and correlates of consciousness would *establish* consciousness to be identical to a state (or function) of the brain. However, causation and correlation are not onto-logical identity. As it happens, nonreductionist philosophies of mind such as dualism and dual-aspect theory (discussed below) *agree* that consciousness (in humans) is causally influenced by and correlates with neural events, but they *deny* that consciousness is nothing more than a state of the brain. This produces a fundamental problem for reductionism. No information about consciousness *other* than its neural causes and correlates is available to neurophysiological investigation of the brain. So if discovery of these neural causes and correlates would not suffice to reduce consciousness to a state of the brain it is difficult to see how such research *could* achieve such a reduction. The *only* evidence about what conscious experiences are like comes from first-person sources, which consistently suggest consciousness to be something other than or additional to neuronal activity. Given this, I con-clude that reductionism (of consciousness to brain) via this route *cannot be made to work* (see Velmans, 1998a, and the full argument in Chapter 3).

Given such fundamental problems with both dualism and reductionism, *nonreductionist* monism deserves serious consideration. An early version of this is Spinoza's dual-aspect theory, which neither splits the universe into two incommensurable substances nor requires consciousness to be anything other than it seems. Rather mind and body are thought to be two aspects of one fundamental 'stuff' (which Spinoza variously refers to as 'Nature' or 'God'). To be scientifically useful, this approach needs to be naturalised.

Creeping up on the correlates of consciousness

There is little doubt that, viewed purely from a third-person perspective, the *proximal* causes and correlates of human consciousness are to be found in the brain, although it is important to remember that causal processes within the brain are embedded within a supporting body and surrounding world. We have examined some of the activating, attentional, perceptual, and represen-tational neural processes that are likely to be involved, in Chapter 11. But, by this third-person route, we cannot discover the nature of consciousness itself. As repeatedly noted, consciousness is in essence a first-person phenomenon.

Only I have direct access to what my own conscious states are like and only you have access to yours. How close can I get to your conscious states by observing your brain? No closer than their neural correlates!

It nevertheless appears to be a natural fact about the world that certain forms of neural activity are accompanied by conscious experiences. Consequently, when such neural activities (the correlates) occur in one's brain one has the corresponding experiences. Given that the neural correlates of consciousness are as close as we can get to consciousness from the outside, and that we do not know exactly what they are, it would be useful to have a few guidelines about what we are looking for. By definition, correlates accompany or *co-occur* with given conscious experiences. This differentiates them from the antecedent causes of consciousness (such as the operation of selective attention, binding, etc.), which may be thought of as the necessary and sufficient *prior* conditions for consciousness in the human brain. Although we do not have complete knowledge about the physical nature of these correlates, there are four plausible, functional constraints imposed by the phenomenology of consciousness itself.

1   **The representational constraint.** Normal human conscious experiences are representational (phenomenal consciousness is always *of* something). Given this, it is plausible to assume that the physical correlates of such experiences are representational states.[1]
2   **The identical referent constraint.** A representational state must represent *something*. For a given physical state to be the correlate of a given experience it is plausible to assume that it represents the *same* thing (otherwise it would not be the correlate of *that* experience).
3   **The information preservation constraint.** For a physical state to be the correlate of a given experience, it is reasonable to suppose that it has the same 'grain'. That is, for every discriminable attribute of experience there will be a distinct, correlated, physical state.[2] As each experience and its physical correlate represent the same thing it follows that each experience and its physical correlate encode the same information about that thing. That is, they are representations with the same *information structure*.
4   **Orderly mapping.** It is reasonable to assume that the formatting of neurally encoded information relates to the formatting of corresponding, phenomenally encoded information in an orderly way, with discoverable neural state space/phenomenal space mappings. An obvious example would be the way that information about spatial location and extension encoded in the brain is mapped into the three-dimensional phenomenal space that we ordinarily experience.[3]

Ever since the pioneering work of Gustaf Fechner (1860), these assumptions have largely been taken for granted in psychological theory, although these assumptions have not always been made explicit in theories of consciousness (cf. Wozniak, 1999). For example, the study of psychophysics, which Fechner founded, takes it for granted that for any discriminable aspect of experience (a just noticeable change in brightness, colour, pitch and so on) there will be a correlated change in some state of the brain. The same is true for the more complex contents of consciousness in the many modern cognitive theories that associate (or identify) such contents with information stored in primary (working) memory, information at the focus of attention, information in a global workspace and so on.

The assumption that experiences and their physical correlates encode identical information also marks an important point of convergence between otherwise divergent theories about the nature of consciousness. This assumption is implicit, for example, in eliminativist and reductionist theories of consciousness (such as Dennett, 1995, and Sloman, 1997a, 1997b, discussed in Chapter 5). It is also explicit in the 'naturalistic dualism' developed by Chalmers (1996) and in the dual-aspect theory developed in Velmans (1991a, 1993b, 1996c) which I elaborate below.

It is important to stress that having an identical referent and information structure does not entail *ontological identity* (as eliminativists and reductionists tend to assume). A filmed version of the play *Hamlet*, recorded on videotape, for example, may have the same sequential information structure as the same play displayed in the form of successive, moving pictures on a TV screen. But it is obvious that the information on the videotape is not ontologically identical to the information displayed on the screen. The information encoded on the tape exists whether or not it happens to be playing and consequently translated into a picture on the screen that one can see. In this instance, the same information is embodied in two different ways (patterns of magnetic variation on tape versus patterns of brightness and hue in individual pixels on the screen), and it is displayed or 'formatted' in two different ways (only the latter display is in visible form). Consequently the choice between eliminativism/reductionism, dualism, and dual-aspect theory has to be made on some other grounds, for example on the basis of which theory accounts for *all* the observable evidence in the most elegant way.

Creeping up on consciousness

Eliminativism and reductionism assume that once one has identified the physical causes and correlates of consciousness in the brain, viewed from a third-person perspective, there is nothing else to understand or explain. For them, the neural correlates of consciousness (or the information structure they embody) are consciousness itself. But, as I have noted in Chapters 3, 4 and 5, this view is *not consistent with our first-person evidence* about what experiences are like. Consequently its protagonists attempt to denigrate the utility, reliability or even the reality of first-person experience. For theories that hope to make sense of first-person experience this is a desperate manoeuvre.

However, if we do not wish to deny the reality of first-person experience we are left with a conceptual problem. Once we arrive at the end of a third-person physical or functional account of how a brain or other system works we still need some credible way to cross the 'explanatory gap' to conscious experience. Luckily, in the human case, this isn't really a *practical* problem, for the reason that we naturally have access to *what lies on both sides of the gap*. We can observe what is going on in the brains of others or in our own brain from an external third-person perspective (via exteroception, aided by a little physical equipment). And we naturally have first-person access to what it is like to have the experiences that accompany such observable brain activity. For many explanatory purposes we just need to switch from one perspective to the other at the appropriate place, and add the first-person to the third-person story in an appropriate way. In everyday life, we are so accustomed to this *perspectival switching* that we often do it without noticing that we are doing it. However, recognising when such switches occur is one important step in making sense of the causal stories that we tell about the interactions between consciousness and brain. In psychophysics, for example, one can examine the neural causes and correlates of a given experience in the brain viewed from a third-person perspective. But to complete the causal story, one then has to switch to the subject's first-person perspective to get an account of the perceptual effect.

Note that this common-sense account of how the 'explanatory gap' is crossed in practice is nonreductive. Third-person evidence about the workings of the brain retains its full privileged status (about the workings of the brain), and first-person evidence about what it is like to have a given experience retains its full privileged status (about the nature of experience). That said, neither third- nor first-person accounts are incorrigible. Once observations or experiences made from either perspective are translated into *descriptions* (observation statements or phenomenological descriptions) there is always a measure of interpretation required – and, as Popper has made clear, even the basic terms used in such descriptions are theory-laden. Interpretation and abstraction are also required to translate such observations/experiences into general descriptive systems, typologies, and 'maps', and further inference and interpretation are required to translate first- or third-person evidence into a *theory about* the workings of mind, consciousness or brain. In all this, the normal rules of scientific engagement apply (see Chapter 9).[4]

The relation between first-person descriptions of experience and third-person descriptions of their physical correlates

While *perspectival switching* from a third-person account of neural events to a first-person account of correlated experiences allows one to cross the 'explanatory gap' we still need to understand how such accounts relate to each other. As I have made clear in Chapters 6 and 9, it is misleading to think of first-person accounts as 'subjective' and third-person accounts as 'objective'. In terms of their *phenomenology*, my observations of your brain states are just my visual experiences of your brain states. Suppose, for example,

I ask you to look at a cat out in the world while I examine the physical correlates of what you see in your brain (in the way shown in Figure 6.3). While I examine your brain I simply report what I see (whether or not I am aided by sophisticated equipment), and while you are looking at the cat you simply report what you see. In this situation, we both experience something out in the world that we would describe as 'physical'. You have a visual experience of a cat, located beyond your body, out in the world. I have a visual experience of the physical correlates (of the cat that you see) beyond my body, in your brain.[5]

Following the representational, identical referent and information preservation constraints suggested above, what you and I see relate to each other in a very precise way. What you see is a phenomenal cat – a visual representation containing information about the shape, size, location, colour and texture of an entity that currently exists out in the world beyond your body surface. What I see is the same information (about the cat) encoded in the physical correlates of what you experience in your brain. That is, the information structure of what you and I observe is identical, but it is displayed or 'formatted' in very different ways. From your point of view, the only information you have (about the entity in the world) is the phenomenal cat you experience. From my point of view, the only information you have (about the entity in the world) is the information I can see encoded in your brain. The way your information (about the entity in the world) is displayed appears to be very different to you and me for the reason that the 'observational arrangements' by which we access that information are entirely different. From my external, third-person perspective I can only access the information encoded in your neural correlates by means of my visual or other exteroceptive systems, aided by appropriate equipment. Because you *embody* the information encoded in your neural correlates and it is already at the interface of your consciousness and brain, it displays 'naturally'[6] in the form of the cat that you experience.

You experience a cat, rather than your neural encodings of the cat, for the reason that it is the information *about the world* (encoded in your neural correlates) that is manifest in your experience rather than the embodying format or the physical attributes of the neural states themselves. As with the TV analogy above, the information encoded on videotape is displayed in the form of a picture on a screen without the magnetic fluctuations on the videotape or the tape itself being displayed upon the screen. I observe/experience the neural encodings of the cat in your brain (rather than the cat) for the simple reason that my visual attention is focused on your brain, not the cat. If I wanted to experience what you experience, I would have to shift my attention (and gaze) away from your brain to the cat (see the thought experiment on 'changing places' in Chapter 9).

From my 'external observer's perspective', can I assume that what you experience is really nothing more than the physical correlates that I can observe? From my external perspective, do I know what is going on in your mind/brain/consciousness better than you do? Not really. I know something about your mental states that you do not know (their physical embodiment). But you know something about them that I do not know (their manifestation in experience). Such first- and third-person information is *complementary*. We need your first-person story and my third-person story for a complete account of what is going on.

The same, basic first- versus third-person relationship of an experience to its neural correlates obtains if you turn your attention away from the cat in the world and attend instead to states of your own body, or to thoughts, images and other inner experiences. The nature of the experience changes, along with the information it encodes (as one changes what the experience is of). Nevertheless, in each case I have access to the neural correlates of what you experience, and you have access to what it is like to have that experience.

If I cannot reduce your story about what you experience to my story about its neural correlates (or vice versa) without loss, are we forced into the conclusion that experiences and their neural correlates are fundamentally different entities or substances? No. I have reviewed the enduring problems faced by such ontological dualism in Chapters 2 and 6. Dualism accepts the reality of first-person experience, but misdescribes its phenomenology. Descartes likens *all* experiences to 'thoughts' (*res cogitans*). However, most of what we experience has little resemblance to thoughts. For example, the way our bodies look and feel is quite unlike phonemic imagery or 'inner speech', and the same is true of the look, sound, touch, taste and smell of entities in the external world such as phenomenal cats. Nor does splitting the universe into two, incommensurable (material and mental) substances help us to understand the *intimate relationship* of consciousness to matter. We return to this below.

An initial way to make sense of the causal interactions between consciousness and brain

This brief analysis of how first- and third-person accounts relate to each other can be used to make sense of the different *forms* of causal interaction that are taken for granted in everyday life or suggested in the clinical and scientific literature. Physical→physical causal sequences describe events from an entirely third-person perspective (they are 'pure third-person' accounts). Mental→mental causal sequences describe events entirely from a first-person perspective (they are 'pure first-person' accounts). Physical→mental and mental→physical causal sequences are *mixed-perspective* accounts employing *perspectival switching*.

Physical→mental causal sequences start with events viewed from a third-person perspective and switch to how things appear from a first-person perspective. For example, a causal account of visual perception starts with a third-person description of the physical stimulus and its effects on the visual system but then switches to a first-person account of what the subject experiences. Mental→physical causal sequences switch the other way. From a subject's point of view, for example, an experienced pain in a tooth might cause a visit to the dentist. It might be possible to give an entirely third-person account of this sequence of events (in terms of dental caries producing pain circuitry activation, efferent signals to the skeleto-muscular system, etc.). But the mixed-perspective account gives a more useful description of what is going on in terms of the knowledge available to the subject.

In principle, complementary first- and third-person sources of information can be found whenever body or mind/brain states are represented in some way in subjective experience.[7] A patient might for example have insight into the nature of a psychological problem (via feelings and thoughts), that a clinician might investigate by observing his/her brain or behaviour. In medical diagnosis, a patient might have access to some malfunction via interoceptors, producing symptoms such as pain and discomfort, whereas a doctor might be able to identify the cause via his/her exteroceptors (eyes, ears and so on) supplemented by medical instrumentation. As with conscious states and their neural correlates the clinician has access to the physical embodiment of such conditions, while the patient has access to how such conditions are experienced. In these situations, neither the third-person information available to the clinician nor the first-person information available to the patient is *automatically* privileged or 'objective' in the sense of being 'observer-free'. The clinician merely reports what he/she observes or infers about what is going on (using available means) and the patient does likewise. Such first- and third-person accounts of the subject's mental life or body states are complementary, and mutually irreducible. *Taken together*, they provide a global, psychophysical picture of the condition under scrutiny.

What is the one thing of which we have two, complementary forms of knowledge?

First- and third-person asymmetries of access, perspectival switching and mixed-perspective explanations provide an initial way to make sense of the different forms of consciousness/brain causal interactions that are taken for granted in everyday life and in therapeutic practices. But they do not resolve some of the more fundamental issues. We can *cross* the explanatory gap by switching between a subject's perspective and an external observer's perspective in an appropriate way, but this says little about the nature of the gap that we cross. Nor does this really resolve the *Causal Paradox*. To achieve this, we have to examine things more deeply.

What dwells within the 'explanatory gap'? The ontological monism combined with epistemological dualism that I adopt assumes that there must be some thing, event or process that one can know in two complementary ways. There must be something that grounds and connects the two views we have of it. Let us call this the 'nature of mind'.

What is mind really like? As Einstein puts it, 'In our endeavour to understand reality we are somewhat like a man trying to understand the mechanism of a closed watch. He sees the face and the moving hands, even hears its ticking, but he has no way of opening the case' (see Chapter 8). One can of course try to develop better instruments to make more refined observations.[8] However, beyond the limits of observation one can only make 'best conjectures'.

If mind grounds and unifies the first- and third-person views we have of it, what can we conjecture about its nature?

- In so far as conscious experiences are of something or about something it is reasonable to suppose that they, and their neural correlates, encode information (see above). If so, the mind encodes information.
- To the extent that brain activities and accompanying experiences are fluid and dynamic (see Chapter 11), the mind can be described as a process, developing over time.[9]

Taken together, these points suggest that mind can be thought of as a form of information processing, and the information displayed in experiences and their physical correlates can be thought of as two manifestations of this information processing – which makes this a *dual-aspect theory of information processing*.

However, this does not fully specify the ontology of the mind. Information processing needs to be encoded in some medium that is capable of carrying out that processing. Given this, what kind of 'medium' is the mind?

One can give a very short list of the observable facts:

- In the human case, minds viewed from the outside seem to take the form of brains (or some physical aspect of brains).[10]
- Viewed from the perspective of those who embody them, minds take the form of conscious experiences.

If first- and third-person perspectives (on the mind) are complementary and mutually irreducible, then the nature of the mind is revealed as much by how it appears from one perspective as the other. If so, the nature of mind is not *either* physical *or* conscious experience, it is at once physical *and* conscious experience. For lack of a better term we may describe this nature as *psychophysical*. If we combine this with the features above, we can say that mind is a psychophysical process that encodes information, developing over time – a view that returns experimental psychology to its beginnings in psychophysics (Box 13.1).

At present, there is little more about 'what dwells within the explanatory gap' that can be said with confidence. We can, of course, develop more detailed theories of mind from either a first- or third-person perspective. Third-person accounts of mental information processing and its neural embodiments are well established in Western science, forming the bulk of cognitive psychology, cognitive neuropsychology and so on. There is also renewed interest in more detailed investigations of first-person, conscious phenomenology (the route

---

Box 13.1 Psychophysical mind

While, in the current reductionist zeitgeist, it might seem unusual to view the nature of mind as *psychophysical*, it is fascinating to note that a similar form of psychophysical, dual-aspect monism was adopted by Gustaf Fechner, and it was this that led him to develop psychophysics – the first and lengthiest scientific research programme in experimental psychology (see Woodward, 1972). It has also recently become clear from previously unpublished letters that a very similar view of the mind–matter relationship was taken by Wolfgang Pauli, one of the founders of quantum mechanics. Pauli, like Fechner, was interested in the ultimate nature of reality, and he concluded that,

> For the *invisible reality* of which we have small pieces of evidence in both quantum physics and the psychology of the unconscious, a *symbolic* psychophysical unitary language must *ultimately* be adequate, and this is the far goal to which I actually aspire. I am quite confident that the final objective is the same, independent of whether one starts from the psyche (ideas) of from physis (matter). Therefore, I consider the old distinction between materialism and idealism as obsolete. . . . It would be most satisfactory if physis and psyche could be conceived as complementary aspects of the same reality.[11]

(Pauli, 1952, cited in Atmanspacher and Primas, 2006)

---

to investigation of the mind that has been traditionally preferred in Eastern philosophies), and in how such first- and third-person investigations can inform each other. However, these investigations deal more with how mind appears viewed from *either* a third- *or* a first-person perspective rather than with what might be the nature of mind itself.

There are nevertheless some useful pointers to what a more complete theory of mind would look like, that we can draw from other areas of science. The struggle to find a model or even a form of words that somehow captures the dual-aspect nature of mind is reminiscent for example of wave–particle complementarity in quantum mechanics – although this analogy is far from exact (Box 13.2). Light appears to behave either as electromagnetic waves or as photon particles, depending on the 'observation arrangements'. And it does not make sense to claim that electromagnetic waves really *are* particles (or vice versa). A complete understanding of light requires both complementary descriptions – with consequent struggles to find an appropriate way of characterising the nature of light which encompasses both descriptions ('wave-packets', 'photon clouds' and so on). This has not prevented physics from developing very precise accounts of light viewed *either* as waves *or* as

---

Box 13.2 Differences between psychological and physical complementarity

While there are close similarities between psychological complementarity and the wave–particle complementarity of quantum mechanics, there are also important differences (see Velmans, 1991a, p. 669, note 18). Psychological complementarity applies to the mind viewed from first- and third-person perspectives. But the wave- and particle-like properties of electrons and photons are both observable from a third-person perspective.

The laws which relate the content of neural and phenomenal representations also seem to have more to do with information than with physical properties such as energy and frequency (although one cannot rule out the possibility of finding bridging laws which blur such distinctions).

At the macrocosmic level, psychological complementarity would seem to be *nonexclusive* – that is, third-person observations of neural correlates by an *external observer* would not exclude simultaneous first-person observations by a *subject* of correlated experiences. That said, self-observation (by a subject observing his own neural correlates via an 'autocerebroscope') might be governed by exclusive complementarity. That is, it might be impossible to simultaneously observe the neural correlates of a given experience and to have that experience. A more detailed discussion of the similarities and differences between psychological and physical complementarity can be found in the replies to Rao in Velmans (1993b) and Velmans (2008b).

---

particles, together with precise formulae for relating wave-like properties (such as electromagnetic frequency) to particle-like ones (such as photon energy). If first- and third-person accounts of consciousness and its physical correlates are complementary and mutually irreducible, an analogous 'psychological complementarity principle' might be required to understand the nature of mind.

At the macrocosmic level, the relation of electricity to magnetism also provides a clear parallel to the form of dual-aspect theory I have in mind. If one moves a wire through a magnetic field this produces an electrical current in the wire. Conversely, if one passes an electrical current through a wire this produces a surrounding magnetic field. But it does not make sense to suggest that the current in the wire is nothing more than the surrounding magnetic field, or vice versa (reductionism). Nor is it accurate to suggest that electricity and magnetism are energies of entirely different kinds that happen to interact (dualist-interactionism). Rather these are two manifestations (or 'dual aspects') of *electromagnetism*, a more fundamental energy that grounds and unifies both, described with elegance by Maxwell's Laws.

Of course, analogies from physics have their limits. A dual-aspect theory of the human mind needs to follow the contours of first-person human consciousness, and third-person manifestations of information processing embodied in human brains. Viewed from a first-person perspective, the contours of human consciousness are defined by the contours of the phenomenal world. This encompasses all that we experience, including inner experiences such as thoughts and images (with a poorly defined location and extension 'in the head'), an extended three-dimensional body, and a surrounding three-dimensional 'physical world' (see Chapter 6). Viewed from a third-person perspective, information about the events represented by such inner, body and external experiences is encoded in the brain. This neural information has its own complex, distributed, but very different contours (the brain's 'map' is not just a miniature version of the world as-experienced). Consequently, the manner in which information displayed in first-person experience is mapped onto information encoded in brains has a distinct topology that needs to be accurately described in any complete theory of mind.

We don't know exactly how all this works, but to make sense of the paradoxical aspects of consciousness/brain causal interactions, we do not really need the details. If consciousness and its physical correlates are actually complementary aspects of a psychophysical mind, we can close the 'explanatory gap' in a way that unifies consciousness and brain while preserving the ontological status of both. It also provides a simple way of making sense of all four forms of physical/mental causation. Operations of mind viewed from a purely external observer's perspective (physical→physical), operations of mind viewed from a purely first-person perspective (mental→mental), and mixed-perspective accounts involving perspectival switching (physical→mental; mental→physical) can be understood as different views (or a mix of views) of a single, psychophysical form of information processing developing over time. In providing a common psychophysical ground for brain and experience, such a process also provides the 'missing link' required to explain psychosomatic effects.

If we combine the analysis presented in Chapters 6 to 10 with the analysis above we can also resolve the *Causal Paradox*. I have discussed this paradox in Chapters 4 and 10, but for ease of reference I will summarise its main features here.

The Causal Paradox summarised

In the psychological literature, consciousness has often been thought to have a *causal role* in brain processing, viewed from a third-person perspective. Indeed, in one or another theory, it has been thought to affect every major phase of human information processing ranging from input (the analysis of novel or complex stimuli, selective attention) and storage (working memory, learning) to transformation (thinking, problem solving, planning, creativity) and output (speech, writing, novel or complex adjustments to the environment). The view that consciousness must have a third-person causal role is also supported by conventional evolutionary theory. After all, if it did not enhance inclusive fitness how could it have evolved?

However, if one examines human information processing purely *from a third-person perspective*, consciousness does not seem to be necessary for any form of processing. As far as we know, the classical physical world is causally closed. The operation of minds and brains seems to be explainable entirely in functional or physical terms that make no reference to what we experience. Once the processing within a system required to perform a given function is sufficiently well specified in procedural terms, one does not have to add an 'inner conscious life' to make the system work. In principle, the same function, operating to the same specification, could be performed by a nonconscious machine. Likewise, if one inspects the operation of the brain from the outside, no subjective experience can be observed at work. Nor does one need to appeal to the existence of subjective experience to account for the neural activity that one *can* observe. The neural correlates of consciousness already fill any 'gaps' that might potentially be filled by consciousness in the activities of brain.

The experimental and introspective evidence regarding how phenomenal consciousness *actually* relates to so-called 'conscious processing' in humans deepens this puzzle. The detailed operations of most processes that we think of as 'conscious' are not available to introspection. In stimulus identification and selection one is not aware of performing feature analysis, accessing long-term memory traces, or making assessments of the relative importance of preconscious stimuli. When remembering, one has no awareness of processes that perform memory search or retrieval. The phonemic images that constitute verbal thinking or 'inner speech' give scant information about the complex information transformations required to solve problems. And the detailed motor programmes controlling the musculature in speech or in complex adjustments to a changing environment have little manifestation in awareness. Rather, what enters awareness appears to *result* from such 'conscious processing'. The entities we perceive are the result of prior feature analysis and feature integration, and the names we assign to such entities 'symbolise' the fact that these have been matched to long-term memory traces in a particular way. The events we remember *have been* searched for and retrieved (from long-term memory). And when we speak, the words that we hear ourselves utter are the *result* of prior semantic, syntactic and phonemic planning, and consequent motor control. In short, once one examines the *timing* of the experiences which accompany 'conscious processing', the experiences seem to come *too late* to affect the processing to which they most obviously relate (by the time you are conscious of this sentence you will already have read it – see Chapter 10).

Given this, something other than the processing which *enables* one to read, speak, think and so on must be taking place at the time that experiences actually arise – perhaps the information integration, and/or the dissemination of information which *results* from focal-attentive processing. However, this still does not solve the puzzle of what phenomenal consciousness does. Conscious experience of given information may *correlate* with information integration and/or dissemination of that information throughout the brain. But we have no conscious experience of carrying out such operations in our own brains, or conscious (introspective) knowledge about *how* we might carry out such brain operations. Consequently, if consciousness does carry out such functions, it must do so *unconsciously* – which doesn't make sense (see 'A conundrum' in Chapter 4).

Yet, from a *first-person perspective*, it seems absurd to deny the role of consciousness in mental life. Nearly all our activities seem to depend directly or indirectly on what we experience. If one examines one's own psychological functioning, consciousness appears necessary for the analysis of novel or complex stimuli, choosing what to attend to or do, and most forms of learning and memory. It also seems necessary for most novel or complex cognitive transformations and output. How could one identify entities or events unless one was aware of them, or decide which ones require urgent attention? How could one think, remember, reflect, plan, dream, feel, be creative, give a lecture or write a paper if one were not conscious? And how, without awareness of the world, could one adjust to a complex, novel or rapidly changing environment? In short, from a third-person perspective, phenomenal consciousness appears to play no causal role in mental life, while from a first-person perspective it appears to be central. This is the 'Causal Paradox'.

How to resolve the Causal Paradox in three steps[12]

Step 1: The sense in which first- and third-person accounts are complementary

If first- and third-person accounts are complementary, some aspects of this paradox are easily resolved. Physical science is, by convention, a 'third-person' science, and if one views the macroscopic material world solely from the perspective of an external observer it appears to be causally closed. Events viewed from a third-person perspective can be entirely explained in terms of data, theories and laws obtainable from that perspective. This applies equally to the workings of the brain. The *conscious experiences* of others cannot be observed, so it is not surprising that, viewed from this perspective alone, the operations of their minds appear to be nothing more than the operation of their brains.

Does this mean that conscious experiences have no 'real' existence, and consequently no causal role? No. I have given many arguments against reductionism (in Chapters 3, 4 and 5). But the deepest argument follows from the interchangeability of an 'external observer' and an 'experiencing subject'. Although reductionists pretend otherwise, 'external observers' are also 'experiencing subjects' and 'experiencing subjects' are also 'external observers'.[13] In a typical psychophysical experiment they simply play different *roles*. External observers are normally interested in events external to themselves (for example the mental states of other people) and consequently focus on what their observations (of other people) *represent*. Subjects are typically asked to focus on the nature of the experiences themselves. However, in terms of *phenomenology* there is no difference between a given individual's 'observations' and 'experiences' (see Chapters 6 and 9). Your visual observations and visual experiences of this book, for example, are one and the same. One cannot reduce first-person experiences to third-person observations for the simple reason that, *without first-person experiences one cannot have third-person observations*. Empirical science *relies* on the 'evidence of the senses'. Eliminate experiences and you eliminate science!

The common-sense alternative is to accept that others experience/observe much as we do ourselves. If we access observed events in similar (symmetrical) ways we are likely to experience/observe them in similar ways. Conversely, if we access given events in different (asymmetrical) ways we are likely to observe/experience them in different ways. Asymmetries typically arise when observed events are within a given subject's body or mind/brain. My observations of your mental processes might be limited to observations of your brain, while your observations of your own mental processes are normally limited to their manifestation in your experience. My account of what is going on may be expressed in neural or information processing terms. Your account of what is going on may be in terms of what you consciously see, feel, think and so on. Viewed from my perspective, an account of your brain states seems to be a complete account of what is going on, and the neural correlates of your experiences fill any gaps that your experiences might fill. Viewed from your perspective, an account of what is going on in terms of what you experience seems to be all that you need to explain what is going on 'in your mind'. Viewed from my perspective, what you experience appears to have no causal effects on what I observe. Viewed from your perspective, what you experience appears to be central. For ontological monism combined with epistemological dualism this presents no paradox. The information encoded in your experiences and their neural correlates is identical. Consequently, first- and third-person accounts of the causal roles of such information need not conflict. They may simply be accounts of the same underlying process developing over time, viewed in two, complementary ways.[14]

Step 2: How to make sense of the functional differences between conscious and nonconscious processing

But this is not the full story. As noted above, many psychological theories claim consciousness to have a *third-person causal role*, exemplified by functional differences between conscious processing and preconscious or unconscious processing. To understand how consciousness enters into causal explanations, we also have to make sense of these differences. As we have seen in Chapters 4 and 10, the role of phenomenal consciousness in so-called 'conscious processing' is subtle. A process might be said to 'be conscious'

(a) in the sense that one is conscious *of* the process;
(b) in the sense that the operation of the process is *accompanied* by consciousness (of its *results*);
(c) in the sense that consciousness *enters into* or *causally influences* the process.

It is sense (c), of course, that is relevant to claims that consciousness has a third-person causal role. But, as noted earlier, one cannot assume a process to be conscious in sense (c) on the grounds that it is conscious in senses (a) or (b). Sense (a) is also very different from sense (b). Sense (a) has to do with what experiences *represent*. Conscious states are always *about something*, that is they provide information to those who have them about the external world, body or mind/brain itself. Some mental processes (problem solving, thinking, planning, etc.), for example, are partially conscious in so far as their detailed operations are accessible to introspection. Sense (b) contrasts different *forms* of mental processing. Some forms of mental processing result in conscious experiences, while others do not. For example, analysis of stimuli in attended channels usually results in a conscious experience of those stimuli, but not in non-attended channels.

Theories that attribute a third-person causal role to consciousness invariably conflate these distinctions. They either take it for granted that if a process is conscious in sense (a) or sense (b) then it must be conscious in sense (c). Or they simply *redefine* consciousness to be a form of processing, such as focal attention, information in a 'limited capacity channel', a 'central executive', a 'global workspace' and so on, thereby begging the question about the functional role of *conscious phenomenology* in the economy of the mind.[15]

How can we make sense of the differences between conscious and preconscious or unconscious processing without conflating these distinctions? To begin with, we have to accept that there are major functional differences between mental processes that are or are not conscious in sense (b). The processing of novel, complex or rapidly changing information normally draws heavily on our cognitive resources and demands our full focal attention. Our focal attention is also drawn to whatever seems most important in our lives at any moment, including not just what we perceive, think and so on, but also what we feel, imagine, remember, and dream. The results of such attentional processing are widely disseminated throughout the mind/brain system. While information not at the focus of attention may also have important effects, non-attended processing generally follows relatively well established or well learnt procedures, and its results remain relatively encapsulated (see Chapters

10 and 11). What is at the focus of our attention enters our consciousness. What is outside the focus of attention remains preconscious or unconscious.

This relatively conventional distinction between attended and non-attended processing accounts for many of the functional differences between 'conscious processing' and 'nonconscious processing' without requiring first-person phenomenal consciousness to have a third-person causal role. If consciousness is a late-arising product of focal-attentive processing, then it is not surprising that processes that are conscious in sense (b) seem to be far more sophisticated and flexible than those that are not. Focal-attentive processing is more sophisticated and flexible than non-attended processing and only the results of focal-attentive processing enter consciousness. Conversely, when consciousness (of given information) is absent, focal-attentive processing (of that information) is absent. And if focal attention is absent one normally cannot read, speak, engage in complex, novel interactions with the world and so on. What enters consciousness also seems important because it *is* important. It is, after all, what has been *selected* for our focal attention.

Step 3: How to make sense of the apparent causal role of the contents of consciousness

Steps 1 and 2 give an initial indication of how one can reconcile the evidence that conscious experiences appear causally effective with the principle that the macrophysical world is causally closed. But there are two further, equally perplexing problems. How can conscious experiences be causally effective if they come too late to affect the mind/brain processes to which they most obviously relate? And how can the contents of consciousness affect brain and body states when one is not conscious of the biological processes that govern those states?

Why do experiences come too late to affect the mind/brain processes to which they most closely relate? For the simple reason that experiences relate most closely to the processes that *produce* them (see Chapter 10). Visual perception becomes 'conscious' once visual processing results in a conscious visual experience; cognitive processing becomes 'conscious' once it produces the inner speech that forms a conscious thought, and so on. Once such experiences arise the processes that have produced them have already taken place.

Why don't we have more detailed experiences of the processes which produce such conscious experiences, or of the detailed workings of our own bodies, minds and brains? Because for normal purposes we don't need them. Our primary need is to interact successfully with the external world and with each other – and for that, the processes by which we arrive at representations of ourselves in the world, or which govern the many internal, adaptive adjustments we have to make, are best left on 'automatic'. This is exemplified by the well accepted transition of skills from being conscious to being nonconscious as they become well learnt (as in reading or driving a car).

Given this, what is consciousness actually contributing to conscious perception, to conscious speech, to conscious thought, to conscious voluntary control, and so on? As noted above, conscious experiences are representations. Some experiences represent states of the external world (exteroceptive experiences), some represent states of the body (interoceptive experiences), and some represent states of the mind/brain itself (volitions, thoughts about thoughts, etc.). Experiences can also represent past, future, real and imaginary events, for example in the form of thoughts and images. Such global representations provide a useful, reasonably accurate representation of what is or might be happening in the world.[16]

Whatever their representational content, current experiences also tell us something important about the current state of our own mind/brain – that it currently has percepts, feelings, thoughts, images, etc., of a given type, and that it has formed current representations with that particular content, as opposed to any others. For example, the thoughts and feelings that enter consciousness at a given moment 'represent' the current state of our own cognitive and affective systems in that they reveal *which* of many possible cognitive and affective states are currently at the focus of attention in a reportable form. If your thoughts and feelings are conscious, and I ask you what you are thinking about and feeling, you can tell me.

In what sense do these contents of consciousness have the causal roles that we normally think them to have? *In everyday life, we behave as 'naïve realists'.* That is we take the events we experience to *be* the events that are actually taking place, although sciences such as physics, biology and psychology might represent the same events in very different ways (see Chapter 8). For everyday purposes, the assumption that the world just *is* as we experience it to be serves us well. When playing billiards, for example, it is safe to assume that the balls are smooth, spherical, coloured, and cause each other to move by mechanical impact. One only has to judge the precise angle at which the white ball hits the red ball to pocket the red. A quantum mechanical description of the microstructure of the balls or of the forces they exert on each other won't improve one's game.

But the experienced world is not the world *itself* – and it is not our experience *of* the balls that governs the movement of the balls themselves. Balls as-experienced and their perceived interactions are *representations* of autonomously existing entities and their interactions, and conscious representations (of what is happening) can only be formed *after* the occurrence of the events they represent. *The same may be said of the events and processes that we experience to occur in our bodies or minds/brains.* When we withdraw a hand quickly from a hot iron, we experience the pain (in the hand) to cause what we do, but the reflex action actually takes place before the experience of pain has time to form. This can also happen with voluntary movements. Suppose, for example, that you are required to press a button as soon as you feel a tactile stimulus applied to your skin. A typical reaction time is 100 ms or so. It takes only a few milliseconds for the skin stimulus to reach the cortical surface, but Libet *et al.* (1979) found that awareness of the stimulus takes at least 200 ms to develop (see Chapter 10). If so, the reaction must take place preconsciously, although we *experience* ourselves as responding *after* we feel something touching the skin. Just as the interactions amongst experienced billiard balls represent causal sequences in the external world, but are not the events themselves, experienced interactions between our sensations and actions represent causal sequences within our bodies and brains, but are not the events themselves. The mind/brain requires time to form a conscious representation of a pain or of something touching the skin and of the subsequent response. Although the conscious representations accurately place the cause (the stimulus) before the effect (the response), once the representations are formed, both the stimulus and the response have already taken place.

A similar pattern applies to experienced thoughts and other inner experiences. The thoughts, images, and feelings that appear in our awareness are both *generated by* processes in our bodies and mind/brains and *represent* the current states of those processes. Thoughts represent the ongoing state of play of our cognitive systems; feelings represent our internal (positive and negative) reactions to and judgements about events (see, for example, Mangan, 1993). Thoughts in the form of 'covert' or 'inner speech' have a similar relation to the cognitive processes which generate them that the words we express have to the processes which generate overt speech. 'It is only when I hear what I say that I know what I think' (see Chapter 10). In each case, once we hear the words or experience the thoughts, the cognitive processes whose ongoing states they represent have already operated.

In sum, conscious representations of inner, body and external events are not the events themselves, but they generally represent those events and their causal interactions sufficiently well to allow a fairly accurate understanding of what is happening in our lives. Although they are only *representations* of events and their causal interactions, for everyday purposes we can take them to *be* those events and their causal interactions. When we play billiards we can line up a shot without the assistance of physics. Although our knowledge of our own inner states is not incorrigible, when we experience our verbal thoughts expressed in covert or overt speech, we usually know all we need to know about what we currently think, without the assistance of cognitive psychology. And when we experience ourselves to have acted out of love or fear, we usually have an adequate understanding of our motivation, although a neuropsychologist might find it useful to give a third-person account of this in terms of its origins in the brain's limbic system. It is not the case that a lower level (microscopic) representation is always better than a macroscopic one (in the case of billiard balls). Nor are third-person accounts always better than first-person ones (in describing our thoughts and emotions). The value of a given representation, description or explanation can only be assessed in the light of the purposes for which it is to be used.

What consciousness does

The above makes sense of why consciousness *seems* to be necessary for complex adaptive functioning (focal-attentive processing is necessary for such functioning, and when consciousness is absent, focal-attentive processing is usually absent). The above analysis also explains why the contents of consciousness seem to enter into many different causal interactions with each other. They do so because the entities, events and processes represented in our experience *really do* enter into many different causal interactions (in the external world, body and mind/brain itself). But this still does not explain what consciousness itself *does*. It remains the case that the macroscopic physical world is causally closed. It remains the case that the neural correlates of consciousness (and the information they encode) would fill any 'gaps' in the working of mind/brain that consciousness might fill. And it remains the case that conscious experiences of real events follow the occurrence of the events themselves. Given this, what does consciousness *add* to the world?

If the above analysis is correct, consciousness is intimately bound up with representation. Phenomenal consciousness is always *of* something. Consciousness is also intimately bound up with knowledge. When we are conscious of what is going on, we also *know* what is going on. That said, consciousness in humans is not *co-extensive* with either representation or knowledge. There are many forms of representation in the brain that are preconscious or unconscious. And we know how to carry out many sophisticated mental tasks, although knowledge of how the mind/brain analyses information, stores it, retrieves it, transforms it, and controls the musculature to make some appropriate response, has little (if any) manifestation in what we experience. A vast reservoir of knowledge about the world and about ourselves is also encoded in long-term memory. While some of this might become conscious, it largely remains unconscious even while it plays a role in ongoing adaptive functioning (in the interpretation of input, the creation of expectations, the planning of appropriate responses and so on). That is, representation and knowledge may be *either* conscious *or* unconscious.

What difference does consciousness make? Suppose we take it away and leave everything else intact. Imagine another universe which is exactly like the one we inhabit with just one fundamental change. Imagine that it has a planet with an earth, sea, and sky, and living creatures just like ours. It also has what appear to be human beings who, viewed from an external observer's perspective, seem just like us. Even their brains appear to operate in the same way. Representations at the focus of their attention are processed differently from non-attended ones, and the neural events that correlate with consciousness (in us) encode information about the world, body and mind/brain, just as we would expect. However *their* 'neural correlates' are not accompanied by conscious experiences. In their universe the mind is entirely physical, not psychophysical.

To 'psychophysicals' like us, such 'physicals' might be impossible to detect, as viewed from our third-person perspective their lack of consciousness would not show. Behaviourally, there would be nothing to distinguish their intelligence or skill from ours. And close inspection of their brains would reveal information encoded, stored, and transformed in the normal way, in spite of the fact that none of this results in a conscious experience. Unlike robots constructed out of silicon that merely simulated our behaviour perfectly, such 'physicals' would be indistinguishable from us both functionally and physically.[17]

So, what is missing? Without behavioural or functional means for distinguishing 'physicals' from ourselves, we can only imagine *what it would be like to be* entirely 'physical'. Leaving our physical and functional structure intact we can, in our imagination, strip consciousness away. If we do, the lights go out. Although we would continue to inhabit and interact with a world, we would not *experience* ourselves to be living in a world. While retaining perfect, functional 'blindsight', without visual experience we would not see the shape of the earth or the light and colour of the sky. While retaining the ability to recognise auditory patterns, we would hear no sound of the wind or of human voices. While maintaining our survival skills, we would feel neither pain nor bodily pleasure. And, although we might have a 'self-model' that distinguishes us from other creatures and locates us in surrounding space, we would have no awareness of ourselves. We would experience no thoughts or emotions, and we would dream no dreams. *No greater loss is imaginable.* But in a purely physical, functional world this would be no loss at all.

This scenario is not entirely hypothetical. In Chapter 8, I have surveyed different ways in which actual experienced worlds are constructed along with the profound changes that can take place if some of the 'experiential materials' are taken away. These materials (sights, sounds, touches, tastes, smells and so on) are the stuff out of which subjective reality is made. As one strips one or another of these away, subjective reality contracts. This happens in cases of sensory impairment, even when some aspects of functioning can be restored by sensory substitution. If blinded, for example, one can learn to know the world in an auditory and tactile way, but none of this restores the grandeur of the visual world as-experienced. Following profound damage to one's hearing, one might learn to lip-read, and yet experience a deep sense of loss of contact with the human voice. If one has some residual hearing in the low frequencies, it may be possible to restore some discrimination of speech and environmental sound with frequency transposition. But one cannot restore the high-frequency 'qualia' of the original sounds: teaspoons still clink in cups but sound like horses clopping, and small songbirds still sing, but in a lower key.

Knowing what it is like to see the beauty in someone's eyes or to hear the nightingale at dawn is a distinct form of knowledge. It differs from abstract knowledge (or 'knowledge by description') in a very obvious way. One can only know the sorrow of losing a child if this sad event actually happens. One can only know what it is like to feel inspired if blessed by an actual inspiration. And one can read about love in innumerable books and scientific papers – but this only becomes subjectively real if one experiences it for oneself. This, I suggest, gets to the heart of the matter. It is only when we *experience* entities, events and processes for ourselves that they become *subjectively real*. It is through consciousness that we *real-ise*[18] the world. And that, and that alone, is its function.

Notes

1 My assumption that normal conscious experiences are representational is driven by a critical realist epistemology (developed in Chapter 8) and not by any commitment to the view that mental states are nothing more than formal computations on representations (a thesis that is currently in dispute). It is worth noting that there is nothing mysterious about experiences being representations of entities and events outside of or within our bodies and brains that differ in some respects from the alternative representations of those entities and events given by science (e.g. by physics). Perceptual processes are likely to have developed in response to evolutionary pressures, and select, attend to, and interpret information in accordance with human adaptive needs. Consequently, they only need to model a subset of the available information. At the same time our perceptual models must be useful, otherwise it is unlikely that human beings would have survived. Given this, it seems reasonable to assume that, barring illusions or hallucinations, the experiences produced by perceptual processing are partial, approximate but nonetheless useful representations of what is 'really there'. The view that some conscious experiences are representational in the sense of being 'intentional' (that they are *of* something) has in any case been widely accepted in philosophy of mind since Brentano reintroduced this medieval notion in the nineteenth century. According to some philosophers not all conscious experiences are intentional. Searle (1994b) for example maintains that 'a feeling of pain or a sudden sense of anxiety, where there is no object of the anxiety, is not intentional' (p. 380). But a conscious experience does not have to be about a specific external object for it to be representational. It may for example represent a state of one's own body or it may represent a global *reaction* to a real, imagined or remembered event. A feeling of pain, for example, represents (in one's first-person experience) actual or potential damage to the body, and it is usually quite accurate in that it is normally subjectively located at or near the site of body damage. A feeling of anxiety is a first-person representation of a state of one's own body and brain that signals actual or potential danger, and so on. Viewed this way, *all* conscious states are about something. On this issue, I adopt the same stance as that developed by Tye (1995). That said, I do *not* assume that the phenomenology (or qualia) of conscious states can be exhaustively described by their representational content *in the world itself* in the manner suggested by Tye (1995, 2007) and other direct realist 'representationalist' philosophers (see extensive discussion in Chapter 7; Seager and Bourget, 2007). Rather, I assume mental states to represent states of affairs (in the external world, body or mind itself) in the broad, functional sense that is widely taken for granted in cognitive science. That representations (in this broad sense) exist in the mind is required to account for many aspects of cognition – for example, to account for the existence of long-term memory, a personal store of knowledge based on prior learning and experience. However, I remain open about the *forms* that these representations might take in the brain, and about the *processes that operate on them*. Neural representations might be iconic, propositional,

feature sets, prototypes, procedural, localised, distributed, static, dynamic, partial, complete or whatever. Operations on representations might be formal and computational, more like the patterns of shifting weights and probabilities that determine the activation patterns in neural networks, or, in some cases, more like learnt sensory-motor skills in the manner suggested by enactive views of perception. In short, I suggest that the correlates of consciousness represent what the phenomenology itself represents, irrespective of how the correlates *embody* those representations.

2 It does not follow of course that the reverse is true, that is, that every differentiable physical state has a corresponding experience. Rather like the pixels on a TV screen, the 'grain' of states which support a given conscious experience may, for example, be finer than that of the experience itself.

3 In vision, some progress has already been made in the discovery of such mappings (see the special issue on the work of Roger Shepard in *Behavioural and Brain Sciences*, 24(4), 2001). While neural state/phenomenal state mappings are likely to differ in different sense modalities (e.g. vision versus audition) and even between different features of a given modality (e.g. colour versus spatial location and extension), there may also be shared, underlying principles (cf. Stoffregen and Benoît, 2001).

4 A renewed concern with first-person evidence also allows added opportunities for triangulation. Theories of brain functioning are constrained not just by input–output relationships, but also by the observable manifestations of such functioning in first-person experience. And theories about the nature of mind are constrained not just by experience but also by the observed workings of the brain. See, for example, Varela (1996, 1999), readings in Varela and Shear (1999), Velmans (2000), Jack and Roepstorff (2003, 2004) and further discussion in Velmans (2007c).

5 As noted in Chapters 6 and 7, neither of us experiences a phenomenal world 'in our head or brain' in addition to the phenomenal world we experience around our bodies. There is no experience *of* a cat 'in your brain', in addition to the phenomenal cat you see in the world. And there are no experiences *of* your neural correlates 'in my brain' in addition to the correlates that I see in your brain.

6 As noted above, I assume that it is simply a 'natural' empirical fact about the world that certain physical events in the brain (the correlates of consciousness) are accompanied by experiences. Consequently, when such neural activities (the correlates) occur in one's brain one has the corresponding experiences. I also assume that the formatting of neurally encoded information relates to the formatting of corresponding, phenomenally encoded information in an orderly way, with discoverable neural state space/phenomenal space mappings. In short, this relationship follows some natural law, however mysterious this presently seems. I return to this issue, and to analogous situations in other branches of science, below.

7 First- and third-person views of body and mind/brain states can complement each other by virtue of the fact that a subject and external observer may have access to different kinds of information about those states (the subject and external observer have asymmetrical access to such states). By contrast, different observers can access events in the external world in a symmetrical way (by means of similar exteroceptive systems). Consequently, their observations can be intersubjective and repeatable, but they are not usually 'complementary' (see Chapter 9).

8 In third-person observations of the brain this usually involves the development of new technologies (fMRI, EEG, PET, etc.). However, such refinements can also be obtained with first-person methods, for example with more highly trained attention to the minutiae of experience (see, for example, readings in Varela and Shear, 1999; Hurlburt and Akhter, 2006; Petitmengin, 2006; Shear, 2007).

9 This does not deny the usefulness of referring to relatively stable, enduring aspects of processing as 'states'.

10 I do not mean to rule out any particular form of physical embodiment in the brain by this claim, for example the possibility that information processing might take place at the quantum mechanical level.

11 See also further discussion in Velmans (2008b). I am grateful to Harald Atmans-pacher for bringing these historical precedents to my attention (personal communication 2007).

12 Following the publication of a similar three-part solution to the Causal Paradox in the first edition of this book, a closely related analysis, applied to a clinically oriented setting, was published in a special issue of the *Journal of Consciousness Studies* along with eight commentaries and a reply (see Velmans, 2002a, 2002b, or, for the full version with commentaries, Velmans, 2003a). A further application of this analysis to an understanding of free will, accompanied by four further commentaries, also appeared in Velmans (2003b) (see also Chapter 14). As far as I can judge, on the basis of commentaries that have been published so far, the analysis below, when properly understood, is not vulnerable to the criticisms that are sometimes directed at dual-aspect theories of conscious causation (see, for example, note 14 below). As I have not detected any genuine vulnerabilities consequent on the published commentaries, I will not review these here. Those with a professional interest in this issue should, however, study these additional resources.

13 See the thought experiment on 'changing places' in Chapter 9.

14 The view that first- and third-person accounts are compatible makes this a form of 'compatibilism' within philosophy of mind. Note that this 'complementary' version of compatibilism is not vulnerable to the problem of 'overdetermination' (the problem that once one has an adequate third-person account of mental processes, any added first-person account is superfluous – see, for example, Kim, 1993, 2005, 2007, for reviews). First-person accounts may not add anything useful to third-person accounts as such. However, if a complete account of mind and its workings (including its dual-aspect manifestations) requires both first- and third-person accounts, then first-person accounts are not superfluous.

15 An extensive discussion of the many different third-person roles suggested for consciousness may be found in the open peer commentaries accompanying Velmans (1991a) and my replies in Velmans (1991b); we have in any case examined this issue in Chapters 4 and 10, so I will not repeat this analysis here.

16 It is reasonable to suppose that the detail of conscious representation has been tailored by evolutionary pressures to be useful for everyday human activities although these representations remain global, approximate and species-specific. To obtain a more intricate knowledge of the external world or body we usually need the assistance of scientific instruments (see Chapter 8).

17 This is, of course, a variation of the familiar 'zombie' scenario. I use this thought experiment solely as a device to clarify what consciousness adds to the world. Removing consciousness, while leaving everything else intact, is conceivable, even if there are no *actual* universes where identical physical and functional conditions are not accompanied by identical experiences (just as removing a magnetic field from the electricity flowing down a wire might be conceivable, but impossible in practice). Chalmers (1996) uses a similar example to mount a case against reductionism. While I share his anti-reductionism (see Velmans, 1991a, 1991b, 1993a, 1993b, 1996c), I do not wish to use this thought experiment as an argument against it. Most reductionists accept that consciousness *seems* to be different from brain states (or functions) but claim that science will *discover* it to be nothing more than a state or function of the brain. In short, they mostly accept that brain states and conscious states are *conceivably* different, but deny that they are *actually*

different (in the universe we happen to inhabit). If so, arguments against reductionism based on 'conceivability' are tangential. My own case against reductionism (in Chapters 3 to 5) focuses on its implausibility in *this universe*, its many false analogies, its self-defeating nature, and the *actual* impossibility of showing conscious experiences and their physical correlates to be ontologically identical. Science might discover the neural causes and correlates of conscious experiences, but causation and correlation do not establish ontological identity.

18 I have hyphenated 'real-ise' to stress that the existence of subjective reality depends on conscious awareness. I develop this theme further in Chapter 14.

14 Self-consciousness in a reflexive universe

A reflexive universe

Chapters 1 to 13 suggest a way to make sense of what consciousness *is* and what consciousness *does* that is consistent with common sense and with the findings of science. According to classical dualism, the universe is split into two separate realms, each composed of different kinds of stuff: physical stuff which has location and extension in space, and the 'thinking' stuff of soul, mind or consciousness which has neither location nor extension in space. In interactionist forms of dualism, these two realms interact with each other somewhere in the human brain. Currently popular forms of physicalism and functionalism attempt to heal this split by attempting to show that soul, mind and consciousness are nothing more than states or functions of the brain. However all these theories agree that the universe is split in a second way: conscious experiences are separate from the world that we can see around our bodies. This world that we can see has extension and location in space, but our experiences of that world are either 'nowhere' or they are 'in the head or brain'.

As we have seen in Chapters 6 and 12, reflexive monism starts in a different place. Although we normally think of the phenomenal world surrounding our body as the 'physical world', it remains part of conscious experience rather than apart from it, which requires a more nuanced understanding of how the phenomenal 'physical world' relates to the *world as described by physics* and the *world itself*. It also requires a different understanding of how experienced phenomena relate to the many entities, events and processes that exist at any given moment but are *not* experienced in the surrounding world, body, and brain. Reflexive monism (RM) suggests a way of understanding these relationships that neither splits the universe into two incommensurable mental and physical substances nor requires consciousness to be anything other than it seems. It neither splits consciousness from matter nor reduces it to a state of the brain. Instead, it suggests a seamless, psychophysical universe, of which we are an integral part, which can be known in two fundamentally different ways. Whether one adopts the perspective of an 'external observer' or a 'subject', the embedding surround, interacting with brain-based perceptual and cognitive systems, provides the supporting *vehicle* for one's conscious view, and what we normally think of as the phenomenal 'physical world' *constitutes* that view. Nor does reflexive monism ultimately separate the observer from the observed. In a reflexive universe, humans are differentiated parts of an embedding wholeness (the universe itself) that, reflexively, have a conscious view of both that embedding surround and the differentiated parts they think of as themselves.

A different perspective on the 'hard problem' of consciousness

The view that these physical and experiential aspects of mind arise from what can best be described as a 'psychophysical ground' also gives RM a different perspective on the classical 'hard problem' of consciousness. In Western science the existence of matter is often taken for granted, while the existence of consciousness is regarded as mysterious. Consequently, the conventional 'hard problem' refers to the difficulty of understanding how consciousness arises from (otherwise, insentient) physical matter, or, in other versions, the seeming irreducibility of first-person accounts of conscious experience to third-person descriptions of the brain. But in truth, the existence of matter is as mysterious as the existence of consciousness, and there are similarly hard problems in physics. Why, for example, should electricity flowing down a wire be accompanied by a magnetic field around the wire; why should electrons sometimes behave as waves and at other times as particles; and why should there be any matter in the universe at all?

We simply assume these to be natural facts that we can observe in the world. We can try to explain them by incorporating them into some body of theory, but we do not agonise over their *existence*. If first-person and third-person accounts of the mind, along with the aspects of mind that they describe, are complementary and mutually irreducible, one would not expect to be able to derive one aspect from, or reduce one aspect to, the other. It might just be a natural fact about the world that certain forms of brain functioning are accompanied by certain forms of first-person experience. That would require us to change a few of our pre-theoretical assumptions about the nature of matter and its relationship to consciousness, and we would still have to investigate the principles that govern the consciousness–brain relationship in great detail. But the fact that given conscious states accompany certain forms of brain functioning would then be 'hard' to understand in the same sense as many facts in physics.

While the parallels are not exact (see Velmans, 2008b), wave–particle complementarity in quantum mechanics provides a rough analogy. One can relate wave and particle properties of electrons to each other with great precision, but within physics, neither is regarded as more basic than, reducible to, or supervenient on the other. As in RM, such properties are regarded as complementary and mutually irreducible – and physics has to grapple with the very same issue of how to specify what it is that these properties *are properties of*. Just as RM opts to describe the fundamental nature of mind as 'psychophysical', physics typically opts for descriptions that somehow combine wave- and particle-like aspects, for example describing photons as 'wave packets' or electrons as 'electron clouds'.

Without foreclosing on the possibility of a deeper understanding of photons and electrons, for example in a mathematical form, quantum mechanics accepts that there is something deeply mysterious about the fundamental nature of matter. Without foreclosing on the possibility of a deeper understanding of mind, RM similarly accepts that there is something deeply mysterious about the way that consciousness and the material forms with which it correlates arise from some 'psychophysical' ground.

Caveats and ancient connections

Needless to say, this analysis of consciousness, mind and world is incomplete and likely to change in some respects as consciousness studies continue to grow. Further empirical advance, for example, is likely to yield a more detailed account of how different forms of consciousness relate to the workings of the brain. There is also a great deal that I have not discussed. I have not for example dealt with how to make sense of extraordinary experiences, altered states of consciousness, and the investigations of consciousness that have been pursued in Eastern traditions over millennia. This is deliberate. My intention is to engage the 'consciousness debate' in the form that it currently presents in Western philosophy and science. Consequently, the only evidence on which I have drawn derives either from ordinary experience or from the findings of science.

Although it addresses current problems, some features of reflexive monism nevertheless appear to be ancient. In one or another form, RM has been present in human thought for more than 3,500 years. One can find versions of it in later Vedic writings such as the Upanishads and, as we will see later, in ancient Egyptian hieroglyphs on a sarcophagus in the British Museum dating back to the period 1850–1650 BC. However this ancient way of thinking about our own nature and the universe in which we live is very different from those currently in fashion. Current Western philosophy and science is largely materialist and reductionist. While this is a successful strategy for unifying our understanding of things in the external world that we are conscious *of*, there appears to be no plausible case for reducing phenomenal consciousness itself to a state or function of the brain. Nor does there seem to be any route whereby an entirely third-person science could *discover* consciousness to be nothing more than a state or function of the brain. In the long run, this may have major implications for our view of our own nature and the nature of the world in which we live. It may also have a subtle impact on science. But the alternative to a reductionist science of consciousness is not non-sense or non-science; it is simply a nonreductionist science of consciousness.

My formal analysis of the mind/body problem and of human consciousness ends at this point. However, given the centrality of consciousness in our lives, I will add a few thoughts that might help to place it in a wider context. Are we the only conscious beings? We know that *we* are conscious, but what is the wider distribution of consciousness? How did consciousness evolve? And what kind of universe could have produced it? Dualists and reductionists alike have expressed many different views on these matters. As all the data needed to *decide* these matters are not currently available, all views are partly speculative. Some aspects of my own thoughts on these matters also have to be speculative, and where this happens, I will make this clear. I have my own 'best guess', but I wish to stress that none of the formal analysis (in Chapters 1 to 13) depends on it.

The distribution of consciousness

Why are all views about the distribution of consciousness on our own planet or in the wider universe partly speculative? Because we do not even know the necessary and sufficient conditions for consciousness in our own brains. As John (1976) pointed out, we do not know the physical and chemical inter-actions involved, how big a neuronal system must be to sustain it, nor even whether it is confined to brains – and thirty years later we are little wiser (see Chapter 11). Given this underdetermination by the data, opinions about the distribution of consciousness have ranged from the ultra-conservative (only humans are conscious) to the extravagantly libertarian (everything that might possibly be construed as having consciousness *does* have consciousness).

The view that only humans have consciousness has a long history in theology, following naturally from the doctrine that only human beings have souls. Some philosophers and scientists have elaborated this doctrine into a philosophical position. According to Descartes only humans combine *res cogitans* (the thinking stuff of consciousness) with *res extensa* (extended material stuff). Nonhuman animals, which he refers to as 'brutes', are nothing more than nonconscious machines. Lacking consciousness, they do not have reason or language (see Chapter 2). Eccles (in Popper and Eccles, 1976) adopted a similar, dualist position – but argued that it is only through human language that one can communicate sufficiently well with another being to *establish* whether it is conscious. Without language, he suggests, the only defensible option is agnosticism or doubt. Jaynes (1979), by contrast, argued that human language is a *necessary condition* for consciousness. And Humphrey (1983) adopted a similar view, arguing that consciousness emerged only when humans developed a 'theory of mind'. He accepts that we might find it useful for our own ethical purposes to treat other animals *as if* they were conscious, but without self-consciousness of the kind provided by a human 'theory of mind' they really have no consciousness at all. There are other, modern variants of this position (e.g. Carruthers, 1998), but we do not need an exhaustive survey. It is enough to note that thinkers of very different persuasions have held this view. Early versions of this position appear to be largely informed by theological doctrine; later versions are based on the supposition that higher mental processes of the kinds unique to humans are necessary for consciousness of any kind.

If the analysis presented in this book is correct, this extreme position has little to recommend it *when applied to humans*, let alone other animals. Phenomenal consciousness in humans is constructed from different extero-ceptive and interoceptive resources and is composed of different 'experiential materials' (what we see, hear, touch, taste, smell, feel and so on – see Chapter 8). It is true that our higher cognitive functions also have manifest-ations in experience, for example, in the form of verbal thoughts. Con-sequently, without language and the ability to reason, such thoughts would no longer be a part of what we experience (in the form of 'inner speech'). But one can lose some sensory and mental capacities while other capacities remain intact (in cases of sensory impairment, aphasia, agnosia and so on). And there is *no* scientific evidence to support the view that language, the ability to reason and a theory of mind are *necessary conditions* for visual, auditory and other sensory experiences (see Chapter 11). Applied to humans, this view is in any case highly counterintuitive. If true, we would have to believe that, prior to the development of language and other higher cognitive functions, babies experience neither pleasure nor pain, and that their cries and chuckles are just the nonconscious output of small biological machines. We would also have to accept that autistic children without a 'theory of mind' never have any conscious experience. To any parent, such views are absurd.

Such views confuse the necessary conditions for the *existence* of con-sciousness with the added conditions required to support its many *forms*. Consciousness in humans appears to be regulated by global arousal systems, modulated by attentional systems that decide which representations (of the external world, body and mind/brain itself) are to receive focal attention. Neural representations, arousal systems, affective systems and mechanisms governing attention are found in many other animals (Jerison, 1985; Panksepp, 2007). Other animals have sense organs that detect environmental information and perceptual and cognitive processes that analyse and organise that information (see Chapter 8). Many animals are also able to communicate and live in complex social worlds. Overall, the precise mix of sensory, per-ceptual, cognitive and social processes found in each species is likely to be species-specific. Given this, it might be reasonable to suppose that only humans can have full *human* consciousness. But it is equally reasonable to suppose that some nonhuman animals have unique, nonhuman forms of consciousness.

Even *self-consciousness* (of a kind) may not be confined to humans. Gallup (1977, 1982), for example, found that individually housed chimpanzees, given access to a full-length mirror, initially threatened and vocalised towards their mirror images as they would another chimpanzee. However, within two or three days their behaviour changed. They began to use their mirror reflections to groom themselves, remove food particles from between their teeth, and inspect parts of their body that they could not otherwise see. On the eleventh day the chimpanzees were anaesthetised and a spot of red dye was placed above one eyebrow and on top of the opposite ear. On recovery, the chimpanzees, who were unable to see the spots, took no notice of them, touching them only rarely. However, once the mirrors were reintroduced they gave clear indications of noticing the change in their appearance. The frequency of touches to the marked spots increased twenty-five-fold, and, on occasion, they would touch the spots and then inspect and lick their fingers (although the dye was an indelible one). In short, after a few days of familiarisation with mirrors, the chimpanzees gave every indication that they recognised the mirror image as a reflection of themselves. Similar findings have been obtained with orang-utans (Tobach *et al.*, 1997), gorillas (Shillito *et al.*, 1999) and tamarins (Hauser *et al.*, 1995); mirror recognition has also been found in elephants (Plotnik *et al.*, 2006) and dolphins (Reiss and Marino, 2001).

Given the evidence for the gradual evolution of the human brain, it seems unlikely that consciousness first emerged in the universe, fully formed, in *homo sapiens*. As the naturalist Thomas Huxley observed in 1874,

> The doctrine of continuity is too well established for it to be permissible to me to suppose that any complex natural phenomenon comes into existence suddenly, and without being preceded by simpler modifications; and very strong arguments would be needed to prove that such complex phenomena as those of consciousness, first make their appearance in man.
>
> (cited in Vesey, 1970, p. 138)

Is consciousness confined to complex brains?

One cannot be *certain* that other animals are conscious – or even that other people are conscious (the classical problem of 'other minds'). However, the balance of evidence strongly supports it (Beshkar, 2008; Dawkins, 1998; Panksepp, 2007). In cases where other animals have brain structures that are similar to that of humans, which support social behaviour that is similar to that of humans (aggression, sexual activity, pair-bonding and so on), it is difficult to believe that they experience nothing at all. But if one does not place the conscious/nonconscious boundary between humans and nonhumans, where should one place it?

It might be that consciousness is confined to animals whose brains have achieved some (unknown) critical mass or critical complexity. In the human case, only representations at the focus of attention reach consciousness, and then only in a sufficiently aroused state (an awake or dreaming state, but not coma or deep sleep). But we need to be cautious about treating such conditions as universal. Within the animal kingdom creatures that sleep include mammals, birds, many reptiles, amphibians and fish, and even ants and fruit flies. However not all active animals appear to sleep (for example, fish that swim continuously in shoals), and while sleep is generally thought to be restorative, its precise biological function remains unknown. Given that sleep is associated with *diminished* consciousness, it seems in any case unlikely that having a sleep–wake cycle is a prerequisite for consciousness.

Selective attention might seem to be a more likely condition, and it is also found in many other animals – even fruit flies (van Swinderen, 2007). In humans the mind/brain receives simultaneous information from a range of sense organs that simultaneously monitor the external and internal environment, and this information needs to be related to information in long-term memory, and assessed for importance in the light of ongoing needs and goals. In short, there are many things going on at once. But we cannot give everything our full, undivided attention. As Donald Broadbent pointed out in 1958, there is a 'bottleneck' in human information processing. The human effector system is also limited. We only have two eyes, hands, legs, etc., and effective action in the world requires precise co-ordination of eye movements, limbs and body posture. As a result, the mind/brain needs to select the most important information, to decide on the best strategy, and to co-ordinate its activity sufficiently well to interact with the world in a coherent, integrated way.

To achieve this, it is as important to *stop* things happening in the brain as it is to make them happen. As William Uttal observed,

> There is an a priori requirement that some substantial portion, perhaps a majority, of the synapses that occur at the terminals of the myriad synaptic contacts of the three-dimensional . . . (neural) . . . lattice must be inhibitory. Otherwise the system would be in a constant state of universal excitement after the very first input signal, and no coherent adaptive response to complex stimuli would be possible.
>
> (Uttal, 1978, p. 192)

To prevent information overload, not to mention utter confusion, attended-to information needs to become *dominantly* active and conscious, while information outside the focus of attention is inhibited (and similar inhibition of eligible activities takes place during dreamless sleep). As we have seen in Chapter 11, activities in the human brain that are eligible for consciousness have to *compete* for dominance, and the mechanisms commonly thought to play a role involve heightened activation of dominant activities, combined with inhibition of non-dominant activities.[1] For example, top-down influences of attentional systems on neural representations of input are likely to be one means by which their activation is heightened and competing activity suppressed. Such neural activities may also become dominant by entering into phase-locked synchrony with other neural assemblies, thereby forming winning coalitions and suppressing competing coalitions. As attention shifts, new information is selectively activated and/or released from inhibition,[2] new coalitions form, become integrated, and conscious.

As noted in Chapter 11, if 'becoming conscious' just requires neurons to become *more* activated (to do more of what they normally do), or to do this in coalition with other assemblies, it may be that selective attention adds nothing *unusual* to the firing patterns of individual neural assemblies to make the information that they encode conscious. 'Eligible neural activities that remain unconscious may not be *different in kind* from those which become conscious, any more than the sound of individual voices at a football stadium is different in kind from the concerted singing of the crowd that drowns them out.' If so, consciousness might be a *natural* accompaniment of certain forms of neural representation, and while having an attentional system allows a choice of *what* will be conscious in complex brains that have many options, this might not be required by simple brains, with few options, to be conscious of anything at all.

It goes without saying that if experiences and their neural correlates encode identical information (Chapter 13) then the neural states that support everyday *human* experiences must be extremely complex. The contents of consciousness are constructed from different sense modalities, and within a given sense modality, experiences can be of unlimited variety and be exquisitely detailed. Complexity might also be a means whereby neural coalitions compete for dominance (Tononi, 2007). However it does not follow from this that *only* brains of similar complexity can support *any* experience. Once again we need to distinguish the conditions for the existence of consciousness from the added conditions that determine the many forms that it can take. The mechanisms required to select, co-ordinate, integrate and disseminate conscious information in the human brain may not be required for simpler creatures, with simpler brains. Complex, highly differentiated brains are likely to be needed to support complex, highly differentiated experiences. But it remains possible that relatively simple brains can support relatively simple experiences.

Frogs, worms and molluscs

The visual system of the frog, for example, appears to be structured to respond to just four stimulus features: a sustained contrast in brightness between two portions of the visual field, the presence of moving edges, the presence of small moving spots, and an overall dimming of the visual field. This is a far cry from the variety and detail provided by the human visual system. But there seems little reason to jump to the conclusion that the frog sees nothing. Rather, as Lettvin *et al.* (1959) proposed, the frog may see just four things relating to its survival. A sudden dimming of the light or a moving edge may indicate the presence of a predator and is likely to initiate an escape response. Sustained differences in brightness may allow the frog to separate water from land and lily pad. And moving spot detectors may allow the frog to see (and catch) a moving fly at tongue's length (see Chapter 8).

As one continues to descend the evolutionary ladder, the plausibility of extrapolating from human to nonhuman animal consciousness becomes increasingly remote. There may, for example, be critical transition points in the development of consciousness which accompany critical transitions in functional organisation (Sloman, 1997a, 1997b). Self-awareness, for example, probably occurs only in creatures capable of self-representation. That said, phenomenal consciousness (of any kind) might only require representation. If so, even simple invertebrates might have some rudimentary awareness, in so far as they are able to represent and, indeed, respond to certain features of the world.

Planarians (flat worms), for example, can be taught to avoid a stimulus light if it has been previously associated with an electric shock (following a classical conditioning procedure). And simple molluscs such as the sea-hare Aplysia, which withdraw into their shells when touched, respond to stimulus 'novelty'. For example, they may habituate (show diminished withdrawal) after repeated stimulation at a given site, but withdraw fully if the same stimulation is applied to another nearby site. Habituation in Aplysia appears to be mediated by events at just one centrally placed synapse between sensory and motor neurons (Uttal, 1978). This is very simple learning, and it is very difficult to imagine what a mollusc might experience. But if the ability to learn and respond to the environment were the criterion for consciousness, there would be no principled grounds to rule this out. It might be, for example, that simple approach and avoidance are associated with rudimentary experiences of pleasure and pain.

Is consciousness confined to brains?

It is commonly thought that the evolution of human consciousness is intimately linked to the evolution of the neocortex (e.g. Jerison, 1985). And, as noted in Chapter 11, it seems likely that mid-brain as well as cortical structures play a central role in determining the forms of consciousness that we experience. However, whether consciousness first emerged with the development of such subcortical and cortical structures, or whether there is something special about the nature of brain cells that somehow 'produces' consciousness, is less certain. As Charles Sherrington has pointed out, there appears to be nothing special about the internal structure of brain cells that might make them uniquely responsible for mind or consciousness. For,

> A brain-cell is not unalterably from birth a brain-cell. In the embryo-frog the cells destined to be brain can be replaced by cells from the skin of the back, the back even of another embryo; these after transplantation become in their new host brain-cells and seem to serve the brain's purpose duly. But cells of the skin it is difficult to suppose as having a special germ of mind. Moreover cells, like those of the brain in microscopic appearance, in chemical character, and in provenance, are elsewhere

concerned with acts wholly devoid of mind, e.g. the knee-jerk, the light-reflex of the pupil. A knee-jerk 'kick' and a mathematical problem employ similar-looking cells. With the spine broken and the spinal cords so torn across as to disconnect the body below from the brain above, although the former retains the unharmed remainder of the spinal cord consisting of masses of nervous cells, and retains a number of nervous reactions, it reveals no trace of recognizable mind. . . . Mind, as attaching to any unicellular life would seem to be unrecognizable to observation; but I would not feel that permits me to affirm that it is not there. Indeed, I would think, that since mind appears in the developing source that amounts to showing that it is potential in the ovum (and sperm) from which the source springs. The appearance of recognizable mind in the source would then be not a creation de novo but a development of mind from unrecognizable into recognizable.

(Sherrington, 1942, cited in Vesey, 1970, p. 323)

Unicellular organisms, fungi and plants

Indeed, given our current, limited knowledge of the necessary and sufficient conditions for consciousness in humans, we cannot, as yet, rule out even more remote possibilities. If the ability to represent and respond to the world, or the ability to modify behaviour consequent on interactions with the world, are the criteria for consciousness, then it may be that consciousness extends not just to simple invertebrates (such as Planaria) but also to unicellular organisms, fungi and plants. For example, the leaflets of the Mimosa plant habituate to repeated stimulation, that is the leaflets rapidly close when first touched, but after repeated stimulation they re-open fully and do not close again while the stimulus remains the same. Surprisingly, this habituation is stimulus-specific. For example, Holmes and Yost (1966) induced leaflet closure using either water droplets or brush strokes, and after repeated stimulation (with either stimulus) habituation occurred. But, if the stimulus was changed (from water drops to brush strokes or vice versa), leaflet closure re-occurred (see also Applewhite, 1975, for a review).

For many who have thought about this matter, the transition from rudimentary consciousness in animal life to sentience in plants is one transition too far. Perhaps it is. It is important to note however that a criterion of consciousness based on the ability to respond to the world does not prevent it. Nor, on this criterion, can we rule out the possibility of consciousness in systems made of materials other than the carbon-based compounds that (on this planet) form the basis for organic life. As we have seen in Chapter 5, silicon-based computers can in principle carry out many functions that, in humans, we take to be evidence of conscious minds. So how can we be certain that they are not conscious?

One should recognise, too, that even a criterion for the existence of consciousness based on the ability to respond or adapt to the world is entirely arbitrary. It might for example be like something to *be* something irrespective of whether one *does* anything. Panpsychists such as Whitehead (1929) have suggested that there is no arbitrary line in the ascent from microscopic to macroscopic matter at which consciousness suddenly appears out of nothing. Rather, elementary forms of matter may be associated with elementary forms of experience. And if they encode information they may be associated with rudimentary forms of mind.

Does matter matter?

Many would regard Whitehead's views as extreme (I give my own assessment below). But there is one position that is even more extreme – the view that the nature of matter doesn't matter to consciousness at all. At first glance, it might seem preposterous to claim that matter doesn't matter for consciousness. But, surprising as it might seem, it is a logical consequence of *computational functionalism*, one of the most widely adopted, current theories of mind. As John Searle has noted, it is important to distinguish this position from the view that *silicon robots* might be conscious. For Searle, human consciousness in spite of its subjectivity, intentionality, and qualia is an emergent *physical* property of the brain. If so, a silicon robot *might* have consciousness. But this would depend not on its programming, but on whether silicon just happens to have the same causal powers (to produce consciousness) as the carbon-based material of brains.

Computational functionalists take the further step that, apart from providing housing for functioning, material stuff is irrelevant. *Any* system that functions *as if* it has consciousness and mind *does* have consciousness and mind. If a non-biological system functions exactly like a human mind then it has a human mind, as the only thing that makes a system a 'mind' is the way that it functions. In its usual reductionist versions, computational functionalism finesses questions about the distribution of first-person consciousness, routinely translating these into questions about how different systems function (see Chapter 5).

However, David Chalmers (1996) has suggested a nonreductionist version of this position that has clear consequences for the distribution of first-person consciousness and mind. Like conventional computational functionalists, Chalmers argues that functional relations alone determine the nature of mind and consciousness, but, for him, consciousness *supervenes* on functioning without reducing to it. In his explanatory system there would be physical laws (about the way systems function), associated conscious experiences, and psychophysical laws or 'bridging principles' which relate the former to the latter. Nothing else, he claims, would be required for a complete theory of mind.[3]

According to Chalmers, a machine that functions in a way that is indistinguishable from that of humans has experiences that are indistinguishable from those of humans (a version of 'strong AI'). This would be true whether the system is made out of silicon chips, or beer cans driven by windmills (to use Searle's memorable phrase), provided only that, in their detailed activity, these systems instantiate the same causal relationships, that is, that they function in the same way. In Chalmers's view, not only machines made of silicon chips could experience in exactly the way that humans do, but so would virtual minds instantiated in the symbol manipulations of programmes.

Chalmers comes to this conclusion on the basis of two thought experiments, which he describes as 'fading qualia' and 'dancing qualia'. In these he considers the familiar scenario in which the neurons of the brain are gradually replaced by silicon chips which exactly replace the functioning of the neurons they replace. As the replacements progress, do the qualia gradually fade? Or, if one were able to switch between one's normal brain and a replacement, silicon brain (with exactly the same functions), would the qualia dance? According to Chalmers if one replaced the functions exactly one could not notice the difference either externally in terms of behaviour, or internally in terms of what one experiences. One would, after all, have to report the same things, otherwise the functioning of the silicon systems would not be the same as that of the neural systems they replace. Hence, functioning of certain sorts is necessarily accompanied by experiences of certain sorts *as there is no way to distinguish any difference.*

This argument was initially put in a special issue of the *Journal of Consciousness Studies* based around Chalmers's 1995 paper, and in Velmans (1995a) (in the same issue) I suggested that Chalmers had presented the options in the silicon replacement experiments in an unnecessarily restrictive way. To begin with, one has to distinguish the question of whether consciousness exists in a silicon brain from whether we can *know* that it exists. As noted in Chapter 5, a silicon robot that functioned in exactly the same way as a human *might* have experiences, but one would not be able to tell from either its behaviour or its internal functioning whether it has (a) experiences just like a human, (b) a distinct silicon experience, or (c) no experience at all. So the third-person route to knowledge about another system's experience is blocked. However, Chalmers puts the stronger view that even if one *were* the system in which brain cells were gradually replaced by silicon chips one would not be able to tell what effects, if any, this might have on one's experience.

The way Chalmers sets up this 'thought experiment' makes the outcome a foregone conclusion. If the replacement of neurons by silicon chips produces no noticeable change in experience that one can report, then Chalmers is right. If the replacement of neurons by silicon chips does make a difference to subjective experience that one can report, one might be tempted to argue that Chalmers is wrong. However, Chalmers argues that the second situation is not functionally equivalent to the first situation. As both the experience and the report have changed, the functioning of the system must have changed. Provided that the 'functioning of the system' refers to the *entire* functioning of the system, there would seem to be nothing wrong with the logic of this argument. If global functioning F_1 is always accompanied by experience C_1

(if F_1 then C_1), then if C_1 is absent F_1 must have changed (if not-C_1 then not-F_1).

How to really find out whether matter matters

That said, whether a given form of experience inevitably accompanies a given form of functioning is an empirical question not a logical one – and to answer this one needs experiments that can actually decide the issue, not thought experiments set up in a way that they cannot fail. By including both experiences and subjective reports of those experiences *within* his definition of 'equivalent system functioning' Chalmers makes his thesis unfalsifiable. No actual experiment designed to investigate the relation of functioning to experience would be carried out that way. In consciousness studies it is usually taken for granted that systems involved in supporting conscious experience are partly dissociable from those involved in *reporting* on conscious experience (that is one of the reasons one has to be cautious about relying only on subjective reports). Given this, it might be possible to replace neural circuitry that supports a given form of experience (say some aspect of vision or audition) with silicon hardware that retained the same internal and external functional relations to the rest of the brain, without affecting the systems that generate subjective reports. Suppose, for example, that we knew exactly how the neural correlates of a particular 'red' experience differed from those of a particular 'green' experience, for example if we were able to identify the precise 'essential nodes' for these experiences in areas V4 and V4a of the visual system. And suppose we replace that neural circuitry with functionally equivalent silicon circuitry, and we hook this up to the rest of the brain in an identical way. We can then present the stimuli that, prior to the experiment, caused that particular red and green experience and note what happens. We might also put in a switch to enable simple neuron/silicon comparisons.[4]

In this situation the silicon replacement might result in (a) no experienced change (red and green look no different), (b) an altered 'silicon' experience ('silicon red' versus 'silicon green?') or (c) no colour experience at all. As the functional input/output relations are unaltered, the ability to identify or discriminate between the two input stimuli should not be affected by the silicon replacement. In case (b), for example, silicon red and green would remain distinct (although unlike any normal colour experience), while in case (c) there would be a novel form of 'blindsight'. One would, of course, make three different reports of what one experiences consequent on outcomes (a), (b) and (c). But that is the whole point of carrying out the experiment, not a weakness as Chalmers claims.[5] Although the verbal reports might differ with different visual effects, the functioning of the visual system would remain the same.

Of course, whether such an experiment is a practical possibility remains to be seen, but as far as I can judge it is logically possible. And if it is logically possible, local functioning of a given kind might *not* be accompanied by experience of a given kind – which undermines Chalmers's case. Indeed, some variant of the experiment above might be the only way to find out whether silicon (or other non-neural) hardware that functions in a given way has a given associated conscious experience. To know what another system experiences one either has to *be* that system, or to *incorporate that system into oneself*. In a small way, such implant experiments might achieve that aim.

The problems of panpsychofunctionalism

Whatever one may think about the 'fading/dancing qualia' arguments, the view that 'matter doesn't matter' for what we experience is highly counter-intuitive. On Chalmers's account, not only would machines made of silicon chips and virtual minds (instantiated in the symbol manipulations of pro-grammes) experience in the way that humans do, but so would systems consisting of symbols written on bits of paper by the population of China, provided only that the causal relationships governing the creation of those symbols mimic those of the human mind. Processes within the human brain that are normally thought of as *unconscious* would also have to be conscious in Chalmers's system (by virtue of their functioning) – in which case the con-scious/nonconscious distinction loses its meaning. The theoretical cost of this position to consciousness studies is considerable. If the conscious/noncon-scious distinction cannot be made, how could one investigate the conditions for consciousness in the human brain, which rely on contrasts between neural conditions adequate or not adequate for conscious experience? And how could one make sense of the extensive experimental literature on the differences between preconscious, conscious and unconscious processing?

Note that Chalmers is forced into this uncompromising position by his fading/dancing qualia argument. Whatever functions is conscious *by virtue of its functioning*. Given this, all brain functions must be conscious. Con-sequently, he maintains that those functions that do not *seem* to enter into our consciousness must be autonomously conscious (they are conscious to themselves). This, in turn, leads to the extravagant claim that there are as many distinct consciousnesses cohabiting in the human brain as there are distinct functions.

Nor does Chalmers see any reason to draw the line at brains or systems that simulate the functioning of the brain. If consciousness of given sorts is invariably associated with functioning of given sorts then *all* forms of func-tioning are associated with experiences, irrespective of their embodiment. This '*panpsychofunctionalism*' (my term for this) is quite different from *panpsychism* (the view that all material forms are accompanied by forms of experience). If true, then not only do thermostats experience in ways that relate to their function (sensing hot and cold), but so do washing machines and vacuum cleaners (whose function is to get clothes and carpets clean). And the rain experiences something that relates to its ability to make the earth wet and make flowers grow – and even rainbows experience something relating to their production of beautiful sensations in the human mind.

The central difficulty for this thesis is that functioning is *observer-relative*. Chalmers's defence is that the structure of physical systems does, to some extent, constrain their potential functioning. But this really misses the point. The operation of a washing machine is constrained by the nature of its physical construction. It also has a useful function to conscious beings like ourselves. But why should the function *we* attribute to it determine *its* consciousness? To put it another way, if it *is* like something to be a washing machine how could that possibly depend on *our* purposes? The same may be said of thermostats or, for that matter, a simulation of the human mind embodied in a symbol-manipulating programme of a virtual machine.[6]

It is not my intention to rule out the possibility that the functioning of a system determines the experience of that system. As noted above, cortical implant experiments might (or might not) support that view. In my estimation, however, *panpsychofunctionalism* (as developed by Chalmers, 1996) is too extreme. If experience depends *solely* on form (or function) and *not at all* on substance (the matter or medium which embodies those functions), then virtual minds embodied in symbol-manipulating programmes would have normal human experiences provided only that they mimic the mind's internal causal relationships. While one cannot rule this out *a priori*, it seems unlikely that the flesh and bone and brain of human embodiment provides no essential contribution to the experienced 'qualia' of human life. In any case, to be a conscious entity or being, one would first have to be an entity or being. And it is by no means self-evident that the population of China passing notes to each other (simulating the symbol manipulation in the human mind) constitutes a 'being' in the required sense.[7] Finally, functioning is observer-relative. So even if a thermostat composed of a bimetal strip does have some 'metallic' experience, there would seem to be no grounds for the assumption that this experience is determined by its functions in human affairs.

Can one draw a line between things that have consciousness and those that don't?

Where then should one draw the line between entities that are conscious and those that are not? Theories about the distribution of consciousness divide into *continuity* and *discontinuity* theories. Discontinuity theories all claim that consciousness emerged at a particular point in the evolution of the universe. They merely disagree about which point. Consequently, discontinuity theories all face the same problem. What switched the lights on? What is it about matter, at a particular stage of evolution, which suddenly gave it consciousness? As noted above, most try to define the point of transition in functional terms, although they disagree about the nature of the critical function. Some think consciousness 'switched on' only in humans, for example once they acquired language or a theory of mind. Some believe that consciousness emerged once brains reached a critical size or complexity. Others believe it co-emerged with the ability to learn, or to respond in an adaptive way to the environment.

As noted above, such theories confuse the conditions for the *existence* of consciousness with the conditions that determine the many *forms* that it can take. Who can doubt that verbal thoughts require language, or that full human self-consciousness requires a theory of mind? Without internal representations of the world, how could consciousness be *of* anything? And without motility and the ability to approach or avoid, what point would there be to rudimentary pleasure or pain? However, none of these theories explains what it is about such biological functions that suddenly switches consciousness on.

Continuity theorists do not face this problem for the simple reason that they do not believe that consciousness suddenly emerged at *any* stage of evolution. Rather, as Sherrington suggests above, consciousness is a 'development of mind from unrecognisable into recognisable'. On this *panpsychist* view, all forms of matter have an associated form of consciousness.[8] In the cosmic explosion that gave birth to the universe, consciousness co-emerged with matter and co-evolves with it. As matter became more differentiated and developed in complexity, consciousness became correspondingly differentiated and complex. The emergence of carbon-based life forms developed into creatures with sensory systems that had associated sensory 'qualia'. The development of *representation* was accompanied by the development of consciousness that is *of* something. The development of *self-representation* was accompanied by the dawn of differentiated self-consciousness and so on. On this view, evolution accounts for the different *forms* that consciousness takes. But, consciousness, in some primal form, did not emerge at any particular stage of evolution. Rather, it was there from the beginning. Its emergence, with the birth of the universe, is neither more nor less mysterious than the emergence of matter and energy.

Most discontinuity theorists take it for granted that consciousness could only have appeared (out of nothing) through some random mutation in complex life forms that happened to confer a reproductive advantage (inclusive survival fitness) that can be specified in third-person functional terms. This deeply ingrained, pre-theoretical assumption has set the agenda for what discontinuity theorists believe they need to explain. Within cognitive psychology, for example, consciousness has been thought by one or another theorist to be necessary for every major phase of human information processing – for example in the analysis of complex or novel input, learning, memory, problem solving, planning, creativity, and the control and monitoring of complex, adaptive response. It should be apparent that continuity theory shifts this agenda. The persistence of different, emergent biological forms may be governed by reproductive advantage. If each of these biological forms has a unique, associated consciousness, then matter and consciousness co-evolve. However, conventional evolutionary theory does not claim that *matter itself* came into being, or persists through random mutation and reproductive advantage. According to continuity theory, neither does consciousness.

Which view is correct? One must choose for oneself. In the absence of anything other than arbitrary criteria for when consciousness suddenly emerged, I confess that I find continuity theory to be the more elegant. Continuity in the evolution of consciousness favours continuity in the distribution of consciousness, although there may be critical transition points in the *forms* of consciousness associated with the development of life, representation, self-representation, and so on.[9]

The role of conscious causation

My preference for continuity theory is also motivated by the detailed analysis given in Chapters 4, 5, 10 and 13 of what consciousness *does*. Discontinuity theory requires a *third-person causal role for consciousness*. However, close scrutiny of the processes that actually carry out analysis, storage, transformation and output of information in the human brain does not support the view that first-person phenomenal consciousness is required for information processing in the human brain (viewed from a third-person perspective). The same functions, operating to the same specification, could be performed by a nonconscious machine. The macroscopic physical world is causally closed. Investigation of the way conscious phenomenology actually relates to so-called 'conscious processing' confirms this view. The detailed operations of most processes that we think of as 'conscious' are not available to introspection. And the conscious experiences themselves seem to come *too late* to affect the processes to which they most obviously relate. Given this, it is not easy to see how conscious experiences confer a third-person, reproductive advantage by *enhancing* the processes to which they most obviously relate.

But this third-person view of what is going on violates our natural intuition that consciousness is *central* to human life. Viewed from a first-person perspective, nearly all our sophisticated mental activities seem to depend on it. We seem to need it whenever our interactions with the world are novel, flexible, or complex. And it is hard to know what it would even mean to think, feel, remember, plan, or dream if one were not conscious. In short, from a third-person perspective, phenomenal consciousness appears to play no causal role in mental life, while from a first-person perspective it appears to be central. This is the 'Causal Paradox'.

In Chapter 13, I have suggested a way to reconcile these seemingly conflicting third- and first-person views about what consciousness does. It is not the case that third-person accounts are true and first-person accounts are false (or vice versa). Rather, one needs the view from both perspectives to obtain a full account of what is going on. Viewed from a third-person perspective, human consciousness appears to be a late-arising product of focal-attentive processing. Focal-attentive processing is far more sophisticated than non-attended processing. Consequently, the difference between focal-attentive and non-attended processing accounts for the functional differences between so-called 'conscious processing' and 'nonconscious processing'. This does not violate the principle that the macrocosmic physical world is causally closed, and it does not require first-person phenomenal consciousness to have a third-person causal role.

But this does not explain the importance of consciousness in human life. Viewed from a first-person perspective, our percepts, thoughts, and emotions seem to affect everything that we do. Why? All our experiences are *of* something. They *represent* what is going on in the external world, the body and the mind/brain itself, in a way that is appropriate for ordinary life. Consequently, for everyday purposes it serves us well to treat our conscious representations as if they *are* the realities they represent. Physics, biology, psychology and other sciences might represent the same entities, events and processes in other ways, so our experiences are not the *things-themselves*. But this does not diminish the value of conscious experiences. In any case, third-person scientific accounts are *also* representations, based on the observations/experiences of external observers. For some purposes, third-person accounts are more useful, but for other purposes, first-person accounts may be more useful. And when these accounts are accurate and of the same thing, they need not conflict. For example, in the precise ways suggested in Chapter 13, first- and third-person accounts of consciousness and its neural correlates may describe the operations of mind, developing over time, viewed in two, complementary ways.

The sense in which conscious free will is an illusion

Viewing conscious experiences as *representations* and viewing first- and third-person accounts as *complementary* is particularly useful in the understanding of *conscious free will*. We normally think of ourselves as being *consciously in charge* of what we do. Yet there is compelling evidence that by the time that we are consciously aware of a wish to do something, the mind/brain has already prepared to do it – and even a decision *not* to do something appears to have its own, preconscious antecedents.[10] This scientific finding has major implications for our understanding of personal agency, ethics and legal systems.

In what sense do such scientific findings make conscious free will an illusion? Only in the sense that the causal role of *any* conscious experience in a 'conscious mental process' can be said to be an illusion. In Velmans (1991a) I have suggested that a mental process might 'be conscious' (a) in the sense that one is conscious *of* it, (b) in the sense that it *results* in a conscious experience, and (c) in the sense that conscious experience plays a *causal role* in that process (see Chapter 10). Once one experiences a wish to do something the volitional processes represented by that experience become conscious in the sense that we become conscious *of* them (sense (a)). Preconscious decision-making processes can also be said to become conscious once they *result* in a conscious free will experience (sense (b)). However the paradoxes surrounding the causal interactions of consciousness and brain give us many reasons to doubt that the experience of will actually *governs* the choices and decisions required for voluntary control (sense (c)). In sum, an experience of will can arise from voluntary processes and represent them without governing them. We nevertheless feel that our conscious experience of will *determines* our decisions and actions. That is the illusion.

Following a long programme of research into experienced free will, the psychologist Daniel Wegner (2002, 2004) has recently come to similar conclusions. Being *representations* of preconscious and unconscious mental processes, conscious experiences can also, occasionally, be *mis*representations, and Wegner provides various examples of misattributed volition (where people believe themselves to have willed an act that was determined by external forces, or believe external forces to have determined acts that they actually carried out themselves). That is a second sense in which experienced free will can be an illusion.

The sense in which conscious free will is not an illusion

Such illusions of free will suggest that it may be causally epiphenomenal, which has threatening consequences for our moral and legal judgements, let alone our visions of our own agency. Consequently, Wegner is concerned, as I am, to discern any *other* sense in which experienced will is not an illusion. According to him, 'conscious will' is a feeling that informs us whether we, or an external agency, are the author of an act, and helps us keep tally of what we are doing and what we have done (Wegner, 2002, p. 328). This in turn helps establish a sense of who we are and gives us a sense of responsibility that leads to morality. I entirely agree – but only because this is a true story told from a *first-person perspective*, which does not, unfortunately, escape epiphenomenalism. Why not? Our conscious sense of 'who we are', of 'authorship', and of 'responsibility' are as much experiences as are experiences of free will. And preconscious and unconscious processes construct our sense of self, authorship, and feeling of responsibility as much as they do our feeling of will. If from the perspective of brain science experienced will is epiphenomenal, then from the perspective of brain science the same can be said of these other experiences.

How can we move beyond this impasse? As noted above, conscious experiences can be representations not just of our own minds, but also of our bodies and the surrounding physical world. In everyday life we behave as 'naïve realists'. We habitually take the events that we experience to *be* the events that are actually taking place. Although sciences such as physics, biology and psychology might represent the same events in very different ways, this approximation usually serves us well.

How does this bear on the status of conscious free will? To the extent that experiences of wishing, deciding and so on accurately represent the operation of our voluntary mental processes they are not an illusion. Human decision-making processes are both sophisticated and flexible. Although conscious representations *of* those processes can be inaccurate, they can also be accurate – and evolution has ensured that mental representations (conscious or not) are more often right than wrong. When we feel we are free to choose or refuse an act, within the constraints of biology and social circumstances imposed on us, we usually *are* free to choose or refuse (having calculated the odds in the light of inner needs and goals, likely consequences, and so on). When we feel that we are not free to choose, for example when under external coercion, or when we feel that we do not have voluntary motor control, for example over muscle twitches, we usually *are not* free to choose or control what we do. In sum, our experienced free will is an accurate, albeit rough and ready, representation of what is going on in our own minds. In this sense, it is *not* an illusion.

How could a preconsciously determined act be 'voluntary'? Voluntary acts imply the possibility of choice, albeit choice within *constraints*. We can only choose to act within the range of human possibility, constrained by heredity and environment, past experience, inner needs and goals, available strategies, current options offered by physical and social contexts and so on. Voluntary acts are also potentially flexible and capable of being novel. In the psychological literature such properties are traditionally associated with controlled rather than automatic processing and with focal-attentive rather than pre-attentive or non-attended processing. I do not deny that voluntary processes are controlled and focal-attentive. Nor do I deny that they are conscious. They are conscious in sense (b) and, to a lesser degree, sense (a) above. They are merely not conscious in sense (c). In Libet's experiments the conscious wish to act appears around 350 milliseconds after the onset of preconscious preparations to act that are indexed by the readiness potential (see Chapter 10). This says something about the timing of the conscious wish in relation to the processes that generate it and about its restricted role once it appears. But it does not argue against the voluntary nature of that preconscious processing. On the contrary, the fact that the act consciously feels as if it is voluntary and controlled suggests that the processes that have generated that feeling *are* voluntary and controlled, as conscious experiences generally provide reasonably accurate representations of what is going on.

In sum, the feeling that we are free to choose or to exercise control is compatible with the nature of what is actually taking place in our own mind/brain, following processes that select amongst available options, in accordance with current needs, goals, available strategies, calculations of likely consequences and so on. While I assume that such processes operate according to determinate principles, the system architecture that embodies them has degrees of freedom that allow us to exercise the choice, flexibility and control that we experience – a form of determinism that is compatible with experienced free will.

What are the consequences for our agency, ethics and legal systems? If preconscious processes in my mind/brain rather than my consciously experienced wishes and decisions are in control of what I do, am I really in charge? And am I ethically and legally responsible for my acts? Yes I am. While my conscious experiences of self, of wishing, deciding and so on might only *represent* the underlying processes that are really responsible, I *am* these underlying processes as well as their manifestation in conscious experience. I (the agent) include the operations of my unconscious and preconscious mind embedded in the world, as well as my conscious wishes, decisions, and my conscious sense of self.

What consciousness adds

The representational function of consciousness get very close to what consciousness adds to our lives, but does not, in my view, quite get to the heart of the matter. As noted in Chapter 13, there is nothing about first-person representations (or third-person representations) that *requires* them to be conscious. One can have representations of oneself or of others from a given observer's perspective that are entirely nonconscious.[11] Conscious experiences nevertheless represent what is going on in a very special way. There is a big difference between having something described to us and experiencing it for ourselves. And there is an even bigger difference between actually experiencing a given situation or state and merely having unconscious information about it (stored, for example, in long-term memory). It is only once we experience something for ourselves that we *real-ise* what it is like. It is only when we experience something for ourselves that it becomes subjectively real. In this, *consciousness is the creator of subjective realities*.

Consciousness and evolution

How does this bear on the role of consciousness in evolution? While there are a number of variants of evolutionary theory, they all account for the persistence of certain life forms or functions in terms of a reproductive advantage that can be described in third-person terms. Viewed from this perspective, the physical correlates of consciousness and the information that they encode *already* account for any role that the information displayed in experience might have in the brain's processing. So it is not obvious what the reproductive advantage of *experiencing* such information might be. As Daniel Dennett puts it, 'it is not a difference that makes a difference'. Viewed from a third-person perspective, 'the creation of subjective realities' is not a function of the 'right kind'.

There is a clear choice at this point. One can either view the role of consciousness exclusively from a third-person perspective, or one has to accept that to make sense of its nature and function, third-person accounts need to be supplemented by first-person accounts. Behaviourist psychology and reductionist philosophy of mind take the first path. I have argued for the second (see also Velmans, 1991a, 1991b, 1993b).

Does the absence of a third-person function for consciousness raise doubts about its existence, evolution or importance? No. Its existence is a primary datum, and its forms may co-evolve with the material forms with which it is associated. Given its first-person nature it is appropriate to assess its importance to life and survival *from the perspective of the beings that have it*. Making things subjectively real has an immediate, all-encompassing, first-person impact (it makes the difference between having a *phenomenal world* or not). From a first-person view, it is obvious how this affects our life and survival. Without it, life would be like nothing. So without it there would be no *point* to survival (Box 14.1).

Box 14.1 Would you choose reproductive fitness or consciousness?

If we leave our theoretical biases to one side for a moment, it is easy to illustrate how consciousness gives meaning to existence.

Imagine that you are 21, in full health but you have no children. Tragically, you catch a fatal illness and have just a few days to live. However the doctors know of two drugs that can save your life, *nocon* and *nokid*. Unfortunately each drug has serious side effects. If you take *nocon* your life would be saved and your biological and behavioural functioning would be entirely normal, including your ability to have many children. However, you for ever, irreversibly lose consciousness. If you take *nokid* your life would be saved and your conscious experience would be entirely normal. Your biological and behavioural functioning would also be normal, with one exception. You for ever, irreversibly lose the ability to have children (by natural or any artificial means). Which drug would you choose?

What makes this little thought experiment interesting is that it directly pits the ability to reproduce (which is absolutely fundamental to evolutionary theory) against the ability to experience. If consciousness is just a means to enhance our reproductive fitness, we should opt to retain this fitness and choose *nocon*. I have tried this thought experiment with many students and they overwhelmingly choose to take *nokid*. Why? Because without the ability to experience anything, life would have no point.

Nor is this scenario entirely fanciful. Imagine that you are about to have a major operation that will require a life support machine, and that there is a serious risk of permanent, irreversible coma. Consequently, before the operation, you make a living will. Once it was *certain* that the coma was permanent and irreversible, would you choose to have the machine switched off?

Accounts of human life or survival in terms of whether it *has a point* fit ill with current, mechanistic accounts of nature. But, I repeat that such mechanistic accounts of how nature appears viewed 'from the outside' simply do not address *what it is like to be* a bit of that nature 'from the inside'. We *know* what it is like to be conscious. The delight in being able to experience ourselves and the world in which we live in an indefinitely large number of ways, or the sorrow of losing one's vision or one's hearing, are *subjectively real*. This reality is not diminished by our inability to explain it in entirely, third-person, inclusive-fitness terms. Our own first-person nature is as much part of the natural world as the functioning of our bodies, and, in the long run, our theories of mind need to accommodate *all* the data. If, after our best efforts, we cannot squeeze what are, in their essence, first-person phenomena into a third-person 'box', so be it. The alternative is to broaden our theories of mind to encompass first-person phenomena. Once one accepts that first- and third-person accounts of the mind are complementary and mutually irreducible, this is easy to do.

Self-consciousness in a reflexive universe

A universe that includes conscious creatures like ourselves has a very different 'feel' from one that simply follows the dead hand of mechanism. This difference becomes evident if we imagine a universe in which conscious creatures are progressively removed. In the ways noted in Chapter 8, the phenomenal world that humans experience is determined by the structure of human sense organs and by the nature of human perceptual and cognitive processing. It is a *representation* of entities, events and processes but it is not the *thing-itself*. In so far as this mix of sensory, perceptual and cognitive processing is unique to humans, this phenomenal reality is species-specific. If we remove human beings, the world would still be there, but the *phenomenal reality* experienced by humans, with its unique sense of being a human self in the world, would no longer exist.

There might, of course, be beings on other planets and there might be many other subjective realities experienced by other animals on our own planet, each with its own mix of sensory, perceptual and cognitive processing. But if we remove all creatures that have a form of self-awareness there would be no sense of 'being a self'. If we then remove all creatures with representational consciousness there would be no consciousness that was *of* anything. And if we removed all sense of what it was like to be something from entities in the universe, it might continue to exist, but it would have no sense of being anything. Such a universe would be without meaning and purpose – and it would be just like the entirely mechanical world described by reductionist, third-person science. In my view, this is *not* a complete view of the universe in which we live.

In 1925, Carl Jung, while travelling in Africa, was moved by similar thoughts:

From Nairobi we used a small Ford to visit the Athi Plains, a great game preserve. From a low hill in this broad savanna a magnificent prospect opened out to us. To the very brink of the horizon we saw gigantic herds of animals: gazelle, antelope, gnu, zebra, warthog, and so on. Grazing, heads nodding, the herds moved forward like slow rivers. There was scarcely any sound save the melancholy cry of a bird of prey. This was the stillness of the eternal beginning, the world as it had always been, in the state of nonbeing; for until then no one had been present to know that it was this world. I walked away from my companions until I had put them out of sight, and savoured the feeling of being entirely alone. There I was now, the first human being to recognize that this was the world, but who did not know that in this moment he had first really created it. . . . There the cosmic meaning of consciousness became overwhelmingly clear to me. 'What nature leaves imperfect, the art perfects,' say the alchemists. Man, I, in an invisible act of creation put the stamp of perfection on the world by giving it objective existence. This act we usually ascribe to the Creator alone, without considering that in so doing we view life as a machine calculated down to the last detail, which, along with the human psyche, runs on senselessly, obeying foreknown and predetermined rules. In such a cheerless clockwork fantasy there is no drama of man, world, and God: there is no 'new day' leading to 'new shores', but only the dreariness of calculated processes. My old Pueblo friend came to mind. He thought that the 'raison d'être' of his pueblo had been to help their father, the sun, to cross the sky each day. I had envied him for the fullness of meaning in that belief, and had been looking about without hope for a myth of my own. Now I knew what it was, and knew even more: that man is indispensable for the completion of creation; that, in fact, he himself is the second creator of the world, who alone has given to the world its objective existence – without which, unheard, unseen, silently eating, giving birth, dying, heads nodding through the millions of years, it would have gone on in the profoundest night of non-being down to its unknown end. Human consciousness created objective existence and meaning, and man found his indispensable place in the great process of being.

(Jung, 1983, p. 284)

In this vision, life and evolution have a purpose that can only be understood in first-person terms. For the reasons set out in Chapters 8 and 13, I find it useful to think of consciousness as the creator of 'subjective realities', rather than 'objective existence', and would argue for a less anthropocentric view. Whether one prefers to think of realities immensely larger than oneself as 'God', the 'Universe', or the 'Natural World' is also a matter of personal choice. But the essential insight is the same: consciousness gives meaning to existence. This is a perennial theme,[12] as old as recorded history. One finds it, for example, in ancient Egypt in 'The revelation of the Soul of

Shu', inscribed on the coffin of Gwa, a physician-sage of the twelfth dynasty (circa 1850–1650 BC):[13]

> *I am SHU*
> *The dweller within the one million beings.*
> *I gain awareness from them.*
> *I disseminate to his own generations the word*
> *Of the one that creates himself from himself.*
> *The generations will identify me.*
> *With the great mystical ship steered*
> *By him who liberates his being from his own Self.*
> *For I have seen the abyss becoming I.*
> *He knew not the place in which I became*
> *Nor did he see me becoming his own face.*
> *I forge my Soul in creating the concept of my Soul*
> *Within the dwellers of the lake of fire.*
> *My becoming is the force of the entire Creation*
> *Which flows forth from the great lord*
> *Of THIS.*

Whatever the full truth of this may be, who can doubt that our bodies *and* our experience are an integral part of the universe? And who can doubt that each one of us has a unique, conscious perspective on the larger universe of which we are a part? In this sense, we participate in a process whereby the universe observes itself – and the universe becomes both the subject and object of experience. Consciousness and matter are intertwined in mind. Through the evolution of matter, consciousness is given *form*. And through consciousness, the material universe is *real-ised*.

Notes

1 See for example the discussion of Posner and Snyder (1975) in Chapter 10 and the discussion of Edelman and Tononi (2000) in Chapter 11.

2 A simple example of the inhibition of conscious experience consequent on re-direction of attention is provided by hypnotic analgesia (see Oakley and Eames, 1985; Crawford *et al.*, 1998). Conversely, dramatic evidence of the effect of release from inhibition on action and consciousness occurs with alien hand syndrome in split-brain patients. Dimond (1980) and Scepkowski and Cronin-Golomb (2003) review evidence that in such patients the left hemisphere continues the attempt to assert dominance over the right in the control of action, although, with the corpus callosum severed and the consequent inability to inhibit right hemisphere activity, it cannot always successfully do so. Sperry *et al.* (1979) also review evidence that once the corpus callosum is sectioned each hemisphere has a distinct associated consciousness of its own (although this issue is controversial). A general review of the role of release from inhibition in selective attention is given by Arbuthnott (1995).

3 It is not easy to categorise this hybrid position. Chalmers generally calls it 'naturalistic dualism' (e.g. Chalmers, 2007) but, sometimes, 'double aspect' theory. As

far as I can judge, these are mutually exclusive positions (see Chapters 2 and 3). On the one hand, Chalmers argues that phenomenal properties and their physical correlates in the brain will be structurally coherent, in the sense that they will encode the same information. On these grounds Chalmers justifiably describes his position as a 'double-aspect theory of information'. In this respect, his 1995 paper and 1996 book appear to recapitulate the 'dual-aspect theory of information' which I presented in a series of *Behavioral and Brain Sciences* papers (1991a, 1991b, 1993b). On the other hand, dual aspects have to be aspects *of* something. Consequently my own analysis adopted a form of nonreductionist monism (ontological monism combined with epistemological dualism). That is, the one thing is the 'nature of mind', which can be known in complementary first- and third-person ways (see Chapter 13). Chalmers prefers to avoid positing some fundamental ground for physical and phenomenal properties and therefore usually describes his position as a form of 'naturalistic dualism' in which consciousness is 'basic' in the same sense that energy is basic in physics. This raises the question, 'If phenomenal and physical properties are equally basic, distinct, and not grounded in something more fundamental, then what is it that *relates* them to each other so precisely?' Alternatively, if phenomenal properties 'supervene' on physical ones (as he argues throughout his 1996 book), then why regard the phenomenal properties as 'basic'? As far as I know, Chalmers has not addressed these fundamental problems. I give a more thorough analysis of Chalmers's arguments in my review of his 1996 book (Velmans, 1997).

4   Note that for this experiment to achieve its aim, it is essential to replace the neural (or other physical) *correlates* of a given conscious experience with the silicon implant rather than any other circuitry that causes or otherwise supports the formation of such correlates. It would not, for example, be instructive (for this purpose) to replace a sense organ with an equivalently functioning implant – as this would merely restore the link between external stimuli and the existing neural circuitry, which would support conscious experience in the normal way. This already happens for example with cochlear implants.

5   This argument is a simplified version of 'A cortical implant for blindsight' (Velmans, 1995a). In his reply to my commentary on his 1995 paper (and to my review of his book) Chalmers suggests that this line of argument is 'weak'. However he does not actually point out any weakness.

6   See, for example, the discussion in Chapter 5 of John Searle's point that for something to be a symbol, it needs to be a symbol *to* someone (otherwise states in a virtual machine are just physical states).

7   What unifies the consciousness of a particular being or entity is a deep question that I will not elaborate on here. In our own case, we have the subjective impression of having a relatively unified consciousness in which the whole of our being participates, although it may be that, at any given moment, only a given subpopulation of cortical neurons form the actual neural correlates of consciousness. Under normal circumstances, we do not have separate hand consciousness, foot consciousness, cellular consciousness and so on (a pain in the foot is 'our' pain rather than the foot's pain). How this occurs is not well understood – although neural binding, inhibition of non-attended states, and widespread dissemination of attended-to information are likely to be contributory factors. It is tempting to speculate that there may also be some more general process associated with the manner in which the individual components of entities lose their separate, physical identities once they are integrated into the higher order entities of which they are parts. In so far as the parts have any associated experiences, these may be integrated, in parallel fashion, into some unified global experience.

8   Although in complex life forms such as ourselves much of this consciousness may be inhibited, for example when information is not at the focus of attention. There

have been many defenders of panpsychism including Spinoza, Leibniz, Lotze, Fechner, Wundt and James. The nonreductive unification of matter and consciousness that is implicit in panpsychism has, in recent years, led to a resurgence of interest in this position, particularly in the form defended by Whitehead (see for example the review of panpsychism by Skrbina, 2005a, 2005b; De Quincy, 2002; and the readings on Whitehead in Weber and Desmond, 2008). A physicalist version of panpsychism has also recently been defended by Strawson (2006).

 9 I should stress again, however, that my theoretical preference is tangential to my formal analysis of consciousness in Chapters 1 to 13. This focuses entirely on ordinary *human* consciousness, so it does not depend on the wider distribution of consciousness.

10 See discussion in Chapter 10 and a further discussion of this issue in Libet (2003b) and Velmans (2003b, 2004).

11 The same point has also been been put by David Galin (in an online conference on first- and third-person approaches to the study of emotion, organised by the University of Arizona, February, 1999) – and Metzinger (1997, 2003) has suggested what some of the functional characteristics of a first-person view might be.

12 See, for example, Neumann (1973), Edinger (1984), and Wilber (1996).

13 This coffin is in the collection of the British Museum – see Reed, 1987, pp. 145–150. I am grateful to the essayist Emilios Bouratinos for bringing this to my attention. The text follows the translation from the original exactly, but, for clarity, I have added my own prose-poem structure.

References

Abernathy, B. (1981) 'Mechanisms of skill in cricket batting', *Australian Journal of Sports Medicine* 13: 3–10.

Abrahamsen, A. and Bechtel, W. (2006) 'Phenomena and mechanisms: putting the symbolic, connectionist, and dynamical systems debate in broader perspective', in R. Stainton (ed.) *Contemporary Debates in Cognitive Science*. Oxford: Basil Blackwell.

Aleksander, I. (1996) *Impossible Minds: My Neurons, My Consciousness*. London: Imperial College Press.

Aleksander, I. (2007) 'Machine consciousness', in M. Velmans and S. Schneider (eds) *The Blackwell Companion to Consciousness*. Malden, MA: Blackwell, pp. 87–98.

Alter, T. (2007) 'The knowledge argument', in M. Velmans and S. Schneider (2007) (eds) *The Blackwell Companion to Consciousness*. Malden, MA: Blackwell, pp. 371–380.

Amoore, J.E. (1977) 'Specific anosmia and the concept of primary odors', *Chemical Senses and Flavor* 2: 267–281.

Applewhite, P.B. (1975) 'Learning in bacteria, fungi, and plants', in W.C. Corning, J.A. Dyal and A.O.D. Willows (eds) *Invertebrate Learning, Vol. 3: Cephalopods and Echinoderms*. New York and London: Plenum Press.

Arbib, M. (ed.) (2002) *The Handbook of Brain Theory and Neural Networks*, 2nd edn. Cambridge, MA: MIT Press.

Arbuthnott, K.D. (1995) 'Inhibitory mechanisms in cognition: phenomena and models', *Cahiers de Psychologie Cognitive* 14(1): 3–45.

Armstrong, D.M. (1968) *A Materialist Theory of Mind*. London: Routledge & Kegan Paul.

Aserinsky, E. and Kleitman, N. (1953) 'Regularly occurring periods of eye motility and concomitant phenomena during sleep', *Science* 118: 273–274.

Ashley, J. (1973) *Journey into Silence*. London: Bodley Head.

Ashmead, D.H., Wall, R., Eaton, R.S., Ebinger, S.B., Snook-Hill, K.A., Guth, M. and Xuefeng, D.Y. (1998) 'Echolocation reconsidered: using spatial variations in the ambient sound field to guide locomotion', *Journal of Visual Impairment and Blindness* 92(9): 615–632.

Atkinson, R.C. and Shiffrin, R.M. (1968) 'Human memory: a proposed system and its control processes', in K.W. Spence and J.T. Spence (eds) *The Psychology of Learning and Motivation, Vol. 2*. New York: Academic Press.

Atmanspacher, H. (2006) 'Quantum approaches to consciousness', in *The Stanford Encyclopedia of Philosophy*, http://plato.stanford.edu/entries/qt-consciousness/

Atmanspacher, H. and Primas, H. (2006) 'Pauli's ideas on mind and matter in the context of contemporary science', *Journal of Consciousness Studies* 13(3): 5–50.

Baars, B.J. (1988) *A Cognitive Theory of Consciousness*. New York: Cambridge University Press.

Baars, B.J. (1991) 'A curious coincidence? Consciousness as an object of scientific scrutiny fits our personal experience remarkably well', *Behavioral and Brain Sciences* 14(4): 669–670.

Baars, B.J. (1994) 'A thoroughly empirical approach to consciousness', *Psyche* 1(6), http://psyche.cs.monash.edu.au/v2/psyche-1-6-baars.html

Baars, B.J. (1997a) 'Some essential differences between consciousness and attention, perception and working memory', *Consciousness and Cognition* 6(2/3): 363–371.

Baars, B.J. (1997b) 'In the theatre of consciousness: global workspace theory, a rigorous scientific theory of consciousness', *Journal of Consciousness Studies* 4(4): 292–309.

Baars, B.J. (2007) 'The global workspace theory of consciousness', in M. Velmans and S. Schneider (eds) *The Blackwell Companion to Consciousness*. Malden, MA: Blackwell, pp. 236–246.

Baars, B.J. and McGovern, K. (1996) 'Cognitive views of consciousness: what are the facts? How can we explain them?', in M. Velmans (ed.) *The Science of Consciousness: Psychological, Neuropsychological, and Clinical Reviews*. London: Routledge.

Baars, B.J. and Newman, J.B. (1994) 'A neurobiological interpretation of global workspace theory', in A. Revonsuo and B. Kamppinen (eds) *Consciousness in Philosophy and Cognitive Neuroscience*. Hillsdale, NJ: Lawrence Erlbaum Associates.

Baars, B.J., Fehling, M.R., LaPolla, M. and McGovern, K. (1997) 'Consciousness *creates access*: conscious goal images recruit unconscious action routines, but goal competition serves to "liberate" such routines, causing predictable slips', in J.D. Cohen and J.W. Schooler (eds) *Scientific Approaches to Consciousness*. Hillsdale, NJ: Lawrence Erlbaum Associates.

Bach-y-Rita, P. (1972) *Brain Mechanisms in Sensory Substitution*. London: Academic Press.

Baddeley, A.D. (1993) 'Working memory and conscious awareness', in A.F. Collins, S.E. Gathercole, M.A. Conway and P.E. Morris (eds) *Theories of Memory*. Hillsdale, NJ: Lawrence Erlbaum Associates.

Baddeley, A.D. (2001) 'Is working memory still working?' *American Psychologist* 56: 851–864.

Bakan, D. (1980) 'On the effect of mind on matter', in R.W. Rieber (ed.) *Body and Mind: Past, Present and Future*. New York: Academic Press.

Banks, W. and Pockett, S. (2007) 'Benjamin Libet's work on the neuroscience of free will', in M. Velmans and S. Schneider (eds) *The Blackwell Companion to Consciousness*. Malden, MA: Blackwell, pp. 657–670.

Barber, T.X. (1984) 'Changing "unchangeable" bodily processes by (hypnotic) suggestions: a new look at hypnosis, cognitions, imagining, and the mind–body problem', in A.A. Sheikh (ed.) *Imagination and Healing*. Farmingdale, NY: Bayworld.

Bechtel, W. and Abrahamsen, A. (2002) *Connectionism and the Mind: Parallel Processing, Dynamics, and Evolution in Networks*, 2nd edn. Oxford: Blackwell.

Beck, F. and Eccles, J. (1992) 'Quantum aspects of brain activity and the role of consciousness', *Proceedings of the National Academy of Science USA, Biophysics* 89: 11357–11361.

Beck, F. and Eccles, J.C. (2003) 'Quantum processes in the brain: a scientific basis of consciousness', in N. Osaka (ed.) *Neural Basis of Consciousness*. Amsterdam and Philadelphia: John Benjamins, pp. 141–166.

Bekoff, M. and Jamieson, D. (eds) (1996) *Readings in Animal Cognition*. Cambridge, MA: MIT Press.

Benjamin, D., Lyons, D. and Lonsdale, D. (2006) 'Embodying a cognitive model in a mobile robot', *Proceedings of the SPIE Conference on Intelligent Robots and Computer Vision*. Boston.

Berkeley, G. (1972 [1710]) *The Principles of Human Knowledge*, ed. and introduced by G.J. Warnock. London and Glasgow: William Collins Sons & Co.

Berry, D.C. and Dienes, Z. (eds) (1993) *Implicit Learning: Theoretical and Empirical Issues*. London: Lawrence Erlbaum.

Beshkar, M. (2008) 'Animal consciousness', *Journal of Consciousness Studies* 15(3): 5–33.

Bindra, D. (1970) 'The problem of subjective experience: puzzlement on reading R.W. Sperry's "A modified concept of consciousness" ', *Psychological Review* 77(6): 581–584.

Bitbol, M. (2008) 'Is consciousness primary?' *NeuroQuantology* 6(1): 53–71.

Bjork, R.A. (1975) 'Short-term storage: the ordered output of a central processor', in F. Restle, R.M. Shiffrin, N.J. Castellan, H.R. Lindman and D.B. Pisoni (eds) *Cognitive Theory, Vol. 1*. Hillsdale, NJ: Lawrence Erlbaum Associates.

Blauert, J. (1983) *Spatial Hearing: The Psychophysics of Human Sound Localization*. Cambridge, MA: MIT Press.

Block, N. (1983) 'Mental pictures and cognitive science', *Philosophical Review* 92: 499–541.

Block, N. (1994) 'Qualia', in S. Guttenplan (ed.) *A Companion to the Philosophy of Mind*. Oxford: Blackwell.

Block, N. (1995) 'On a confusion about a function of consciousness', *Behavioral and Brain Sciences* 18(2): 227–272.

Block, N. (1997) 'Biology versus computation in the study of consciousness', *Behavioral and Brain Sciences* 20(1): 159–166.

Bock, J.K. (1982) 'Towards a cognitive psychology of syntax: information processing contributions to sentence formulation', *Psychological Review* 89: 1–47.

Boff, R., Kaufman, L. and Thomas, J.P. (1986) *Handbook of Perception and Human Performance, Vol. 1: Sensory Processes and Perception*. New York: Wiley.

Bogen, J. (1995) 'On the neurophysiology of consciousness: I. An overview', *Consciousness and Cognition* 4(1): 52–62.

Boghossian, P. and Velleman, J.D. (1989) 'Color as a secondary quality', *Mind* 98: 81–103.

Bongard, J., Zykov, V. and Lipson, H. (2006) 'Resilient machines through continuous self-modeling', *Science* 314: 1118–1121.

Boomer, D.S. (1970) 'Review of F. Goldman-Eisler *Psycholinguistics: Experiments in spontaneous speech*', *Lingua* 25: 152–164.

Boring, E. (1942) *Sensation and Perception in the History of Experimental Psychology*. New York: The Century Co.

Bousbia-Salah, M. and Fezari, M. (2007) 'A navigation tool for blind people', in T. Sobh (ed.) *Innovations and Advanced Techniques in Computer and Information Sciences and Engineering*. Berlin: Springer, pp. 333–337.

Bower, G. (1972) 'A selective review of organizational factors in memory', in E. Tulving and W. Donaldson (eds) *Organization of Memory*. New York: Academic Press.

Braun, A.R., Balkin, T.J., Wesensten, N.J., Carson, R.E., Varga, M. and Baldwin, P. (1997) 'Regional cerebral blood flow throughout the sleep–wake cycle. An H$_2$^{15}O PET study', *Brain* 120: 1173–1197.

Braun, A.R., Balkin, T.J., Wesensten, N.J., Gwadry, F., Carson, R.E., Varga, M., Baldwin, P., Belenky, G. and Herscovitch, P. (1998) 'Dissociated pattern of activity in visual cortices and their projections during human rapid eye movement sleep', *Science* 279: 91–95.

Brewer, W.F. (1974) 'There is no convincing evidence for operant or classical conditioning in adult humans', in W.B. Weimer and D.S. Palermo (eds) *Cognition and the Symbolic Process*. Hillsdale, NJ: Lawrence Erlbaum Associates.

Bridgman, P.W. (1936) *The Nature of Physical Theory*. Princeton, NJ: Princeton University Press.

Broad, C.D. (1925) *The Mind and Its Place in Nature*. London: Routledge & Kegan Paul.

Broadbent, D.E. (1958) *Perception and Communication*. New York: Pergamon Press.

Brugger, P. (1994) 'Heautoscopy, epilepsy, and suicide', *Journal of Neurology, Neurosurgery, and Psychiatry* 57: 838–839.

Byrne, A. (1994) 'Behaviourism', in S. Guttenplan (ed.) *A Companion to the Philosophy of Mind*. Oxford: Blackwell.

Campion, J., Latto, R. and Smith, Y.M. (1983) 'Is blindsight an effect of scattered light, spared cortex, and near-threshold vision?' *Behavioral and Brain Sciences* 6: 423–486.

Carr, T.H. and Bacharach, V.E. (1976) 'Perceptual tuning and conscious attention: systems of input regulation in visual information processing', *Cognition* 4: 281–302.

Carruthers, P. (1998) 'Natural theories of consciousness', *European Journal of Philosophy* 6(2): 203–222.

Castaigne, P., Lhermitte, F., Buge, A., Escourolle, R., Hauw, J.J. and Lyon-Caen, O. (1981) 'Paramedian thalamic and midbrain infarcts: clinical and neuropathological study', *Annals of Neurology* 10(2): 127–148.

Chalmers, A. (1990) *Science and its Fabrication*. Buckingham: Open University Press.

Chalmers, A. (1992) *What Is This Thing Called Science?* 2nd edn. Buckingham: Open University Press.

Chalmers, D. (1995) 'Facing up to the problem of consciousness', *Journal of Consciousness Studies* 2(3): 200–219.

Chalmers, D. (1996) *The Conscious Mind: In Search of a Fundamental Theory*. New York and Oxford: Oxford University Press.

Chalmers, D. (2007) 'Naturalistic dualism', in M. Velmans and S. Schneider (eds) *The Blackwell Companion to Consciousness*. Malden, MA: Blackwell, pp. 359–368.

Chappell, V.C. (ed.) (1962) *Philosophy of Mind*. Englewood Cliffs, NJ: Prentice-Hall.

Cheesman, J. and Merikle, P.M. (1984) 'Priming with and without awareness', *Perception and Psychophysics* 36: 387–395.

Cheesman, J. and Merikle, P.M. (1986) 'Distinguishing conscious from unconscious perceptual processes', *Canadian Journal of Psychology* 40: 343–367.

Chella, A. and Macaluso, I. (2006) Sensations and perceptions in Cicerobot, a museum guide robot. *Brain Inspired Cognitive Systems Conference (BICS, 2006)*. Canada: ICSC Academic Press.

Cherry, C. (1953) 'Some experiments on the reception of speech with one and with two ears', *Journal of the Acoustical Society of America* 25: 975–979.

Chomsky, N. (1959) 'A review of B. F. Skinner's *Verbal Behavior*', *Language* 35(1): 26–58.

Chomsky, N. (1968) *Language and the Mind*. New York: Harcourt Brace Jovanovich.

Churchland, P. (1989) *Neurophilosophy: Toward a Unified Science of the Mind/Brain*. Cambridge, MA: MIT Press.

Clark, A. (1997) *Being There: Putting Brain, Body and World Together Again*. Cambridge, MA: MIT Press.

Clifford, W.C.K. (1901 [1878]) 'On the nature of things-in-themselves', in L. Stephen and F. Pollock (eds) *Lectures and Essays by the late William Kingdom Clifford*. London: Macmillan & Co.

Colvin, M. and Gazzaniga, M. (2007) 'Split-brain cases', in M. Velmans and S. Schneider (eds) *The Blackwell Companion to Consciousness*. Malden, MA: Blackwell, pp. 181–193.

Conrad, R. (1979) *The Deaf School Child: Language and Cognitive Functions*. London: Harper & Row.

Corteen, R.S. (1986) 'Electrodermal responses to words in an irrelevant message: a partial reappraisal', *Behavioral and Brain Sciences* 9: 27–28.

Corteen, R.S. and Wood, B. (1972) 'Autonomic responses to shock-associated words in an unattended channel', *Journal of Experimental Psychology* 94: 308–313.

Craig, K.D. (1978) 'Social modelling influences on pain', in R.A. Sternbach (ed.) *The Psychology of Pain*. New York: Raven Press.

Crawford, H.J., Knebel, T. and Vendemia, J.M.C. (1998) 'The nature of hypnotic analgesia: neurophysiological foundation and evidence', *Contemporary Hypnosis* 15(1): 22–23.

Cresswell, P. (1998) 'A more convivial perspective system', in J. Wood (ed.) *The Virtual Embodied*. London: Routledge.

Crick, F. (1984) 'Function of the thalamic reticular complex: the searchlight hypothesis', *Proceedings of the National Academy of Science USA* 81: 4586–4590.

Crick, F. (1994) *The Astonishing Hypothesis: The Scientific Search for the Soul*. London: Simon & Schuster.

Crick, F. and Koch, C. (1990) 'Toward a neurobiological theory of consciousness', *Neurosciences* 2: 263–275.

Crick, F. and Koch, C. (1998) 'Consciousness and neuroscience', *Cerebral Cortex* 8: 97–107.

Crick, F. and Koch, C. (2007) 'A neurobiological framework for consciousness', in M. Velmans and S. Schneider (eds) *The Blackwell Companion to Consciousness*. Malden, MA: Blackwell, pp. 567–579.

Crook, J.H. (1980) *The Evolution of Human Consciousness*. Oxford: Clarendon Press.

Cytowic, R.E. (1995) 'Synesthesia: phenomenology and neuropsychology: a review of current knowledge', *Psyche* 2(10): http://psyche.cs.monash.edu.au/v2/psyche-2-10-cytowic.html

Damasio, A. (1999) *The Feeling of What Happens: Body, Emotion and the Making of Consciousness*. San Diego: Harcourt.

Damasio, A.R., Grabowski, T.J., Bechera, A., Damasio, H., Ponto, L.L.B. and Parvisi, J. (2000) 'Subcortical and cortical brain activity during the feeling of self-generated emotions', *Nature Neuroscience* 3: 1049–1056.

Danckert, J., Ferber, S., Doherty, T., Steinmetz, H., Nicolle, D. and Goodale, M.A. (2002) 'Selective, non-lateralized impairment of motor imagery following right parietal damage', *Neurocase* 8(3): 194–204.

Danto, A.C. (1985) 'Consciousness and motor control', *Behavioral and Brain Sciences* 8(4): 540–541.

Davidson, D. (1970) 'Mental events', in D. Davidson, *Essays on Actions and Events*. Oxford: Oxford University Press.

Dawkins, M.S. (1998) *Through Our Eyes Only? The Search for Animal Consciousness*. Oxford: Oxford University Press.

Dawson, M.E. and Schell, A.M. (1982) 'Electrodermal responses to attended and unattended significant stimuli during dichotic listening', *Journal of Experimental Psychology: Human Perception and Performance* 8: 315–324.

de Gelder, B., de Haan, E. and Heywood, C. (eds) (2001) *Out of Mind: Varieties of Unconscious Processes*. New York: Oxford University Press.

Dehaene, S. and Naccache, L. (2001) 'Towards a cognitive neuroscience of consciousness: basic evidence and a workspace framework', *Cognition* 79: 1–37.

Dell, G.S. (1986) 'A spreading activation theory of retrieval in sentence production', *Psychological Review* 93: 283–321.

Dement, W.C. and Kleitman, N. (1957) 'The relation of eye movements during sleep to dream activity: an objective method for the study of dreaming', *Journal of Experimental Psychology* 53(3): 339–346.

Dennett, D.C. (1978) *Brainstorms: Philosophical Essays on Mind and Psychology*. Cambridge, MA: MIT Press.

Dennett, D.C. (1991) *Consciousness Explained*. London: Allen Lane.

Dennett, D.C. (1994) 'Instead of qualia', in A. Revonsuo and M. Kampinnen (eds) *Consciousness in Philosophy and Cognitive Neuroscience*. Hillsdale, NJ: Lawrence Erlbaum Associates.

Dennett, D.C. (1995) 'Cog: steps toward consciousness in robots', in T. Metzinger (ed.) *Conscious Experience*. Thorverton: Imprint Academic.

Dennett, D.C. (2003) 'Who's on first? Heterophenomenology explained', *Journal of Consciousness Studies* 10(9–10): 10–30.

Dennett, D.C. and Kinsbourne, M. (1992) 'Time and the observer: the where and when of consciousness in the brain', *Behavioral and Brain Sciences* 15: 183–200.

De Quincy, C. (2002) *Radical Nature: Rediscovering the Soul of Matter*. Montpelier, VT: Invisible Cities Press.

Deutsch, J.A. and Deutsch, D. (1963) 'Attention: some theoretical considerations', *Psychological Review* 70: 80–90.

Dewar, E.M. (1976) 'Consciousness in control systems theory', in G.G. Globus, G. Maxwell and I. Savodnik (eds) *Consciousness and the Brain*. New York: Plenum.

Dewey, J. (1991 [1910]) *How We Think*. Buffalo, NY: Prometheus.

Dimond, S.J. (1980) *Neuropsychology: A Textbook of Systems and Psychological Functions of the Human Brain*. London: Butterworths.

Dixon, N.F. (1981) *Preconscious Processing*. Chichester: Wiley.

Dooremalen, H. (2003) 'Evolution's shorthand. A presentational theory of the phenomenal mind', doctoral thesis, Tilburg University, The Netherlands.

Droscher, V.B. (1971) *The Magic of the Senses: New Discoveries in Animal Perception*. London: Panther Books.

Ducasse, C. (1960) 'In defence of dualism', in S. Hook (ed.) *Dimensions of Mind*. New York: Collier Books.

Eccles, J.C. (1980) *The Human Psyche*. New York: Springer.

Eccles, J.C. (1989) *Evolution of the Brain: Creation of the Self*. London: Routledge.

Edelman, G.M. and Tononi, G. (2000) *A Universe of Consciousness: How Matter Becomes Imagination*. New York: Basic Books.

Edinger, E.F. (1984) *The Creation of Consciousness: Jung's Myth for Modern Man*. Toronto: Inner City Books.

Einstein, A. and Infeld, L. (1938) *The Evolution of Physics: From Early Concepts to Relativity and Quanta*. New York: Clarion Books, Simon & Shuster.

Engel, A.K. and Singer, W. (2001) 'Temporal binding and the neural correlates of sensory awareness', *Trends in Cognitive Sciences* 5(1): 16–25.

Ericsson, K.A. (2003) 'Valid and non-reactive verbalisation of thought during performance of tasks: towards a solution to the central problems of introspection as a source of scientific data', in A. Jack and A. Roepstorff (eds) *Trusting the Subject? Volume 1: The Use of Introspective Evidence in Cognitive Science*. Exeter: Imprint Academic, pp. 1–18.

Ericsson, K.A. and Simon, H. (1984) *Protocol Analysis: Verbal Reports as Data*. Cambridge, MA: MIT Press.

Eysenck, M.W. and Keane, T. (2005) *Cognitive Psychology: A Student's Handbook*. Hove and New York: Psychology Press.

Falkenstein, M., Hoormann, J. and Hohnsbein, J. (1999) 'ERP components in Go/Nogo tasks and their relation to inhibition', *Acta Psychologia* 101: 267–291.

Farthing, J.W. (1992) *The Psychology of Consciousness*. Englewood Cliffs, NJ: Prentice-Hall.

Fechner, G.T. (1860) *Elemente der Psychophysik*. Leipzig: Breitkopf und Härtel; reprinted, Bristol: Thoemmes Press, 1999.

Feldman, H., Goldin-Meadow, S. and Gleitman, L.R. (1978) 'Beyond Herodotus: the creation of language by linguistically deprived children', in A. Lock (ed.) *Action, Gesture, and Symbol: The Emergence of Language*. London: Academic Press.

Ffytche, D.H., Howard, R.J., Brammer, M.J., David, A., Woodruff, P. and Williams, S. (1998) 'The anatomy of conscious vision: an fMRI study of visual hallucinations', *Nature Neuroscience* 1: 738–742.

Flew, A. (ed.) (1978) *Body, Mind, and Death*. New York: Macmillan.

Fodor, J.A., Bever, T.G. and Garrett, M.F. (1974) *The Psychology of Language*. New York: McGraw-Hill.

Fontana, D. (2007) 'Mystical experience', in M. Velmans and S. Schneider (eds) *The Blackwell Companion to Consciousness*. Malden, MA: Blackwell, pp. 163–172.

Foster, J. (1991) *The Immaterial Self: A Defence of the Cartesian Dualist Concept of Mind*. London: Routledge.

Franklin, S. (2003) 'IDA: a conscious artefact?', *Journal of Consciousness Studies* 10(4–5): 133–172.

Fuster, J.M. (1989) *The Prefrontal Cortex*. New York: Raven.

Gallagher, D. (2007) 'Phenomenological approaches to consciousness', in M. Velmans and S. Schneider (eds) *The Blackwell Companion to Consciousness*. Malden, MA: Blackwell, pp. 686–696.

Gallup, C.G. (1977) 'Chimpanzees: self-recognition', *Science* 167: 86–87.

Gallup, C.G. (1982) 'Self-awareness and the emergence of mind in primates', *American Journal of Primatology* 2: 237–248.

Ganis, G., Thompson, W.L. and Kosslyn, S.M. (2004) 'Brain areas underlying visual mental imagery and visual perception: an fMRI study', *Cognitive Brain Research* 20: 226–241.

Gardiner, J. (1996) 'On consciousness in relation to memory and learning', in M. Velmans (ed.) *The Science of Consciousness: Psychological, Neuropsychological, and Clinical Reviews*. London: Routledge.

Gardner, H. (1987) *The Mind's New Science*. New York: Basic Books.

Glicksohn, J. (1993) 'Putting consciousness in a box: once more around the track', *Behavioral and Brain Sciences* 16(2): 404.

Goldman-Eisler, F. (1968) *Psycholinguistics: Experiments in Spontaneous Speech*. New York: Academic Press.

Goodale, M. (2007) 'Duplex vision: separate cortical pathways for conscious perception and the control of action', in M. Velmans and S. Schneider (eds) *The Blackwell Companion to Consciousness*. Malden, MA: Blackwell, pp. 616–627.

Goodale, M.A. and Milner, A.D. (2004) *Sight Unseen: An Exploration of Conscious and Unconscious Vision*. New York: Oxford University Press.

Gray, C.M. (1994) 'Synchronous oscillations in neural systems: mechanisms and functions', *Journal of Computational Neuroscience* 1: 11–38.

Gray, J. (1995) 'The contents of consciousness: a neurophysiological conjecture', *Behavioral and Brain Sciences* 18(4): 659–722.

Gray, J. (2004) *Consciousness: Creeping up on the Hard Problem*. Oxford: Oxford University Press.

Green, D.M. (1976) *An Introduction to Hearing*. Hillsdale, NJ: Erlbaum.

Green, R.T. (1981) 'Beyond Turing', *Speculations in Science and Technology* 4(2): 175–186.

Greene, B. (2004) *The Fabric of the Cosmos: Space, Time, and the Texture of Reality*. New York: Knopf.

Greenwald, A.G. (1992) 'New Look 3: unconscious cognition reclaimed', *American Psychologist* 47: 766–790.

Greenwald, A.G. and Liu, T.J. (1985) 'Limited unconscious processing of meaning'. Paper presented at the annual meeting of the Psychonomic Society, Boston, MA, November.

Greenwald, A.G., Klinger, M.R. and Liu, T.J. (1989) 'Unconscious processing of dichoptically masked words', *Memory and Cognition* 17: 35–47.

Gregory, R.L. (1966) *Eye and Brain: The Psychology of Seeing*. London: Weidenfeld & Nicolson.

Gribbin, J. (1995) *Schrodinger's Kittens and the Search for Reality: Solving the Quantum Mysteries*. New York: Little, Brown & Co.

Groeger, J.A. (1984a) 'Preconscious Influences on Language Production', Ph.D. thesis, Queen's University of Belfast.

Groeger, J.A. (1984b) 'Evidence of unconscious semantic processing from a forced error situation', *British Journal of Psychology* 75: 305–314.

Groeger, J.A. (1988) 'Qualitatively different effects of undetected and unidentified auditory primes', *Quarterly Journal of Experimental Psychology* 40A: 323–329.

Grosjean, F. (1980) 'Spoken word recognition processes and the gating paradigm', *Perception and Psychophysics* 28: 267–283.

Grush, R. and Churchland, P.S. (1995) 'Gaps in Penrose's toilings', in T. Metzinger (ed.) *Conscious Experience*. Thorverton: Imprint Academic.

Gunderson, K. (1970) 'Asymmetries and mind–body complexities', in M. Radner and S. Winokur (eds) *Analyses of Theories and Methods of Physics and Psychology, Minnesota Studies in the Philosophy of Science, Vol. 4*. Minneapolis: University of Minnesota Press.

Guo, Y.X. and Kawasaki, M. (1997) 'The representation of accurate temporal information in the electrosensory system of the African electrical fish, *Gymnarchus Niloticus*', *Journal of Neuroscience* 17(5): 1761–1768.

Guttenplan, S. (ed.) (1994) *A Companion to the Philosophy of Mind.* Oxford: Blackwell.

Güzeldere, G. (1997) 'The many faces of consciousness: a field guide', in N. Block, O. Flanagan and G. Güzeldere (eds) *The Nature of Consciousness: Philosophical Debates.* Cambridge, MA: MIT Press.

Güzeldere, G. and Nahmias, E. (2000) 'Introspection reconsidered', in M. Velmans (ed.) *Investigating Phenomenal Consciousness: New Methodologies and Maps.* Amsterdam: John Benjamins.

Haber, R.N. (1979) 'Twenty years of haunting eidetic imagery: where's the ghost?' *Behavioral and Brain Sciences* 2: 583–619.

Haggard, M. and Eimer, M. (1999) 'On the relation of brain potentials and awareness of voluntary movements', *Experimental Brain Research* 126: 128–133.

Haldane, E. and Ross, G.R.T. (1931) *The Philosophical Works of Descartes.* Cambridge: Cambridge University Press.

Hameroff, S.R. and Penrose, R. (1996) 'Conscious events as orchestrated space-time selections', *Journal of Consciousness Studies* 3(1): 36–53.

Hardcastle, V.G. (1991) 'Epiphenomenalism and the reduction of experience', *Behavioral and Brain Sciences* 14(4): 680.

Harnad, S. (1990) 'The symbol grounding problem', *Physica* D42: 335–346.

Harnad, S. (1991) 'Other bodies, other minds: a machine incarnation of an old philosophical problem', *Minds and Machines* 1: 43–54.

Hart, W.D. (1995) 'Dualism', in S. Guttenplan (ed.) *A Companion to the Philosophy of Mind.* Oxford: Blackwell, pp. 265–269.

Hartelius, G. (2007) 'Quantitative somatic phenomenology', *Journal of Consciousness Studies* 14(12): 24–56.

Hashish, I., Finman, C. and Harvey, W. (1988) 'Reduction of postoperative pain and swelling by ultrasound: a placebo effect', *Pain* 83: 303–311.

Hauser, M.D., Kralik, J., Botto-Mahan, C., Garrett, M. and Oser, J. (1995) 'Self-recognition in primates: phylogeny and the salience of species-typical features', *Proceedings of the Academy of Sciences of the United States of America* 92: 10811–10814.

Hawking, S. (1988) *A Brief History of Time.* Toronto: Bantam Books.

Heath, R.G. (1996) *Exploring the Mind–Body Relationship.* Baton Rouge, LA: Moran Printing.

Hebb, D. (1949) *The Organization of Behavior.* New York: John Wiley and Sons.

Hershenson, M. (1998) *Visual Space Perception.* Cambridge: MA: MIT Press.

Hilgard, E.R. (1986) *Divided Consciousness: Multiple Controls in Human Thought and Action.* New York: Wiley-Interscience.

Hobbes, T. (1991 [1651]) *Leviathan*, ed. R. Tuck. Cambridge: Cambridge University Press.

Hobson, J.A. (2007) 'Normal and abnormal states of consciousness', in M. Velmans and S. Schneider (eds) *The Blackwell Companion to Consciousness.* Malden, MA: Blackwell, pp. 101–113.

Hoche, H.-U. (2007) 'Reflexive monism versus complementarism: an analysis and criticism of the conceptual groundwork of Max Velmans's model of consciousness', *Phenomenology and the Cognitive Sciences* 6: 389–409.

Hocken, S. (1977) *Emma and I*. London: Victor Gollancz.

Holender, D. (1986) 'Semantic activation without conscious identification in dichotic listening, parafoveal vision, and visual masking', *Behavioral and Brain Sciences* 9: 1–66.

Holland, O. (2007) 'A strongly embodied approach to machine consciousness', *Journal of Consciousness Studies* 14(7): 97–110.

Holmes, E. and Yost, M. (1966) 'Behavioral studies in the sensitive plant', *Worm Runners Digest* 8: 38.

Holstege, G., Georgiadis, J.R., Paans, A.M., Meiners, L.C., van der Graaf, F.H. and Reinders, A.A. (2003) 'Brain activation during human male ejaculation', *Journal of Neuroscience* 23: 9185–9193.

Honderich, T. (2006) 'Radical externalism', *Journal of Consciousness Studies* 13(7–8): 3–13.

Hopfield, J. (1982) 'Neural networks and physical systems with emergent collective computational abilities', *Proceedings of the National Academy of Sciences, USA* 79: 2554–2558.

Hughes, G. (2008) 'Is consciousness required to inhibit an impending action? Evidence from event-related brain potentials', PhD thesis, Goldsmiths, University of London.

Hughes, G., Velmans, M. and de Fockert, J. 'Unconscious priming of a no-go response', *Psychophysiology* (in press).

Hume, D. (1965 [1739]) *A Treatise of Human Nature*, ed. L.A. Selby-Bigge. Oxford: Oxford University Press.

Humphrey, N. (1983) *Consciousness Regained*. Oxford: Oxford University Press.

Hurlburt, R.T. and Akhter, S.A. (2006) 'The Descriptive Experience Sampling method', *Phenomenology and the Cognitive Sciences* 5: 271–301.

Husserl, E. (1931) *Ideas. General Introduction to Pure Phenomenology*, trans. [from Husserl 1913] W.R. Boyce Gibson. New York: Collier Books.

Jack, A. and Roepstorff, A. (eds) (2003) *Trusting the Subject? Vol. 1: The Use of Introspective Evidence in Cognitive Science*. Exeter: Imprint Academic.

Jack, A. and Roepstorff, A. (eds) (2004) *Trusting the Subject? Vol. 2: The Use of Introspective Evidence in Cognitive Science*. Exeter: Imprint Academic.

Jackson, F. (1986) 'What Mary didn't know', *Journal of Philosophy* 83: 291–295.

James, W. (1890) *The Principles of Psychology*. New York: Henry Holt.

James, W. (1970 [1904]) 'Does "consciousness" exist?', in G.N.A. Vesey (ed.) *Body and Mind: Readings in Philosophy*. London: Allen & Unwin.

Jaynes, J. (1979) *The Origin of Consciousness in the Breakdown of the Bicameral Mind*. London: Allen Lane.

Jeannerod, M. (2007) 'Consciousness of action', in M. Velmans and S. Schneider (eds) *The Blackwell Companion to Consciousness*. Malden, MA: Blackwell, pp. 540–550.

Jerison, H.J. (1985) 'On the evolution of mind', in D.A. Oakley (ed.) *Brain and Mind*. London: Methuen.

John, E.R. (1976) 'A model of consciousness', in G. Schwartz and D. Shapiro (eds) *Consciousness and Self-Regulation*. New York: Plenum Press.

Johnson-Laird, P.N. (1988) 'A computational analysis of consciousness', in A. Marcel and E. Bisiach (eds) *Consciousness and Contemporary Science*. Oxford: Oxford University Press.

Jones, W.H.S. (1923) *Hippocrates, Vol. 2*, Cambridge, MA: Harvard University Press and William Heinemann.

Julien, R.M. (2004) *A Primer of Drug Action: A Concise, Non-technical Guide to the Actions, Uses, and Side Effects of Psychoactive Drugs*, 10th edn. New York: W.H. Freeman.

Jung, C.G. (1983) *Memories, Dreams, Reflections.* London: Harper Collins.

Kahneman, D. (1973) *Attention and Effort.* Englewood Cliffs, NJ: Prentice-Hall.

Kahneman, D. and Treisman, A. (1984) 'Changing views of attention and automaticity', in R. Parasuraman and D.R. Davies (eds) *Varieties of Attention.* Orlando, FL: Academic Press.

Kant, I. (1978 [1781]) 'Paralogisms of pure reason', in *Immanuel Kant's Critique of Pure Reason*, trans. N.K. Smith. London: Macmillan.

Karrer, R., Warren, C. and Ruth, R. (1978) 'Slow potentials of the brain preceding cued and non-cued movement: effects of development and retardation', in D.A. Otto (ed.) *Multidisciplinary Perspectives in Event-Related Potential Research.* Washington, DC: US Government Printing Office.

Kihlstrom, J.F. (1987) 'The cognitive unconscious', *Science* 237: 1445–1452.

Kihlstrom, J.F. (1996) 'Perception without awareness of what is perceived, learning without awareness of what is learned', in M. Velmans (ed.) *The Science of Consciousness: Psychological, Neuropsychological, and Clinical Reviews.* London: Routledge.

Kihlstrom, J.F. and Cork, R.C. (2007) 'Consciousness and anesthesia', in M. Velmans and S. Schneider (eds) *The Blackwell Companion to Consciousness.* Malden, MA: Blackwell, pp. 628–639.

Kihlstrom, J.F., Dorfman, J. and Park, L. (2007) 'Implicit and explicit memory and learning', in M. Velmans and S. Schneider (eds) *The Blackwell Companion to Consciousness.* Malden, MA: Blackwell, pp. 525–539.

Kim, J. (1993) *Supervenience and Mind.* Cambridge: Cambridge University Press.

Kim, J. (2005) *Physicalism, or Something Near Enough.* Princeton, NJ: Princeton University Press.

Kim, J. (2007) 'The causal efficacy of consciousness', in M. Velmans and S. Schneider (eds) *The Blackwell Companion to Consciousness.* Malden, MA: Blackwell, pp. 406–417.

Kish, D. (2002) 'Echolocation: how humans can "see" without sight', www. worldaccessfortheblind.org/echolocationreview.rtf

Kiverstein, J. (2007) 'Could a robot have a subjective point of view?', *Journal of Consciousness Studies* 14(7): 127–140.

Knutson, B., Burgdorf, J. and Panksepp, J. (2002) 'Ultrasonic vocalisations as indices of affective states in rats', *Psychological Bulletin* 128: 961–977.

Kohler, I. (1962) 'Experiments with goggles', *Scientific American* 206: 62–72.

Köhler, S. and Moscovitch, M. (1997) 'Unconscious visual processing in neuropsychological syndromes: a survey of the literature and evaluation of models of consciousness', in M.D. Rugg (ed.) *Cognitive Neuroscience.* Hove: Psychology Press.

Köhler, W. (1966) 'A task for philosophers', in P.K. Feyerabend and G. Maxwell (eds) *Mind, Matter and Method: Essays in Philosophy of Science in Honour of Herbert Feigl.* Minneapolis: University of Minnesota Press.

Kolb, B. and Whishaw, I.Q. (2003) *Fundamentals of Human Neuropsychology*, 5th edn. New York: Worth Publishers.

Konttinen, N. and Lyytinen, H. (1993) 'Brain slow waves preceding time-locked visuo-motor performance', *Journal of Sport Sciences* 11: 257–266.

Kornhuber, H.H. and Deeke, L. (1965) 'Hirnpotentialänderungen bei willkürbewegungen und passiven bewegungen des menchen: bereitschaftspotential und reafferente potentiale', *Pflügers Archiv für die Gesampte Physiologie des Menschen und Tiere* 284: 1–17.

Kosslyn. S.M. and Thomson, W.L. (2003) 'When is early visual cortex activated during visual mental imagery?' *Psychological Bulletin* 129: 723–746.

Kucera, H. and Francis, W.M. (1967) *Computational Analysis of Present-day American English*. Providence, RI: Brown University Press.

Külpe, O. (1901) *Outlines of Psychology*. New York: Macmillan.

La Berge, D. (1981) 'Automatic information processing: a review', in J. Long and A. Baddeley (eds) *Attention and Performance IX*. Hillsdale, NJ: Erlbaum.

Lachman, R., Lachman, J.L. and Butterfield, E.C. (1979) *Cognitive Psychology and Information Processing: An Introduction*. Hillsdale, NJ: Erlbaum.

Lackner, J. and Garrett, M.F. (1973) 'Resolving ambiguity: effects of biasing context in the unattended ear', *Cognition* 1: 359–372.

Lashley, K.S. (1958) 'Cerebral organization and behavior', in *The Brain and Human Behavior, Proceedings of the Association for Research on Nervous and Mental Disease*. Baltimore: Williams & Wilkins.

Lavie, N. (2007) 'Attention and consciousness', in M. Velmans and S. Schneider (eds) *The Blackwell Companion to Consciousness*. Malden, MA: Blackwell, pp. 489–503.

Laws, P. (1972) 'On the problem of distance hearing and the localization of auditory events inside the head', dissertation, Technische Hochschule, Aachen.

Leask, J., Haber, R.N. and Haber, R.B. (1969) 'Eidetic imagery in children: II. Longitudinal and experimental results', *Psychonomic Monograph Supplements* 3: 25–48.

LeDoux, J. (1998) *The Emotional Brain: The Mysterious Underpinnings of Emotional Life*. London: Weidenfeld & Nicolson.

Lee, H.W., Hong, S.B., Seo, D.W., Tae, W.S. and Hong, S.C. (2000) 'Mapping of functional organisation in human visual cortex: electrical cortical stimulation', *Neurology* 54(4): 849–854.

Lehar, S. (2003) 'Gestalt isomorphism and the primacy of subjective conscious experience: a gestalt bubble model', *Behavioral and Brain Sciences* 26(4): 375–444.

Lehar, S. (2006) 'The dimensions of visual experience: a quantitative analysis'. Presented at the Tucson 2006 conference Toward a Science of Consciousness. http://sharp.bu.edu/~slehar/Tucson2006/Tucson2006Narration.html

Leibniz, G.W. (1923 [1686]) *Discourse of Metaphysics, Correspondence with Arnauld, and Monadology*, trans. M. Ginsberg. London: Allen & Unwin.

Lenarz, T. (1997) 'Cochlear implants: what can be achieved', *American Journal of Otology* 18(6): S2–S3.

Lenhart, M. (2007) 'High-frequency stimulation in sensorineural hearing loss', *The Hearing Review*. www.hearingreview.com/issues/articles/2007–11_01.asp

Lenneberg, E.H. (1967) *Biological Foundations of Language*. New York: Wiley.

Lettvin, J.Y., Maturana, H.R, McCulloch, W.S. and Pitts, W.H. (1959) 'What the frog's eye tells the frog's brain', *Institute of Radio Engineer's Proceedings* 47: 1940–1951.

Lewes, C.H. (1970 [1877]) 'The physical basis of mind', in G.N.A. Vesey (ed.) *Body and Mind: Readings in Philosophy*. London: George Allen & Unwin.

Lewis, D. (1972) 'Psychophysical and theoretical identifications', *Australasian Journal of Philosophy* 50: 249–258.

Lewis, D. (1994) 'Reduction of mind', in S. Guttenplan (ed.) *A Companion to the Philosophy of Mind*. Oxford: Blackwell.

Libet, B. (1985) 'Unconscious cerebral initiative and the role of conscious will in voluntary action', *Behavioral and Brain Sciences* 8: 529–566.

Libet, B. (1996) 'Neural processes in the production of conscious experience', in M. Velmans (ed.) *The Science of Consciousness: Psychological, Neuropsychological, and Clinical Reviews*. London: Routledge.

Libet, B. (2002) 'The timing of mental events: Libet's experimental findings and their implications', *Consciousness and Cognition* 11(2): 291–299.

Libet, B. (2003a) 'Timing of conscious experience. Reply to the 2002 commentaries on Libet's findings', *Consciousness and Cognition* 12(3): 321–331.

Libet, B. (2003b) 'Can conscious experience affect brain activity?' *Journal of Consciousness Studies* 10(12): 24–28.

Libet, B., Wright Jr, E.W., Feinstein, B. and Pearl, D.K. (1979) 'Subjective referral of the timing for a conscious experience: a functional role for the somatosensory specific projection system in man', *Brain* 102: 193–224.

Liotti, M. and Panksepp, J. (2004) 'Imaging human emotions and affective feelings: implications for biological psychiatry', in J. Panksepp (ed.) *Textbook of Biological Psychiatry*. Hoboken, NJ: Wiley, pp. 33–74.

Lissman, H.W. (1963) 'Electrical location by fishes', *Scientific American* 208(3): 50–59.

Lock, A. (1975) *Action, Gesture, and Symbol: The Emergence of Language*. London: Academic Press.

Locke, J. (1975 [1690]) *An Essay Concerning Human Understanding*, ed. P.H. Nidditch. Oxford: Clarendon Press.

Loizou, P.C. (1998) 'Introduction to cochlear implants', *IEEE Signal Processing Magazine*, pp. 101–130. www.utdallas.edu/~loizou/cimplants/tutorial/

Loizou, P.C. (2006) 'Speech processing in vocoder-centric cochlear implants', *Advances in Oto-Rhino-Laryngology* 64: 109–143. www.utdallas.edu/~loizou/cimplants/tutorial/

Luquet, G.H. (1996) 'Prehistoric mythology', in *The Larousse Encyclopedia of Mythology*. London: Chancellor Press.

McCorduck, P. (1979) *Machines Who Think: A Personal Enquiry into the History and Prospects of Artificial Intelligence*. San Francisco: W.H. Freeman.

McCrone, J. (1999) *Going Inside: A Tour around a Single Moment of Consciousness*. London: Faber & Faber.

McGinn, C. (1995) 'Consciousness and space', in T. Metzinger (ed.) *Conscious Experience*. Thorverton: Imprint Academic.

Mach, E. (1897 [1885]) *Contributions to the Analysis of Sensations*, trans. C.M. Williams. Chicago: Open Court Publishing Co.

McMahon, C.E. and Sheikh, A. (1989) 'Psychosomatic illness: a new look', in A. Sheikh and K. Sheikh (eds) *Eastern and Western Approaches to Healing*. New York: Wiley-Interscience.

McNamara, J. (1973) 'Nurseries, streets and classrooms: some comparisons and deductions', *Modern Language Journal* 57: 250–251.

Mandler, G. (1975) *Mind and Emotion*. New York: Wiley.

Mandler, G. (1985) *Cognitive Psychology: An Essay in Cognitive Science*. Hillsdale, NJ: Erlbaum.

Mandler, G. (1991) 'The processing of information is not conscious, but its products often are', *Behavioral and Brain Sciences* 14(4): 688–689.

Mandler, G. (1997) 'Consciousness redux', in J.D. Cohen and J.W. Schooler (eds) *Scientific Approaches to Consciousness*. Hillsdale, NJ: Lawrence Erlbaum Associates.

Mangan, B. (1993) 'Taking phenomenology seriously: the "fringe" and its implications for cognitive research', *Consciousness and Cognition* 2(2): 89–108.

Mangan, B. (2003) 'The conscious fringe: bringing William James up to date', in B.J. Baars, W.P. Banks and J.B. Newman (eds) *Essential Sources in the Scientific Study of Consciousness*. Cambridge, MA: MIT Press, pp. 741–759.

Mangan, B. (2007) 'Cognition, fringe consciousness, and the psychology of William James', in M. Velmans and S. Schneider (eds) *The Blackwell Companion to Consciousness*. Malden, MA: Blackwell, pp. 673–685.

Marcel, A.J. (1980) 'Conscious and preconscious recognition of polysemous words: locating the selective effects of prior verbal context', in R.S. Nickerson (ed.) *Attention and Performance VIII*. Hillsdale, NJ: Lawrence Erlbaum Associates.

Marcel, A.J. (1986) 'Consciousness and processing: choosing and testing a null hypothesis', *Behavioral and Brain Sciences* 9: 40–41.

Margenau, H. (1970) 'Einstein's concept of reality', in A. Schilpp (ed.) *Albert Einstein: Philosopher-Scientist*. La Salle, IL: Open Court.

Marslen-Wilson, W.D. (1984) 'Function and process in spoken word recognition – a tutorial review', in H. Bouma and D.G. Bouwhuis (eds) *Attention and Performance X*. Hillsdale, NJ: Lawrence Erlbaum Associates.

Marslen-Wilson, W.D. and Tyler, L.K. (1980) 'The temporal structure of spoken language understanding', *Cognition* 8: 1–71.

Mattison, C. (1998) *The Encyclopaedia of Snakes*. London: Blandford.

Melzack, R. (1973) *The Puzzle of Pain*. Harmondsworth: Penguin.

Melzack, R. (1975) 'The McGill Pain Questionnaire: major properties and scoring methods', *Pain* 1: 277–299.

Melzack, R. (1987) 'The short-form McGill Pain Questionnaire', *Pain* 30: 191–197.

Merikle, P.M. (2007) 'Preconscious processing', in M. Velmans and S. Schneider (eds) *The Blackwell Companion to Consciousness*. Malden, MA: Blackwell, pp. 512–524.

Merikle, P.M. and Daneman, M. (1998) 'Psychological investigations of conscious perception', *Journal of Consciousness Studies* 5(1): 5–18.

Merikle, P.M. and Joordens, S. (1997) 'Parallels between perception without attention and perception without awareness', *Consciousness and Cognition* 6(2/3): 219–236.

Metzinger, T. (1995) 'Faster than thought: holism, homogeneity and temporal coding', in T. Metzinger (ed.) *Conscious Experience*. Thorverton: Imprint Academic.

Metzinger, T. (1997) 'Phenomenal consciousness: the problem landscape'. Paper given at the International Brain and Self Workshop: Toward a Science of Consciousness, Elsinore, Denmark.

Metzinger, T. (2003) *Being No One: The Self-Model Theory of Subjectivity*. Cambridge, MA: MIT Press.

Meyer, D.E., Schvaneveldt, R.W. and Ruddy, M.G. (1975) 'Loci of contextual effects on visual word recognition', in P.M.A. Rabbitt and S. Dornic (eds) *Attention and Performance V*. New York: Academic Press.

Miller, G. (1962) *Psychology: The Science of Mental Life*. Gretna, LA: Pelican Books.

Moncrieff, R.W. (1967) *The Chemical Senses*, 3rd edn. London: L. Hill.

Moore, G.E. (1922) 'The refutation of idealism', in *Philosophical Studies*, London: Routledge and Kegan Paul.

Moore, G.E. (1970 [1910]) 'Some more problems of philosophy', in G.N.A. Vesey (ed.) *Body and Mind: Readings in Philosophy*. London: George Allen & Unwin.

Morrison, P. and Morrison, E. (1961) *Charles Babbage and his Calculating Engines*. New York: Dover.

Mouritsen, H. and Ritz, T. (2005) 'Magnetoreception and its use in bird navigation', *Current Opinion in Neurobiology* 15(4): 406–414.

Moutoussis, K. and Zeki, S. (2002) 'The relationship between cortical activation and perception investigated with invisible stimuli', *Proceeding of the National Academy of Sciences* 99: 9527–9532.

Nagel, T. (1974) 'What is it like to be a bat?' *Philosophical Review* 83: 435–451.

Nagel, T. (1986) *The View from Nowhere*. New York: Oxford University Press.

Neeley, J.H. (1977) 'Semantic priming and retrieval from lexical memory: roles of inhibitionless spreading activation and limited capacity attention', *Journal of Experimental Psychology: General* 106: 226–254.

Neisser, U. (1967) *Cognitive Psychology*. Englewood Cliffs, NJ: Prentice-Hall.

Neumann, E. (1973) *The Origins and History of Consciousness*. Princeton, NJ: Princeton University Press.

Newborn, M. (1997) *Kasparov Versus Deep Blue: Computer Chess Comes of Age*. New York: Springer.

Newell, A. and Simon, H.A. (1963 [1956]) 'The logic theory machine', *IRE Transactions on Information Theory*, September; reprinted in E.A. Feigenbaum and J. Feldman (eds) *Computers and Thought*. New York: McGraw-Hill.

Newell, A. and Simon, H.A. (1972) *Human Problem Solving*. Englewood Cliffs, NJ: Prentice-Hall.

Newell, A., Shaw, J.C. and Simon, H.A. (1960) 'Report on a general problem solving program for a computer', in *Information Processing: Proceedings of the International Conference on Information Processing*. Paris: UNESCO.

Nieuwenhuis, S., Yeung, N., Van den Wildenberg, W. and Ridderinkhof, K.R. (2003) 'Electrophysiological correlates of anterior cingulate functioning in a go/no-go task', *Cognitive, Affective, and Behavioral Neuroscience* 3(1): 17–26.

Nissen, M.J. and Bullemer, P. (1987) 'Attentional requirements of learning: evidence from performance measures', *Cognitive Psychology* 19: 1–32.

Noë, A. (ed.) (2002) 'Is the visual world a grand illusion?' Special issue of the *Journal of Consciousness Studies* 9(5/6). Thorverton: Imprint Academic.

Noë, A. (2004) *Action in Perception*. Cambridge, MA: MIT Press.

Noë, A. (2007) 'Inattentional blindness, change blindness, and consciousness', in M. Velmans and S. Schneider (eds) *The Blackwell Companion to Consciousness*. Malden, MA: Blackwell, pp. 504–511.

Norman, D. (1969) *Memory and Attention: An Introduction to Human Information Processing*. New York: Wiley.

Oakley, A.D. and Eames, L.C. (1985) 'The plurality of consciousness', in D.A. Oakley (ed.) *Brain and Mind*. London: Methuen.

O'Regan, J.K., Myin, E. and Noë, A. (2004) 'Towards an analytic phenomenology. The concepts of "bodiliness" and "grabbiness" ', in A. Carsetti (ed.) *Seeing, Thinking and Knowing*. Dordrecht: Kluwer, pp. 103–114.

Pace-Schott, E.F. and Hobson, J.A. (2007) 'Altered states of consciousness: drug-induced states', in M. Velmans and S. Schneider (eds) *The Blackwell Companion to Consciousness*. Malden, MA: Blackwell, pp. 141–153.

Panksepp, J. (1998) *Affective Neuroscience: The Foundations of Human and Animal Emotions*. Oxford: Oxford University Press.

Panksepp, J. (2005) 'Affective consciousness: core emotional feelings in animals and humans', *Consciousness and Cognition* 14: 30–80.

Panksepp, J. (2007) 'Affective consciousness', in M. Velmans and S. Schneider (eds) *The Blackwell Companion to Consciousness*. Malden, MA: Blackwell, pp. 114–129.

Pashler, H. (1999) *The Psychology of Attention*. London: MIT Press.

Penfield, W. (1975) *The Mystery of the Mind: A Critical Study of Consciousness and the Human Brain*. Princeton, NJ: Princeton University Press.

Penfield, W. and Rassmussen, T.B. (1950) *The Cerebral Cortex of Man*. New York: Macmillan.

Penrose, R. (1994) *Shadows of the Mind: A Search for the Missing Science of Consciousness*. Oxford: Oxford University Press.

Penrose, R. and Hameroff, S. (1995) 'What "gaps"? – Reply to Grush and Churchland', *Journal of Consciousness Studies* 2(2): 98–111.

Perenin, M.T. and Jeannerod, M. (1978) 'Visual function within the hemianopic field following early cerebral hemidecortication in man: 1 – Spatial localization', *Neuropsychologia* 16: 1–13.

Petitmengin, C. (2006) 'Describing one's subjective experience in the second person: an interview method for the science of consciousness', *Phenomenology and the Cognitive Sciences* 5: 229–269.

Petitmengin-Peugeot, C. (1999) 'The intuitive experience', in F. Varela and J. Shear (eds) *The View from Within*. Exeter: Imprint Academic, pp. 43–77.

Petrides, M.B., Alivisatos, B., Evans, A.C. and Meyer, E. (1993) 'Dissociation of human mid-dorsolateral from posterior dorsolateral frontal cortex in memory processing', *Proceedings of the National Academy of Sciences of the United States of America* 90: 873–877.

Pierce, C.S. and Jastrow, J. (1885) 'On small differences in sensation', *Memoirs of the National Academy of Sciences* 3: 317–329.

Place, U. (1956) 'Is consciousness a brain process?' *British Journal of Psychology* 47: 44–50.

Plotnik, J.M., de Waal, F.B. and Reiss, D. (2006) 'Self-recognition in Asian elephant', *Proceedings of the National Academy of Sciences of the United States of America* 103: 17053–17057.

Pockett, S., Banks, W.P. and Gallagher, S. (eds) (2006) *Does Consciousness Cause Behavior?* Cambridge, MA: MIT Press.

Pope, K.S and Singer, J.L. (eds) (1978) *The Stream of Consciousness: Scientific Investigations into the Flow of Experience*. New York: Plenum Press.

Popper, K.R. (1959) *The Logic of Scientific Discovery*. London: Hutchinson.

Popper, K.R. (1972) *Objective Knowledge: An Evolutionary Approach*. Oxford: Clarendon.

Popper, K.R. and Eccles, J.C. (1993 [1976]) *The Self and its Brain*. London: Routledge.

Posner, M.I. and Boies, S.W. (1971) 'Components of attention', *Psychological Review* 78: 391–408.

Posner, M.I. and Petersen, S.E. (1990) 'The attentional system of the brain', *Annual Review of Neuroscience* 13: 25–42.

Posner, M.I. and Raichle, M.E. (1993) *Images of Mind*. New York: Scientific American Library.

Posner, M.I. and Snyder, C.R.R. (1975) 'Facilitation and inhibition in the processing of signals', in P.M.A. Rabbitt and S. Dornick (eds) *Attention and Performance V*. New York: Academic Press.

Posner, M.I. and Warren, R.E. (1972) 'Traces, concepts, and conscious constructions', in A.W. Melton and E. Martin (eds) *Coding Procsses in Human Memory*. Chichester: Winston and Wiley.

Posner, M.I., DiGirolamo, G.J. and Fernandez-Duque, D. (1997) 'Brain mechanisms of cognitive skills', *Consciousness and Cognition* 6(2/3): 267–290.

Pribram, K.H. (1971) *Languages of the Brain: Experimental Paradoxes and Principles in Neuropsychology*. Englewood Cliffs, NJ: Prentice-Hall.

Pribram, K.H. (1974) 'How is it that sensing so much can do so little?', in F.O. Schmitt and F.G. Worden (eds) *The Neurosciences Third Study Program*. Cambridge, MA: MIT Press.

Pribram, K.H. (1979) 'Behaviorism, phenomenology and holism in psychology: a scientific analysis', *Journal of Social and Biological Structures* 2: 65–72.

Pribram, K. (2004) 'Consciousness reassessed', *Mind and Matter* 2(1): 7–35.

Primas, H. (2002) 'Hidden determinism, probability, and time's arrow', in H. Atmanspacher and R.C. Bishop (eds) *Between Chance and Choice*. Exeter: Imprint Academic, pp. 89–113.

Prince, M. (1970 [1885]) 'The nature of mind and human automatism', in G.N.A. Vesey (ed.) *Body and Mind: Readings in Philosophy*. London: George Allen & Unwin.

Putnam, H. (1960) 'Minds and machines', in S. Hook (ed.) *Dimensions of Mind*. New York: Collier Books.

Putnam, H. (1975) *Philosophical Papers. Vol. 2: Mind, Language and Reality*. Cambridge: Cambridge University Press.

Pynte, J., Do, P. and Scampa, P. (1984) 'Lexical decisions during the reading of sentences containing polysemous words', in S. Kornblum and J. Requin (eds) *Preparatory States and Processes*. Hillsdale, NJ: Lawrence Erlbaum Associates.

Rakover, S. (1996) 'The place of consciousness in the information processing approach: the mental-pool and the cognitive-pool thought experiment', *Behavioral and Brain Sciences* 19(3): 537–538.

Ramsdell, D.A. (1947) 'The psychology of the hard-of-hearing and the deafened adult', in H. Davis (ed.) *Hearing and Deafness*. New York: Murray Hill.

Reber, A.S. (1993) *Implicit Learning and Tacit Knowledge: An Essay on the Cognitive Unconscious*. Oxford: Oxford University Press.

Reber, A.S. (1997) 'How to differentiate implicit and explicit modes of acquisition', in J.D. Cohen and J.W. Schooler (eds) *Scientific Approaches to Consciousness*. Hillsdale, NJ: Lawrence Erlbaum Associates.

Reed, B. (1987) *The Field of Transformations*. Rochester, VT: Inner Traditions International, Ltd.

Rees, G. and Frith, C. (2007) 'Methodologies for identifying the neural correlates of consciousness', in M. Velmans and S. Schneider (eds) *The Blackwell Companion to Consciousness*. Malden, MA: Blackwell, pp. 553–566.

Rees, R. and Velmans, M. (1993) 'The effects of frequency transposition on the untrained auditory discrimination of congenitally deaf students', *British Journal of Audiology* 27: 53–60.

Reiss, D. and Marino, L. (2001) 'Mirror self-recognition in the bottlenose dolphin: a case of cognitive convergence', *Proceedings of the Scientific Academy of the United States of America* 98: 5937–5942.

Ress, D. and Heeger, D.J. (2003) 'Neuronal correlates of perception in early visual cortex', *Nature Neuroscience* 6(4): 414–420.

Revonsuo, A. (1995) 'Consciousness, dreams, and virtual realities', *Philosophical Psychology* 8(1): 35–58.

Revonsuo, A. (2006) *Inner Presence: Consciousness as a Biological Phenomenon.* Cambridge, MA: MIT Press.

Rey, G. (1991) 'Reasons for doubting the existence of even epiphenomenal consciousness', *Behavioral and Brain Sciences* 14(4): 691–692.

Richardson, J. (2000) 'Intersubjectivity and the therapeutic relationship: an exploration of theory and clinical practice', in D. Peters (ed.) *The Placebo Response: Biology and Belief in Clinical Practice.* London: Harcourt Brace, pp. 167–192.

Robertson, L. (2004) *Space, Objects, Minds, and Brains.* New York and Hove: Psychology Press.

Rock, I. (1997) *Indirect Perception.* Cambridge, MA: MIT Press.

Rockwell, W.T. (2005) *Neither Brain not Ghost.* Cambridge, MA: MIT Press.

Romanes, G.J. (1896 [1885]) 'Mind and motion (Rede Lecture)', in G.J. Romanes, *Mind and Motion and Monism.* London: Longmans, Green & Co.

Rose, D. (2006) *Consciousness: Philosophical, Psychological and Neural Theories.* Oxford: Oxford University Press.

Russell, B. (1987 [1946]) *A History of Western Philosophy.* London: Unwin Hyman Ltd.

Russell, B. (1948) *Human Knowledge: Its Scope and its Limits.* London: Allen & Unwin.

Ryle, G. (1949) *The Concept of Mind.* London: Hutchinson.

Sales, G. and Pye, D. (1974) *Ultrasonic Communications by Animals.* London and New York: Chapman and Hall; Wiley.

Scepkowski, L.A. and Cronin-Golomb, A. (2003) 'The alien hand: cases, categorizations, and anatomical correlates', *Behavioral and Cognitive Neuroscience Reviews* 2(4): 261–277.

Schacter, D.L. (1990) 'Toward a cognitive neuropsychology of awareness: implicit knowledge and anosognosia', *Journal of Clinical and Experimental Neuropsychology* 12(1): 155–178.

Schacter, D.L. (1992) 'Consciousness and awareness in memory and amnesia: critical issues', in A.D. Milner and M.D. Rugg (eds) *The Neuropsychology of Consciousness.* London: Academic Press.

Schiff, N.D. (2007) 'Global disorders of consciousness', in M. Velmans and S. Schneider (eds) *The Blackwell Companion to Consciousness.* Malden, MA: Blackwell, pp. 589–604.

Schiff, N.D. and Plum, F. (2000) 'The role of arousal and "gating" systems in the neurology of impaired consciousness', *Journal of Clinical Neurophysiology* 17: 438–452.

Schneider, D. (1974) 'The sex-attractant receptors of moths', *Scientific American* 231(1): 28–35.

Schooler, J. and Schreiber, A. (2004) 'Experience, meta-consciousness, and the paradox of introspection', in A. Jack, and A. Roepstorff (eds) *Trusting the Subject? Vol. 2: The Use of Introspective Evidence in Cognitive Science.* Exeter: Imprint Academic, pp. 17–39.

Schwender, D., Madler, C., Klasing, S., Peter, K. and Pöppel, E. (1994) 'Anesthetic control of 40-Hz brain activity and implicit memory', *Consciousness and Cognition* 3(2): 129–147.

Seager, W. and Bourget, D. (2007) 'Representationalism about consciousness', in M. Velmans and S. Schneider (eds) *The Blackwell Companion to Consciousness.* Malden, MA: Blackwell, pp. 261–276.

Searle, J. (1980) 'Minds, brains and programs', *Behavioral and Brain Sciences* 3: 417–457.

Searle, J. (1987) 'Minds and brains without programs', in C. Blakemore and S. Greenfield (eds) *Mindwaves*. Oxford: Blackwell.

Searle, J. (1990) 'Consciousness, explanatory inversion and cognitive science', *Behavioral and Brain Sciences* 13(4): 585–642.

Searle, J. (1992) *The Rediscovery of the Mind*. Cambridge, MA: MIT Press.

Searle, J. (1994a) 'The problem of consciousness', in A. Revonsuo and M. Kamppinen (eds) *Consciousness in Philosophy and Cognitive Neuroscience*. Hillsdale, NJ: Lawrence Erlbaum Associates.

Searle, J. (1994b) 'Intentionality (I)', in S. Guttenplan (ed.) *A Companion to the Philosophy of Mind*. Oxford: Blackwell, pp. 379–386.

Searle, J. (1997) *The Mystery of Consciousness*. London: Granta Books.

Searle, J. (2007) 'Biological naturalism', in M. Velmans and S. Schneider (eds) *The Blackwell Companion to Consciousness*. Malden, MA: Blackwell, pp. 325–334.

Shallice, T.R. (1972) 'Dual functions of consciousness', *Psychological Review* 79: 383–393.

Shallice, T.R. (1978) 'The dominant action system: an information processing approach to consciousness', in K.S. Pope and J.L. Singer (eds) *The Stream of Consciousness: Scientific Investigations into the Flow of Experience*. New York: Plenum.

Shallice, T.R. (1988) 'Information processing models of consciousness: possibilities and problems', in A. Marcel and E. Bisiach (eds) *Consciousness and Contemporary Science*. Oxford: Oxford University Press.

Shanks, D.R. and St John, M.F. (1994) 'Characteristics of dissociable human learning systems', *Behavioral and Brain Sciences* 17(3): 367–447.

Shastri, L. and Ajjanagadde, V. (1993) 'From simple associations to systematic reasoning: a connectionist representation of rules, variables and dynamic bindings using temporal synchrony', *Behavioral and Brain Sciences* 16(3): 417–494.

Shear, J. (2007) 'Eastern methods for investigating mind and consciousness', in M. Velmans and S. Schneider (eds) *The Blackwell Companion to Consciousness*. Malden, MA: Blackwell, pp. 697–710.

Shear, J. and Jevning, R. (1999) 'Pure consciousness', *Journal of Consciousness Studies* 6(2/3): 189–213.

Sheikh, A.N., Kunzendorf, R.G. and Sheikh, K.S. (1996) 'Somatic consequences of consciousness', in M. Velmans (ed.) *The Science of Consciousness: Psychological, Neuropsychological, and Clinical Reviews*. London: Routledge.

Sheldrake, R. (2005) 'The sense of being stared at. Part 2: Its implications for theories of vision', *Journal of Consciousness Studies* 12(6): 32–49.

Shepard, R.N. and Hut, P (1997) 'Turning the "hard problem" upside down and sideways', *Journal of Consciousness Studies* 3(4): 313–329.

Sherrington, C.S. (1942) *Man on His Nature*. Cambridge: Cambridge University Press.

Shiffrin, R. (1997) 'Attention, automatism, and consciousness', in J.D. Cohen and J.W. Schooler (eds) *Scientific Approaches to Consciousness*. Hillsdale, NJ: Lawrence Erlbaum Associates.

Shillito, D.J., Gallup, G.G. and Beck, B.B. (1999) 'Factors affecting mirror behaviour in western lowland gorillas', *Animal Behavior* 55: 529–536.

Simons, D.J. and Chabris, C. (1999) 'Gorillas in our midst: sustained inattentional blindness for dynamic events', *Perception* 28(9): 1059–1074.

Simons, D.J. and Levin, D.T. (1998) 'Failure to detect changes to people in a real-world interaction', *Psychonomic Bulletin and Review* 5: 644–649.

Simons, G. (1983) *Are Computers Alive?* Boston: Birkhäuser.

Singer, W. (2007) 'Large-scale temporal coordination of cortical activity as a prerequisite for conscious experience', in M. Velmans and S. Schneider (eds) *The Blackwell Companion to Consciousness*. Malden, MA: Blackwell, pp. 605–615.

Skinner, B.F. (1953) *Science and Human Behavior*. New York: Macmillan.

Skinner, B.F. (1957) *Verbal Behavior*. New York: Appleton-Century-Crofts.

Skrabanek, P. and McCormick, J. (1989) *Follies and Fallacies in Medicine*. Glasgow: Tarragon Press.

Skrbina, D. (2005a) 'Panpsychism', in *Stanford Encyclopedia of Philosophy*, http://plato.stanford.edu/entries/panpsychism/

Skrbina, D. (2005b) *Panpsychism in the West*. Cambridge, MA: MIT Press.

Sloman, A. (1991) 'Developing concepts of consciousness', *Behavioral and Brain Sciences* 14(4): 694–695.

Sloman, A. (1997a) 'Design spaces, niche spaces and the "hard" problem', http://66.102.9.104/search?q=cache:wo--I9fMte8J:www.cs.bham.ac.uk/research/projects/cogaff/Sloman.design.and.niche.spaces.ps+Design+spaces,+niche+spaces+ and+the+% 22hard%22+problem%27,&hl=en&ct=clnk&cd=3

Sloman, A. (1997b) 'What sorts of machine can love? Architectural requirements for human-like agents both natural and artificial', http://66.102.9.104/search?q=cache:TEfwTa36DlUJ:www.cs.bham.ac.uk/research/projects/cogaff/Sloman.voicebox.2page.ps+What+sorts+of+machine+can+love&hl=en&ct=clnk&cd=1

Sloman, A. and Chrisley, R.L. (2003) 'Virtual machines and consciousness', *Journal of Consciousness Studies* 10(4–5): 113–172.

Sloman, A. and Logan, B. (1998) 'Architectures for human-like agents'. Paper presented to European Conference on Cognitive Modelling, Nottingham, April.

Smart, J.J.C. (1962) 'Sensations and brain processes', in V.C. Chappell (ed.) *Philosophy of Mind*. Englewood Cliffs, NJ: Prentice-Hall.

Smith, C.U.M. (2008) 'The "hard problem" and the quantum physicists. Part 2: Modern times', *Brain and Cognition* (in press).

Smith, S.M., Brown, H.O. and Toman, J.E.P. (1947) 'The lack of cerebral effects of d-tubocurarine', *Anesthesiology* 8: 1–14.

Smolensky, P. (1994) 'Computational models of mind', in S. Guttenplan (ed.) *A Companion to the Philosophy of Mind*. Oxford: Blackwell.

Spanos, N.P., Ham, M.H. and Barber, T.X. (1973) 'Suggested ("hypnotic") visual hallucinations: experimental and phenomenological data', *Journal of Abnormal Psychology* 81: 96–106.

Sperry, R.W. (1969) 'A modified concept of consciousness', *Psychological Review* 76(6): 532–536.

Sperry, R.W. (1970) 'An objective approach to subjective experience', *Psychological Review* 77(6): 585–590.

Sperry, R.W. (1984) 'Consciousness, personal identity and the divided brain', *Neuropsychologia* 22(6): 661–663.

Sperry, R. (1985) *Science and Moral Priority: Merging Mind, Brain and Human Values*. New York: Praeger.

Sperry, R.W., Zaidel, E. and Zaidel, D. (1979) 'Self-recognition and social awareness in the disconnected minor hemisphere', *Neuropsychologia* 17: 153–166.

Spinoza, B. (1876 [1677]) *The Ethics*, in *The Ethics of Benedict Spinoza*. New York: Van Nostrand.

Stanovich, K.E. (1991) 'Damn! There goes that ghost again!' *Behavioral and Brain Sciences* 14(4): 696–697.

Stapp, H. (1993) *Mind, Matter and Quantum Mechanics*. New York: Springer-Verlag.

Stapp, H. (2007a) 'Quantum mechanical theories of consciousness', in M. Velmans and S. Schneider (eds) *The Blackwell Companion to Consciousness*. Malden, MA: Blackwell, pp. 300–312.

Stapp, H. (2007b) 'Quantum approaches to consciousness', in P.D. Zelago, M. Moscovitch and E. Thompson (eds) *The Cambridge Handbook of Consciousness*. Cambridge: Cambridge University Press, pp. 881–908.

Stapp, H. (2007c) *Mindful Universe: Quantum Mechanics and the Participating Observer*. New York: Springer.

Stevens, R. (2000) 'Phenomenological approaches to the study of conscious awareness', in M. Velmans (ed.) *Investigating Phenomenal Consciousness: New Methodologies and Maps*. Amsterdam: John Benjamins, pp. 99–120.

Stevens, S.S. (1966) 'Quantifying the sensory experience', in P.K. Feyerabend and G. Maxwell (eds) *Mind, Matter and Method: Essays in Philosophy of Science in Honour of Herbert Feigl*. Minneapolis: University of Minnesota Press.

Stoffregen, T.A. and Benoît, G.B. (2001) 'On specification of the senses', *Behavioral and Brain Sciences* 24(2): 195–261.

Stratton, G.M. (1897) 'Vision without inversion of the retinal image', *Psychological Review* 4: 341–360.

Strawson, G. (2006) 'Realistic monism: why physicalism entails panpsychism', *Journal of Consciousness Studies* 13(10/11): 1–31.

Stroop, J.R. (1935) 'Studies of interference in serial verbal reactions', *Journal of Experimental Psychology* 18: 643–662.

Styles, E. (1997) *The Psychology of Attention*. Hove: Psychology Press.

Swinney, D.A. (1979) 'Lexical access during sentence comprehension: (re)consideration of context effects', *Journal of Verbal Learning and Verbal Behaviour* 18: 645–659.

Swinney, D.A. (1982) 'The structure and time-course of information interaction during speech comprehension: lexical segmentation, access, and interpretation', in J. Mehler, E.C.T. Walker and M. Garrett (eds) *Perspectives on Mental Representation*. Hillsdale, NJ: Lawrence Erlbaum Associates.

Tarnas, R. (1993) *The Passion of the Western Mind*. New York: Ballantyne Books.

Thomas, A. (2007) 'Quantum decoherence', www.ipod.org.uk/reality/reality_decoherence.asp

Titchener, E.B. (1915) *A Beginner's Psychology*. New York: Macmillan.

Tobach, E., Skoilnick, A.J., Klein, I. and Greenberg, G. (1997) 'Viewing of self and nonself images in a group of captive orangutangs (Pongo pygmaeus Abellii)', *Perceptual and Motor Skills* 84: 355–370.

Tononi, G. (2007) 'The information integration theory', in M. Velmans and S. Schneider (eds) *The Blackwell Companion to Consciousness*. Malden, MA: Blackwell, pp. 287–299.

Torrance, S. (2007) 'Two conceptions of machine phenomenality', *Journal of Consciousness Studies* 14(7): 154–166.

Treisman, A.M. (1964) 'Verbal cues, language, and meaning in attention', *American Journal of Psychology* 77: 206–214.

Turing (1982 [1950]) 'Computing machinery and intelligence', in D.R. Hofstadter and D.C. Dennett (eds) *The Mind's I: Fantasies and Reflections on Self and Soul.* Harmondsworth: Penguin.

Tye, M. (1995) *Ten Problems of Consciousness: A Representational Theory of the Phenomenal Mind.* Cambridge, MA: MIT Press.

Tye, M. (2007) 'Philosophical problems of consciousness', in M. Velmans and S. Schneider (eds) *The Blackwell Companion to Consciousness.* Malden, MA: Blackwell, pp. 23–35.

Underwood, G. (1977) 'Contextual facilitation from attended and unattended messages', *Journal of Verbal Learning and Verbal Behaviour* 16: 99–106.

Underwood, G. (1991) 'Attention is necessary for word integration', *Behavioral and Brain Sciences* 14(4): 698.

Uttal, W.R. (1978) *The Psychobiology of Mind.* Hillsdale, NJ: Lawrence Erlbaum.

Van de Laar, T. (2003) 'The concept of projection in theories of phenomenal consciousness', http://66.102.9.104/search?q=cache:x6kwqq1zZcwJ:www.eurospp.org/2003/papers/Doc2003/van%2520Laar.doc+Dooremalen+Velmans&hl=en&ct=clnk&cd=1

Van de Laar, T. (2007) 'Explicit science: methodology implying assumptions behind scientific research into consciousness and conscious intentional action', PhD dissertation, Radbout University, Nijmegen. http://handle.net/2066/29993

van der Heijden, A.H.C., Hudson, P.T.W. and Kurvink, A.G. (1997) 'On widening the explanatory gap', *Behavioral and Brain Sciences* 20(1): 157–158.

Van Gulick, R. (2007) 'Functionalism and qualia', in M. Velmans and S. Schneider (eds) *The Blackwell Companion to Consciousness.* Malden, MA: Blackwell, pp. 381–395.

van Swinderen, B. (2007) 'Attention-like processes in Drosophilia require short-term memory genes', *Science* 315: 1590–1593.

Varela, F.J. (1996) 'Neurophenomenology: a methodological remedy for the hard problem', *Journal of Consiousness Studies* 3(4): 330–350.

Varela, F.J. (1999) 'Present-time consciousness', *Journal of Consciousness Studies* 6(2/3): 111–140.

Varela, F. and Shear, J. (eds) (1999) *The View from Within: First Person Approaches to the Study of Consciousness.* Exeter: Imprint Academic.

Varela, F., Thomson, E. and Rosch, E. (1993) *The Embodied Mind.* Cambridge, MA: MIT Press.

Vaughan, R. and Zuluaga, M. (2006) 'Use your illusion: sensorimotor self-simulation allows complex agents to plan with incomplete self-knowledge', *Proceedings of the Ninth International Conference on Simulation of Adaptive Behaviour.* SAB, Rome, Italy, pp. 298–312.

Velmans, M. (1973a) 'Speech imitation in simulated deafness, using visual cues and recoded auditory information', *Language and Speech* 16: 224–236.

Velmans, M. (1973b) 'Aids for deaf persons', British Patent Office, No. 1340105.

Velmans, M. (1975) 'Effects of frequency recoding on the articulation learning of perceptively deaf children', *Language and Speech* 18(part 2): 180–199.

Velmans, M. (1990a) 'Consciousness, brain, and the physical world', *Philosophical Psychology* 3: 77–99.

Velmans, M. (1990b) 'Is the mind conscious, functional, or both?' *Behavioral and Brain Sciences* 13: 629–630.

Velmans, M. (1991a) 'Is human information processing conscious?', *Behavioral and Brain Sciences* 14(4): 651–669.

Velmans, M. (1991b) 'Consciousness from a first-person perspective', *Behavioral and Brain Sciences* 14(4): 702–726.

Velmans, M. (1993a) 'A reflexive science of consciousness', in *Experimental and Theoretical Studies of Consciousness*, Ciba Foundation Symposium No. 174. Chichester: Wiley.

Velmans, M. (1993b) 'Consciousness, causality and complementarity', *Behavioral and Brain Sciences* 16(2): 409–416.

Velmans, M. (1995a) 'The relation of consciousness to the material world', *Journal of Consciousness Studies* 2(3): 255–265.

Velmans, M. (1995b) 'The limits of neuropsychological models of consciousness', *Behavioral and Brain Sciences* 18(4): 702–703.

Velmans, M. (ed.) (1996a) *The Science of Consciousness: Psychological, Neuropsychological and Clinical Reviews*. London: Routledge.

Velmans, M. (1996b) 'What and where are conscious experiences?', in M. Velmans (ed.) *The Science of Consciousness: Psychological, Neuropsychological and Clinical Reviews*. London: Routledge.

Velmans, M. (1996c) 'Consciousness and the "causal paradox" ', *Behavioral and Brain Sciences* 19(3): 537–542.

Velmans, M. (1997) 'Review of D. Chalmers *The Conscious Mind*', *Network* 64: 57–60; reprinted in *Consciousness and Experiential Psychology* (1998) 1(1): 14–17. Also available at http://cogprints.org/386/

Velmans, M. (1998a) 'Goodbye to reductionism', in S. Hameroff, A. Kaszniak and A. Scott (eds) *Towards a Science of Consciousness II: The Second Tucson Discussions and Debates*. Cambridge, MA: MIT Press.

Velmans, M. (1998b) 'Physical, psychological and virtual realities', in J. Wood (ed.) *The Virtual Embodied*. London: Routledge.

Velmans, M. (1999a) 'Intersubjective science', *Journal of Consciousness Studies* 6(2/3): 299–306.

Velmans, M. (1999b) 'When perception becomes conscious', *British Journal of Psychology* 90(4): 543–566.

Velmans, M. (ed.) (2000) *Investigating Phenomenal Consciousness: New Methodologies and Maps*. Amsterdam: John Benjamins.

Velmans, M. (2001) 'Heterophenomenology versus critical phenomenology: a dialogue with Dan Dennett', online debate at http://cogprints.soton.ac.uk/documents/disk0/00/17/95/index.html

Velmans, M. (2002a) 'How could conscious experiences affect brains?', *Journal of Consciousness Studies* 9(11): 3–29.

Velmans, M. (2002b) 'Making sense of causal interactions between consciousness and brain', *Journal of Consciousness Studies* 9(11): 69–95.

Velmans, M. (2003a) *How Could Conscious Experiences Affect Brains?* Exeter: Imprint Academic.

Velmans, M. (2003b) 'Preconscious free will', *Journal of Consciousness Studies* 10(12): 42–61.

Velmans, M. (2004) 'Why conscious free will both is and isn't an illusion', *Behavioral and Brain Sciences* 27(5): 677.

Velmans, M. (2007a) 'Where experiences are: dualist, physicalist, enactive and reflexive accounts of phenomenal consciousness', *Phenomenology and the Cognitive Sciences* 6(4): 547–563.

Velmans, M. (2007b) 'How experienced phenomena relate to things themselves: Kant, Husserl, Hoche, and reflexive monism', *Phenomenology and the Cognitive Sciences* 6: 411–423.

Velmans, M. (2007c) 'Heterophenomenology versus critical phenomenology', *Phenomenology and Cognitive Science* 6: 221–230.

Velmans, M. (2008a) 'Reflexive monism', *Journal of Consciousness Studies* 15(2): 5–50.

Velmans, M. (2008b) 'Psychophysical nature', in H. Atmanspacher and H. Primas (eds) *Wolfgang Pauli's Philosophical Ideas and Contemporary Science*. Berlin: Springer, pp. 115–134.

Velmans, M. and Marcuson, M. (1983) 'Comparing the acceptability of a spectrum preserving and a spectrum destroying transposer for the deaf', *British Journal of Audiology* 17: 12–26.

Velmans, M. and Schneider, S. (eds) (2007) *The Blackwell Companion to Consciousness*. Malden, MA: Blackwell.

Velmans, M., Wienrich, A. and Duggan, C. (1982) 'Field trials with a new frequency transposing hearing aid', *Report No. 2 to the Department of Health and Social Security*, London, Contract No. R/E 1049/84.

Velmans, M., Marcuson, M., Grant, J., Kwiatkowski, R. and Rees, R. (1988) 'The use of frequency transposition in the language acquisition of sensory-neural deaf children', *Report to the Medical Research Council*, Grant No. G8319832N.

Vermersch, P. (1999) 'Introspection as practice', *Journal of Consciousness Studies* 6(2/3): 17–42.

Vesey, G.N.A. (ed.) (1970) *Body and Mind: Readings in Philosophy*. London: George Allen & Unwin.

Voerman, S. (2003) 'We are better off without reflexive monism', www.savoerman.nl/pdf/reflexivemonism.pdf

Von der Malsburg, C. (1986) 'Am I thinking assemblies?', in G. Palm and A. Aertsen (eds) *Brain Theory*. New York: Springer.

Von Frisch, K. (1971) *Bees: Their Vision, Chemical Senses and Language*. Ithaca, NY: Cornell University Press.

Von Neumann, J. (1955/1932) *Mathematical Foundations of Quantum Mechanics*. Princeton, NJ: Princeton University Press (trans. Robert T. Beyer from the 1932 German original, *Mathematiche Grundlagen der Quantummechanik*. Berlin: J. Springer).

von Senden, M. (1960 [1932]) *Space and Sight*, trans. P. Heath. London: Methuen/Free Press.

Wall, P.D. (1996) 'The placebo effect', in M. Velmans (ed.) *The Science of Consciousness: Psychological, Neuropsychological and Clinical Reviews*. London: Routledge.

Warnock, G. (1972) *Berkeley*. Harmondsworth: Peregrine Books.

Warrington, E. and Weiskrantz, L. (1978) 'Further analysis of the prior learning effect in amnesic patients', *Neuropsychologia* 16: 169–177.

Watson, J.B. (1913) 'Psychology as the behaviorist views it', *The Psychological Review* 20: 158–177.

Waugh, N.C. and Norman, D.A. (1965) 'Primary memory', *Psychological Review* 72: 89–104.

Weber, M. and Desmond Jr, W. (eds) (2008) *Handbook of Whiteheadian Process Thought*. Frankfurt: Ontos Verlag.

Wegner, D. (2002) *The Illusion of Conscious Will*. Cambridge, MA: MIT Press.

Wegner, D. (2004) 'Précis of The illusion of conscious will', *Behavioral and Brain Sciences* 27(5): 1–11.

Weiskrantz, L. (1986) *Blindsight: A Case Study and Implications*. London: Open University Press.

Weiskrantz, L. (1988) 'Neuropsychology of vision and memory', in A.J. Marcel and E. Bisiach (eds) *Consciousness in Contemporary Science*. Oxford: Oxford University Press.

Weiskrantz, L. (1997) *Consciousness Lost and Found*. Oxford: Oxford University Press.

Weiskrantz, L. (2007) 'The case of blindsight', in M. Velmans and S. Schneider (eds) *The Blackwell Companion to Consciousness*. Malden, MA: Blackwell, pp. 175–180.

Wheeler, M. (2005) *Reconstructing the Cognitive World*. Cambridge, MA: MIT Press.

Whitehead, A.N. (1957 [1929]) *Process and Reality*. New York: Macmillan.

Whitehead, A.N. (1932) *Science and the Modern World*. Cambridge: Cambridge University Press.

Wilber, K. (1996 [1984]) *Up From Eden: A Transpersonal View of Human Evolution*. Wheaton, IL: Theosophical Publishing House.

Wilson, T.D. (2002) *Strangers to Ourselves: Discovering the Adaptive Unconscious*. Cambridge, MA: Harvard University Press.

Wiltschko, R. and Wiltschko, W. (1995) *Magnetic Orientation in Animals*. Berlin: Springer Verlag.

Wimsatt, W. (1976) 'Reductionism, levels of organization, and the mind–body problem', in G.G. Globus, G. Maxwell and I. Savodnik (eds) *Consciousness and the Brain*. New York: Plenum.

Wittgenstein, L. (1953) *Philosophical Investigations*, trans. G.E.M. Anscombe. Oxford: Basil Blackwell.

Woodward, W.R. (1972) 'Fechner's panpsychism: a scientific solution to the mind–body problem', *Journal of the History of the Behavioral Sciences* 8: 367–386.

Wozniak, R.H. (1999) *Classics in Psychology, 1855–1914: Historical Essays*. Bristol: Thoemmes Press.

Wright, W. (2003) 'Projectivist representationalism and color', *Philosophical Psychology* 16: 515–529.

Zahavi, D. (2007) 'Killing the straw man: Dennett and phenomenology', *Phenomenology and the Cognitive Sciences* 6(4): 331–347.

Zaidel, E., Jacoboni, M., Zaidel, D.W. and Bogen, J. (2003) 'The callosal syndromes', in K.M. Heilman and E. Valenstein (eds) *Clinical Neuropsychology*, 4th edn. New York: Oxford University Press, pp. 347–403.

Zajonc, A. (1993) *Catching the Light: An Entwined History of Light and Mind*. London: Bantam Press.

Zeki, S. (2007) 'A theory of microconsciousness', in M. Velmans and S. Schneider (eds) *The Blackwell Companion to Consciousness*. Malden, MA: Blackwell, pp. 580–588.

Zeki, S. and Bartels, A. (1999) 'Towards a theory of visual consciousness', *Consciousness and Cognition* 8: 225–259.

Zeman, A. (2003) *Consciousness: A User's Guide*. London: Yale University Press.

Note

Most of the Velmans papers are available online at http://cogprints.soton.ac.uk/ (via an author search).

Author index

Subject index

Page numbers in *italic* indicate Figures.